The Terror of the Coast

Hul'qumi'mum First Nations place names mentioned in the text.

The Terror of the Coast

Land Alienation
and Colonial War
on Vancouver Island
and the Gulf Islands,
1849-1863

Chris Arnett

Talonbooks

1999

Talonbooks
#104—3100 Production Way
Burnaby, British Columbia, Canada V5A 4R4

Typeset in Garamond Condensed and printed and bound in Canada by Hignell Printing Ltd.

First Printing: August 1999

Talonbooks are distributed in Canada by General Distribution Services, 325 Humber College Blvd.,
Toronto, Ontario, Canada M9W 7C3; Tel.:(416) 213-1919; Fax:(416) 213-1917.

Talonbooks are distributed in the U.S.A. by General Distribution Services Inc., 4500 Witmer Estates,
Niagara Falls, New York, U.S.A. 14305-1386; Tel.:1-800-805-1083; Fax:1-800-481-6207.

The publisher gratefully acknowledges the financial support of the Canada Council for the Arts; the
Government of Canada through the Book Publishing Industry Development Program; and the
Province of British Columbia through the British Columbia Arts Council for our publishing activities.

Canadian Cataloguing in Publication Data

Arnett, Chris.
  The terror of the coast

  Includes bibliographical references.
  ISBN 0-88922-318-1

  1. Indians of North America--British Columbia--Government
relations--History. 2. Vancouver Island (B.C.)--History. 3. Indians of
North America--Land tenure--British Columbia. I. Title.
E78.B9A76 1999 971.1'2004979 C99-910227-3

To my taua (grandmother), Jane Meri Arnett
and to my father and mother,
John and Norma Arnett.

ki mua ki muri

We look to the past (ki mua)
and take that with us into the unknown future (ki muri).

Contents

Acknowledgements

I would like to acknowledge the following individuals whose input and interest facilitated the creation of this book: Bob Akerman, Dennis Alphonse, Grahame Brazier, Anne Cullingham, the late Tommy Paul, Chief Jill Harris, Bob and Emily Rice, Oshiane Mitchell, Roy Edwards, Henry Edwards, Rocky Wilson, Mary Joe, Lawrence George, Herb George, Frank Norris, Robert Daniels, April Miller, Mark Kiemele, Cindy Johnny, Charles Kahn, Les Laronde, Beth Lischeron, Paul Schmid, James Hendrickson, Brenda Timbers, Grant Keddie, Andrew Loveridge, Bruce Watson, Harry Conn, Wayne Suttles, and Audrey Ginn. Special thanks to my neighbour Lawrie Neish for his assistance in guiding me through the intricacies of the Tandy 1000 personal computer to produce the original manuscript. The following individuals and institutions also provided invaluable assistance: Mary Daisy Day of the Reprographic Section of the Public Records Office in London, Mary Davidson and staff of the Salt Spring Island Archives, staff of the British Columbia Archives and Records Service, staff at the Surveyors General Branch in Victoria, Dan Savard of the Royal British Columbia Museum, Lynn Maranda of the City of Vancouver Museum, and Vera McIver of the Diocese of Victoria Archives.

I thank Karl Siegler and Christy Siegler of Talonbooks for their ongoing support of this project and their assistance, with the valuable editing skills of Ryan Wadsworth, in transforming "a veritable babble of tongues" into a finished manuscript.

A $4,000 short-term writer's grant from the Canada Council in 1995 allowed me to expand on the initial archival research. This was supplemented by a further $500 from the Annie York Trust Fund.

Last, but in no way least, I thank my wife, Barbara, and our two sons, John and Carl, for their loving support and patience throughout the creation of this book.

—Christopher Anderson Arnett
Salt Spring Island, June 8th, 1999

A Note on Orthography:

There are a number of writing systems used to convey the Hul'qumi'num language. For the sake of consistency in the narrative, the anglicized names of villages and individuals are used throughout the text. Other Hul'qumi'num words follow the writing system developed by Thomas E. Hukari and Ruby Peters (1995). Stress is generally on the first or second syllable. In this system the letter "i" is pronounced as "ee" in English. Thus "hwunitum" (white person) is pronounced "hwu-nee-tum."

Introduction

One aspect of British Columbia history which has not been examined in much detail is the alienation of aboriginal lands and resources during the colonial period, from 1849, when the Colony of Vancouver Island was established, to 1871 when British Columbia entered the Canadian confederation. The official policy of the imperial and colonial governments regarding aboriginal lands is fairly well-known, but how this policy was enacted on the ground, particularly in the face of aboriginal opposition, is less familiar.

The Hudson's Bay Company, in its role as the proprietor of Great Britain's only colony on the western shores of North America, negotiated fourteen land sale agreements with First Nations on Vancouver Island between 1850 and 1854. These agreements guaranteed to aboriginal people the undisturbed use of their lands and resources in exchange for allowing white settlement within their territories. The ceded lands of 1850-1854 constituted the various districts of the Colony of Vancouver Island, but as the colony sought to expand into adjacent territories of Hul'qumi'num First Nations on the east coast of Vancouver Island and the Gulf Islands there was less willingness by hwulmuhw ("people of the land") to negotiate the sale of their lands and resources to the hwunitum, a Hul'qumi'num word for people of European ancestry, which translates literally as "the hungry people."

Frustrated by this opposition, the colonial government embarked on a policy of illegal surveys and land sales in the Cowichan Valley and an illegal pre-emption system directed at Salt Spring Island and the Chemainus Valley in 1859. This policy provoked militant opposition by young warriors from the villages of Quamichan on the Cowichan River, and Lamalcha and Penelakut on Kuper Island. This book will demonstrate how the first "treaty process" in what is now British Columbia collapsed, not for lack of funds as is often supposed, but through the use of armed force to end hwulmuhw opposition to the occupation of their lands by hwunitum.

The Terror of the Coast consists of two parts. The first four chapters describe the arrival of hwunitum and the erosion of hwulmuhw sovereignty and jurisdiction after contact. The remainder of the book details the colonial war of 1863 against the Lamalcha and Penelakut warriors of Kuper Island and the subsequent trials and public executions of hwulmuhw participants.

The hwunitum point of view has dominated the historic record of the colonial period and this book is a revision of that record based on primary sources intended to place the events leading up to 1863 in their proper context. The period covered by this book is reconstructed using the oral history of hwulmuhw elders and the hwunitum written record as preserved in government and police correspondence, the editorials, letters, and articles from four colonial newspapers, and the ship's logs and "Letters of Proceedings" written by Royal Navy officers. The details of the period from 1849 to 1858 are based largely on government correspondence, particularly that of Governor James Douglas, and hwulmuhw oral history. From 1858 onward the story is augmented by the colonial print media in Victoria and New Westminster. The questions of land alienation and the war of 1863 were covered by pioneer journalists such as Amor De Cosmos, D.W. Higgins, John Robson and others, who published first and second-hand accounts by hwunitum and hwulmuhw informants as well as their own commentary. The voice of the colonial press contains important details often missing from official correspondence, not the least of which was the wide-spread support by hwunitum for the equitable settlement of hwulmuhw land claims.

In a similar manner, valuable information is preserved in the writing of various Anglican and Roman Catholic clergy who recorded hwulmuhw points of view even as they worked to undermine the culture.

Despite the preponderance of hwunitum primary sources, the bias they contain can sometimes be transcended by the use of what one historian has termed, "embalmed evidence." Contemporaneous hwulmuhw perspectives were often recorded in newspapers and official correspondence, even if they were ignored as the dominant interpretation took hold. For example, letters to the editors of colonial newspapers, such as those written during the conflict by William Smithe, a settler in the unceded lands of the Cowichan Valley and future premier of British Columbia, preserve with remarkable clarity hwulmuhw points of view.

Literature recording hwulmuhw archaeology, ethnography and the oral history of Hul'qumi'num First Nations can also be drawn upon to augment and balance the hwunitum record. Valuable in this regard are a series of interviews with hwulmuhw elders by Beryl Cryer in the 1930s. Cryer's interviews preserve hwulmuhw accounts of events leading up to the war and crucial perspectives relating to the conflict itself.

Most important is the oral history preserved among Hul'qumi'num First Nations today.

As much as possible, the primary sources are woven verbatim into the text to document the events of long ago from the perspectives of the participants and to avoid paraphrasing, which all too often clouds what really happened by omitting important details. This approach might be seen as empiricist but it is justifiable in order to establish a chronology of events often overlooked.

The war against the Kuper Island warriors was small compared to those raging elsewhere in North America. While Napoleon III laid waste to Central Mexico, the American Civil War was entering its third year of bloodshed, dominating the Victoria and New Westminster newspapers with descriptions of battlefields piled high with unburied dead. But this short-lived, almost forgotten war, waged by the British colony of Vancouver's Island against the Lamalcha of Kuper Island, was significant in the history of British Columbia. The war marked the first time that military force was used to eliminate hwulmuhw opposition to hwunitum settlement. The defeat of the Lamalcha and Penelakut warriors removed the most strident opposition to hwunitum expansion and paved the way, without mutual agreement, for the alienation of hwulmuhw land on eastern Vancouver Island and the Gulf Islands. The assistance of hwulmuhw allies in bringing the war against the Lamalcha to an early conclusion was quickly forgotten and their lands alienated without agreement.

Although well documented in newspapers, government, police and naval correspondence, the colonial war of 1863 and its impact on British Columbia history has been all but ignored by hwunitum historians who, if they recognize it at all, relegate the incident to that of a "police action" to apprehend "murderers"— a peripheral event outside the public mainstream of colonial history. The manufactured evidence, used in 1863 to incriminate the Lamalcha and to justify the military, or "police," action against them, is perpetuated. To cover up a bungled military operation (the attack on Lamalcha by HMG *Forward*) and to pave the way for hwunitum settlement, the Lamalcha people were vilified as "murderers" and "outlaws." For over a century, one of the Lamalcha leaders, Acheewun, was characterized in popular histories as "a bloodthirsty villain," while the efforts of the colonial police and Royal Navy to maintain "law and order" in these matters were championed. Issues surrounding the erosion of hwulmuhw sovereignty and jurisdiction in the face of ongoing hwunitum migration are seldom addressed— relegated to a "shadow history." It is this "shadow history" of the received version, the story of hwulmuhw resistance, which this book seeks to reveal.

There are other reasons why this story did not make its mark in the history of British Columbia. Although the Royal Navy, one of the most powerful military organizations in the world, figured prominently in the conflict, it produced no glorious victories or naval heroes. In the one pitched battle that did occur, naval forces were defeated by lesser armed opponents and there was little desire to publicize this fact, when elsewhere in the world Britain's imperial war machine was trampling aboriginal armies. Aristocratic naval officers hoping to carve distinguished careers for themselves in the Pacific Northwest saw little glory or pride in hunting down small bands of fugitives and then flogging them to extract confessions.

Similarly, the war and the trials that followed were not a proud legacy for the aging colonial regime of Governor James Douglas, which was in its final year. The trials and executions of three teenagers and four men in the spring and summer of 1863 were controversial and condemned by many hwunitum as a "gross injustice." The active influence of the colonial executive, manifest in the person of James Douglas, over a supposed independent judiciary (the Chief Justice of the Supreme Court, David Cameron, was his brother-in-law) insured that there would be no due process of law against hwulmuhw defendants, particularly those who actively opposed hwunitum occupation of their lands. Douglas, in his official correspondence with the Colonial Office in London, suppressed information and downplayed hwulmuhw opposition to colonization. Shortly after the conflict with the Lamalcha warriors broke out, Douglas was informed that he was being eased into retirement by the Colonial Office. Within months he was gone from the political scene, and the events of the final year of his long career as "the father of British Columbia" were forgotten by "mainstream" British Columbians.

Finally, there remains the colonial myth that, contrary to what happened south of the 49th parallel, the British resettlement of British Columbia was benign, bloodless and law-abiding. For their part, the Lamalcha warriors faced the most powerful weaponry ever used against North American indigenous people. Naval warships such as the 185 foot HMS *Cameleon* with its seventeen breech-loading, rifled cannon, firing thirty-two to forty pound shells of exploding shrapnel, were the nineteenth century equivalent of modern-day naval destroyers and capable of causing mass destruction within seconds. Granted, the "Indian Wars" of British Columbia came nowhere near the wholesale slaughter of aboriginal people that too often characterized the inter-racial conflict in the western United States, but as one historian has observed, "human conflict does not decline in complexity as it does in scale." Our history books do not record the words of a hwunitum newspaperman who wrote, at the end of the trial which sent four Lamalcha and Penelakut warriors to the gallows: "We have disgraced our humanity, our religion, our law, and our free constitution by staining our hands with innocent blood." The trials of 1863, detailed in the pages of this book, will demonstrate how those who could not be killed by the armed forces of the colony were prosecuted and killed by its judiciary.

Hul'qumi'num First Nations have always known that the colonial government made solemn promises to negotiate treaties with them and that these promises were broken. They have not forgotten the time when the Royal Navy bombarded their villages, took hostages and prisoners, tortured and hanged them—and the reason why. As Emily Rice recalls:

Mom was saying they attacked Kuper. Took the ladies away. Killed the men and the kids. They were just trying to get rid of the Indians so they could take their land.

Details are few—eradicated by generations of exposure to the residential school system which separated many young people from their elders and the natural flow of oral history. The colonial war of 1863 was also a "civil war" that pitted family against family, and people can be reluctant to talk about such conflicts for fear of renewing old feuds. "It's best not to talk about it," an elder said. "It brings back bad feelings." Others recall with pride how a lone rifleman "held off the gunboat" at Lamalcha when the *Forward* attacked the village.

Land claims by First Nations have been an ongoing issue in British Columbia since colonial times but their origins and issues are not well understood by the majority of people in the province. On Salt Spring Island, the largest of the Gulf Islands, there is a belief persistent among the hwunitum population that the island was only used occasionally by Hul'qumi'num First Nations, as if such limited use diminished their ownership. This myth, invented by the first hwunitum settlers to justify their own claims to the land, reflected a hwunitum point of view that hunter-gatherer societies represented an idle, wandering way of life when in fact the exploitation of seasonal resources owned by specific families were essential parts of the hwulmuhw economy. Permanent settlements fluctuated over time, but there were few parts of Salt Spring Island that were not owned by a hwulmuhw family, be they from Saanich, Cowichan, Halalt, Lamalcha, Penelakut or Lyacksen. As Roy Edwards explains:

Salt Spring Island was used by many different peoples because it was so full of food there. Ducks, black ducks, plants, oysters, clams. It was quite rich. It had all the food that the Indians wanted.

The land and the resources it provided were extremely valuable, and it was its loss that impoverished the people of the land.

Chapter One

Tthu tumuhw 'i' tthu hwulmuhw
'i' tthu hwunitum
(The Land, the People of the Land,
and the Hungry People)

Our interests are guided by the teachings of the elders. They have passed down a system of land tenure that emphasizes stewardship and harmony with the earth. The land and its resources are a gift from the Creator and therefore our traditional lands have a special and distinct place in our cultural, spiritual and economic well-being. The environment we lived in meant that we guarded our territory with our lives. The first traders who came to participate in our economy were there at our pleasure and had to conform to the environment we lived in for survival. Hul'qumi'num had and maintained a vibrant economy and a culture that was the bond to the land and the resources. This era in our history had little poverty, as the land supplied every element of our needs.

—Hul'qumi'num Treaty Group, LANDS,
Opening Statement, March 30th, 1998 [1]

The east coast of Vancouver Island is a rolling forested plain that narrows towards the south where the mountainous spine of the great island edges towards the sea, and two rivers, the Cowichan and Chemainus, drain the ancient forests through valleys and fertile deltas. Offshore, a maze of smaller islands forms a seemingly impassable wall along the Gulf of Georgia—the inland sea which separates Vancouver Island and the Gulf Islands from the distant mountains of the continental mainland.

A rain shadow cast by the Olympic Peninsula provides the east coast of Vancouver Island and the Gulf Islands with a distinctive climate characterized by mild, wet winters and long, cool summers. Natural resources of the sea and land abound although they pale in comparison with those of a century ago. Throughout the year, intertidal shorelines harbour numerous species of shellfish. In winter, ducks by the thousands once flocked to wetlands and natural harbours. On the land, deer and elk flourished in the forests and meadows, which were filled with many species of edible and medicinal plants. In spring, the myriad herring spawn in sheltered waters, attracting chinook salmon followed by stellar sealions and human beings in search of them all. The cycle culminates each summer with the great migration of sockeye salmon to the Fraser River and the return of the chum salmon to the creeks and rivers of Vancouver island.

But it was not always so. In the shwi'em' (time of the ancient stories) when the world was made "there was nothing on it—just ground and water."[2]

Then Heel's, the Changer, "came down to the world to finish things ... he went about fixing things, making lakes and rivers, and all things that grow, and then he made animals and all things like that."[3] Heel's dropped the first people from the sky to populate the land. A man named Syalutsa' landed on a grassy field called Tsuqwulu on the southwest side of the mountain Swuqus overlooking the Cowichan Valley.[4] A little further north Stutsun fell from the sky and landed on the mountain Skwaakwnus above the Chemainus River.[5] Other people came out of the land itself. At Penelakut on Kuper Island two great cedar logs lay by the shore. Warmed by the rays of the sun, the bark on one of the logs cracked and out came the first man on the island. Within a short time he was joined by the first woman, who emerged from the sand between the two logs.[6] Syalutsa', Stutsun, and the others who landed atop the mountains and hills of Vancouver Island or emerged from the driftwood and sands of Kuper Island are the ancestors of the Hul'qumi'num First Nations.[7]

Heel's created the resources used by the first people and introduced the snuw'uy'ul (the cultural teachings), which governed all manner of conduct and interaction with the spiritual and physical realm, including the use of specific places and resources by specific families. As Cowichan elder Angus Smith explains:

> Where you dropped is where you belong ... Particular areas were peculiar to certain groups or families, where our ancestors were dropped on earth. They were carrying the cultural teachings ... Several peoples would go up the Cowichan River to the lake gathering their food. They knew where food was available. They gathered elk, deer and trout at the lake. Each place was designated to them. The cultural teachings were shown them, instructing them what was good for their life. It was showing the first people what they could use. It was only from the Elders; they would decide as they would go up to the Lake area. That's the way it was with our ancestors; that's why the Cowichan people carry this tradition. All the places have names.[8]

Hwulmuhw place-names describe "either what grows there, or how the land was shaped, or what had happened to the land form."[9] To give but a few examples:

Hwaaqwum (merganser duck place) is the ancient name for Burgoyne Bay on Salt Spring Island and described the valued food resource found there at a certain time of the year; Prevost Island is called Hwes'hwum (place having hair seals), named for the seals sought for meat, oil and skins; Stsath (halibut) was the name given Long Harbour on Salt Spring Island to indicate the fish found there; and, at the north end of the same island, Pqunup (white ground) described the white shell beaches created by millions of discarded, bleached shells produced by the harvesting and processing of clams.[10]

Upon completion of his work, Heel's left the earth and, over time, with the retreat of the glaciers and the stabilization of the present land mass, the seasonal cycles of resource extraction by Hul'qumi'num First Nations became established. Nowhere else, in what is now British Columbia, was food procurable in such variety and abundance. People accessed these resources throughout the year. As elder Henry Edwards explains:

> Some things are ready at a certain time of year and that's when you go and get them. It was like that on Salt Spring Island. People would go when that food was ready. They went in the springtime and the summer, even winter. That's where they got their groceries.[11]

The preservation of large quantities of food during the bountiful months of summer, supplemented by localized resources, allowed the occupation of year-round village sites and the development, over at least 5,000 years, of a complex society.[12]

The ancestor Syalutsa' and other first people established villages on the Cowichan River and its delta.[13] They called themselves Cowichan after the mountain which looms to the east of the river delta and resembles a great frog "basking in the sun," or squw'utsun'.[14] House sites on the delta fluctuated with the changes in the river but by the time of first contact with hwunitum, over a dozen villages and house sites including the major settlements of Clemclemalits, Taitka, Comiaken, Quamichan, Khenipsen and Somenos, occupied the shores of Cowichan Bay or the banks of the Cowichan River.[15] Individual families owned fish weirs on the river but hunting and food-gathering on the delta was accessible to all.

Beyond the river and the delta, individual Cowichan families owned land and resources on the south end of Salt Spring Island from Hwaaqwum to Tsuween and on various Gulf Islands at Hwes'hwum, Sqtheq and elsewhere.[16] Food and other resource gathering sites extended across the Gulf of Georgia to such places as Theethuts'ton on the lower Fraser River where the majority of Cowichan people migrated every summer, to fish the great runs of sockeye salmon.[17]

To the north of the Cowichan, a closely-related group of people occupy villages on the east coast of Vancouver Island and the adjacent Gulf Islands of Kuper,

Ancestral Mountains Swuqus (left) and Skwaakwnus overlooking Chemainus Valley.
Photo by Barbara Arnett.

Penelakut, Kuper Island, 1983, looking towards Valdez Island, Porlier Pass and Galiano Island.
The old village occupied the shoreline at one end of Penelakut Spit where foundations and one
longhouse remain.   *Photo by Chris Arnett.*

Housepost at Penelakut village with carved representation of ancestor.
Photo by Elouise Street-Harises, 1924. Courtesty of Vancouver Museum, PN 12.

Galiano and Valdez. These people claim descent from Stutsun and other ancestors who fell from the sky onto the mountain Skwaakwnus overlooking the Chemainus River delta.[18] The hwunitum call them "Chemainus," but the people refer to themselves individually by the names of their winter villages—Halalt, Chemainus, Sickameen, Taitka (Lyacksen), Penelakut, Yuhwula'us or Lamalcha. Families from these villages at one time controlled various lands and resources on the east coast of Vancouver Island from Sthihum to Kwhwuyt and throughout the Gulf Islands.[19] Just as the Cowichan River was the focus of much economic activity for the Cowichan people, the smaller Chemainus River (Silaqwa'l) was a focus for food and other resource gathering for Hul'qumi'num First Nations. Families from Penelakut owned aerial duck nets and fish sites on Bonsall Creek, but the tidal flats and resources at the mouth of the river were shared by all. Upriver, resources and hunting grounds were said to be used exclusively by Halalt, Sickameen, and Chemainus families only.[20] On the islands, Lamalcha and Penelakut families controlled access to certain lands and resources on both sides of Trincomalee Channel from Sqthaqa'l to Kulman, including the north end of Salt Spring Island from stulan on the west side to Shiyahwt on the east, and all of Galiano Island.[21] Taitka (closely related to the Cowichan village of the same name) controlled Valdez Island and shared with the Penelakut the annual sealion hunt at Porlier Pass.[22] All of these people crossed the Gulf of Georgia each summer to Hwlitsum (Canoe Pass), on the south arm of the Fraser River Delta, Tluktinus, and further up the river at Qiquyt, to fish the sockeye.[23]

The Hul'qumi'num First Nations of Vancouver Island and the Gulf Islands lived in villages ranging in size from one to fifteen large rectangular houses constructed of cedar posts and beams covered with split cedar planks. Each house contained one or more nuclear families which occupied its own section, referred to as lelum'unup, or 'the place where you are from."[24] Together these nuclear families of brothers, cousins and brothers-in-law living in one great house formed the hw'nuchalewum, or house group, the "highest unit of common allegiance" within the village.[25]

Despite shared ancestry, name and identification with a localized territory, the village was not an isolated, self-contained social unit under a single leader, but a loose alliance of hw'nuchalewum which might co-operate in food-gathering activities, labour exchange, or mutual defence. However, as anthropologist Wayne Suttles explains, "they were not obliged to do so by any formal village organization. There was no office of village chief and no village council. Co-operation was *ad hoc*. Leadership was for specific purposes and was exercised by virtue of specific skills, property rights, or supposed superhuman powers."[26]

The institution of marriage connected hw'nuchalewum to house groups in other villages throughout the territories of Hul'qumi'num First Nations and beyond. As a result, "individual and family status was as dependent upon ties of marriage and kinship with other villages as upon economic rights and traditional identity with one's own village."[27] These intervillage ties constituted the hwulmuhw community more so than the village itself.

Hul'qumi'num First Nations evolved a society divided into three distinct levels of status.[28] The majority of people were considered to be "high class people," individually addressed as si'em. The si'em descended from distinguished ancestors from whom they inherited important names which came with rights and privileges, including access to certain lands and resources. The si'em greatly outnumbered the commoners, or stashum, "low class" people who had "lost their history" and "had no claim to the most productive resources of the area and no claim to recognized inherited privileges."[29] The stashum often lived in separate houses in their own section of the village or in a different location altogether where they remained subservient to the "high class" people.[30] Slaves, or skwuyuth, persons captured in war or purchased, were few in number and lived in the houses of the wealthy where they were regarded as private property.

Si'em owned the property rights to the most productive food gathering areas in the surrounding countryside, but high status came from the sharing of food. Their rights and privileges were validated through the cultural institution of stlun'uq, or potlatch, an occasion when people from other villages were invited by a host hw'nuchalewum "to receive gifts of wealth to validate changes of status and exercise inherited privileges."[31] Suttles writes that the stlun'uq:

> ... played an important part within this system of sharing access to resources. By potlatching, a group established its status vis-à-vis other groups, in effect saying "we are an extended family (or village of several extended families) with title to such-and-such a territory having such-and-such resources." And when a leading member assumed a name that harked back to the beginning of the world when the ancestors of the group first appeared on the spot, this not only demonstrated the validity of the group's title but perhaps also announced in effect "this is the man in charge of our resources."[32]

Within the total socio-economic system, the most important function of the stlun'uq, as Suttles has demonstrated, was not the drive for high status but the redistribution of wealth derived from family-owned resources within the inter-village community—the recipients of which would, at some future date, be obliged to return.

Hwulmuhw land tenure was not a matter of exclusive title by individuals to separate pieces of land, but was based on the ownership of resources by individual hw'nuchalewum. Land was not viewed as a commodity, but was valued for the resources it provided to feed, house, clothe, and equip an individual and his extended family. Access and management of clam beds, seal rocks, fishing sites, camas and wild clover patches, and other resources formed the basis of a family's wealth. The exploitation and redistribution of these resources was the foundation of the basis of the hwulmuhw economy.

The boundaries of family-owned lands and resources were well-known. As Robert Akerman explains:

> Lots of people say that the Indians didn't own the land because it wasn't surveyed. But they had it surveyed by landmarks, rivers, creeks, mountains and rocks—That sort of thing.[33]

Although there were hunting and gathering areas within the vicinity of the winter villages which were accessible to all, access to privately-owned resources was restricted and the penalty for unauthorized trespassing, at least in the first half of the nineteenth century, was harsh. An early account of Hul'qumi'num First Nations property rights comes from the son of a noble Quamichan woman and an Englishman named John Humphreys who settled in the Cowichan River delta possibly as early as 1856. According to his information "as told by the Indians themselves":

> Every family had its own hunting and fishing grounds, and the tract of land which each one claimed was in proportion to the size of the family, if it was a large family it had a large tract of land, and vice versa. Sometimes one family had to its credit many miles of land, for its hunting and fishing purposes. If one Indian found another man poaching on his land he immediately shot and killed him as it was within the law to do so. There were very few laws but what there were, were strictly kept, as the punishment for breaking them was very strict. Also every man could get nearly all the game he wanted on his own property and consequently did not have to trespass on his neighbour's land.[34]

Recognition of family ownership was important, but access to family-owned resources was not denied those who followed protocol. When permission was asked of the owners to access a resource, it was rarely refused. Consider the resources owned by a "high class" Clemclemalits family at Hwaaqwum (Burgoyne Bay) on Salt Spring Island:

> They owned the property and they used to stay there. The Indians didn't just use the land occasionally—they owned it. If others wanted to fish or hunt in that area they'd have to get permission.[35]

The land was the source of economic well-being and deeply venerated for its spiritual values. The landscape preserved the teachings of Heel's in strange rock formations, contained the bones of the ancestors, and was the abode of stlutle'luqum (dangerous little beings.) [36] Wealth and success in life depended on supernatural power bestowed by stlutle'luqum, but it was only accessible to those who trained hard and maintained strict standards of conduct. This power enabled men and women to excel in their particular talents. Salt Spring Island, the largest of the Gulf Islands, harboured many sacred sites on its mountains and lakes where youths sought supernatural power.

In the late eighteenth and early nineteenth centuries, hwulmuhw prophets foresaw the impending change which would upset forever the established economic cycles and social order—contact with the expanding Christian trading empires of Europe and America:

> A Shaman dreamed that a great canoe came to his village, moving without paddles. A man with a black face, black with hair and with white skin underneath, smiled and called the old man friend. The stranger gave the old man a little box, painted in bright colours, then departed in his great canoe.
>
> The old man tried to open the box, but could not discover how the lid was fastened down. Suddenly the box flew open and out roared a great wind that dried up the springs and creeks. The fish left the waters of the sea and rivers and the deer ran to the other side of the mountains.
>
> The great wind dried the old man's throat, so that he thirsted for whiskey, a drink he had never tasted. The warriors fell to quarrelling with one another and none would listen to wise advice.
>
> Finally, out of the little box came the spotted sickness, and the shaman knew that the white man's gift was—death. [37]

Long before the hwunitum settled on the Gulf of Georgia, their presence had a deadly impact on the aboriginal people in the form of smallpox, which reached the area about 1782 overland from the Columbia River region to the south. [38] The plague was spent by the time it reached the northern reaches of the Georgia Strait but, in its wake, hwulmuhw population centres were decimated. Untouched Kwakwaka'wakw populations to the north took advantage of the situation and launched devastating raids into the territories of their disabled southern neighbours in search of slaves and wealth. [39] The end of the plague coincided with the rise of the maritime fur trade, the main centre of which was the Nuuchahnulth territories on the west coast of Vancouver Island. Although only indirectly involved with the European and American traders at first, the Kwakwaka'wakw procured European/American trade goods, and particularly muskets, which further augmented their military superiority over their southern opponents, causing great social unrest in the region.

The establishment of the Hudson's Bay Company at Fort Langley on the Fraser River in 1827 gave hwulmuhw increased access to European trade goods and muskets and restored the balance of power between hwulmuhw and Kwakwaka'wakw fighting forces. Muskets allowed hwulmuhw warriors to match their opponents' fighting abilities and allowed pre-emptive raids into Kwakwaka'wakw homelands which, over time, checked their southward advance. [40]

The increase in musket-dominated warfare created innovations in hwulmuhw tactics. Hwulmuhw warriors quickly learned the advantages of volley firing, whereby men fired their muskets in unison at a single target. Smoothbore muskets, by themselves heavy and slow to load, were almost less effective in combat than bows and arrows, but fired en masse their effect was devastating, especially when fired upon an unsuspecting foe from a concealed position. This tactic, the surprise volley, became a trademark of hwulmuhw warfare and was responsible for several important victories over the Kwakwaka'wakw. [41]

The introduction of firearms also caused modifications in defense works, such as the construction of earthwork trenches in combination with loopholed block-houses. Built of stout squared timbers, loopholed for muskets and cannon, the blockhouse allowed warriors to mass their firepower from a protected strategic strong point against an exposed, unprotected enemy. In the Saanich village of Tsouwat, each household built a blockhouse with plank walls "outside its own house. It had doors with locks and loopholes. It was about twenty feet high in front but lower in back, about the height of a man's reach." [42] These early blockhouses seem to have been simply smaller versions of the shed-roofed plank house. Possibly the most elaborate fortifications built by hwulmuhw were those erected by the Cowichan warrior, Tsosieten, at Taitka on the Cowichan River delta. Taitka was "surrounded by pickets and bastions out of which there poked three large cannon." [43]

The continuous fighting between Kwakwaka'wakw and Hul'qumi'num First Nations gave rise among the latter to a number of famous warrior si'em, including Hulkalatkstun of Penelakut, Tsosieten of Taitka, Lohar of Comiaken and Tzouhalem of Khinepsen. Born of a Quamichan man and a Comiaken woman, Tzouhalem, under the guidance of his grandmother, trained to be a warrior. His "old granny ... taught him how to bathe himself every day, rubbing his skin with hemlock boughs, and to run in the woods and away back in the hills where the spirits would come and talk to him." [44] Tzouhalem met a cannibal spirit that told him: "When you fight and when you kill people, I shall be with you," whereupon Tzouhalem "went back to his cave home and sang his mystery song ... which signified that he had been given human flesh to eat. When he danced he flourished his gun and knife." [45]

Tzouhalem's seemingly invincible fighting ability and unruly behaviour led to his being asked to leave the village of Quamichan, which he did, establishing himself and his followers in a single fortified house at Khinepsen at the mouth of the Cowichan River near Comiaken, the village of his mother.[46] Tzouhalem maintained his association with Quamichan. An 1853 hwunitum census identified him as the preeminent "chief," and it seems likely that Tzouhalem's fighting prowess helped to establish Quamichan as the largest and wealthiest of the Cowichan villages with a reputation for opposition to hwunitum encroachment.[47]

Hwulmuhw military ascendency culminated in the battle of Hwtlupnets (c.1840), when an unprecedented alliance of Hul'qumi'num First Nations, Nanaimo, Saanich, Songhees, Esquimalt, Musqueam and Squamish warriors gathered to defeat an invading armada of Kwakwaka'wakw-speaking Lekwiltok and their Comox allies.[48] The mobilization occurred when word reached the south that an invasion by a large force of northerners was imminent. After entering the territories of Hul'qumi'num First Nations, the northerners reached Hwtlupnets (Maple Bay) where they made camp on the beach. Under the leadership of Tzouhalem and Tsosieten, the hwulmuhw army divided into two divisions, one on either side of the bay. A third party, dressed to appear as women, canoed into the bay where they were sighted by the northerners who set off in pursuit only to be caught as the hwulmuhw allies, following a system of pre-arranged signals, closed in to slaughter them.[49] It was the first and last time such a diverse group of First Nations united to defeat a common enemy. The battle of Hwtlupnets ended large-scale raids by northern peoples into the south, although smaller raids and violent encounters with Hul'qumi'num First Nations continued for another three decades.

Worried by the pending American annexation of the Columbia River region, where Fort Vancouver was the Pacific Ocean depot for the Hudson's Bay Company, George Simpson, the company's governor, directed that another fort be established on the southern end of Vancouver Island. Acting on these instructions, Chief Factor James Douglas in March of 1843 left Fort Vancouver in the Hudson's Bay Company steamer *Beaver* and proceeded to Vancouver Island. Born in 1803, in British Guiana of a Scottish father and an Afro-American mother, Douglas had been in the service of the Hudson's Bay Company in the Pacific Northwest since 1821. As a result of his long tenure with the country, he understood intimately many aspects of aboriginal culture. Over six feet tall, this "stout powerful man of good conduct and respectable abilities" who was "furiously violent when aroused" loomed larger than any other over the early history of British Columbia.[50]

Upon his arrival on southern Vancouver Island on March 14th, 1843, the 39-year-old Douglas selected land owned by Lekwungaynung-speaking people adjacent to a protected harbour for what was to be the site of Fort Victoria. The first meeting between the British and the owners of the land involved a degree of confrontation and uncertainty. As one member of the expedition observed:

> It was about four o'clock in the afternoon when we arrived there. At first we saw only two canoes; but, having discharged two cannon shot, the aborigines left their retreats and surrounded the steamboat. The following day canoes arrived from all sides. [51]

A mutual understanding was soon reached. Douglas "informed them of our intention of building in this place which appeared to please them very much."[52] With their co-operation and assistance, a log stockade was soon erected and the fort's buildings were under way. On the evening of March 17th, a "luminous column" appeared in an arc across the sky.[53] Having heard about the hwunitum and attracted by the celestial event, some 1,200 Cowichan, Clallam, and Saanich people converged on the site where they were greeted by the first Roman Catholic priest to set foot on Vancouver Island, Father Jean Baptiste Bolduc. He conducted mass on Sunday the 18th, and proceeded to a nearby village where he performed 102 baptisms. A young man told Bolduc that his arrival had been prophesied many years earlier.[54]

Hwulmuhw welcomed the presence of the new hwunitum fort on Vancouver Island because it meant increased access to hwunitum merchandise, particularly firearms, ammunition, blankets, hardware and liquor. Within a year, however, a dispute arose over jurisdiction which threatened to erupt in violence and all-out war between the hwunitum traders and the coalition of warriors who had recently defeated the northern raiders at Hwtlupnets. To provide meat for a feast, a hwulmuhw hunting party shot what a Hudson's Bay Company employee claimed were "some of our best working oxen & horses." The animals were not in the fort, which the hwulmuhw seemed to acknowledge as hwunitum property, but were "left feeding on the surrounding grounds": fair game, as it were, for the hwulmuhw owners of the land outside the Hudson's Bay Company establishment. Roderick Finlayson, who had recently assumed the position of Chief Trader, responded by suspending trade and issuing ultimatums: "I then sent a message to the chiefs demanding the delivery of the perpetrators of this unprovoked deed, or payment to be made for the animals killed which they declined doing—I then suspended trade or any dealing with them until this matter was settled—Whereupon they sent word to some of the neigbouring tribes—to come to their assistance, as they intended to attack the Fort."[55] The hwulmuhw in the vicinity of Fort Victoria called for a gathering of the same alliance of warriors who had recently defeated the Kwakwaka'wakw and their allies at Hwtlupnets.

The hwulmuhw soon received these reinforcements, including a contingent of Cowichan warriors under Tzouhalem, who assumed command of the military operation. After two days of negotiations, the warriors of the alliance "opened fire

on the Fort riddling the stockade & roofs of the House with their musket balls."
The fusillade was intense and according to Finlayson, "it was with the greatest
difficulty I could prevail on our men not then to return the Fire, but wait for my
orders." The Chief Trader knew that any response on the part of the Fort would
plunge the Hudson's Bay Company into a disastrous war against a numerically
superior and well-armed foe. Finlayson decided on a display of force to intimidate
the attackers, without harming them, in order to re-open negotiations. He loaded
a cannon with grape shot and fired it at a nearby empty hwulmuhw house,
completely demolishing it. The firing ceased and the two sides agreed to a parley.
The dispute was settled according to hwulmuhw law, whereby compensation was
accepted for alleged wrong. Finlayson later wrote that he "was determined to have
the offenders punished, or payment made for the animals killed—They preferred
the latter, and before that day closed furs to the full amount were delivered at the
gate. After which we smoked the pipe of peace." [56]

On June 15th, 1846, in the face of increasing militancy by American squatters in
the Oregon and Washington Territories, the Treaty of Washington was signed by the
United States and Great Britain, conceding to the Americans the 49th parallel as the
boundary from the Rocky Mountains to the Pacific, but leaving Vancouver Island
within the British sphere of influence. In that same year the Governor of the
Hudson's Bay Company, Sir John Pelly, wrote to Earl Grey, the Colonial Secretary of
Great Britain, informing him that:

> The Hudson's Bay Company having formed an establishment on the
> southern point of Vancouver's Island, which they are annually enlarging,
> are anxious to know whether they will be confirmed in the possession of
> such lands, as they may find it expedient to add to those which they
> already possess. [57]

Earl Grey agreed that the interests of Great Britain in the region would best be
served by an active policy of British immigration and colonization to check
American settlement. Despite controversy over the plan, on January 13, 1849,
Queen Victoria signed the grant making the Hudson's Bay Company "the true and
absolute lords and Proprietors" of Vancouver Island, "together with all royalties of
the seas upon these coasts within the limits aforesaid, and all mines royal thereto
belonging." [58]

The days of the fur trade were coming to an end as the Hudson's Bay Company
operations diversified to include farming, salmon-curing, logging and now
colonization. The company was to assume responsibility for all civil and military
affairs in the new colony, the costs of which were to be borne by land sales. The
grant would be reviewed every five years and, if cancelled, the imperial government
"might repurchase the Island, provided it reimbursed the Company for its expenditures and for its establishments and property." [59]

The only reference to the island's aboriginal owners in the letters patent was a statement that British colonization under the auspices of the Hudson's Bay Company "would induce greatly ... to the protection and welfare of the native Indians residing within that portion of Our territories," presumably in contrast to the state of war then existing between aboriginal people and Americans to the south, in the company's former domains of the Oregon and Washington Territories. [60] In London little was known regarding the aboriginal people of the region, and the question of extinguishing aboriginal title prior to occupation of the land was left to local Hudson's Bay Company officials. However, the intent of the Colonial Office regarding this issue is revealed in a confidential draft of a parliamentary paper prepared in March 1849, for the consideration of cabinet, which stated that:

> ... in parting with the land of the island Her Majesty parts only with her own right therein, and that whatever measures she was bound to take in order to extinguish the Indian title are equally obligatory on the Company. [61]

Recognition that such title did indeed exist was acknowledged in discussions concerning the creation of legislation to provide for the administration of justice in the new colony which referred to "that part of the Indian Territories called Vancouver's Island." [62]

. Chapter Two

The Entire Property of the White People Forever

It appears decreed that the white and red man are never to live in amity together, the history of the colonization and settlement of every portion of North America is but a continued chronicle of forcible occupations; it matters little whether the means employed be arms or negotiation, the poor savage is invariably in the end driven out of his patrimony, and the negotiation merely consists in the dictation of certain conditions by the more powerful, which the weaker has no choice but to accept; and which conditions are violated by the invader whenever it suits his convenience, or whenever he wishes a more extended boundary. Hitherto, in Vancouver Island the tribes who have principally been in intercourse with the white man, have found it for their interest to keep up that intercourse in amity for the purposes of trade, and the white adventurers have been so few in number, that they have not at all interfered with the ordinary pursuits of the natives. As the Colonial population increases ... the red man will find his fisheries occupied, and his game, on which he depended for subsistence, killed by others; the fishers will probably cause the first difficulty, as all the tribes are singularly jealous of their fishing privileges, and guard their rights with the strictness of a manorial preserve. Collisions will then doubtless take place, and the Tscallum [Klallam] and the Cowitchin will be numbered with the bygone braves of the Oneida and Delaware.

—Captain Walter Colquhoun Grant,
first independent settler on Vancouver Island, 1849[1]

According to British imperial policy, before settlement could take place on the lands "granted" to the Hudson's Bay Company, the aboriginal title to those lands had to be extinguished.[2] This policy was established in North America by the Royal Proclamation of 1763, which also stipulated that aboriginal land could only be ceded or sold to the Crown. However, events far across the Pacific Ocean in New Zealand set the precedent for the alienation of aboriginal territories on Vancouver

Island. The 1840 Treaty of Waitangi, which established British sovereignty, confirmed and guaranteed to "the Chiefs and tribes of New Zealand and to the respective families and individuals thereof the full exclusive and undisturbed possession of their Lands and Estates, Forests, Fisheries and other properties which they may collectively or individually possess ... so long as it is their wish and desire to retain the same in their possession."[3]

After the 1840 Treaty of Waitangi, the British government advanced money to the New Zealand Company to purchase Maori land on behalf of the Crown, land which would then be sold at a profit to pakeha [European] settlers. The largest land sale in New Zealand took place on the South Island in June 1848, when 13,551,400 acres of Ngai Tahu lands were conveyed to the New Zealand Company for £2,000.[4] The rangatira (chiefs) initially rejected the offer but later agreed on the condition that they would be guaranteed their places of residence, their mahinga kai (places where food is produced or procured), and ample reserved land for their descendants. The rangatira insisted that these conditions be written into the deed of conveyance. The British, as was required by the Treaty of Waitangi, agreed. The original deed was written in Maori by Tracy Kemp, who negotiated the agreement on behalf of the New Zealand Company, and it was read aloud to the assembled signatories who affixed their marks and signatures to the document at Akaroa on June 12th, 1848. Only later did the Ngai Tahu realize that the conditions would be ignored; that the actual amount of lands sold far exceeded what they had been led to believe; and that they would be denied access to traditional food gathering areas.[5]

Although the new colony of Vancouver Island was administered by a governor appointed by the Colonial Office in London, control of land and settlement was entrusted to the Hudson's Bay Company and it fell upon the company's highest ranking official in the colony, James Douglas, Chief Factor of Fort Victoria, to negotiate with the aboriginal people for the sale of their lands.

Douglas was probably aware of the New Zealand land sales and understood the necessity of undertaking similar agreements in the newly established colony of Vancouver Island.[6] On September 3rd, 1849, Douglas wrote to the Secretary of the Hudson's Bay Company, Archibald Barclay, that:

> Some arrangement should be made as soon as possible with the native Tribes for the purchase of their lands ... I would also strongly recommend, equally as a measure of justice, and from a regard to the future peace of the colony, that the Indian Fisheries, Village Sites and Fields, should be preserved for their benefit and fully secured to them by law.[7]

Before Douglas' letter reached London, Barclay wrote to him regarding the new colony and offered guidelines regarding the aboriginal people and their land according to the prevailing point of view of Britain's colonial administrators:

With respect to the rights of the natives, you will have to confer with the chiefs of the tribes on that subject, and in your negotiations with them you are to consider the natives as the rightful possessors of such lands only as they are occupied by cultivation, or had houses built on, at the time when the Island came under the undivided sovereignty of Great Britain in 1846. All other land is to be regarded as waste, and applicable to the purposes of colonization ... The Natives will be confirmed in the possession of their Lands as long as they occupy and cultivate them themselves but will not be allowed to sell or dispose of them to any private person, the right to the entire soil having been granted to the Company by the Crown. The right of fishing and hunting will be continued to them and when their lands are registered, and they conform to the same conditions with which other settlers are required to comply, they will enjoy the same rights and privileges.[8]

Barclay's instructions to Douglas were much influenced by the question of land alienation in New Zealand where British colonists managed to alienate Maori land despite the guarantees of property rights, including ownership and control of their economic resources, enshrined in the Treaty of Waitangi. Ignorant of aboriginal land tenure and the seasonal exploitation of food resources, colonist organizations lobbied for the alienation of land outside the perimeters of native settlements and agricultural plots which, under Pakeha (European) concepts of land tenure, were regarded as waste. Part of the problem was British acceptance of the social theory developed by Vattel, an eighteenth-century French legalist, who argued that cultivation alone gave the right to hold title to land. Hunting or food gathering were considered "idle" forms of existence. "Those who yet hold to the idle mode of life," wrote Vattel, "usurp more land than they would require with honest labour, and cannot complain if other nations, more laborious and too much pent-up, come and occupy a portion of it."[9]

Barclay drew on the report of a select committee of the House of Commons which examined Maori title in this regard and concluded that the Maori had only "qualified Dominion" over their lands. Barclay quoted directly from the select committee's report in his December 16th letter when he instructed Douglas that the "uncivilized inhabitants of any country have ... a right of occupancy only, and ... until they establish among themselves a settled form of government and subjugate the ground to their own uses by the cultivation of it ... they have not any individual property in it."[10]

When the secretary's letter arrived at Fort Victoria in the spring of 1850, Douglas lost no time in assembling the si'em of Songish, Clallam and Sooke families who occupied the lands surrounding the Fort and along the coast, west to Sherringham Point. Between April 29th and May 1st, 1850, Douglas negotiated nine agreements whereby he arranged, at least according to his point of view, that "the whole of their lands ... should be sold to the Company."[11] For his part, Douglas essentially made the same guarantees to the hwulmuhw leaders of southern Vancouver Island as Kemp made to the Ngai Tahu in New Zealand. On May 16th, he reported to Barclay that:

> I summoned to a conference, the chiefs and influential men of the Songees Tribe, which inhabits and claims the District of Victoria, from Gordon Head on Arro [Haro] Strait to Point Albert on the Strait of De Fuca as their own particular heritage. After considerable discussion it was arranged that the whole of their lands, forming as before stated the District of Victoria, should be sold to the Company, with the exception of Village sites and enclosed fields, for a certain remuneration, to be paid at once to each member of the Tribe. I was in favour of a series of payments to be made annually but the proposal was so generally disliked that I yielded to their wishes and paid the sum at once.
>
> The members of the Tribe on being mustered were found to number 122 men or heads of families, to each of whom was given a quantity of goods equal in value to 17s Sterling and the total sum disbursed on this purchase was £103.14.0 Sterling at Dept. price. I subsequently made a similar purchase from the Clallum Tribe, of the country lying between Albert Point and Soke [Sooke] Inlet. In consequence of the claimants not being so well known as the Songees, we adopted a different mode of making the payments, by dealing exclusively with the Chiefs, who received and distributed the payments while the sale was confirmed and ratified by the Tribe collectively. This second purchase cost about £30.0.8. I have since made a purchase from the Soke Tribe of the land between Soke Inlet and Point Sherringham, the arrangement being concluded in this as in the preceeding purchase with the Chiefs or heads of families who distributed the property among their followers.[12] The cost of this tract which does not contain much cultivable land was £16.8.8. The total cost, as before stated, is £150.3.4.
>
> I informed the natives that they would not be disturbed in the possession of their Village sites and enclosed fields, which are of small extent, and that they were at liberty to hunt over the unoccupied lands, and to carry on their fisheries with the same freedom as when they were the sole occupants of the country.
>
> I attached the signatures of the native Chiefs and others who subscribed the deed of purchase to a blank sheet on which will be copied the contract or Deed of conveyance, as soon as we receive a proper form, which I beg may be sent out by return of Post.[13]

In response to Douglas's request for a "contract or Deed of conveyance" to append the 'X's made by the si'em, Barclay sent Douglas a hand-written English translation of Kemp's Deed of 1848, with blank spaces for the names of the tribes, lands, payments and dates. In the accompanying letter Barclay informed Douglas that the "Governor and Committee [of the Hudson's Bay Company] very much approve of the measure you have taken in respect of the lands claimed by the natives. You will receive herewith the form or contract or deed of Conveyance to be used on future occasions when lands are to be surrendered to the Company by the native tribes. It is a copy with hardly any alteration of the Agreement adopted by the New Zealand Company in their transactions of a similar kind with the natives there." [14] Barclay's version of Kemp's Deed became the text of the so-called "Douglas Treaties:"

Form of Agreement for purchase of Land from Natives of Vancouver's Island

Know all men. We the Chiefs and People of the tribe called ___ who have signed our names and made our marks to this Deed on the ___ day of ___ one thousand Eight hundred and ___ do consent to surrender entirely and for ever to James Douglas the Agent of the Hudson's Bay Company in Vancouver's Island that is to say, for the Governor Deputy Governor and Committee of the same the whole of the lands situate and lying between ___.

The condition of, or understanding of the sale is this, that our village sites and Enclosed Fields are to be left for our own use, for the use of our Children, and for those who may follow after us; and that the lands shall be properly surveyed hereafter; it is understood however that the land itself with these small exceptions becomes the Entire property of the White people for ever; it is also understood that we are at liberty to hunt over the unoccupied lands, and to carry on our fisheries as formerly. We have received as payment £___.

In token whereof we have signed our names and made our marks at ___ on the ___ day of ___ One thousand Eight hundred and ___. [here follow the Indian signatures] [15]

Upon receipt of Barclay's letter, Douglas adapted the text of the New Zealand-derived deed to each of the nine land sale agreements already negotiated. [16]

The question arises as to whether or not the native people of southern Vancouver Island knew what they were doing when they made these agreements with Douglas. Given the economic and spiritual significance of their ancestral territories, plus the fact that they did not share European concepts of land ownership, it is likely that the "Chiefs and headmen" were unaware of hwunitum intentions. Hwulmuhw leaders, however, were not opposed to hwunitum settlement and, like their counterparts in New Zealand, recognized the value of making agreements with the most powerful nation on earth as a means of establishing peace in a region plagued by ongoing wars. [17] As New Zealand historian James Belich suggests, sovereignty has two distinct shades of meaning which can be distinguished by adding the words "nominal" and "substantive." Nominal sovereignty is the theoretical dominion of a sovereign such as a monarch who "reigns but does not govern." Substantive sovereignty, on the other hand, refers to the actual dominion of a controlling power … which exercises a decisive, though not necessarily absolute, influence over the whole of a country." [18] Undoubtedly, Douglas had the latter meaning in mind when he forged his agreements, but it is likely that the former meaning was closer to the understanding of the Songees, Clallam and Sooke—a recognition of British nominal sovereignty in exchange for confirmation and acknowledgement of their substantive sovereignty over ancestral lands and resources.

There has been much emphasis on the low monetary value of these "transactions" which were, as Douglas himself indicated, based on the "Department" (i.e. wholesale) price of the goods, or seventeen shillings per three blankets, the number given each si'em. [19] The hwunitum price was irrelevant and, in the minds of the hwulmuhw recipients, had nothing to do with the value of the land which Douglas believed was being sold. The aboriginal leaders who took part in these early land sale agreements accepted the Hudson's Bay Company blankets not as payment for "the whole of their lands," but as a symbolic payment comparable to the blankets and other goods distributed at the stlun'uq, or potlatch, for the witnessing of important events. In this instance, the acceptance of three blankets by each si'em validated Douglas' word that "they would not be disturbed in the possession of their Village sites and enclosed fields … and that they were at liberty to hunt over the unoccupied lands, and to carry on their fisheries with the same freedom as when they were the sole occupants of the country." [20] Hwulmuhw families saw the agreements as a confirmation of their ownership of ancestral village sites and the food-gathering resources which were the foundation of their economy.

Positive word of the "Douglas Treaties" spread to neighbouring First Nations. "The Cowetchin [Cowichan] and other Tribes," wrote Douglas, "have since expressed a wish to dispose of their lands, on the same terms; but I declined their proposals in consequence of our not being prepared to enter into possession." [21]

Two years later, as the lands in the ceded territories around Fort Victoria were occupied by hwunitum, apparently without, any objection by hwulmuhw, Douglas, who was now Governor of the Colony of Vancouver Island, looked to extinguish the title of the Saanich people whose land and resources lay northeast of Fort Victoria. Douglas and other Hudson's Bay Company employees became shareholders in the "Vancouver's Island Steam Saw Mill Company," which commenced logging operations on lands owned by Saanich families near Cadboro Bay. The Saanich objected to this unauthorized use of their resources. According to a Saanich elder, the late Dave Elliot Senior:

> Our people got together and they said "What are we going to do about those beautiful trees? Are we just going to sit here and just let them do it?" So they talked back and forth and said, "No, we can't just let it go, we have to say something." So they decided to do something about it.[22]

Four canoes of Saanich warriors proceeded to the site of the logging operation and ordered the hwunitum to leave—which they did. Douglas then sought to make a land sale agreement with the Saanich along the same lines as the previous agreements of 1850. He informed the Hudson's Bay Company that:

> The steam saw mill Company having selected as the site of their operations the section of land … which being within the limits of the Sanitch country, those Indians came forward with a demand for payment, and finding it impossible to discover among the numerous claimists the real owners of the land in question, and there being much difficulty in adjusting such claims, I thought it adviseable to purchase the whole of the Sanitch Country, as a measure that would save much future trouble and expence. I succeeded in effecting that purchase in a general convention of the Tribe; who individually subscribed the Deed of Sale, reserving for their use only the village sites and potato patches, and I caused them to be paid the sum of £109.7.6 in woolen goods, which they preferred to money.[23]

When Douglas invited the headmen of the various winter villages of the Saanich Peninsula to Fort Victoria on February 7th and 11th, 1852, they were under the impression that the hwunitum leader wished to negotiate a peace treaty:

> When they got there, all these piles of blankets plus other goods were on the ground. They told them these bundles were for them plus about $200 but it was in pounds and shillings.
>
> They saw these bundles of blankets and goods and they were asked to put X's on this paper. They asked each head man to put an X on the paper. Our people didn't know what the X's were for. Actually they didn't call them X's they called them crosses. So they talked back and forth from one to the other and wondered why they were being asked to put crosses on the paper and they didn't know what the paper said. What I imagined from looking at the document was that they must have gone to each man and asked them their name and then they transcribed it in a very poor fashion and then asked them to make an X.
>
> One man spoke up after they discussed it, and said, "I think James Douglas wants to keep the peace."

They were after all almost in a state of war, a boy had been shot. [24] Also we stopped them from cutting timber and sent them back to Victoria and told them to cut no more timber.

"I think these are peace offerings. I think Douglas means to keep the peace. I think these are the sign of the cross."

He made the sign of the cross. The missionaries must have already been around by then, because they knew about the 'sign of the cross'! "This means Douglas is sincere."

They thought it was just a sign of sincerity and honesty. This was the sign of their God. It was the highest order of honesty.

It wasn't much later they found out actually they were signing their land away by putting those crosses out there. They didn't know what it said on the paper ... Our people were hardly able to talk English at that time and who could understand our language? [25]

Unlike the previous land sale agreements, those arranged with the Saanich were made with the actual text of the deed in place at the time they were signed. However, according to the oral history, the Saanich "did not know what it said on the paper." Even if interpreters were available to explain the wording of the deed of conveyance to the Saanich headmen there is still no assurance that the full implications of its contents were accurately conveyed to or understood by the Saanich. But with the guarantee that their winter villages, potato fields and traditional food gathering sources would be protected, the Saanich si'em saw no reason not to sign. The British had, after all, stopped cutting timber at Cadboro Bay when the Saanich protested. In any event, the oral history is clear on the point that it was the acceptance by Saanich leaders of Douglas' perceived sincerity that convinced them to agree to accept the blankets and thereby validate the agreement.

Across the Pacific Ocean, four years earlier, the Ngai Tahu had similarly debated "Kemp's Deed," and, in the final analysis, some, though by no means all, accepted its promise of undisturbed Maori occupation of their lands and continued access to resources based on the word of high-ranking British officials. Among aboriginal people such as the Ngai Tahu and the Saanich, the word of a man of recognizable high rank such as Douglas was sacrosanct and entirely dependable. To break one's word was to lose the most important aspect of a high-ranking person's life—his honour and the respect accorded him by others.

After the treaty with the Saanich had been executed, Douglas turned his attention to territories further north on Vancouver's Island.

From time immemorial, the Nanaimo people knew of the coal deposits in their territory and associated them with qwunus, the killer whale. The elders warned that interference with deposits would bring dire consequences:

So the head men said, "Never touch that black rock no matter where you see it, for it belongs to the great black fish, and if we touch that rock, all the fish will surely come and kill us."[26]

Qwunus did not come to kill the people, but the discovery of the valuable coal-bearing "Douglas vein" at Wentuhuysen Inlet in present day Nanaimo focused hwunitum interest on the territories of Hul'qumi'num First Nations along the east coast of Vancouver Island and hastened the alienation of those lands.

Although the existence of the rich coal deposits were confirmed in May 1850, the hwulmuhw lands which lay between Nanaimo and the Saanich Peninsula, including the extensive Cowichan and Chemainus Valleys and the offshore labyrinth of islands, remained relatively unknown to hwunitum. Douglas was aware of the agricultural potential of the region as early as 1849 when he informed the Hudson's Bay Company that the Cowichan Valley "is reported by the Indians to be much superior to this part of Vancouver's Island in respect to extent of cultivated land."[27] Potato cultivation, introduced decades earlier, had reached such heights that hwulmuhw farmers harvested them by the ton from extensive fields in the Cowichan and Chemainus Valleys and traded the surplus to the hwunitum.[28]

In May 1851, Douglas instructed two Hudson's Bay employees, Joseph MacKay and Tomo Antoine, to explore the Cowichan Valley "with a view to opening [it] to settlers."[29] Both men were seasoned veterans of the company and Antoine, of Chinook/Iroquois ancestry, would play an important role in the alienation of hwulmuhw lands. A "slight, actively built man, with a dark copper-coloured face, lit up by keen, intelligent eyes," Antoine served the Company "in several capacities, as guide, hunter, and interpreter in all of which capacities he [stood] unrivalled."[30] MacKay and Antoine, the first outsiders to explore the Cowichan Valley, made their reconnaissance "under the protection of 'Hosua'[Tsosieten] chief of the Cowitchen tribe," and reported land suitable for agriculture along the river.[31]

The first hwunitum to live in the area was a Quebecois, Father Honore Timothy Lempfrit of the Roman Catholic order, Oblates des Mary Immaculate. Described by Douglas as "a very able and zealous teacher," Lempfrit had been "loaned" to the diocese of Vancouver Island until the arrival of the consecrated Bishop Modeste Demers.[32] In October 1851, without the authorization of the Bishop who was in Europe, Lempfrit left Victoria to establish a mission among the Cowichan. His arrival amongst the Cowichan at the beginning of their winter dances eventually created "a great lack of cordiality between the pastor and his flock."[33] Fearing that Lempfrit's continued presence in the Cowichan Valley would endanger the peace of the colony, Douglas, in May 1852, dispatched a constable and ten men to rescue him in the first armed intervention in Cowichan affairs by hwunitum.[34] Shortly thereafter Lempfrit left for Oregon.[35] Following this experience, Douglas discouraged missionary activities outside of the Colony of Vancouver Island where, in unceded territories, he was unable to guarantee their safety.

His activities drew censure from the church, but Lempfrit's short-lived mission planted the seeds of Catholicism amongst Hul'qumi'num First Nations. As one church historian observed, during his stay, Lempfrit "in his inexperience and for the lack of someone to counsel him … baptized over four thousand Indians, and married as many of them as must receive the Church's blessing on their union, after only eight days of instruction and probation." [36]

Douglas was anxious to explore the area for himself, particularly in light of the discovery of extensive coal deposits at Nanaimo. In early August 1852, he "carried out the project which [he had] long entertained, of a canoe expedition, through the Canal de Arro and along the East Coast of Vancouver's Island, for the purpose of examining the country and communicating with the native tribes, who inhabit that part of the Colony." [37] Douglas soon discovered that he was literally entering uncharted territory where, up until Lempfrit's mission, few hwunitum had ventured. Using the latest map of Vancouver Island as a chart, Douglas soon noted its "extreme incorrectness" beyond Cowichan Head on the east coast of the Saanich Peninsula. "From that point," he wrote, "all resemblance to the Coast ceases." [38]

Passing beneath the prominent steep slopes of the south end of Salt Spring Island, Douglas was informed that the place was called Tsuween (land [mountain] comes down to the water.) [39] Douglas anglicized the Hul'qumi'num place name to "Chuan" and used it to refer to the entire island.

Proceeding up the Arro Canal (Sansum Narrows), Douglas' canoe expedition "touched at the Cowegin [Cowichan] River, which falls into the Canal … and derives its name from the tribe of Indians which inhabit the neighbouring country." [40] Douglas was impressed by the extent of Cowichan agriculture. "These Indians," he wrote, "partially cultivate the alluvial Islands near the mouth of the river, where we saw many large and well kept fields of potatoes, in a very flourishing state, and a number of fine cucumbers which had been raised in the open air, without any particular care." [41]

North of the Cowichan territory, Douglas briefly explored the mouth of the Chemainus River which he recognized as being smaller than the Cowichan River, and "navigable to a short distance only from the Coast. It is inhabited by a branch of the Cowegin [Cowichan] Tribe, whom we did not see." [42] Douglas then proceeded to Nanaimo where he examined the coal deposits and experienced "a feeling of exultation in beholding so huge a mass of mineral wealth." [43]

Upon his return to Fort Victoria, Douglas was optimistic that further exploration of the east coast of Vancouver Island and the Gulf Islands would benefit the colony.

In his August 17th letter to Sir John Packington, Her Majesty's Principal Secretary of State for the Colonial Department, Douglas wrote that:

> A correct survey of these channels will remove many of the difficulties that would at present be experienced by sailing vessels navigating these straits and, should Her Majesty's Government, at any time, direct surveys to be made in this quarter, I think the Arro Archipelago will be found to have peculiar claims to their attention, as there is a prospect of its soon becoming the channel of a very important trade.[44]

The relative isolation of Hul'qumi'num First Nations from overt hwunitum influence on Vancouver Island's east coast and the adjacent islands was over. The discovery and development of the Hudson Bay Company's coal mining operations at Nanaimo focused hwunitum attention on securing title to the valuable coal-bearing deposits. On the 24th of August, 1852, with the vast majority of the Nanaimo people away at the Fraser River sockeye fishery, Douglas instructed Joseph MacKay "to proceed with all possible diligence to Wintuhuysen Inlet, commonly known as Nanymo [Nanaimo] Bay, and formally take possession of the coal beds lately discovered there for and in behalf of the Hudson's Bay Company."[45] Professional miners began work after September 6th under the direction of Scottish immigrant John Muir, and six days later the first commercial shipment of coal from Nanaimo territory left Colvilletown, as the new settlement was called, for Fort Victoria.[46] Upon their return from the Fraser River fishery, some of the Nanaimo people also began actively gathering coal from surface deposits "with a surprising degree of industry" to trade "for clothing and other articles of European manufacture."[47] Douglas himself returned to the area less than five months later, only this time he did not travel in a canoe, but aboard the Hudson's Bay Company steam vessel *Beaver* in command of a military expedition.

On November 5th, 1852, at the Lake Hill sheep station near Fort Victoria, an employee of the Hudson's Bay Company, Peter Brown, was shot several times in the chest and killed by a Nanaimo man named Siamasit and an unknown Cowichan companion, after Brown "had insulted the squaws of the Indians."[48] When Douglas learned of the attack he immediately informed Company headquarters in London of his plans to secure the suspects in the killing, believed to be "two Indians of the Cowegin [Cowichan] tribe":

> I propose dispatching messengers to the chiefs of the Cowegin tribe tomorrow to inform them of the foul deed that has been committed, and to demand the surrender of the criminals. I shall also offer a reward for their discovery. Should these measures fail, I shall be under the painful necessity of sending a force to seize upon the murderers.[49]

At Esquimalt, Captain Augustus L. Kuper, commander of the thirty-six-gun British frigate *Thetis*, acknowledged Douglas' request for assistance, informing him "that in the event of your finding it necessary to resort to more stringent measures to enforce the surrender of the murderers, you may depend upon my hearty co-operation in this matter, as at all times when you may consider it to be necessary for the security and benefit of the colony of Vancouver Island."[50]

Douglas sent his ultimatum to the Cowichan on November 7th, and within a few days "Soseeah [Tsosieten] the Chief, who possesses the greatest degree of influence with his people," arrived in Victoria to confer with the hwunitum leader:

> … he expresses the utmost regret, that such an unhappy event should have taken place, as his people are not disposed to quarrel with the whites to whom they are under so many obligations, and he assured me that all his Tribe, with the exception of one little party called Thlim Thlimclits [Clemclemalits] who are related to one of the assassins have resolved to give up the murderers, and should the latter attempt to screen them from justice, the rest of the Tribe are not disposed to aid or assist them in any manner in resisting the Queen's authority.[51]

This came as welcome news to Douglas, who was desirous "to avoid implicating the Tribe in the guilt of individuals … The Thlim Thlimclits [Clemclemalits] may also see the folly of taking part with the murderers, and shun a contest, which would be disagreeable to us, and calamitous to them."[52]

The attack on Brown raised fears among the hwunitum of Fort Victoria and the surrounding farms that an all-out attack by Cowichan warriors against the colony was imminent. Douglas stopped the sale of gunpowder to hwulmuhw and announced that he was suspending all trade with the Cowichan until the matter was resolved. Another month was to pass when, after learning the identities of the two killers and realizing that their relations would not give them up, Douglas organized a military expedition to secure their capture.

Although the campaign was to take place "at a very unfavorable season," it could not be delayed as the departure of the warship *Thetis* from the colony was imminent. "I feel convinced," wrote Douglas, "of making the present attempt to capture the murderers, in order to alarm the Indians and to prevent further murders and aggressions, which I fear may take place if the Indians are emboldened by present impunity. Every exertion will be made to avoid hostilities and to bring the Indians to a friendly compromise and unless the Queen's authority be speedily respected the tribe will be neither molested or attacked."[53]

At 7 a.m. on Tuesday, January 4th, 1853, the expeditionary force left Esquimalt under Douglas' command. The *Thetis* was thought to be too large to navigate the uncharted waters of Sansum Narrows, so the Hudson's Bay Company steam vessel *Beaver* was detailed to tow the brigantine *Recovery* and the pinnace, barge, and launch of the *Thetis* to Cowichan Bay. On board the various craft were one hundred and thirty sailors and marines of the *Thetis* under the command of Lieutenants John Moresby and Arthur Sansum. The regulars were accompanied by the local Hudson's Bay Company militia—ten men of the Victoria Voltigeurs—under the command of Joseph MacKay. [54]

After stopping at the Saanich village of Tsawout, where Douglas made a speech and "distributed a few presents among the chiefs" to reassure them of his peaceful intentions, the force was delayed another day "in consequence of a violent head wind and strong ebb." [55] Finally, on Thursday morning, January 6th, the British flotilla arrived in Cowichan Bay, where they caused "great excitement among the Indians who shunned the vessels." [56]

Knowing that the suspect was from the village of Clemclemalits, Douglas sent a message ashore by canoe, inviting the Cowichan si'em on board the *Beaver* "to a conference in which I hope to be able to prevail upon them to surrender the murderer quietly and without a recourse to violent measures, which I consider justifiable only as a last resource." [57] The bearer of this message may have been Tomo Antoine, who was enlisted in the Voltigeurs as an interpreter. Fluent in English, French and Hul'qumi'num dialects, Antoine may also have been instrumental in obtaining the co-operation of certain Cowichan si'em to resolve the dispute, possibly by the distribution of gifts. [58] The messengers returned to the vessels in the evening "with the intelligence that the chiefs of the Camegins [Cowichans] agreed to hold a conference near the mouth of the river; when they will meet us tomorrow morning, instead of coming on board the boat which they fear to do." [59]

Early the next morning, Friday, January 7th, the British troops landed and marched past the village of Comiaken where they were greeted by Tsosieten before taking up position on the rocky knoll behind the village (Comiaken Hill) where the ancestors of the place came down from the sky in the distant past. [60] Douglas records what transpired that morning:

> The tent was immediately pitched, a fire lighted, on a pretty rising oak ground and at the suggestion of "Soseiah" [Tsosieten] the Camegin chief … the sailors and marines were thrown a little back from the river in order to conceal their numbers, as he expressed a fear that the Camegins would be afraid to come if they saw so large a force. These arrangements being completed and the ground occupied, we prepared to receive the Indians as they arrived. [61]

> In the course of two hours the Indians began to drop down the River in their war canoes, and landed a little above the position we occupied; and last of all arrived two large canoes crowded with the relatives and friends of the murderer, hideously painted, and evidently prepared to defend him to the last extremity; the criminal himself being among the number. On

landing they made a furious dash towards the point I occupied, a little in advance of the Force and their demeanour was altogether so hostile that the marines were with little difficulty restrained from opening fire upon them. When the first excitement had a little abated, the murderer was brought into my presence and I succeeded after a good deal of trouble, in taking him into custody; and sent him a close prisoner on board the steam vessel. [62]

The "good deal of trouble" mentioned by Douglas was not a physical struggle but protracted speeches on both sides with Tomo Antoine as interpreter. Moresby, the gunnery lieutenant of the *Thetis*, records that Douglas threatened the Cowichan with violence if the wanted man was not given up. According to Moresby, Douglas raised his hand and said: "Hearken, O Chiefs! I am sent by King George who is your friend, and who desires right only between your tribes and his men. If his men kill an Indian, they are punished. If your men do likewise, they must also suffer. Give up the murderer, and let there be peace between the peoples, or I will burn your lodges and trample out your tribes." [63]

According to Douglas, the Cowichan man alleged to have been the warrior who shot Brown "was produced by his friends armed cap a pie [head to foot] and was heard in his defence, which went to declare that he was innocent of the crime laid to his charge. I listened to all that was alleged in his defence, and promised to give him a fair hearing at Nanaimo. He was on those terms surrendered." [64]

What Douglas may or may not have known was that the man surrendered to him that day was not the warrior who killed Brown, but a slave (skwuyuth) offered instead as compensation. [65] According to hwulmuhw law it would be inappropriate to hand over a man of high rank to atone for the death of a person of low rank which Brown, in the Hudson's Bay hierarchy, clearly was. Possibly Douglas was aware of what was going on but agreed to the exchange as a way to avoid hostilities with the Cowichan who were recognized as the most militarily capable threat against the infant colony. In doing so he resolved the dispute between the hwunitum and the Clemclemalits according to hwulmuhw law.

With the slave in custody, Douglas "remained on the ground for several hours," addressed the two hundred assembled Cowichan and distributed gifts signifying to the si'em that a peaceful balance between the Fort Victoria hwunitum and the Cowichan was restored. [66] How much of the following speech by Douglas, given its content, was correctly translated by Tomo Antoine is not known:

I afterwards addressed the Indians who were there assembled, on the subject of their relations with the Colony and the Crown. I informed them that the whole of their country was a possession of the British crown, and that Her Majesty the Queen had given me a special charge, to treat them with justice and humanity and to protect them against violence of all foreign nations which might attempt to molest them, so long as they remained at peace with the settlements. I told them to apply to me for redress, if they met with any injury or injustice at the hands of the Colonists and not to retaliate and above all things, I undertook to impress upon the minds of the chiefs that they must respect Her Majesty's warrant, and surrender any criminal belonging to their respective tribes, on demand of the Court Magistrate and that resistance to the Civil power, would expose them to be considered enemies. I also told them that being satisfied with their conduct in the present conference, peace was restored and they might resume their trade with Fort Victoria. The distribution of a little tobacco and some speechifying on the part of the Indians, expressions of their regard and friendship for the whites closed the proceedings and the conference broke up.[67]

Two days later the expedition continued towards Nanaimo in search of Siamasit, the other man involved in Peter Brown's death. Siamasit was the son of a si'em of Tiwulhuw on the Nanaimo River, and "was regarded as the Hero of the Tribe."[68] Siamasit's relations, according to hwulmuhw law, offered furs in compensation for the death of the low ranking Hudson's Bay employee, but Douglas was not prepared to negotiate. He regarded the Nanaimo as posing little threat to hwunitum interests "not having the reputation of being so numerous or warlike in their habits as the Cowegin [Cowichan] Tribe."[69] Douglas seized Siamasit's father and "another influential Indian" as hostages. After some difficulty, including a bloodless assault by marines and colonial militia on Kwulsiwul, the furthest downstream village on the Nanaimo River, Douglas marched on the village of Tiwulhuw and informed the people "that they should be treated as enemies, and their villages destroyed, if they continued longer to protect the murderer."[70] Siamasit was soon tracked down at his place of refuge on the Chase River where he was captured by Basil Botineau of the Victoria Voltigeurs:

A few inches of snow had fallen and his footmarks were traced, he was chased in fact, to a river (since named from this incident, Chase River); here the scout Basil Botineau found himself at fault, and, as it was getting dark, would have abandoned the search had not the Indian, who was hiding under the driftwood, snapped his flint-lock musket at him, but the priming and charge were damp and neither exploded. The scout followed the direction of the sound, but in the dusk could not see the Indian, who tried a second shot at him when the priming only exploded, but the flash exposing his hiding place, he was immediately discovered, knocked down and handcuffed.[71]

On the cold morning of January 17th, 1853, there was a brief trial on the quarter-deck of the *Beaver*, where a jury of naval officers found their prisoners guilty of the murder of Peter Brown. Siamasit and the slave shared "the melancholy distinction of being the first persons in British Columbia to be condemned by a jury and sentenced to death."[72] Siamasit's mother begged the British to hang her husband instead as "he was old and could not live long ... and one for one was Indian law."[73] In a deliberate move to intimidate the local population, the men were executed at the south end of Protection Island, across from the site of the first coal shaft sunk on Nanaimo Harbour in the "presence of the whole Nanaimo Tribe, the scene appearing to make a deep impression on their minds."[74]

Douglas was pleased at the outcome of the brief campaign, particularly the encounter with the Cowichan. In a letter to the Colonial Office, Douglas wrote:

> I am happy to report that I found both the Cowegin and Nanaimo Tribes more amenable to reason than was supposed; the objects of the Expedition having, under Providence, been satisfactorily attained, as much through the influence of the Hudson's Bay Company's name, as by the effect of intimidation. The surrender of a criminal, as in the case of the Cowegin murderer, without bloodshed, by the most numerous and warlike of the Native Tribes on Vancouver's Island, at the demand of the Civil powers may be considered, as an epoch, in the history of our Indian relations, which augers well for the future peace and prosperity of the Colony. That object however could not have been effected without the exhibition of a powerful force.[75]

Douglas also informed the Hudson's Bay Company headquarters in London that the recent expedition succeeded in allaying the fears of hwunitum colonists and impressing upon hwulmuhw factions the efficacy of British military power: "War was carried to their door last winter and they are sensible that at any moment we can repeat the experiment."[76]

The 1853 expedition to the Cowichan River and Wentuhuysen Inlet also established the pattern of British exploitation of interfamily rivalry to achieve results that were, it appears, mutually beneficial to the parties involved. Blankets and other gifts were used to enlist co-operation. While seen as bribery by British standards, from a hwulmuhw point of view the exchange of gifts was a solemn recognition of alliance between hwulmuhw and hwunitum interests for common purpose. One of the single largest expenditures of the entire expedition was fourteen pounds, six shillings "for secret service by Indians at Cowegin and Nanaimo."[77] Where "bribery" failed, the British resorted to hostage-taking and threats of deadly force to achieve their ends.

The British strategy of "divide and conquer" was crucial to their success in a land where they were vastly outnumbered by hwulmuhw populations. A comparison of population figures compiled from the 1853 and 1854 census illustrates the disparity in numbers between the Hwunitum of the Colony of Vancouver Island and Hul'qumi'num First Nations inhabiting the east coast of Vancouver Island and the Gulf Islands. Of a total hwunitum population of 774, half of whom were under the age of twenty, 232 lived at Fort Victoria, 151 at Nanaimo, with the balance distributed amongst outlying farms in the ceded territories.[78] By comparison, the following excerpt of a census entitled "Original Indian Population of Vancouver Island 1853" from Douglas' private papers, reveals the populations of various Hul'qumi'num First Nations south of Nanaimo.[79] According to these figures, several villages alone outnumbered the entire hwunitum population of the Colony.

FAMILY PLACE OF HABITATION	MEN WITH BEARDS	WOMEN	BOYS	GIRLS
Komiaken [Comiaken]	100	120	87	113
Thlimthim Comiaken Valley	160	160	153	162
Quamichan	430	450	400	450
Sawmina [Somenos]	80	75	63	80
Tataka Comiaken Gap	160	162	160	165
Penalahats [Penelakut]	200	219	205	195
Chemanis [Chemainus]	200	203	264	283
Sumlumalcha [Lamalcha]	20	22	36	44

While the British exerted their power and influence over various groups of Hul'qumi'num First Nations people, there were similar shifts of power amongst the people themselves. Shortly after the hwulmuhw census of 1853, Tzouhalem, who was listed in Douglas' census as the highest ranking si'em at Quamichan, was killed at Lamalcha on Kuper Island by Shelm-tum when Tzouhalem raided the village in an attempt to kidnap Shelm-tum's wife, Tsae-Mea-Lae.

It was like this. Over on Kuper Island there was a Indian village where the Lamalchas lived. Now, one of the Lamalchas was a man named Shelm-Tum and he had a big, fine-looking wife called Tsae-Mea-Lae. For many months Tzouhalem had wanted that woman, and at last he made up his mind to go and take her. One day he started off with his second brother a man named Squa-Lem ... Well, away they went, and when they got to Lamalcha, Tzouhalem ran to the house where Tsae-Mea-Lae lived and began singing and dancing, for the great Tzouhalem to take away.

There were not many of the Lamalchas in the house, and when they heard Tzouhalem's voice they ran away and hid, only the brave Tsae-Mea-Lae waited, hiding behind the door. Pretty soon Tzouhalem came to the door, looked in, but could see no one. He turned to go away when, quickly Tsae-Mea-Lae leaned out and putting a thick clam stick around his breast, held him from behind and shouted to her husband to come and kill him.

It did not take Schelm-Tum long to get his axe, and with one blow he cut off Tzouhalem's head. Later the Lamalchas sent the head back to Quamichan, but they kept the body on Kuper Island. [80]

The death of Tzouhalem, the most feared and powerful warrior amongst the Cowichan, gave the people of Lamalcha a certain notoriety despite the small population of the village. Over the next few years, Lamalcha attracted disaffected warriors who, for one reason or another, could not live in their own villages. Although the Lamalcha had killed the one man who posed the greatest military threat to hwunitum, within a few years another formidable warrior, equally antagonistic towards the hwunitum, would become associated with the village and lead a small band of warriors against hwunitum incursions into his people's territories. His name was Acheewun, a man described by the hwunitum as "the terror of all the tribes around" and "a perfect fiend"—a man who "seemed likely to assume the mantle of Tzouhalem." [81]

In the wake of the successful campaign against the Nanaimo, Douglas acted quickly to consolidate the Hudson's Bay Company's occupation of the coal-bearing deposits on Wentuhuysen Inlet. In January of 1853, the Hudson's Bay Company, concerned that the coal fields would revert to the Crown's possession when and if its charter was revoked, instructed Douglas to extinguish the aboriginal title and purchase the land from the Crown. [82] Douglas' first attempt to arrange a land sale agreement was unsuccessful but he assured the company that he would re-open negotiations "as soon as I think it safe and prudent to renew the question of Indian rights, which always give rise to troublesome excitements, and has on every occasion been productive of serious disturbances." [83] The late expedition and subsequent executions precluded immediate negotiations and almost two years would pass before Douglas was able to make an agreement with the people who owned the land in question. These people inhabited Saalaquun, the furthest upriver of five villages on the Nanaimo River. They "held aloof from the other four villages and appear to have been the most self-sufficient and dominant group," controlling the only salmon fish weir on the river. [84]

Douglas focused on building a fort by the coal shaft to protect the coal-miners from hwulmuhw attacks. By June 1853, two company employees, Leon Labine and Jean Baptiste Fortier, with a crew of labourers, built a two-story octagonal bastion of squared timbers armed with two six-pound carronades overlooking the dock facilities, the coal workings and the fledgling hwunitum settlement. The guns from this two-story bastion were used to intimidate the native population with random displays of gunnery towards Protection Island and Gallows Point. [85]

Coal production continued in a haphazard way, with Saalaquun labourers mining coal at open deposits and trading it to the British until November 27th, 1854, when twenty-three hwunitum families recruited from the Brierly Hill Colliery in Staffordshire, England arrived in Colvilletown. [86]

Shortly after the arrival of the Staffordshire miners, Douglas was finally able to conclude a treaty with the people who owned the site of the coal mining operation. Just before Christmas in 1854, Douglas met with the Saalaquun si'em, Suquen-es-then, and others to formally purchase the land occupied by the coal mine "from Commercial Inlet 12 miles up Nanaimo River." [87] The land sale agreement had taken almost two years to negotiate and was the most expensive. It was witnessed and signed by 159 si'em, each of whom received four blankets, twice as many as those given to the Sooke and Clallam si'em, and one more than both the Songees and Saanich si'em received. [88] It was also the only land sale agreement that bears the signature of James Douglas.

As in the previous agreements signed at Fort Victoria, the Nanaimo were misled with regards to the significance of the agreement they signed with the British. What follows is the Saalaquun version of the land sale agreement signed at Colvilletown on December 23rd, 1854, as recalled by Suquen-es-then's daughter, Tstass-Aya, and her husband, Quen-es-then, who was present as a small boy:

> Well, one day a Hudson's Bay man came to see my father. "We want to talk to you and your people about this coal," he said. "We will have a meeting. You and all your people, and you must get another chief and his people, and on a certain day we will all talk this thing over."

> So my father, Chief Suquen-Es-Then, called all his people, and he told another chief, whose name was Chief Schwun-Schn, to call his tribe, and together they went to the meeting."

> Now, you know where the big wharf is now—where the steamers come? Well, down there is a rock, in the water. In those old days it was part of the land, and at that place was a very big house. To that house there went all the Hudson's Bay men, and the two chiefs with their people.

> Here Quen-Es-Then interrupted. "I was at that meeting," he said, "I can remember all the people in that house, and lots outside, but I was only a small boy standing beside my father."

> Then the Hudson's Bay men talked to the Indians. "This coal that is here," they said, "is no good to you, and we would like it; but we want to be friends, so, if you will let us come and take as much of this black rock as we want, we will be good to you." They told my father, "The good Queen, our great white chief, far over the water, will look after your people for all time, and they will be given much money, so that they will never be poor."

Then they gave each chief a bale of Hudson's Bay blankets and a lot of shirts and tobacco, just like rope! "These are presents for you and your people, to show we are your good friends," they said. The chiefs took the things and they cut the blankets, which were double ones, in half, to make more, and gave one to every chief man, then the shirts, and to those who were left they gave pieces of the rope tobacco; so that every man in the tribes had a present.

"Now you know," said Tstass-Aya, "we think there was some mistake made at that meeting, or, maybe, the people could not understand properly what was said; but later, when our people asked for some of the money for their coal, the Hudson's Bay men said to them,"Oh, we paid you when we gave you those good blankets!" But those two chiefs knew that the man had said, "The Queen will give you money." [89]

According to the Nanaimo version of the agreement, Douglas made verbal promises that were not honoured. The New Zealand-derived conveyance form, if it was ever attached to the Nanaimo agreement, has since been lost. However, it seems probable that the same provisions were included and that "the conveyance obtained in 1854 was obtained on the strength of a promise that the Indians would be entitled to retain their village sites and enclosed fields, and the Indians would have the right to hunt over the unoccupied lands, as well as to carry on their fisheries as before." [90] In short, they would retain their sovereignty and jurisdiction over their people and lands.

That the Nanaimo signatories were familiar with the text of the deed of conveyance is strongly suggested in the wording of an address given by Nanaimo si'em to Douglas' successor Arthur Kennedy, on the subject of land alienation on November 15th, 1864:

We want to keep our land here and up the river ... All our other land is gone, and we have been paid very little for it. God gave it to us a long time ago, and now we are very poor, and do not know where our houses will be if we leave this. We want our land up the river to plant for food. Mr. Douglas said it would be ours, and our children's after we are gone. [91]

In other words, the Nanaimo were demanding that the government live up to the promise of the 1854 "Douglas Treaty," that villages, fields, and food gathering areas would, as the deed of conveyance put it, "be kept for our own use, for the use of our children, and for those who may follow after us." [92]

With the arrival of the Staffordshire miners and the Nanaimo land sale agreement in place, the coal-mining operations began in earnest to supply company steamers and, increasingly, warships of the Royal Navy on patrol and survey duties for the imperial government. 1854 not only heralded the first ceded territories among

Hul'qumi'num-speaking people (the Saalaquun), but also marked the beginning, thanks to the Crimean War, of the naval base in Esquimalt where a hospital had been constructed in expectation of casualties following an allied assault on the Petrovask Peninsula. More than the bastion looming over Colvilletown, the formidable, increasingly frequent appearance of Royal Navy warships coaling at the docking facilities below served to discourage hwulmuhw resistance to hwunitum newcomers.

The town of Colvilletown, soon to be called Nanaimo, grew to be the second largest hwunitum settlement in the Colony of Vancouver Island. In addition to its coaling facilities, the town's proximity to the heartland of Hul'qumi'num First Nations made it an important trading and distribution centre for hwunitum goods, not the least of which was alcohol.

Alcohol was an important trade item, highly valued and eagerly sought by hwulmuhw. It had become a symbol of wealth: one gallon was equal to two three-point Hudson's Bay blankets.[93] Its consumption permeated many aspects of hwulmuhw culture, including the stlun'uq (potlatch) and funerals. Amidst the disruption of traditional society, "drunkenness appeared as a desireable thing which outweighed its unpleasant consequences. It had preeminent value in the feast situation. The more intoxicated the guests became, the more conspicuously did they attest to the strength of the host's liquor and to their wealth which permitted them to be so lavish with hard-to-come-by whiskey and rum."[94]

Colonial legislation "prohibiting the Gift or Sale of Spiritous Liquors to Indians" was introduced by Douglas and approved by the Council of the Colony of Vancouver Island on August 3rd, 1854, but despite this measure the illegal trade in alcohol to hwulmuhw continued unabated.[95] Liquor consumption by hwunitum was widespread and the profits associated with bootlegging too attractive. Commenting on the constant traffic of coastal schooners over the following decade, a former dealer stated that it "was potent to anyone of common sense that the main objective of these vessels making voyages is for gain by whiskey selling."[96]

Between 1850 and 1854, the Hudson's Bay Company, with increasing difficulty, negotiated fourteen land sale agreements with aboriginal people on Vancouver's Island. The Colony of Vancouver Island composed eight districts created from these lands, but the 1854 agreement at Nanaimo would be the last of the "Douglas Treaties." With Nanaimo to the north and Victoria to the south, the unceded territories of Hul'qumi'num First Nations along the east coast of Vancouver Island were flanked by centres of hwunitum power and influence, who were increasingly envious of the rich agricultural lands along the Cowichan and Chemainus Rivers and the large offshore island known to the hwunitum as Chuan or Salt Spring.

Kenipsen, Cowichan Bay, 1934. Birthplace and residence of the famous Cowichan warrior Tzouhalem.   *Royal British Columbia Museum, Photo 6047.*

Clemclemalits, 1984. One of the larger Cowichan villages, families from Clemclemalits owned lands and resources on the south end of Salt Spring Island. In 1853, a si'em from the village killed Peter Brown, a Hudson's Bay Company employee. Douglas accepted a slave substitute to settle the dispute.   *Photo by Chris Arnett.*

Interior of Fort Victoria. Site of the land sale agreements of 1850 and 1852 by which hwulmuhw on southern Vancouver Island, from Sooke to North Saanich, ceded their lands to hwunitum.

British Columbia Archives and Records Service, Photo HP 10601.

Chapter Three

The Imperial Chain

South of the Colony of Vancouver Island, across Juan de Fuca Strait in the Washington Territory, the influx of 4,000 hwunitum to the shores of Puget Sound set the stage for an escalation of inter-racial conflict. Although Dwamish, Suquamish, and other native leaders made treaties with the newcomers, other leaders such as Leschi of the Nisqually waged war against the hwunitum in the fall of 1855.[1] These developments were watched with interest and not a little anxiety by the colonial regime of James Douglas which provided financial and material support, including the Hudson's Bay Company steamers *Otter* and *Beaver*, to aid the American forces. "I confess that it was not motives of humanity alone that induced me to lend such aid," wrote Douglas to the Colonial Office, "other reasons of sound policy were not wanting ... such as the conviction on my mind that the triumph of the Native Tribes would certainly endanger the position of this colony, which in that case could not be maintained without a vast increase of expence for military defences. It is therefore clearly to our interest that the American cause should triumph, and the natives be made to feel that they cannot successfully contend against the power of the whites."[2]

The town of Seattle, the major American settlement on Puget Sound, was attacked on January 26th, 1856, and the hwulmuhw were defeated after a day-long fight. Further south, not even the presence of the *Beaver*, carrying thirty United States regulars and Washington Territory Volunteers, could prevail over Leschi and thirty-eight well-armed warriors entrenched on the beach at Steilacoom where, after a bloodless stand-off, the hwunitum wisely withdrew. During the unrest, hwunitum settlers and soldiers constructed sixty-one stockades and blockhouses, and sporadic fighting continued until October 1856.[3] Hwulmuhw on Vancouver Island were well aware of what was taking place to the south. Douglas wrote that Hul'qumi'num First Nations were "elated with the recent successes of the Oregon Tribes over the United States Troops, [and that] the natives of this Colony were also becoming insolent and restive."[4]

At Fort Victoria, Douglas was also faced with large flotillas of well-armed aboriginal people from the north, heading south to trade. Some of these migrating families had ongoing feuds with Hul'qumi'num First Nations and fights, often with loss of life, occurred. Douglas informed the Colonial Office of an incident that took place in July 1856, when "a gang of Queen Charlotte Islanders ... attacked and nearly destroyed a native Cowegin village situated about 50 miles north of this place. The Cowegins, few in number, fought desperately and were all slaughtered on the spot, and the assailants made off toward their own country with a number of captive women and children."[5] Hul'qumi'num First Nations warriors retaliated by occupying strategic points "on the borders of the settlements, and shot every northern Indian, without respect to tribe or person, who ventured abroad."[6] Douglas was obliged to provide the steamship *Otter* as an escort for some 300 "northern Indians" to insure their safe passage through Hul'qumi'num First Nations territories.

The inter-racial conflict in the Washington Territories and ongoing conflict between First Nations on Vancouver Island created "a well-grounded apprehension of danger, in the minds of the Colonists," and Douglas likened the situation to "a smouldering volcano which at any moment may burst into fatal activity."[7]

Douglas was particularly worried about hwunitum men who went to live amongst hwulmuhw in those areas where land sale agreements had not been made. By 1856, a few hwunitum had established themselves in the Cowichan Valley where they married Cowichan women and lived amongst the people, acquiring rights to land according to hwulmuhw custom. Since a si'em with a hwunitum son-in-law presumably gained easier access to hwunitum goods, such arrangements were initially accorded some prestige. One of these early settlers, an unidentified "Scotchman," held "an expensive piece of land from an Indian Chief on the terms of—giving him two blankets and accepting one of his daughters."[8] Another was an Englishman named Thomas Williams, a former Hudson's Bay Company employee, who had worked at the Uplands farm between 1852 and 1855 before moving to the Cowichan Valley in 1855 or 1856.[9] Douglas tried to prevent what he described as "the irregular settlement of the country" lest the rule of law "so conscientiously nurtured by himself" be put to risk through unauthorized contact between hwunitum and hwulmuhw.[10]

Douglas' worst fears were realized when, on August 22nd, 1856, Thomas Williams was brought to Fort Victoria "in, it is feared, a fatally wounded state, having been shot through the arm and chest by 'Tathlasut,' an Indian of the Saumina [Somenos] tribe who inhabit the Upper Cowegin District."[11] The dispute centred around a woman, possibly Tathlasut's intended bride, who went to live with Williams and "refused to be parted from him."[12] Williams, it seems, was not well-liked and had tried to exert his own authority over Cowichan people through intimidation. As the late August Jack of Chemainus explained:

> This fellow he wants to be the big chief over all the Indians in this country. Everybody's scared of this fellow and they do what he says. One chief, he's not scared any more, so he shoots this fellow in the arm, and the bullet goes right through and makes a big hole in his chest.
>
> A medicine man says, "I fix you so you don't die." Then he plugs up the hole in this fellow's chest with cedar bark, and he takes him to Victoria. [13]
>
> This fellow's arm goes no good, and the white doctor cuts it off, but this fellow doesn't die.
>
> The Governor gets mad, so he sends ships with guns to catch the chief who shoots this fellow, and he hangs this chief up in a tree. [14]

When Williams was brought to Fort Victoria Douglas was informed that Tathlasut "felt assured of escaping with impunity. He in fact told his friends that they had nothing to fear from the enmity of the whites, as they would not venture to attack a powerful tribe, occupying a country strong in its natural defences, and so distant from the coast." [15] Douglas planned a quick response. Two recently arrived Royal Navy vessels, HMS *Monarch* (eighty-four guns) and HMS *Trincomalee* (twenty-four guns), gave Douglas the opportunity to launch the largest display of hwunitum military force seen up to that time on the east coast of Vancouver Island. Douglas called on the services of Admiral Henry William Bruce, commander of the Pacific Station, informing him that:

> ... the Civil Power will require the support of a larger military force than the Colony can provide ... a force sufficient to answer the ends of justice, and to teach the savages to respect the lives and property of Her Majesty's subjects. [16]

A message was sent to Nanaimo "ordering Thos. Oumtony [Tomo Antoine] to proceed at once to Victoria to act as an interpreter." [17]

Within a week, Douglas was in Cowichan Bay aboard the HMS *Trincomalee*, the sailing frigate commanded by Captain Wallace Houston. The sail-powered *Trincomalee* was deemed unsuitable to navigate the channels and capricious currents en route to Cowichan Bay and was towed to her destination by the Hudson's Bay Company steamer, *Otter*. On board under the command of Captain Matthew Connolly were 437 sailors and marines from the *Trincomalee* and the *Monarch*, a field battery of two twelve-pound howitzers and eighteen Victoria Voltigeurs under the command of William J. McDonald. The force was three times larger than the expedition of 1853. [18]

On September 1st, the small army disembarked and camped on strategic Comiaken Hill, the site of the previous altercation in 1853. The timing of the expedition was fortuitous for the British, as the majority of the Cowichan people were absent at the Fraser River sockeye fishery. As Douglas later observed, "the Cowegin [Cowichan] Tribe can bring into the field about 1400 Warriors but nearly 1000 of these were engaged upon an expedition to Fraser's River, when we entered their Country." [19] While the troops bivouacked, hwulmuhw allies were despatched to determine the whereabouts and disposition of the various Cowichan families in the villages along the river channels of the delta. The scouts returned with conflicting reports but Douglas was able to determine that Tathlasut was near the village of Somenos, some five miles inland.

Although there is no mention in the official dispatches, Cowichan oral history records that the guns of the *Trincomalee* opened fire on Cowichan houses to terrorize and intimidate the people.

[The HMS *Trincomalee*] bombarded the Indian houses, causing the Indians to flee in terror into the woods. The Indian account reflects vividly the awe experienced on the flash of fire, together with the smoke and the echoing rumble of the guns. The people ran from their houses and, not knowing which way to turn to avoid the danger, they joined together in groups within the fringes of the wood, taking comfort in the presence of each other as though by mutual support they might be able to steady the quailing of their bodies and silence the crash of doom which rumbled so ominously in their ears. Then the terrified Indians were glad enough to point out the hiding-place of the murderer. [20]

It was Lohar, a prominent si'em from the village of Comiaken, who was prevailed upon to assist the British in either securing Tathlasut or facing destruction. According to Lohar's daughter, Stockl-whut:

The captain of the man-of-war came and talked to my father, and said to him, "Some of your people are hiding that bad man. If you don't give him up I will take my big guns and blow up all your villages." Now Lohar knew where that Somenos man was hiding, and as he did not want all his people's houses to be broken, and wanted to help the white man do what was right, he went to the place where that bad man was to be found. [21]

An official account by Douglas describes the British advance up the Cowichan River on the following day, September 2nd:

In marching through the Thickets of the Cowegin Valley the Victoria Voltigeurs were, with my own personal Staff, thrown well in advance of the Seamen and Marines, formed in single file to scour the Woods [to] guard against surprise, as I could not fail to bear in mind the repeated disasters, which last Winter befell the American Army while marching through the Jungle against an enemy much inferior in point of numbers and spirit to the Tribes we had to encounter. [22]

The Troops marched some distance into the Cowegin Valley, through thick bush and almost impenetrable forest. Knowing that a mere physical force demonstration would never accomplish the apprehension of the culprit I offered friendship and protection to all the natives except the culprit, and such as aided him or were found opposing the ends of justice. That announcement had the desired effect of securing the neutrality of the greater part of the Tribe who were present, and after we had taken possession of three of their largest Villages the surrender of the culprit followed. [23]

Tathlasut was seized by a band of warriors led by Lohar: "Come out!" he called to him. "Don't be afraid; it is your friend and chief Lohar." The man came out from his hiding place, holding his musket behind his back with one hand. "We are friends," said Lohar, and held out his hand. The Somenos man took the hand held out to him. Lohar quickly pulled him closer, and reaching round behind him, caught the musket and took it from him. Then he shouted to other men who had gone with him, and they ran up and took the Somenos man and tied him so that he could not get away. [24]

Tathlasut resisted capture and during the struggle "Lohar was wounded in the arm. He got cut with a knife when he captured this person." [25]

After securing the village of Somenos, the British force marched a half mile further west and set up camp to await the arrival of the two artillery pieces being transported up the south arm of the Cowichan River from Comiaken by canoe. Soon the British were approached by "a formidable force of armed Indians" with "their faces blackened ... and painted for war, shouting and gesticulating." But there was no fighting as Tathlasut was handed over. [26]

The trial and execution of Tathlasut took place behind the village of Quamichan where a "drum-head courtmartial was convened" with a jury of naval officers, while sailors rigged a make-shift block and tackle gallows to a large oak tree. [27] Although the newly appointed Chief Justice David Cameron was present, he did not preside but instead yielded to the authority of his brother-in-law Douglas who acted as judge. [28] According to Douglas, Tathlasut "was tried before a special Court convened on the spot and was found guilty of 'maiming Thomas Williams with intent to murder,' an offence which the Statute 1st, Victoria Cap 83, Section 2 considers felony and provides that the offender should suffer death. He was accordingly hanged and the sentence was carried into effect, near the spot where the crime was committed, in the presence of the Tribe upon whose minds, the solemnity of the proceedings, and the execution of the criminal were calculated to make a deep impression."[29] As Lohar's descendant, Dennis Alphonse relates, Tathlasut's execution made a deep impression on everyone, not just the hwulmuhw:

> There's a story that when they hung this person—he must have been a very strong person because he started singing and it was a nice clear day and all of a sudden it got dark. There was thunder and lightning and it started raining and that's when they hung him. Anyway, they got kind of scared with what was going on when they hung him.[30]

After Tathlasut's body was taken down, his mother breathed into his nostrils and began "feeding him with salmon" in an attempt to revive him.[31] The rain continued to fall as the gun crews of the two artillery pieces "practised shooting to frighten the Indians."[32]

MacDonald, the militia Captain, recalled that those Cowichan present at Tathlasut's execution showed "many indications that their approval was withheld and that they yielded only to force."[33] Douglas, on the other hand, recorded that "the expedition remained at Cowegin two days after the execution of the offender, to re-establish friendly relations with the Cowegin Tribe, and we succeeded in that object, to my entire satisfaction."[34] It was later alleged that an unnamed si'em only consented to the hanging after Douglas "had a number of blankets given to him after the man was hung, or before."[35]

Douglas informed the Colonial Office in London that the recent expedition employed "the same principles of action" used in 1853, "that is, by striving to impress on the minds of the Natives that the terrors of the law would be let loose on the guilty only, and not on the Tribe at large, provided they took no part in resisting the Queen's authority nor in protecting the Criminal from justice."[36] Douglas maintained that he "was not influenced by the love of military display ... but solely by a profound sense of public duty, and a conviction, founded upon experience, that it is only by resorting to prompt and decisive measures of punishment, in all cases of aggression, that life and property can be protected and the Native Tribes of this Colony kept in a proper state of subordination."[37]

The response of the Colonial Office to Douglas' action against the Cowichan was less than enthusiastic. Douglas later informed Admiral Bruce that he had received:

> ... the approval of the authorities at the Colonial Office expressed however in measured terms intended to show that Her Majesty's Ministers do not like the hazard of military expeditions into the Indian Country. I dare say that few persons who know their character have any partiality for such expeditions, but however inglorious these episodes may be they are

Oficers and crew of the HMS Trincomalee *engaged in gunnery practice.*
British Columbia Archives and Records Service, HP 1-51758.

Dennis Alphonse ("Lohar") on Comiaken Hill gesturing towards Cowichan Bay where HMS
Trincomalee *threatened to bombard Cowichan villages.*   *Photo by Chris Arnett.*

Site of the trial and execution of Tathlasut near Quamichan village.

Photo by Chris Arnett.

nevertheless essential parts of the system by which our Empire over the Indian mind is to be supported. [38]

Lohar, the si'em who captured Tathlasut, was convinced that the Cowichan could not win a war against the British whose naval guns, sailors and marines would make short work of any resistance. When the British threatened to bombard the villages around Cowichan Bay if Tathlasut was not given up, Lohar "as a leader took it upon himself to save the Cowichan people." [39] He used his influence as a "paramount chief of the Cowichan tribe" to curb retaliation against hwunitum by Tathlasut's relatives:

> Now the Indians saw that it would not do to harm the white man; that if they did so, they would be punished and for some time there was no trouble. [40]

Other hwulmuhw leaders reacted with anger and called for vengeance against hwunitum who transgressed their laws. Referring to Thomas Williams:

> Everybody says this is a bad thing, and the chief at Chemainus says he's going to shoot this fellow dead if he comes around there. Then nobody's scared of him anymore. [41]

The 1856 military expedition against the Somenos profoundly influenced the future of the Cowichan people by bringing "the whites into their midst, for one of the principal legacies of the expedition was the discovery of the expanse and fertility of the Cowichan plain." [42]

Upon his return to Fort Victoria, Douglas wrote enthusiastically to his friend and colleague, James Murray Yale, that "Cowegin is a fine valley far more extensive and valuable as an agricultural country than I had any idea of"—a statement which reflects his enthusiasm for the potential of the Cowichan Valley to alleviate the crucial shortage of agricultural land, the main impediment to hwunitum settlement facing the Colony of Vancouver Island. [43] Douglas predicted that the valley could support 50,000 settlers: "I have therefore bright hopes for our future," he wrote, "and no longer despair of the Colony." [44]

The major obstacle was hwulmuhw ownership. Rear Admiral Bruce shared Douglas' optimism and made the improbable claim that the Cowichan people would welcome hwunitum settlers. "Its present population consists of 4,000 Indians," he wrote, "who are friendly to the English, and desirous for their residence among them; notwithstanding the summary infliction of justice they so recently witnessed at our hands." [45] Bruce was probably referring to Lohar who, according to his daughter, "was always very friendly to the white men ... He wanted them to come and live in our land." [46] Other Cowichan si'em were opposed to any land sale agreements and preferred to exercise their own sovereignty and jurisdiction over their lands.

None of this seemed to matter to Douglas who, after two successful military campaigns against Cowichan people, went ahead with his plans to alienate from hwulmuhw ownership the majority of the Cowichan Valley. In 1857 Douglas authorized the Surveyor General, Joseph Despard Pemberton, a Protestant Irish immigrant who had been in the colony since 1851, to undertake a reconnaissance of the area and to report on the feasibility of settlement. Tomo Antoine led the small party up the Cowichan River to Cowichan Lake and down the Nitinaht River to its outlet on the west coast of Vancouver Island. Pemberton's exploration confirmed British impressions regarding the potential of the Cowichan Valley as a future addition to the colony.[47] Douglas was now prepared to allow other agents of colonization to enter the territories of Hul'qumi'num First Nations as a preliminary stage in the alienation of their lands.

Hwunitum desire for hwulmuhw land was matched by the quest for their souls. Quebecois Roman Catholic clergy contributed to the destabilization of hwulmuhw culture in ways equally as effective as Douglas' hangings and naval bombardments. The success of the Quebecois missionaries in obtaining numerous converts while simultaneously undermining traditional hwulmuhw culture was partly the result of the drastic decline in hwulmuhw population. Hwulmuhw witnessed disease, alcoholism, violence and subsequent high mortality rates, wreaking havoc among them while the hwunitum suffered little and in fact prospered. The acceptance of Christian deities seemed necessary to restore order in a world out of balance.[48]

As early as 1843, when Father Jean-Baptiste Bolduc arrived at the future site of Fort Victoria and offered to baptize a large congregation of hwulmuhw assembled there, an elder addressed him saying:

> Your words are good; but we have been told that those that were baptized of the Kwaitlens and the Kawitshins (on the Fraser River) died almost immediately; however, as you say it is a good thing, we believe it. Since that will make us see the Master on high after death, baptize all those in our camp; do them this charity; they are to be pitied; almost all die.[49]

When the Bishop of Vancouver Island, Modeste Demers, arrived in the colony in September, 1852, on the heels of Timothy Honore Lemprit's ill-fated Cowichan mission, he began to make frequent visits to the Cowichan Valley, and possibly other areas, where he was well received.

Born in the little village of St. Nicholas in Lower Canada in 1809, Demers arrived in the Pacific Northwest overland in 1838.[50] From his base in the Oregon Territory he travelled extensively throughout the land, "contacting and converting the Indian tribes from the northern boundary of Oregon to Stuart Lake in what is now the

Interior of British Columbia."[51] Demers and another priest, Blanchet, employed and elaborated "Chinook," a five hundred word trade jargon invented by Hudson's Bay Company employees to facilitate communication with indigenous peoples.[52] Demers created a vocabulary, composed canticles, and translated prayers into Chinook which "enabled the two first missionaries to do a great deal of good among the Indians and half-breeds."[53] In 1847 Demers was consecrated Bishop of Vancouver Island.

Upon his arrival in the Colony of Vancouver Island, Bishop Demers found himself chronically short-handed and, receiving no assistance from the largely Protestant Hudson's Bay Company establishment, Demers worked on his own:

> Losing no time in undertaking his arduous activities … he, himself, began his frequent visitations to the natives of the East Coast of the Island to whom, in a very short time, he became so well known and beloved as the "Great Priest with the long hat and the crooked stick, the Man of Prayer" … soon his visits to the natives took on the nature of triumphal processions in which the tribes would vie with one another in their demonstrations of faith.[54]

A church historian provides a description of a typical visit by the Bishop to a hwulmuhw village:

> In the eyes of the aborigines, the priest was above all the "man of God," a being quite apart in creation, upon whom too much honour could scarcely be lavished. As soon as his canoe, manned by a crew hailing from the last village visited, was in sight, a volley of musketry saluted the temperance flag which floated in the wind over the frail skiff. Then the men on shore separated from the women and, forming lines distinct from theirs in front of the village, received a hearty handshake from the missionary, after each person had blessed himself with a generously proportioned sign of the cross. As he passed along, the priest had to be very careful lest he should forget even the smallest babe in the distribution of his fatherly attentions.
>
> Then the chief welcomed the envoy from Heaven in the name of his people, and the missionary reciprocated by telling the villagers of his happiness in meeting his children, and delicately hinted at the great expectations he entertained with regard to their docility to the voice of God, whose instrument he was to be among them.[55]

Hul'qumi'num First Nations were generally unfamiliar with the Chinook trade jargon and Demers' missionary activities were facilitated to a large degree by the Hudson's Bay Company interpreter Tomo Antoine, of whom the bishop wrote, "the Iroquois named Thomas, a devout young man, assisted by interpreting sermons and teaching them hymns and prayers in their own tongue."[56] An early convert was Jean-Baptiste Glasetatem, a si'em of Comiaken, who was appointed by Demers "to act as a priest among his own people" pending the establishment of a resident priest.[57] Lohar, the other prominent si'em of Comiaken, also "liked the priests and always tried to help them; they were his good friends ... Lohar did all the priests told him."[58] Another early convert to Catholicism was the Kuper Island warrior and si'em Hulkalatkstun from Penelakut who, as a young man, "had been taught by the priests and 'got religion.'"[59] It was said that Hulkalatkstun, who was baptized Pierre, was "the first chief to welcome Roman Catholic missionaries to the Pacific Coast."[60]

In 1858, Bishop Demers authorized Father Pierre Rondeault, a secular priest and recent arrival from Lower Canada, to establish a mission at Comiaken on Cowichan Bay. A Cowichan elder, Quon-us, recalled Rondeault's (Londo's) reception:

> That good man came when I was a little boy. My people told me how he paddled all alone from Saanich up to Comiaken. He had nothing with him, just a sack of flour and his Book, a gun to get food with, and maybe a blanket. When the Cowichan people heard he was coming, everybody went down to the water to look at him, and to tell him how glad they were that he had come! and everybody wanted to shake his hand. All that day Father Londo was shaking hands and talking to the people. My father's friend Tsulchamel, who the priests by and by called Gabriel—he told father Londo to come and live in his house at Comiaken, and there he stayed until he could make his own house.[61]

The Comiaken si'em, Lohar, and Jean-Baptiste Glasetatem invited Rondeault to use their houses to perform mass and baptisms which were well-attended.[62] Samuel Harris, a hwunitum trader who established himself in the valley around 1858, reported seeing "over 900 clean-washed, well-dressed Indians at mass in one of their own lodges."[63] Others travelled long distances "to hear the priest and to see him ... From the islands they came, and from all parts of the coast—big canoes full of men, women and children. He likes best to see the little children come. 'Bring them all,' he told the old people, and he held them and washed (baptized) them and gave them names like the white man."[64]

Rondeault visited villages outside of the Cowichan Valley to preach and baptize. Hulkalatkstun developed a special relationship with Rondeault who "used to come to Penelekhut. Ah, Hul-ka-latkstun did like that man! Often he used to come and talk to the Cowichans."[65]

Hwulmuhw converts soon pooled their labour to build a church, St. Ann's, on the summit of the hill overlooking the village of Comiaken. Built of logs, the church measured "about 50 feet by 20," and "some distance from it, in front, a huge wooden Latin cross stood in the ground."[66] When St. Ann's was finished the people built "a humble shanty adjoining the church" for Father Rondeault's living quarters. Si'em from various villages contributed, as Quon-as recalled:

> For this house the Indians gave one board from each village; one from Comiaken, one from Quamichan, one from Yekoloas and Penelekhut on Kuper Island, and so on, and in that way every place helped to make a house for that good man.[67]

Other Catholic missionaries assisted Rondeault to convert hwulmuhw on the east coast of Vancouver Island. The Oblate priest, Father Casimar Chirouse from the Puget Sound Tulalip Mission came north to visit Rondeault in May 1859. During his brief visit, it was sais that Chirouse, the "Apostle of Puget Sound":

> ... baptized about four hundred children and induced over two thousand adults publicly to renounce gambling, conjuring and murdering. So successful was his preaching and so sincere were the Indians in their promises, that they loaded his canoe with the paraphernalia of the medicine-man, or conjurer, as well as with knives, gambling discs and similar accessories to sin.[68]

Chirouse made a similar trip in April 1860 with another priest, Father Fouquet.

By the end of 1860, as a result of their efforts and Rondeault's mission at Comiaken, the traditional way of life was effectively undermined and the majority of Hul'qumi'num First Nations were, at least nominally, Roman Catholics. Over time, as Roman Catholic influence grew, the ancient system of hereditary si'em and inherited rights and privileges was displaced in part by si'em appointed by the Bishop.[69]

Protestant missionaries arrived late on the scene and found their labours hampered by the influence their Catholic rivals had over the hwulmuhw. One of them, an Irishman named Alexander Garrett, arrived in the colony in 1860 at the invitation of the Anglican Bishop, George Hills.[70] Garrett established a school for aboriginal children at the Songhees reserve across from the town of Victoria and made occasional visits to the Cowichan Valley, but his ministrations met with little success. An arrogant, dishevelled man, Garrett despised and distrusted the French-speaking Roman Catholic priests whom he often referred to as "foreigners."

Others were much more charitable in their regard for the labours of the Romanist missionaries. The hwunitum trader, Samuel Harris, wrote a letter on March 26th, 1861, in which he described the profound influence of the Roman Catholic priests on Cowichan society after only two years residence among them:

> I reside in the above district [Cowichan] in the midst of about 2,000 Indians who, eighteen months ago, carried on a system of drunkenness

and murder too horrible to relate. At this date they may be said to be a reclaimed people. Drink is forbidden by them, and a penalty attached to drunkenness by order of their chiefs. Consequently, other crimes are of rare occurrence. And to what is all this owing? To the honest and persevering labours of a poor Catholic priest who receives no salary, and is fed by the Indians as far as their means will enable them. Within eighteen months he has baptized upwards of 250 children and 50 adults who can repeat the catechism in their own language. Besides cutting timber, they have subscribed their dollars to build a substantial church, capable of containing 400 people, and it is, every Sabbath, full to overflowing. I have seen hundreds standing in the rain to catch a sound of the priest's exhortation. They are now collecting funds to furnish their church and make it like the white man's place of worship. [71]

As Harris points out, the Quebecois priests took an active role in suppressing the liquor trade which plagued the Cowichan people. On one occasion, "illicit whiskey dealers, who, attempting to land alcohol from their sloops, were driven off and their casks rolled into the sea." [72]

The fundamental influence of the church, however, was not so much spiritual as economic. The Roman Catholic Mission of St. Ann's diverted attention from traditional food resources by encouraging the people to cultivate cash crops such as potatoes, tobacco, timber and dairy products. [73] As a result, a growing percentage of people stayed in their winter villages during the annual summer migration to the Fraser River in order to tend their crops under the guidance of the priests.

Similarly, the Church competed with the stlun'uq (potlatch)—the complex system by which wealth was redistributed amongst the people in exchange for witnessing and thereby validating important changes in status. The priests:

... recognized that the giving that was the foundation of Indian religious beliefs was a field of strength that was worth their while to cultivate. Potlatching is a two-way process. Within this present world you give, and sooner or later, you receive in return. The priests attempted to replace potlatching with the practice of giving worldly goods to the church in exchange for everlasting life ... When they gave, the priest would promise that it would all be returned in the next world ... But the Church wanted cash, not swaddling blankets for the Baby Jesus. So the devout learned to turn their goods into cash ... When the goods were turned into cash which flowed across the seas and upward toward the heavens, the cycle that had perpetuated itself for so long was broken. The imperial chain was complete. [74]

Modeste Demers, first Roman Catholic Bishop of Vancouver Island.
British Columbia Archives and Records Service, Photo HP 2533.

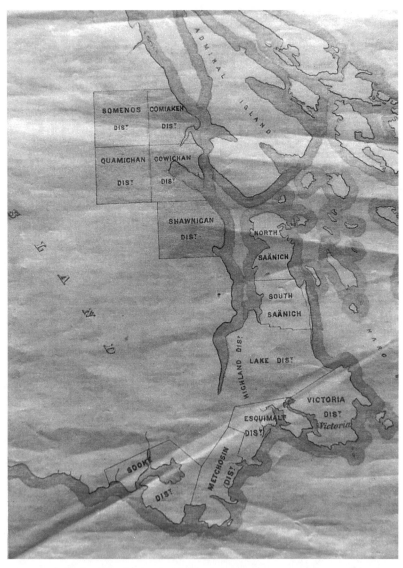

*Vancouver Island Colony showing area of land purchase agreements, from 1850 to 1852,
and illegally acquired Cowichan territories, July 22nd, 1859.*

Courtesy of Surveyors General Branch, Victoria.

Chapter Four

After the Gold Rush

While Roman Catholic missionaries infiltrated the territories of Hul'qumi'num
First Nations, two inter-related events prompted Douglas to begin the process
of alienating aboriginal lands without mutual agreements. Reports of the discovery
of gold on the mainland reached Great Britain, and in 1857 a bill was passed in
parliament to establish a second colony in the Pacific Northwest. It was also decided
that the Royal Licence to Vancouver Island given to the Hudson's Bay Company
would be terminated on May 30th, 1859, along with the company's right to
exclusive trade with the aboriginal people. The subsequent influx of hwunitum
miners to the Fraser River in 1858, and the end of the Hudson's Bay Company
charter, altered forever the balance of power between the indigenous people and
the newcomers and hastened the erosion of hwulmuhw sovereignty in the unceded
territories adjacent to the Colony of Vancouver Island.

Throughout the spring and summer of 1858, upwards of thirty thousand
hwunitum flooded into Victoria before pressing on through hwulmuhw territories
and across the Gulf of Georgia to the gold fields of the newly created Colony of
British Columbia.

Aboriginal people on the east coast of Vancouver Island and on the Gulf Islands
struggled to maintain their sovereignty and jurisdiction during the onset of the
Gold Rush. The gold seekers travelled the long-established canoe route between
Vancouver Island and the mainland which, before reaching the Gulf of Georgia,
passed through territories and waterways owned by Saanich, Cowichan, Penelakut,
and Lamalcha families. Some hwulmuhw welcomed the foreigners as trading
partners or employers, and offered their skills as canoeists, teamsters and
commissaries. At Elelen[1] (Miners' Bay), on the Mayne Island side of Active Pass,
Saanich owners allowed hwunitum to use the beach as a temporary camp and
staging area for the perilous journey across the Gulf of Georgia. Other hwulmuhw
resented the trespass and enforced their jurisdiction over the land and waterways.
Enforcement ranged from verbal threats to homicide according to the dictates of
personalities, situations, and the seriousness of transgression of hwulmuhw law.

Those most actively opposed to the hwunitum invasion included members of Cowichan, Penelakut and Lamalcha families whose traditional food-gathering territories lay along the route taken by the hwunitum miners through the southern Gulf Islands.

Active Pass, the body of water separating Galiano and Mayne Islands, was the major route through the Gulf Islands and a traditional ambush site.[2] In 1858 "a certain bad Indian ... in company with several others" is said to have killed "three white men at Plumper's Pass [Active Pass] and sunk their canoe."[3] According to information later given by a hwulmuhw informant to a hwunitum settler, great care was taken by the assailants to remove all traces of their work:

> It seems that it is the practice of these pirates, after committing a murder, to sink the bodies of their victims in deep water, by means of a stone tied around the neck, and also to scuttle any vessel that may, in such a manner, fall into their clutches, and sink her to avoid their crime being discovered and punished.[4]

Another incident, not well-documented, was said to have taken place near Active Pass in 1858, where eight Lamalcha and Penelakut warriors fired upon the Hudson's Bay Company steamer *Otter*.[5] There were no casualties and no reprisals, which suggests that the encounter was a symbolic demonstration of hwulmuhw sovereignty. The colonial government recognized these warriors as a serious obstacle to hwunitum settlement but took no direct action against them for fear of jeopardizing land sale agreements and to avoid the danger that a war would pose to the thousands of hwunitum en route to the mainland through the unceded territories of the Gulf Islands.[6]

The announcement that the Hudson's Bay Company charter to Vancouver Island would be revoked on May 30th, 1859, prompted the colonial government to take active measures to acquire as much additional hwulmuhw land for the company as possible before the charter expired. By the middle of 1858, unbeknownst to the people living there, the Colony of Vancouver Island initiated the appropriation of land in the Cowichan Valley by issuing scrip to hwunitum speculators which would entitle them to purchase land in the area at the going rate of one pound (five dollars) an acre upon completion of a survey.[7] The "Cowichan Scrip" was issued on a first-come-first-served basis to Hudson's Bay Company associates, politicians, merchants and Royal Navy officers.[8] Douglas made no attempt to arrange land sale agreements with the Cowichan people but went ahead with the sale of their lands solely, it seems, to secure for the Hudson's Bay Company and its friends the prime agricultural lands within the unceded Cowichan territories. This was in direct violation of imperial policy established in North America since the Royal Proclamation of 1763.

Most of the "Cowichan Scrip" was issued, and initial installments paid, before the actual survey took place. The first purchaser, Thomas J. Skinner, Bailiff for the Puget Sound Company's farm at Esquimalt and member of the Legislative Assembly for that district, bought his "Cowichan Scrip" on June 25th, 1858. He, like Thomas Gardinier a week later, "paid into the office ... $250 ... to secure installment proper on 1,000 acres of land at Cowichan when surveyed." [9]

Because hwulmuhw title had not been formerly extinguished, as occurred elsewhere in the colony, purchasers were only required to pay one quarter of the purchase price with the balance payable "when the Indian question of title of the land was settled." [10] The Surveyor General, Joseph Pemberton, who apparently handled many of these sales, reassured the buyers that a resolution of the title was imminent. When questioned by Douglas two years later concerning statements he made to purchasers "with regards to extinguishing the Indian title at Cowichan," Pemberton wrote in reply "that if in 1858 any Purchaser of the lands in question [asked] whether within a reasonable time the Indian title to those lands would be extinguished as had been previously the practice I should have replied in the affirmative." [11]

On Wednesday, March 16th, 1859, Pemberton and his assistant surveyor, Oliver Wells, along with a party of five men, left Victoria for the Cowichan Valley for a preliminary inspection prior to the actual survey of the land. [12] The surveying party apparently calculated their arrival to coincide with a seasonal migration of the Cowichan people, "large bodies of whom were absent at the Herring fisheries." [13]

Pemberton returned to Victoria and on March 22nd, 1858, Wells began his survey at Mill Creek Bay at the mouth of the Saanich Inlet and worked his way north. [14] By May 14th all of the coastal land lying north of the mouth of Saanich inlet to present-day Crofton was surveyed into one hundred acre lots comprising five districts named after hwulmuhw winter villages: Shawnigan, Cowichan, Quamichan, Somenos, Comiaken and Chemainus. [15] Shawnigan was the southernmost district above Mill Bay. To the north, the Cowichan District surrounded Cowichan Bay, encompassing the heartland of the Cowichan people, including the fertile river delta and most of the winter villages and potato fields. West of Cowichan District was another quadrant of lots drained by the Cowichan and Koksilah Rivers. It contained the winter villages of Somenos and Koksilah and was named Quamichan after the village of the same name which the surveyors placed at its eastern boundary. Somenos was the name given to the district directly above Quamichan, a region without permanent winter villages, but with numerous food gathering areas, which embraced the fertile lands surrounding Somenos lake at the base of the ancestral mountain Swuqus (Mount Prevost.) East of Somenos District was the less arable land of Comiaken District, unoccupied by permanent hwulmuhw settlements but used extensively for hunting and the gathering of edible and medicinal plants.

The surveyors had intended to proceed into the so-called Chemainus District, encompassing the Chemainus Valley, but on the 31st of May, a day after the Hudson's Bay Company grant to Vancouver Island expired, Pemberton wrote Wells to congratulate him "on the admirable progress you are making" and instructed him to "omit the survey of unsaleable land" in the Chemainus District. [16] The survey of the most valuable land was complete. In his official report Wells stated that 57,658 acres of land had been surveyed of which "45,000 acres of plain and prairie lands may be set down as superior agricultural districts, the remaining 17,600 acres being either open or thickly wooded land, partly arable, will likewise be chiefly occupied. There is thence a sufficient quantity of good level land laid out in this valley to provide farms for a population of from 500 to 600 families at an average of about 100 acres each." [17]

Although most hwulmuhw inhabitants were away at the herring fishery during his survey, Wells claimed that "the Indians have shown throughout a perfectly friendly disposition, and a strong desire to see the white man settled among them. Their services may prove of utility to the early settler by way of cheap labour." [18]

In marked contrast to Wells' positive report, Douglas informed the Colonial Office on May 25th that "much excitement prevails among the Cowitchen Tribes in consequence of a detailed Survey of the Cowitchen Valley which is now being executed by the Colonial Surveyor of Vancouver Island." Douglas reported that there was:

> ... a general belief among the "Cowitchens" that their lands are to be immediately sold and occupied by white settlers, an impression which it is difficult to remove and that gives rise to much contention amongst themselves about the disposal of their lands; one party being in favour of a surrender of a part of their country for settlement; while another party comprising nearly all the younger men of the Tribe strongly oppose that measure and wish to retain possession of the whole country in their own hands, and I anticipate much trouble in the adjustment of those disputes before the land can be acquired for settlement. [19]

By July 1859, 9,880 acres in what were now called the "Eastern Districts," including a large portion of the Cowichan Valley, had been selected and sold to nineteen purchasers. [20] The ownership of these lots was for a time purely symbolic, for none of the purchasers could occupy their claims. Cowichan families rightly resented hwunitum trespass on and occupation of their potato fields, food gathering resources and burial sites and they removed the surveying stakes placed by Wells. [21] Lieutenant Richard Mayne, who had a downpayment of £25 on his own section, visited the area in the summer of 1859, and wrote:

[The Cowichan] have shown no favour to those settlers who have visited their valley. Although it has been surveyed it cannot yet be settled as the Indians are unwilling to sell, still less to be ousted from their land. [22]

Meanwhile, events in the Colony of British Columbia put extra pressure on the Vancouver Island colony to alienate hwulmuhw land for hwunitum settlers. Within months of the initial rush to the gold-bearing bars of the Fraser Canyon, most of the hwunitum returned to the Colony of Vancouver Island. By the fall of 1858, the majority of them booked passage south, leaving behind their less fortunate comrades. As one observer explained:

The tens of thousands that had pressed into the city in '58, were diminished to not more than 1,500, embracing "the waifs and strays" of every nationality, not excepting a good many whose antecedents were not above suspicion. [23]

To deal with this influx of potentially troublesome unemployed, Douglas ordered the construction in Victoria of a Police Court and Barracks, "the most expensive government building in the Colony," and gave authority to Augustus Frederick Pemberton, a Protestant Irish immigrant, and uncle of the Surveyor General, to raise the first police force in western Canada. [24] Clothed in blue uniforms trimmed with brass buttons, the colonial police were organized "on the London Metropolitan model" which, in addition to Pemberton as Commissioner of Police, included an inspector, two sergeants, and eleven constables. [25] Their salaries were to be paid, Douglas informed the Colonial Secretary, "by the Hudson's Bay Company out of the proceeds of Land Sales effected in Vancouver's Island." [26] The Victoria colonial police had the daunting task of enforcing British law on the ground in the colony and in the unceded territories. The new Commissioner of Police soon gained "a reputation for fearlessness and determination" and it was claimed "that next to Governor Douglas there is no man to whom the country is more greatly indebted for the establishment of a law-abiding course than to Mr. Pemberton." [27] Unfortunately, long hours and low wages "caused senior officers to succumb all too frequently to graft or bribery." [28]

During the winter of 1858-59 the unemployed miners, who far outnumbered resident hwunitum in the colony, eked out a living as best they could. Jonathan Begg of Scotland, who arrived in the colony from California, worked at odd jobs and grew cabbages on vacant city lots. [29] Other industrious men, such as William Brady of the United States, turned to hunting elk and deer to supply the demand for fresh venison. [30] Those less scrupulous turned to the lucrative and illegal business of selling alcohol to hwulmuhw customers.

Others had had enough of gold mining and wished to take up farms and make a living from the land. It seemed to many, however, that arable land was accessible only to those associated with the Hudson's Bay Company. Unemployed hwunitum began to organize into committees to pressure the government for access to the agricultural land in the Cowichan Valley which had been surveyed and sold but not opened to settlement because the government had yet to extinguish hwulmuhw title. A petition of July 2nd, 1859, called for the creation of a pre-emption system, whereby individuals (and not "capitalists") could select land for a nominal fee and, over time, as the land was developed or "improved," acquire title. [31]

Douglas informed the petitioners "that if there are a hundred farmers ready to settle in the Cowitchen valley, let them present themselves, and facilities will be afforded them, the Indian title extinguished as soon as practicable; that no immediate payment will be required for the land." [32] Douglas, however, was still unable to negotiate a land sale agreement with Hul'qumi'num First Nations.

The unemployed found support in the columns of the *British Colonist*, a Victoria newspaper founded in 1858 by an eccentric Nova Scotian immigrant and future premier of British Columbia named Amor De Cosmos. In an article published on the fourth of July, 1859, De Cosmos exclaimed:

Why is Indian title to Cowichan not extinguished at once? This [demand] is repeated over and over again, and yet no response is heard from the government. It may require judicious management, but it has to be done. The country expects it without delay. We want farmers,—and the best way to get them is to open the lands of Cowitchen to actual settlers by extinguishing the Indian title.

A committee of "Messrs. Copeland, Sparrow, and Manly" was appointed at a July 11th meeting in Victoria "to present a petition to the Governor to permit them to settle in Cowichan," but the committee was informed "that it could not be done at present." [33] No explanation was given but, aside from opposition by Hul'qumi'num First Nations to settlement in their territories, the revocation of the Hudson's Bay Company's grant placed the colonial government in an awkward position, legally, to grant title. [34]

The *British Colonist* of July 13th, 1859, had no sympathy for the plight of the Hudson's Bay Company and berated the government for its inability to open the Cowichan Valley to hwunitum settlement. It echoed the cry of land-hungry hwunitum frustrated at the government's delay in providing agricultural land for settlers:

All are convinced that if the Company had last year fulfilled the conditions of the grant, or the government done its duty, the Cowichan Valley would today have been filled with thrifty farmers ... the united voice of this community advocates the claim of the hardy pioneers who wish to settle in Cowichan.

Douglas saw in the petitioners an opportunity to concentrate them in a settlement within unceded Hul'qumi'num First Nations territories, and he began to formulate a plan. The Surveyor General had advised Douglas not to permit hwunitum settlers into the Cowichan Valley until suitable arrangements, such as a land sale agreement, could be made with the Cowichan.[35] However, Douglas writes in a letter to Newcastle that:

> [I do not] feel disposed to adopt Mr. Pemberton's suggestion respecting the Cowitchen Country. It has for good reasons been the invariable policy of the Government to concentrate as much as possible the white population when forming settlements in Districts inhabited by powerful tribes of Indians, but that object is attainable now as fully as at any former period in the history of the Colony, and I therefore do not consider it expedient or adviseable to close, for some time, the Cowitchen valley against the settlement of Whites, as Mr. Pemberton suggests. To adopt such a course would naturally give rise to much clamour and dissatisfaction among the people, and in effect retard the legitimate progress of the Colony.[36]

However, Douglas did not direct settlers to the Cowichan Valley, but instead announced that the "Chemainus District," left unsurveyed by Oliver Wells a few months previous, would be thrown open to settlement. "They were offered the Chemainus country," the *British Colonist* explained, "which is unsurveyed and commences ten miles north of the southern end of Cowichan, towards Nanaimo. The land is reported good. Whether this will be accepted [by the petitioners] has not been decided."[37] The hwunitum were unfamiliar with the "Chemainus District," which included the Chemainus Valley and Salt Spring Island, and on July 18th thirty prospective settlers left Victoria, "for the purpose of exploring the unsurveyed Chemainus lands."[38] One of them, Jonathan Begg, a principal organizer of the land reform movement, described their impression of Salt Spring Island:

> The band of adventurers ... including myself finding the island beautifully situated in the midst of an archipelago more beautiful than the 1000 islands of the St. Lawrence we determined to form a settlement here this being the most convenient to Victoria.[39]

The exploring party may also have visited the mouth of the Chemainus River where they would have noticed the flourishing potato fields of hwulmuhw farmers.

The hwunitum returned to Victoria on July 24th to announce that they were "highly pleased with the country and consider it a beautiful agricultural country."[40] There was no mention of the aboriginal inhabitants, most of whom, at this time of year, would have been absent at the Fraser River sockeye fishery.

Within days of the return of the hwunitum explorers, Douglas and Pemberton devised a "make-shift pre-emption system," which was limited to the unsurveyed land of Hul'qumi'num First Nations in the Chemainus Valley and on Salt Spring Island.[41]

Douglas deliberately aimed the first pre-emption system in western Canada directly at the territories owned by those most actively opposed to hwunitum settlement. The open prairie land of Hwtlelum (place having salt), on the north east side of Salt Spring Island, chosen by the hwunitum as an ideal site for settlement, was an important food-gathering area used by Lamalcha and Penelakut families. The resources of the Chemainus River were also accessed by families from Kuper Island, and the valley itself was home to the Halalt and other people. [42] Douglas hoped that his unofficial pre-emption strategy would satisfy the unemployed miners-turned-settlers and, at the same time, establish *de facto* hwunitum presence in unceded hwulmuhw territories.

The colonial government's pre-emption policy within the unceded territories of Hul'qumi'num First Nations "was never officially proclaimed, nor was its authorization sought from the Imperial Government" possibly because Douglas knew that it was illegal. [43] In official correspondence to the Colonial Office Douglas only asked for authorization to apply the new pre-emption strategy to vacant lands already ceded by hwulmuhw in the treaties of 1850, 1852, and 1854—lands that were, by and large, unsuitable for agriculture. [44] This suggests that Douglas, frustrated by hwulmuhw unwillingness to part with their lands, planned to circumvent the land sale agreement process to provoke reaction from militant hwulmuhw factions which would, in turn, allow for military retaliation and the forceful alienation of their lands without agreement. Douglas seemed confident that any hwulmuhw resistance would be futile.

Once again, the British chose the time of year when the majority of Hul'qumi'num First Nations would be involved in the sockeye fishery at the Fraser River.

On July 26th, 1859, Pemberton informed Copland that he had received the names of twenty-five persons "for whom you are agent and who apply through you for permission to settle on the unsurveyed lands of Tuam or Salt Spring Island ... The permission asked for I am empowered to give." Pemberton added that "none of these persons shall occupy or allow other persons to occupy lands at any time occupied by Indians," an interesting caveat given that all of the land in question was unceded and owned by numerous families. [45]

On July 27th, 1859, eighteen men left Victoria on board the *Nanaimo Packet* for the fertile prairies of Hwtlelum on Salt Spring Island. [46] Due to the shoaling sandstone shoreline, the schooner landed them on a sandy beach two miles south, the site of a major hwulmuhw clam harvesting and processing site which the hwunitum named "Walker's Hook," after Edward Walker, master of the *Nanaimo Packet*. After exploring the land they "drew choices of [lot] selection." [47]

When the Penelakut and Lamalcha returned to their villages on Kuper Island, there was anger over the unannounced arrival of hwunitum in their midst. In light of information received from Jonathan Begg, the *New Westminster Daily Times* wrote:

> We have to urge upon the Government the necessity of some immediate measures being adopted to settle the Indian claims, if any exist, upon these islands as the settlers are subjected to constant annoyance and insult from these claimants more especially by the "Penalichar [Penelakut] tribe," who boldly tell the settlers that the Island is their's, and that Gov. Douglas has "cap-swallowed" it, which, in the elegant Chinook jargon (we believe), means stolen it. The subject deserves immediate attention. [48]

On the southern part of the island, where 5,000 acres had been surveyed between Hwaaqwum (Burgoyne Bay) and Hwne'nuts (Fulford Harbour), Douglas promised compensation to Kwi'alhwat, the Clemclemalits si'em whose family owned the land and resources in the Burgoyne Valley, on condition that he leave. [49] According to Robert Akerman, a descendant:

> My Grandmother [Tehokwiya] said that Douglas promised her dad [Kwi'alhwat] compensation for the Burgoyne Valley if he'd leave it and go back to his camp at Cowichan Bay. So he left ... Douglas must have recognized that the Indians owned the land or why else would he offer to buy it. [50]

Local opposition to the hwunitum settlements at Hwaaqwum and Hwtlelum on Salt Spring Island was soon tempered by marriage between many of the settlers to the daughters of local si'em from Penelakut and elsewhere. At Hwtlelum (Salt Spring Settlement), one of the settlers, Henry Sampson, eventually married Lucy, the daughter of Hulkalatkstun, a si'em at Penelakut. [51] Others followed his example. The Anglican Bishop George Hills, visiting the settlement a year later, found "sixteen settlers mostly young men" and observed that "nearly all are living with Indian women." [52] Intermarriage made legitimate, according to hwulmuhw custom, hwunitum occupation of family-owned lands. The rights to the land and access to local resources "came" with the women upon marriage and were transferred to the men. [53]

Similarly, in the Burgoyne Valley marriages between Roman Catholic hwunitum settlers such as Michael Gyves, Theodore Traige and John Maxwell, and the daughters of Clemclemalits si'em, allowed these men to occupy their claims unmolested. [54]

Other hwunitum on Salt Spring Island who did not marry into hwulmuhw families were tolerated because of their value as trading partners. Jonathan Begg followed the example of Samuel Harris at Cowichan Bay and opened a trading post on his north end claim, catering not only to the settlers but to nearby hwulmuhw clients. In a March 10th, 1860, letter to family in the United States, he boasted that:

"It is very cheap living here as the Indians who are very useful and very good to white men bring us large quantities of the best the water, woods and forest can produce for a mere song."[55] Begg's store and farm became such a fixture that the Salt Spring settlement on the north end of the island was often referred to as Begg's Settlement.

The Salt Spring Island Stone Company Ltd. laid claim to a thousand acres of land encompassing the entire northwest tip of the island, a region characterized by dry rocky outcrops, forested ravines, and little arable land. Owned by Lamalcha and Penelakut families who "had shacks here and there," this area was valued for the hunting of deer and elk and the gathering of food plants and other resources.[56] Pqunup (Southey Point, Cupple's Beach) was an important clam digging area and the site of a burial ground.[57] The stone cutters' claim was technically made up of five lots but because the area was controlled by the Lamalcha it remained unsurveyed and the four or five Englishmen employed by the company occupied only a tiny area of the shoreline north of Stonecutter's Bay on the west side of the island. How the company managed to occupy traditional Lamalcha territory is not known but it seems likely that some sort of payment or mutually beneficial agreement was made.

The Salt Spring Island Stone Company may have commenced operations as early as 1859 under the direction of John Lee, "a first class mechanic who understood stone as anyone would bread and butter." He and his four co-workers "true to nature and instinct … built a house of stone," parts of which still stand at the top of a sloping incline above the shore where they cut sandstone blocks.[58] The stonecutters understood too well their precarious situation; archaeological investigations of their stone house reveal blocks of stone specially cut to provide embrasures for rifles fitted into the wall facing the sea.[59]

At the Admiralty Bay settlement, which spread across the centre of the island, there was much less tolerance towards the newcomers. The lands occupied by hwunitum and qihuye' (black) settlers encompassed Shiyahwt (Admiralty Bay) and Stulan (Booth Canal), both of which were important camps and food-gathering areas accessed by Hul'qumi'num First Nations. According to Lamalcha elder Henry Edwards, "People from all over the world go there [Shiyahwt] to harvest seafood. Families had cabins built all along the shore—each one had a smokehouse for clams, herring, ducks [and] seal. People from Lamalcha, Penelakut, Valdez, Saanich people, all went to Shiyahwt."[60] The land between the head of Booth Canal and Admiralty Bay (now Ganges Harbour) was used as a canoe portage by Lamalcha families. According to Roy Edwards, "They used Booth Bay when they went to fish at the Fraser River. They went to the head of the bay and they used skids to pull their canoes over to Ganges."[61] Hwunitum occupation of these areas interfered with established hwulmuhw use of the land. There was also little, if any, trade between the two peoples and no intermarriage.

Jonathan Beggs' store at the Salt Spring Settlement (now Fernwood) on the northeast side of Salt Spring Island, 1860. Sketch by Edward Mallandaine.
British Columbia Archives and Records Service, Photo PDP 1278.

Section of stone blocks from the walls of the stonecutter's house on Salt Spring Island overlooking Houston Passage, showing embrasures for rifles.　　*Photo by Chris Arnett.*

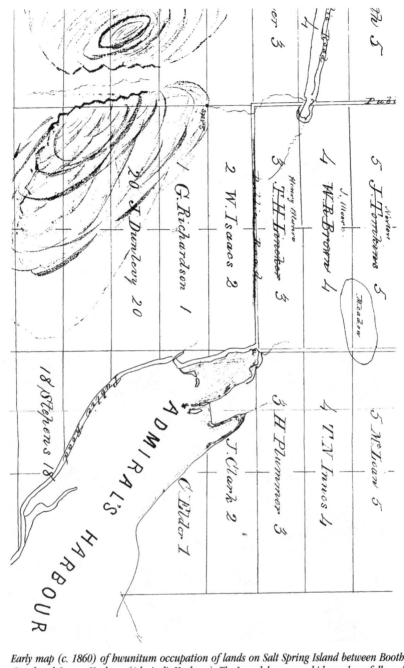

Early map (c. 1860) of bwunitum occupation of lands on Salt Spring Island between Booth Canal and Ganges Harbour (Admiral's Harbour). The Lamalcha canoe skid may have followed the route of the public road between lots 2 and 3.   Courtesy of Salt Spring Island Archives.

At Shiyahwt, shortly after the hwunitum occupied their claims, hwulmuhw owners arrived and erected houses along the beach at the head of the harbour to remind the settlers of the true ownership of the land.[62] Henry Lineker, whose two hundred acre claim occupied the Lamalcha canoe portage, built the first house in the Admiralty Bay settlement in November 1859, but his family was often visited by Lamalcha people who made themselves at home in the family's log cabin:

> Bands of Indians might come to the cabin and quite fill up the small space. Before the fire they would sit perhaps a whole day, for no one dared ask them to move. They talked among themselves, and intimated by suggestively drawing a hand across the throat, what would happen to the unlucky mortal who ventured to disturb them. The family did not stay very long on the island.[63]

Another hwunitum settler, James Shaw, took up land on the east side of the island in December 1859, cleared some land, built a house and planted potatoes, but within months was forced to leave when he found his claim "inconvenient and unprotected from Indians" who continued to access their lands despite his residence.[64]

At least six qihuye' families, recently immigrated from the United States, also took up land in the vicinity at the Admiralty Bay settlement towards Vesuvius Bay.[65] They did not intermarry with hwulmuhw and their presence was likewise only barely tolerated. A few months after their arrival in early 1860, Lamalcha or Penelakut warriors robbed "some of the black settlers" at the "Ganges Harbour settlement."[66] Black or white, those settlers lacking marriage or economic ties to hwulmuhw had no rights to the land and the resources and were fair game for depredation. The Lamalcha, in particular, "would await settlers landing at Vesuvius Bay with their sacks and boxes of supplies—swoop down and depart with the supplies before the startled settler knew what had happened."[67] The hostility directed towards the hwunitum by the true owners of the land was the main reason for the high absenteeism and turnover of hwunitum pre-emptions on Salt Spring Island.[68]

A short time after the Salt Spring pre-emptions, another two hundred and twelve hwunitum applied for pre-emption rights in the Chemainus Valley. A survey was made of the valley between August 11th, and August 25th, 1859, while the majority of hwulmuhw inhabitants were absent at the Fraser River.[69] It was soon revealed that the government had greatly overestimated the amount of suitable agricultural land in the Chemainus Valley, much of which was "heavy timbered land" confined by precipitous slopes to within three miles of the shore. There was barely enough arable land to accommodate the needs of twenty-five hwunitum, let alone two hundred and twelve, and much of it was occupied by hwulmuhw potato fields.[70]

In the middle of November 1859, Robert Watson and thirteen other pre-emptors "laid in about twelve months provisions and started for Chemainus, with the intention of making it our home on our arrival." [71] They arrived as the winter dances were beginning, and the villages on the Chemainus River (at Halalt on Willy Island) and at Lamalcha on Kuper Island were full. The hwunitum were watched and not made welcome. Eventually they were forced to leave. According to Watson:

> ... we experienced considerable difficulty with the Indians, as they did not wish us to settle on the land until they were paid for it, as there were only certain portions they would allow us to settle on. Only six of the party remained. I then accompanied one of the Chiefs to the Governor to have our reasons for being there explained to them. The Governor made him some trifling presents which smothered matters a little for some time, when the party went to work, built houses, and prepared a large amount of fencing, with a view to putting in crops for the spring. About the latter end of February [1860] the settlers were informed by the friendly portion of the Indians, that their Indians meditated taking our lives. The whole party returned to Victoria with the expectation that some settlement would be made with the Indians in time to allow us getting in spring seeds, but after purchasing cattle, ploughs, and other necessary implements and seed, we were informed that although the Government was favourable to the settlement, and wished us to go on with our improvements, that they had no money at their disposal to extinguish the Indian title, without which I consider the land system only a farce, as the Indians occupy all the fronts of the small valleys, and their potato patches, although not exceeding ten acres, spread over as many thousand acres ... I am not one of those who attach all blame to the Governor in retarding settlement of the colony; it is those legislators that refuse the necessary means to extinguish the Indian title to the soil that keeps Cowichan and Chemainus from being thriving settlements instead of as they now are—merely hunting grounds for the red man. [72]

As Watson reveals, Douglas made some sort of promise to local si'em but it was not carried through and the settlers were forced to leave their claims. Commenting on the eviction of the Chemainus Valley settlers, the *Victoria Gazette* of April 13th, 1860, recognized the need to extinguish hwulmuhw title as "a pragmatic political gesture rather than a strict legal necessity": [73]

> However much the title may be disputed, it is and has been usual to subsidize the Indian upon taking possession of his patrimony, and thus while denying a right *de jure*, admitting it *de facto*. The system of giving presents for purchase of or in exchange for lands, is attended with the happiest results. By it the friendship of the Indian is gained, he is

convinced of our honour, justice, and integrity, and his confidence is at once acquired. The injurious effects of non-extinguishment of title in other districts is shown by the fact of Chemainus settlers having been obliged to leave that part of the country. To suppress a serious broil and bring the offenders to justice would cost more than the sum required to extinguish the title and gain the confidence of the native. Economy invites the Indian title to be extinguished, custom calls for it ... We ask the Executive at once to extinguish the title to the land in the Chemainus district ... Do it now, for it can be done at small cost. But let priests and missionaries once gain the ear of the Indian then farewell to so easy and so inexpensive an arrangement. [74]

However, money was not the issue. The aboriginal owners of the Chemainus Valley wanted to keep their lands and had set aside areas for hwunitum settlement. Robert Watson accompanied a si'em to Victoria, where Douglas assured them that he would make a land sale agreement with the Halalt, Chemainus, Sickameen, Penelakut, and Lamalcha owners that would recognize their rights to their lands and resources. Douglas presented the si'em with gifts in recognition of his promise, but did not act on his word.

As a Victoria newspaper later observed, "promises were made both to Indians and settlers that compensation should be paid to the former for the loss of their summer homesteads, potato plots, and fishing stations, and broken and broken again; and to this day the redskin and the white man have not had that justice which common sense, truth, and honour ought to have compelled the Government to give them, without one day's necessary delay." [75]

In the first week of April 1860, HMS *Plumper* took time out from its surveying duties to visit the Admiralty Bay settlement, "as it had been reported that some Indians had been troublesome there." The British, as Lieutenant Mayne recalled, "found however, that the Indians had done nothing more than tell the settlers occasionally, as Indians do everywhere, that they (the whites) had no business there except as their guests, and that all the land belonged to them." [76] Mayne was sympathetic to hwulmuhw claims for compensation for alienated land on Salt Spring Island and he realized the difficulty of applying hwunitum concepts of ownership against the ancient and complex indigenous system of land tenure.

It appeared to be most desirable here, as at other places, that the Indians should be duly paid for their land. This is not so simple as it may seem, however, even supposing the money necessary for such a purpose to be forthcoming. In New Zealand the Government spent many thousand pounds purchasing the land, appointing agents, commissioners, &c., and something of the same is no doubt as necessary here. Vancouver Island, however, has no revenue available or sufficient for such a purpose, and of course the revenue of British Columbia cannot, while the two colonies are distinct, be applied to it. Another difficulty would be found in the conflicting claims of the various tribes, arising from their habits of polygamy and inheritance from the female side, together with the absence of any documentary or satisfactory evidence of title.

If, therefore, any one chief or tribe were paid for a piece of land without the acknowledgement on the part of adjacent tribes of the vendor's right to the land sold, five or six other claimants would in all probability come forward asserting the land to be theirs, and founding their title to it upon some intermarriage of its former possessors. The difficulty arising from the Indian custom of descent from the female side are most perplexing ... Admiral Island, [Salt Spring Island] for instance, of which I am now speaking, would, in all probability, be claimed by no less than four tribes, viz., the Cowitchin, the Penalikutson [Penelakut], a small tribe living among these islands, the Nanaimos, and Saanitch Indians. On the occasion of our present visit, the settlers, in reference to this subject, said the Indians had never been there before, and that they had established a village there [at the head of Ganges Harbour] for the sole purpose of asserting their claim to compensation to the land. Upon our telling one of them this, he pointed to a small stump by which we were standing, and said it marked his father's grave, where he had buried him three years ago [1857]—long before any white settler came to the place. [77]

The unregulated mixing of transient hwunitum and hwulmuhw residents in the Gulf Islands led to more incidents of violence as hwunitum, often in ignorance, transgressed hwulmuhw laws and paid the penalty. Following the gold rush of 1858, an unknown number of hwunitum were killed for trespass, insults, molestation of women or in retaliation for other wrongs, real or imagined. Some attacks had the acquisition of wealth as their objective. However, as one hwunitum observed: "nine-tenths of the outrages perpetrated by natives upon the superior race, and supposed to be the result of insensate cruelty, can be traced to some wanton violation of the personal or domestic rights of the Indians on the part of the whites." [78]

Alcohol, a major feature of inter-racial contact, often served as a catalyst for violence. Oshiane Mitchell relates an incident that occurred in one of the houses at Penelakut:

The boat with the white people anchored off the big house. Like the big house down here at Chemainus. One man came in and wanted to sell. Nobody's talking. Don't understand what he say. "You guys drinkin'? I'd like to give you a drink," that apple cider was in a can. "Here you are." In the big house, this was the women [indicates a line], this was the man's [another separate line]. Not drinking, the women. The men drink some more, they got very drunk. The whites want to give some of that to the women. No [said the men, indicating the line of women] this is the women. We want more, you got lots. We want some more, more. They try and dump it. Then they went out to the boat and got all the things. Some got the hatchets, some got the long knives. The white people, they died.[79]

People from the village of Lamalcha at the south end of Kuper Island "did not like these white men coming."[80] Because their lands on Salt Spring Island were being occupied and used, in most cases without their permission, certain individuals associated with the eight households of Lamalcha emerged as leading opponents of hwunitum colonization. The preeminent Lamalcha si'em, Squ'acum, was described as "a powerful chief," and is remembered today as a "war man" who was "mean to the whites."[81]

While the Lamalcha opposed hwunitum occupation of their land, they embraced hwunitum technology. They adopted hwunitum clothes, used whaleboats as well as canoes, and practiced hwunitum carpentry. At the centre of the village was a large blockhouse built of squared timbers "well-morticed and tennoned," and loopholed on three sides for muskets and rifles.[82] Eight feet in height, it may have been modelled after hwunitum blockhouses built the previous decade on Whidbey and San Juan Islands. Rifle pits surrounded the fort. In addition to these defences, Lamalcha was well-situated geographically, with the houses of the village at the head of a crescent-shaped bay, flanked by two points of land. On each point were "lookouts" where warriors kept watch. Lamalcha is "the look-out place."[83]

One incident took place between 1858 and 1860 when a Lamalcha warrior named Palluk, his Lamalcha wife Semallee, and a Nanaimo man named Skiloweet, killed a hwunitum man at S'tayus (Pender Island.) The unidentified victim was on the island to hunt, probably without permission, when the hwulmuhw party saw him one morning as they passed by in a canoe and landed. The men conversed amiably for some time. According to a hwulmuhw witness, the hwunitum gave "no offence, and made use of no angry expressions whatever" when Palluk, without warning, "fired and wounded him in the arm while he was sitting by his tent at the fire … When the white man jumped up to get his gun, Palluk rushed upon him" and Skiloweet went to his aid. The hwunitum hunter grabbed Palluk and Skiloweet by the hair and "was knocking their heads together," when Semallee "seized an axe and struck him on the back."[84] Skiloweet then cut the man "across the abdomen with a knife. He fell dead. His intestines came out. The body was left there and not buried or concealed."[85]

During these turbulent times, violence was not only directed against hwunitum newcomers but continued within hwulmuhw society as well. This "warfare" took the form of retaliatory violence whereby individual acts of violence drew response according to a principle "of a duty ... to retaliate in kind for the killing of a member of the nation or kin group."[86] As legal historian Hamar Foster elaborates, although "retaliatory violence is a form of social control ... kinship and other relationships usually kept such violence—which was governed by customary expectations and principles of liability—within acceptable limits."[87] Because of complex inter-village kinship, warfare amongst Hul'qumi'num First Nations was practically non-existent. When it did occur, it was most often limited to quarrels "between nobles of different villages." In general, these disputes between si'em of nearby villages were "patched up through the intervention of common kinsmen, and seldom resulted in open feuds."

Where villages and kinship ties were more remote, feuds were more likely to occur but, as hwulmuhw elders informed anthropologist Diamond Jenness:

> ... they were feuds between individual nobles, as a rule, in which the villages as a whole played the part of spectators only. One noble would challenge another to approach his village and settle their quarrel by single combat; or he would send word through a messenger that he would attack his enemy in his home. The principals then fought out their duel on the beach, while their retainers stood by to guard against treachery.[88]

Around 1858, there was a feud between a Penelakut man named Acheewun and one Ashutstun, of Valdez Island, that was to have far-reaching consequences for Hul'qumi'num First Nations and the people of Lamalcha in particular.

Ashutstun, for some unknown reason, had killed a man who was making a canoe.[89] The victim was a friend or relation of Acheewun, who made plans to avenge his death. Sometime around 1858, Acheewun, accompanied by his brother Shenasaluk and two companions, arrived at "Swamuxum," a "village" or "camp" in the vicinity of Porlier Pass, where Ashutstun was present with his son, Sewholatza, and others. Sewholatza claimed that Acheewun "came to the camp drunk."[90] As the people gathered to watch, Acheewun and Ashutstun faced each other with their weapons and a fight ensued.

Acheewun later claimed that Ashutstun made the first move: "He first got angry and struck me in the face with a knife."[91] Acheewun then struck Ashutstun "who bled very much from the effect of the blow." Ashutstun was incapacitated and some of "the lookers on" went to carry him to his house. Acheewun "walked proudly about" before firing upon them.[92] Sewholatza, who watched the fight from inside the house, recalled that "just as he was being carried to the door, A-chee-wun fired his musket at him, the ball wounding one of the men who was assisting and struck his father on the right side, passing out the left. After receiving the wound his father staggered into the house and fell dead on the ground."[93] Two more shots were fired into the house. Acheewun called on Sewholatza "to come out and he would serve him the same," but the fight ended with no further casualties. [94]

It was a traditional fight between two men of lineage on the beach in front of their followers, but there was no compensation or retaliatory violence for the death of Ashutstun until 1863, when Sewholatza would exploit British naval forces to seek revenge on Acheewun.

After this fight, Acheewun fell out of favour with Hulkalatkstun, the si'em of his house at Penelakut, who, perhaps on account of the death of Ashutstun, characterized Acheewun as "a bad and cruel man." [95]

Acheewun moved to Porlier Pass where he may have lived at Khinepsen, a small village site at the north end of Galiano Island named for the home village of the famous warrior Tzouhalem. [96] Acheewun also possessed "a number of retreats and hiding places on Galiano and other islands," including an almost inaccessible "tunnel" high up Mount Sutil at the south end of Galiano Island. [97] He married Sally, the daughter of Statumish, a si'em who lived at the "upper settlement" on the Chemainus River. [98] By 1859, with the hwunitum occupation of the north end of Salt Spring Island and the Chemainus River, Acheewun became "the leader of a small band" militantly opposed to hwunitum colonization. [99] As one of his descendants put it, Acheewun "could see what was coming and fought against it to the bitter end." [100] Several of his followers were from Lamalcha and Acheewun himself gravitated towards "the look-out place."

The looser social structure at Lamalcha, [101] and its growing reputation as a centre of opposition to hwunitum, made it a desireable place for persons who, for one reason or another, were unable to live in their home villages. Lamalcha attracted displaced persons from Penelakut, Nanaimo, and other places, which gave the village a reputation as a place for "men and women who [had] been expelled from their own tribes on account of bad conduct." [102] The colonial government saw them as an obstacle to land sale agreements and as a threat to the safety of hwunitum.

Chapter Five

Pay the Indians for the Land
or We'll Have an Indian War

Douglas realized that before hwunitum settlement of the Cowichan and Chemainus valleys could occur, and to ensure the safety of hwunitum settlers on Salt Spring Island, hwulmuhw title to the land would have to be extinguished. In an address to the House of Assembly on March 1, 1860, he asked the House "to provide means for extinguishing, by purchase, the native Title to the Lands in the Districts of Cowichan, Chemainus and Salt Spring Island which are now thrown open for settlement. The purchase should be effected without delay, as the Indians may otherwise regard the settlers as trespassers and become troublesome." [1]

In early June 1860, Douglas instructed Sheriff George W. Heaton to make reconnaissance of the area and conduct a census of Hul'qumi'num First Nations, presumably in preparation for a land sale agreement and to assess hwulmuhw opposition to hwunitum settlement. As usual, the colonial officials went during seasonal migrations by the majority of families to their food gathering properties. "The taking of this census," wrote Heaton, "was attended with considerable difficulty in consequence of the Indians, as is usual at this season, being scattered in all directions for the purpose of fishing." [2] Accompanied by local trader Samuel Harris, Heaton visited all the major hwulmuhw settlements on the east coast of Vancouver Island from the Cowichan River north to Nanaimo, including those on Willy Island and Kuper Island.

Heaton described the majority of the people he met as "perfectly civil and friendly on the occasion of my visit ... well supplied with all the neccesities of life—adding to the fish with which their waters are so abundantly supplied the produce of numerous patches of potato ground." [3] However, at the village of Quamichan, which Heaton described as "the most numerous of the Cowichan families," he found "a turbulent spirit and, among the younger men of the tribe—one antagonistic to the whites." [4]

Leaving the Cowichan territory, the two hwunitum travelled further north along the east coast of Vancouver Island to the villages of Halalt, Sunuwnets, and Chemainus. At Penelakut, on Kuper Island, where there was anger over the recent occupations of territories on Salt Spring Island, Heaton and Harris encountered more hostility. In contrast to many of the people he met, the Penelakut, wrote Heaton, were "an exception to the general civility. They declined to furnish their numbers or to allow them to be taken."[5]

Heaton met a similar reception from the Lamalcha people on the south end of the island whom he described as "ci-devant [former] slaves ... considered by the neighbouring Indians to have no territorial rights."[6]

It is interesting to note that Heaton emphatically states that the Lamalcha were a village of ex-slaves with "no territorial rights." While some Lamalcha households may have been less well-connected to lands and resources, elders today recognize that Lamalcha families owned resources on the north end of Salt Spring Island, Secretary and Galiano Islands, and accessed other locations through marriage.[7] Heaton's claim seems calculated in light of the reputation of the Lamalcha as strong opponents of hwunitum settlement, and the fact that land desired by hwunitum settlers, particularly in the Chemainus Valley and on the north end of Salt Spring Island, lay within their territories. In fact, Heaton drew attention to the wealth of natural resources within the Lamalcha territory that could be exploited by hwunitum:

> There is an excellent site for a white fishing station on their island; fresh water favourable to oyster beds, cod, rock-cod, salmon, halibut—cuttle-fish (occasionally), herring, dogfish, sea cow, porpoises and whales in their greatest abundance in the neighbouring waters.[8]

Heaton's report of June 12th, 1860, gave Douglas valuable information regarding Hul'qumi'num First Nations on the eve of the alienation of their land and resources. For example, a comparison of the population figures of the various villages with those of Douglas' 1853 census revealed that in seven short years hwulmuhw populations on the east coast of Vancouver island and adjacent islands had dropped by fifty per cent.

Based on the population figures contained in Heaton's census, and according to his own calculation that £3 worth of goods to each si'em would be sufficient, Douglas estimated that it would cost £3,000 to extinguish the title of lands belonging to Hul'qumi'num and Nanaimo First Nations.[9] The House of Assembly had agreed with his earlier request to set aside funds for the purchase of hwulmuhw lands and included £2,000 in the budget estimates, but the item was struck out during a meeting on July 3rd.[10] Some members apparently believed that the funds should be supplied by the British government and not raised locally.

Whether the House of Assembly approved the funds or not, Douglas faced even greater obstacles, not the least of which were internal divisions amongst the Hul'qumi'num First Nations regarding negotiations with the hwunitum.

Following the eviction of hwunitum settlers from the Chemainus Valley, a series of violent confrontations between native people in the Gulf Islands in the spring and summer of 1860 reminded hwunitum settlers of their precarious position in the unceded lands. The Battle of Hwtlupnets had put an end to large scale raids by Kwakwaka'wakw people, but violence continued between hwulmuhw populations and smaller migratory bands of people en route from the north to hwunitum establishments in Victoria. Alcohol was a factor in many of these confrontations and hwulmuhw insisted that, among Kwakwaka'wakw-speaking people, "whiskey" was "the principal reason of their going south to Victoria." [11]

In the early spring of 1860, there was a raid on Penelakut by "northern Indians" which left several people killed and one of the si'em badly wounded. [12] Penelakut was put on military alert and it was only by chance that two Roman Catholic missionaries, Fouquet and Chirouse, were not killed in an ambush during a visit to the village shortly after the raid. [13] Around this time Hulkalatkstun, another si'em of the village, was wounded in a fight with northern people near Esquimalt, setting the stage for retaliation. [14]

A potent reminder to hwunitum settlers of hwulmuhw sovereignty occurred on the 4th of July, 1860, when resident Lamalcha and Penelakut warriors attacked the occupants of a Bella Bella canoe at the head of Ganges Harbour on Salt Spring Island, killing ten of them. According to one of the settlers, the attack was in retaliation for previous events, the hwulmuhw warriors having "owed them a grudge for some injury done years ago." [15]

A canoe carrying "nine men, two boys and three women of the Bella Bella tribe" was on its way to Victoria when a hwunitum by the name of McCawley met them at the Salt Spring Settlement where he convinced the Bella Bella to take him to Victoria. Lieutenant Mayne, who described the passenger as "one of the settlers on the north end of Saltspring Island," writes that McCawley "asked them to take him to Victoria, calling at the settlement in Ganges Harbour on the way. They were willing to take him to Victoria, but objected going to Ganges Harbour on account of the Cowitchins. The settler, however, overruled their objections, and they finally assented to his wish." [16]

Thomas Lineker, the settler with whom McCawley "had business," recalled that there were fifty Indians of the Cowichan tribe encamped there," no doubt in their houses at the head of the harbour. [17] Lineker noted that they "manifested an unfriendly spirit" when the Bella Bella canoe arrived, but "professed friendship, which misled the Bella Bella." [18] According to Lineker, "while McCawley was up at my house, we were startled by the sound of firearms on the beach. The Indians by this time had got into a regular fight, which lasted about an hour and terminated in the Cowichans killing eight men and plundering the canoe, which they carried off with the women and boys, whom they took prisoners. This occurred close to the beach. They fired some 200 shots, some of the bullets flying close to our heads." [19]

Two of the female Bella Bella prisoners were subsequently killed. [20] There were no hwulmuhw casualties. [21]

In a letter written to Governor Douglas five days after the fight, Lineker outlined the precarious position of the settlers. [22] The Penelakut and/or Lamalcha warriors had departed and without their protection Lineker feared for the safety of the settlers in the event of a retaliatory attack by relatives of the vanquished Bella Bella. He wrote: "The Indians have all left here, probably anticipating an attack, in such an event we should be anything but safe, especially should they in any way molest the Settlers. We number here twenty-six men, scattered over about two miles square. Considering their defenseless position the Settlers trust that Your Excellency will deem it expedient to afford them such protection as you in your wisdom may think necessary." [23]

The HMS *Satellite*, a twenty-four-gun corvette, was dispatched to the area, where its commander, Captain James Charles Prevost, ensured that the settlers were safe. On the shores of Ganges Harbour, Prevost located the bodies of six victims, noting that they "were slaughtered with the most barbarous wanton cruelty … there were marks of bullets discernible all around their hearts, and … their heads were fearfully battered in." [24] The British negotiated the release of the sole surviving Bella Bella woman from "the offending tribe" and re-united her with the sole male survivor who, it turned out, was her husband. [25]

Douglas was later informed that the hwunitum at Ganges Harbour "though greatly alarmed suffered no molestation whatsoever from the Victorious Tribe, who, before leaving the settlement expressed the deepest regret for the affray, pleading in extenuation that they could not control their feelings, and begging that their conduct might not be represented to this government in an unfavourable light." [26] Apparently it was not. The Battle of Shiyahwt [Ganges Harbour] was an important victory for the Lamalcha/Penelakut. Most significant was the fact that the fight occurred in the midst of the largest hwunitum settlement outside of the Colony of Vancouver Island. The settlers were endangered by the fighting. Bullets flew over the heads of the Lineker family and hit the walls of their cabin. [27] The fact that there were no reprisals or censure made against the Kuper Island people suggests British recognition of hwulmuhw jurisdiction and sovereignty over their lands on Salt Spring Island. Although there were calls for a resident magistrate on Salt Spring Island, Douglas refused. As he pointed out in correspondence to the

Colonial Office, he only selected magistrates "from the respectable class of Settlers," and that none of the resident settlers on Salt Spring Island had "either the status or the intelligence requisite to enable them to serve the public with advantage in the capacity of local Justices." [28] Douglas knew that any interference with local hwulmuhw jurisdiction could precipitate an attack on hwunitum settlers.

Douglas took no direct action against the Lamalcha and Penelakut, but the fight at Ganges Harbour and other violence caused by the presence of northern people in the south prompted him to request that the three British warships, HMS *Plumper*, HMS *Termagant* and HMS *Alert*, then present in the colony, be sent north under the command of Captain George Henry Richards to visit the major northern aboriginal settlements "to extract promises from their chiefs that they would live according to the [British] law and stop fighting each other, especially during the annual voyages to Victoria." The success of the cruise was negligible. Although it has been claimed that the cruise "put an end to marauding expeditions among Northwest Coast Indians," the fact is that internecine violence continued well into the following decade. [29]

The HMS *Termagant* arrived in the colony on July 12th, 1860, as an escort for two gunboats, the *Forward* and the *Grappler*, both of which were to play an important role in the subjugation of hwulmuhw populations and the enforcement of hwunitum law. The one-hundred-foot steam-powered gunboats were part of a large group of small warships specially built for service in the shallow waters of the Black Sea and the Baltic during the 1854-56 Crimean War with Russia. [30] It was soon realized by the Admiralty that the these "Crimean Gunboats" would be equally useful in similar conditions along the Pacific Coast. In addition to state-of-the-art steam engines, the gunboats were equipped with simple fore and aft rigs and were reported to sail "remarkably well for the small amount of canvas [they] could spread." [31] They were armed with a thirty-two-pound rifled cannon located aft on a pivoting carriage, which enabled the gunboat to fire exploding shrapnel and other projectiles in any direction, and two twenty-four-pound howitzers amidships. With thirty-six well-armed sailors and marines, commanded by aristocratic naval officers, the gunboats were formidable opposition to lightly-armed aboriginal forces. The *Forward* and *Grappler* represented a permanent force which the colonial government could rely upon to assist the civil power in exercising its jurisdiction over aboriginal people.

For the British seaman, service on board these small gunboats was unpleasant: "With the machinery and boilers taking up over half the space between decks, the crew of thirty-six were squeezed into the remainder at the extremities, officers aft, the men forward. In an age when seamen had nothing in the way of luxuries afloat, life on these little craft was well below the already low average and pretty unpopular." [32]

Shortly after its arrival, the *Forward* was involved in its first fight against aboriginal people at Tsuqlotn on Quadra Island when its commander, Charles Robson, went in pursuit of Lekwiltok warriors who had robbed some boats off Salt Spring Island owned by Chinese traders.[33] Robson found the Lekwiltok in a fortified position at Cape Mudge on the south end of Quadra Island and a fire-fight ensued. "Had it not been for the rifle-plates," wrote Lieutenant Mayne, "a good many might have been hit, as the Indians kept up a steady fire upon them for a considerable time."[34] Mayne observed that the Lekwiltok "are alone as yet in standing out after the appearance of a man-of-war before their village," but Tsuqlotn would not be the last battle fought between the *Forward* and aboriginal fighters.

The gunboats added to a growing British military presence in the region, augmented by the arrival from operations in China of two companies of the First Brigade of Royal Marines, to counter the growing threat from American expansion.[35]

Royal Navy officers became interested in land speculation, particularly in the unceded lands of Hul'qumi'num First Nations. Three officers, Mayne, Lyall, and Bedwell, had purchased "Cowichan Scrip," and the Navy sought to establish a naval depot in the heart of their territories on Stu'kin (Thetis Island.) As early as June 30th, 1859, the senior naval officer, Captain Michael Decourcy, of HMS *Plyades*, "made application on behalf of the Lords of the Admiralty to be put in possession of the title deed of Thetis Island."[36] Within a few years, another young, wealthy naval officer, Lieutenant Commander the Honourable Horace Lascelles, pre-empted large acreages surrounding the Hudson's Bay Company coalfields at Nanaimo with the intention of developing additional coal mining operations.

On the 6th of February, 1861, a petition was prepared by the House of Assembly to formally request that the British imperial government provide funds for the purchase of hwulmuhw lands at Cowichan, Chemainus (including Salt Spring and other islands) and Barclay Sound. It was addressed to the Principal Secretary of State for the Colonies, the Duke of Newcastle. The petition and a dispatch sent by Douglas to accompany it warned of the possibility of inter-racial war if the aboriginal title to the lands in question was not properly extinguished:

> WE, Her Majesty's faithful and loyal subjects, the members of the House of Assembly of Vancouver Island in Parliament assembled, would earnestly request the attention of Your Grace to the following considerations:
>
> 1. THAT many Colonists have purchased land, at the rate of One Pound Sterling per acre, in districts to which the Indian title has not yet been extinguished.

2. THAT, in consequence of the non-extinction of this title, those persons, though most desirous to occupy and improve, have been unable to take possession of their lands—purchased, in most cases, nearly three years ago; and of this they loudly and justly complain.

3. THAT the Indians, well aware of the compensation heretofore given for lands, appropriated for colonization, in the earlier settled districts of Vancouver Island, as well as in the neighbouring territory of Washington, strenuously oppose the occupation by settlers of lands still deemed their own. No attempts of the kind could be persisted in, without endangering the peace of the Country, for these Indians, though otherwise well disposed and friendly, would become hostile if their supposed rights as regards land were systematically violated; and they are still much more numerous and warlike than the petty remnants of tribes, who in 1855 and 1856, in the western part of the adjacent United States territory of Washington, kept up for nearly a year, a desultory and destructive warfare which compelled the whole agricultural population of the Country to desert their homes, and congregate in blockhouses.

4. THAT within the last three years, this Island has been visited by many intending settlers, from various parts of the world. Comparatively few of these have remained, the others having, as we believe, been, in great measure, deterred from buying land as they could not rely on having peaceable possession; seeing that the Indian Title was still unextinguished to several of the most eligible agricultural districts of the Island.

5. THAT the House of Assembly respectfully considers, that the extinction of the aboriginal title is obligatory on the Imperial Government.

6. THAT the House of Assembly, bearing in mind, that from the dawn of modern colonization until the present day, wars with aborigines have mainly arisen from disputes about land, which by timely and moderate concession on the part of the more powerful and enlightened of the disputants concerned, might have been peaceably and economically adjusted; now earnestly pray, that Her Majesty's Government would direct such steps to be taken, as may seem best, for the speedy settlement of the matter at issue, and the removal of a most serious obstacle to the well being of this Colony." [37]

Confident that the British government would provide the necessary means for the extinguishment of hwulmuhw title, the colonial government went ahead with its plans for an official pre-emption system to apply to the ceded lands of the colony and to unceded hwulmuhw land including Salt Spring Island, "the Chemainus," and James Island in Haro Strait. A full eighteen months had passed since the first allowance of pre-emptive rights by Pemberton in Chemainus and on Salt Spring Island and the official proclamation of the new policy. On February 19th, 1861, Douglas issued the first Land Proclamation Act in which he announced that he was "empowered by Her Majesty's Government to fix the upset price of country land within the colony of Vancouver Island and its dependencies at 4s. 2d. per acre," far less than the previous price of £1, and more in line with American prices. The proclamation announced that "British subjects may enter upon and occupy land, not being otherwise reserved, in certain quantities and in certain districts—That from and after the date hereof, male British subjects, and aliens who shall take the oath of allegiance before the Chief Justice of Vancouver Island, above the age of eighteen years, may pre-empt unsold Crown lands in the districts of Victoria, Esquimalt, the Highlands, Sooke, North Saanich and South Saanich, Salt Spring Island, Sallas [James] Island, and the Chemainus (not being an Indian reserve or settlement.)" Interestingly enough, the Cowichan territories of the Cowichan Valley were not included. Single men were allowed to occupy up to one hundred and fifty acres and married men with a wife "resident in the colony" were allowed two hundred acres with an additional ten acres for each child. [38]

When the House of Assembly petition for assistance to extinguish hwulmuhw title was sent to London on March 25th, 1861, Douglas accompanied it with the following dispatch. Besides being "evidence that Governor Douglas was prepared to vouch for the fact that the Indians had their own legal system, and that each tribe had title to its own territory and that its rights with regard to its territory were recognized by all other tribes," his letter underlined the importance of a land sale agreement to avoid a situation "that would endanger the peace of the Country."

My Lord Duke,

I have the honour of transmitting a Petition from the House of Assembly of Vancouver Island to Your Grace praying for the aid of Her Majestey's Government in extinguishing the Indian Title to the public lands in this Colony: and setting forth, with much force and truth, the evils that may arise from the neglect of that very necessary precaution.

2. As the Native Indian population of Vancouver Island have distinct ideas of property in land, and mutually recognize their several exclusive possessory rights in certain districts, they would not fail to regard the occupation of such portions of the Colony by white settlers, unless with the full consent of the proprietary Tribes, as national wrongs; and the sense of injury might produce a feeling of irritation against the Settlers, and perhaps disaffection to the Government, that would endanger the peace of the Country.

3. Knowing their feelings on that subject, I made it a practice, up to the year 1859, to purchase the Native rights in the land, in every case, prior to the settlement of any District; but since that time in consequence of the termination of the Hudson's Bay Company's Charter, and the want of funds, it has not been in my power to continue it. Your Grace must indeed be well aware that I have, since then, had the utmost difficulty in raising money enough to defray the most indispensable wants of Government.

4. All the settled Districts of the Colony, with the exception of Cowitchen, Chemainus, and Barclay Sound, have been already bought from the Indians, at a cost in no case exceeding £2.10 sterling for each family. As the land has since then increased in value, the expence would be relatively somewhat greater now, but I think that their claims might be satisfied with a payment of £3 to each family; so that taking the Native population of those districts at 1000 families, the sum of £3000 would meet the whole charge.

5. It would be improper to conceal from your Grace the importance of carrying that vital measure into effect without delay.[39]

Frustrated with the perceived inaction of the colonial and imperial governments, Amor De Cosmos, the editor of the *British Colonist*, wrote that "nothing but negligence has prevented the extinction of the Indian title long ago" at Cowichan and Chemainus. He scoffed at the notion of an "Indian War" if funds could not be found to extinguish native title on lands desired by hwunitum farmers. De Cosmos likened the threat of war to being "frightened by a bugbear ... 'Pay the Indians for the land or we'll have an Indian war.' We don't believe it. We hold it to be our best policy to pay them, to avoid even the possibility of a war. But our government says it cannot provide the means. Granting such to be the case, shall we allow a few red vagrants to prevent forever industrious settlers from settling on the unoccupied lands?"[40]

The Land Proclamation Act of 1861 encouraged a few hwunitum to occupy lands in the unceded territories. Christian Mayer, a native of Plöchingen in the Kingdom of Württemburg, and James Messenger Greary each registered one hundred acres of land on the site of Elelen at Miner's Bay on Mayne Island. They encountered no opposition by hwulmuhw owners, possibly on account of the fact that Mayer married a local hwulmuhw woman named Matilda. Mayer and Greary named their farm "New Brighton," raised hogs and cattle, and employed local hwulmuhw as labourers.[41]

Other less desirable individuals also began to occupy unceded lands. A "crazy surveyor" named Rowe occupied land on Salt Spring Island where he proclaimed himself "Czar of the whole concern—Vancouver Island included."[42] Armed with two revolvers and a double-barrelled shotgun, Rowe threatened hwunitum and hwulmuhw alike, his bizarre behaviour putting the unstable peace of the island at risk. By October, 1861, Rowe had disappeared and it was rumoured that he "was murdered by Cowichan Indians for his money, and that the body had been interred near his cabin."[43] His weapons were also missing.

On the delta of the Cowichan River, an Irish immigrant named Patrick Brennan was granted, on July 27th, 1861, "a legal claim ... to not less than 200 acres of land improved by him at the entrance of the Cowichan River." Brennan had no respect for hwulmuhw and was "very violent and harsh in his treatment of the Indians."[44]

A party of hwunitum prospectors exploring the Chemainus River in early April 1861, found only a single hwunitum, George MacCauley, resident in the valley. The hwunitum prospectors commented on hwulmuhw frustration over Douglas' failure to negotiate a land sale agreement prior to hwunitum occupation of the land as he had done elsewhere in the Colony of Vancouver Island.

> The Cowichan Indians complain loudly of the treatment they receive from the Government, and are determined not to give up their valley to the whites without sufficient renumeration, and are quite indignant with Governor Douglas for not redeeming the promise he has repeatedly made them of paying them a visit. There appears to be trouble brewing in this area.[45]

There was a growing sense of urgency, as revealed in the following excerpt of a motion in the House of Assembly on July 17th, 1861, by the member for Victoria District, William Tolmie. Regarding the late petition to London, which was still unanswered, Tolmie wondered "what course the Government intends pursuing in a matter so pressing by requiring attention in the Chemainus and Cowichan Districts, as until the Indian is in some way compensated, there will be no settlement in these fertile districts, although large portions of each are already taken up."[46]

In October of 1861 the Duke of Newcastle turned down the request by the Colony of Vancouver Island for financial assistance to extinguish hwulmuhw title. Newcastle wrote that while he "was fully sensible of the great importance of purchasing without loss of time the native title to the soil of Vancouver Island," he felt that "the acquisition of title is a purely Colonial interest, and the Legislature must not entertain any expectation that the British taxpayer will be burthened to supply the funds or British credit pledged for the purpose."[47] Newcastle had actually been in favour of the colony's request but the Lords of the Treasury had turned it down.[48]

The refusal to allow imperial money to be used in the extinguishment of aboriginal title in the territories of Hul'qumi'num First Nations became part of the myth which claimed that British Columbia's first "treaty process" collapsed through lack of funds. Clearly, this was not the case. In 1860 and 1861 the House of Assembly approved the provision of £2,000 to purchase hwulmuhw lands in the Chemainus and Cowichan Valleys, but the funds were never used. [49] Similarly, in 1863 and 1864, the House approved the expenditure of $9,700 as "payment for Lands at Chemainus, Cowichan, &c," but, as in previous years, the amount was "unexpended." [50] Why the colonial government went to such lengths to petition the imperial government over a "trifling" amount of money to settle land claims is curious and suggests that the hwunitum of the colony were glossing over the fact that more was at stake in alienating hwulmuhw land than just money.

The real reason that land sale agreements were not made was because many Cowichan, Halalt, Lamalcha, Penelakut, Chemainus and other si'em would not sell their people's land at any price. The aboriginal system of land tenure, whereby families owned houses in permanent villages and distant food and resource gathering areas, sometimes overlapping language boundaries, made negotiations impossible. Hul'qumi'num First Nations in the Chemainus Valley had set aside portions of their land for hwunitum settlement, but the land was considered neither big enough, or good enough, to satisfy the hwunitum. The Colony of Vancouver Island was obliged to look at other strategies to alienate hwulmuhw lands.

Within months, the "land question" became less of an issue as the colonial government became pre-occupied with the events of the American Civil War. The hwunitum population of Victoria was openly sympathetic with the Confederacy. Money was raised on its behalf and a popular drinking establishment named the Confederate Saloon flew secessionist flags. Douglas himself dreamed of invading Puget Sound to seize former Hudson's Bay territories until he was directed by the Colonial Office to maintain the strictest neutrality. [51]

The winter of 1861-1862 was particularly harsh, and with insufficient food supplies hwunitum settlers on Salt Spring Island suffered greatly. By May of 1862, a third of the settlers had left. [52]

However, a greater catastrophe lay in store for the aboriginal populations of the two colonies in March, 1862, when an American miner from San Francisco arrived in Victoria with smallpox. [53] Immediate steps were taken to vaccinate local hwulmuhw populations, but when the disease broke out among aboriginal people visiting from the north, their camps were burned and the people ordered to leave. On May 12th "the Northern Indian huts on the reserve were fired and burned to the ground. Probably 100 huts were thus destroyed. We should not be in the least surprised if the disease were to visit and nearly destroy every tribe of Indians between here and Sitka." [54] A June 2nd report stated that no local hwulmuhw had died but among the northern visitors there was "much more devastation." [55] Sent north by force, Kwakwaka'wakw, Haida, Bella Bella, Tsimshian and Tlingit carried the seeds of destruction to their home communities and beyond. By the time the disease ran its course, a third of the aboriginal population along the coast north of Comox and into the British Columbia interior had perished. [56]

On June 11th the last group of Northern Indians, three hundred men, women, and children, some with smallpox, were ordered to leave Cadboro Bay outside Victoria. The gunboat *Forward,* under the command of Lieutenant Commander the Honourable Horace Lascelles, was detailed to tow the twenty-six canoes "and protect the Indians until they have—passed Nanaimo—the Indians of which place have many old scores to wipe out in consequence of outrages received at the hands of the Northern braves in years gone by." [57]

Newly appointed Superintendent of Police, Horace Smith, would accompany the cruise.

While "passing up by Ganges Harbour, Salt Spring Island," the *Forward* and its flotilla of "Hydah" canoes was fired upon by either Lamalcha or Penelakut warriors led by "two ringleaders." [58] Their gunfire "whistled over the heads of the *Forward*'s people." They "would not desist at the commands of Superintendent Smith ... The guns of the *Forward* then being loaded with grape, they obeyed the order." [59] Lascelles sent a boat's crew after the two leaders "by which they were captured, taken aboard the *Forward*, and given three dozen [lashes] each as a gentle reminder to keep their bullets at home in future. The flogging exercised a very wholesome influence among other tribes to whom the news was communicated." [60]

Next to hanging, public flogging with the cat-o'-nine-tails was the most feared of hwunitum punishments, described as "the most humiliating that can be inflicted upon these savages." [61] As an early issue of the *Victoria Gazette* explained, hwulmuhw viewed the hwunitum practice of flogging "with terror not only from the pain involved, but singularly enough, from a species of degradation which ... they connect with it." [62]

The *Forward*'s altercation with Hul'qumi'num First Nations at Shiyahwt may have precipitated the violence that was to ensue during the coming year as those who suffered the indignity of flogging sought revenge for their humiliation.

When Douglas addressed the opening of the House of Assembly on March 19, 1862, he announced that he had entered into negotiations with hwulmuhw families who owned land and resources in the recently surveyed Malahat District south of the Cowichan area. There had been "agrarian disputes endangering the public peace and safety," and Douglas "deemed it expedient, in order to remove the immediate cause of contention, to enter into arrangements with the natives for the satisfaction of their claims on the land, upon terms agreeable to them, and advantageous to the Colony. As an essential part of that arrangement, I propose that a portion of land shall be reserved for their exclusive use and benefit—a measure which will remove almost the only cause likely to disturb the harmony existing between the settlers and the natives. Arrangements will, if found necessary, be made for the settlement of native claims in Cowichan District."[63]

The House of Assembly unanimously passed a resolution stating "that this House would view with approval the extinguishment by His Excellency the Governor of Indian Title at Cowichan, from the proceeds of land sales." However, the question of raising funds was complicated by the overlapping jurisdictions of hwunitum governments. The colonial legislature could not raise the money itself, as it had no authority over land sales which, following the cancellation of the Hudson's Bay Company grant in 1859, were now under the control of the Colonial Office in London. There was, at least, the appearance of a willingness to negotiate in good faith with First Nations. Included in the colonial estimates for 1862 were £2000 for "Cowichan Road and Settlement of Indian Titles," of which only £998/13s. was spent by the end of the year—on the road.[64]

The Cariboo gold rush of 1862, promoted by sensational articles written by Donald Fraser[65] for the *London Times*, brought another migration of hwunitum men to the colonies from Canada, Great Britain and the United States. Faced again with the prospects of hundreds, if not thousands, of unemployed hwunitum clamouring for land, the colonial government decided to forego any further delay in occupying the unceded territories of the Cowichan.

Petitions from "Cowichan Landholders" who were unable to occupy their four-year-old claims in the Cowichan Valley, pressured the government to resolve the question of extinguishing hwulmuhw title. Commenting on these demands, Surveyor General Pemberton informed Douglas:

> That during the four years that have elapsed since the payment of the first Installment it would have been difficult for a farmer to make residence in that Country profitable; his property would have been liable to annoyance from Indians on account of the unsettled Land Claims—It has also been difficult to find out with accuracy the position of any particular section the land marks having been carefully removed by Indians.[66]

Douglas despaired of ever finding a consensus among Hul'qumi'num First Nations to negotiate land sale agreements similar to those made at Victoria and Nanaimo the previous decade. Consequently, the colonial regime made plans to convey a large party of hwunitum settlers with naval gunboats and occupy sections of the surveyed districts of Shawnigan, Somenos, and Quamichan without consultation with the native owners. Late August was chosen as the date for the occupation. The British would take advantage of the seasonal migration to the Fraser River sockeye fishery in order to occupy the Cowichan lands.

A public notice, issued June 8th, 1862, announced that those who no longer wished to settle in the Cowichan Valley would have their holdings sold at public auction "as advertised under the pre-emption act of 1861, with a promise that the clauses relating to occupation shall not be enforced until the Indians are settled with."[67] The next day the government announced that the holdings of the original purchasers of 1858-59 were in arrears and that if payment was not received by August 11th their claims would be forfeited and put up for auction the following day at "the upset price," the pre-emption rate of four shillings and two pence an acre. The government also informed the holders that if they paid the second installments now owed, the money would "be applied in settling the claims made by the Indian Titles."[68]

On July 29th, 1862, Douglas called a meeting of the Colonial Executive to discuss the establishment of the hwunitum colony in the Cowichan Valley. First they had to deal with the "Cowitchen Land Claims," the 8,000 acres technically purchased by scrip in 1858 and 1859 by hwunitum speculators. Since these men had paid one quarter down, with the balance payable upon extinguishment of hwulmuhw title, they were given the opportunity of selecting land equal to the amount already paid, which amounted to some 2,000 acres. George Cary, the Attorney-General, was "to ascertain whether it be practicable to obtain a body of Settlers to proceed to Cowichan," and, "in such a case," the Surveyor General, Pemberton, was directed "to arrange position of land which Settlers can take up under pre-emption Act." Aside from a reference to "certain promises respecting Indian Title," there was little else recorded regarding their discussion of hwulmuhw ownership except for the last order of business—that "an application will be made to Admiral in command to send a Gun Boat to Cowichen to protect Settlers."[69]

That night, three hundred hwunitum crowded the courthouse in the government building complex known as the "bird-cages" to hear Cary outline the government's plan. Most of the concerns of the crowd focused on fears of reprisal by the resident Cowichan against potential settlers but Cary and other speakers reassured the meeting that "the government would no doubt compensate [the Cowichan] for their land," and that the settlers would be protected by a Royal Navy escort. Cary opened the meeting with a summary of the government's position regarding the upcoming occupation:

> Mr. Cary commenced by saying that there was a large number of persons here who were desireable of settling upon the Crown Lands, and becoming citizens of Vancouver Island, and as there was only one place upon which they could settle, and as there were many obstacles in their way at present, several had suggested to him that a plan be introduced by which the Cowichan District might be settled up, and that Government had decided, if 70, 80, or 100 men could be obtained who were willing to

settle there, that they should be put in possession of the land. A great deal of land was bought formerly by speculators at $5 per acre, on which they had only paid $1, but promised to pay the balance when the Indian question as to the title of the land was settled. These purchasers had bought originally 8000 acres, and they had since consented to give up all but about 2000 acres—leaving some 6000 acres for the new-comers whom it was proposed to take thither. Each man would be allowed to pre-empt 150 acres; if he has a wife, 50 additional acres, and 10 for every child. A gunboat would accompany the party, and also a competent party to deal with the Indians. All that the government wanted was an assurance that a sufficient number of men would go up in a fortnight and a vessel would be provided to take them, and he did not fancy that there would be the least trouble in taking possessions of the lands. In Somenos and Comiaken districts no trouble with the Indians was to be feared. In Quamichan and Cowichan, however, there were numerous Indian potato patches, and a competent surveyor would accompany the party and set apart the land for these patches. What was to be avoided was ill feeling between the settlers and Indians … Mr. Cary concluded by saying that a list would be opened for the reception of the names of all those willing to go up and Government would do all it could to help them. [70]

In response to more questions from the audience concerning danger of attack by Cowichan warriors, Cary stated that "the settlers should settle as near as possible to each other for mutual protection," and that "they would be amply protected in their rights to the land by the employment of a little moral force backed up by a little physical force," primarily the cannon, marines and sailors of the gunboat *Grappler* and the HMS *Hecate*, a five-gun paddle-wheel sloop named for the ancient Greek Goddess of Hell.

Surveyor General Joseph Pemberton came forward and tempted the audience with descriptions of the natural resources owned by the Cowichan people while assuring them that they would be welcomed by the aboriginal residents.

Mr. Pemberton said there were from 50,000 to 60,000 acres of good land in Cowichan Valley—the best on Vancouver Island … There were from 15,000 to 20,000 acres perfectly open, and the land was well watered. The fisheries were extensive and would turn out to be valuable; it was a great country for game, and although he was a poor shot he had always been able to supply himself while there with game of every description. The timber was of the best kind, and minerals were believed to abound there.

Regarding the hwulmuhw, "[Pemberton said] the Indians were anxious to have the whites come among them as soon as they were settled with for the land … Mr.

Pemberton believed the present was a good opportunity for 100 to 200 men to go there, and government was anxious to give them every assistance."

> In answer to questions, Mr. Pemberton said that the Indians had made very moderate proposals to him and that they were very anxious for a white population to settle there, government would no doubt compensate them reasonably for the land ... there was no danger of a fight, the moral effect of the presence of the whites was enough to keep them in order.

Cary stood up again to speak and "said that when a list of names had been obtained, at the end of a fortnight, Government would know whether any arrangements could be made with the Indians, and if so, the party would start." [71]

There were more comments from the floor regarding the Cowichan people: "A gentleman in the audience spoke very forcibly on the necessity of cultivating friendly relations with the Indians. He liked the project, but Indians were treacherous, and the settlers should be protected. He wanted to have the matter fully stated." George Pidwell, a holder of "Cowichan Scrip," "made a few forcible and well-timed remarks with regard to those great bugbears, the Indians ... He believed that the Indians were very much overrated."

> Mr. Cary again stated that Government would see that an ammicable arrangement with the Indians was made before the party started.

> Mr. Pemberton remained on the platform for some time thereafter, and continued to answer questions, some of which bore on the shooting of a settler many years ago, and the subsequent hanging of the culprit by men-o'-war's men. [72]

Pemberton, Cary, and Franklyn convinced the crowd of prospective settlers that there would be no fear of retaliation by Hul'qumi'num First Nations, assuring them that an ammicable arrangement with the Indians was made before the party started.

Henry Press Wright, the Anglican Archdeacon who was present at the meeting, asked the Reverend Alexander Garrett "to go and visit [the Cowichan], for the double purpose of preaching to them, and of ascertaining their feelings with regard to the proposed settlement of the whites among them." [73]

Garrett visited the region in company with "a young medical friend" by horse-back along a trail recently "blazed through the forest." Upon their arrival at Cowichan Bay, Garrett was surprised to meet one of the Catholic missionaries attached to the mission at Comiaken. His reminiscence of their encounter reveals the mistrust between the two denominations and alleges that by this time Catholic clergy were encouraging hwulmuhw to resist incursions by Protestant hwunitum and not to provide them with food or water. [74]

Garrett made another reconnaissance with Verney, the commander of the gunboat *Grappler*, on Saturday the 16th of August, probably to acquaint Verney with the lay of the land prior to the upcoming occupation. They approached from North Saanich by canoe and, after spending the night near one of the Clemclemalits camps "on the South side of the Cowichan mouth," they proceeded upriver to the village of Quamichan "and generally rambled about," returning to Victoria the following day. Verney was not impressed. "I saw little of the land," he wrote, "and certainly came to the conclusion that the land is not as good and as clear as the settlers have been led by the government to expect ... I fear that this effort to settle the Cowitchin Valley will be a failure, and that many poor fellows will lose their all: the government looks to me for help, and they shall get all I can give them for the sake of the settlers: I fear there is some underhand dealing among officials in this matter." [75]

On the morning of Monday, August 18th, some 100 prospective hwunitum settlers boarded HMS *Hecate* for the journey to their new homes in the unceded homelands of the Cowichan. Governor Douglas, Surveyor General Pemberton, Attorney-General Cary, and, as Verney noted, "a lot of other Generals," accompanied the settlers in the *Hecate*. [76] In tow behind the *Hecate* was the schooner *Explorer*, carrying the settlers' luggage, provisions and implements. Garrett, in light of his recent visits to the area, "was taken along as Chaplain to His Excellency and gave such information as he could." [77] Fearing opposition by resident hwulmuhw, a "Public Notice" issued four days before the departure date called on the settlers to occupy land "in such a manner as is not likely to lead to any misunderstanding or difficulty with the natives." [78]

The occupation of the Cowichan territory was carried out with military precision: "The expedition reached Cowichan at 4 o'clock, p.m. ... and the settlers, divided into three parties [which], under the guidance of the Surveyor General and his assistant, and the Attorney-General, were landed at the localities in which it is intended they shall inspect and select lands for farming purposes."

> One party of the settlers was despatched to Shawnigan District, another to Somenos District, and a third to Quamichan ... They were given to understand by His Excellency that actual residence on the land would alone entitle them to hold it. [79]

"The Governor also disembarked and encamped, and the party were regaled with fresh butter, milk, eggs, and other home-raised luxuries by one of the Cowichan farmers." [80] Douglas made his camp on the hill above the village of Comiaken which had served as his base of operations in 1853 and 1856, and was now the site of the Catholic mission of St. Ann's. Douglas addressed those Cowichan present and promised them that they would be compensated "for the lands taken up by the settlers" in a similar fashion to the treaties negotiated previously with the Songees, Clallam, Sooke, Saanich and Nanaimo. The *British Colonist* reported:

> The few natives at present in the district (the major portion of the tribes being absent fishing) agreed without hesitation to the surrender of their lands to the Government, with the exception of their village sites and potato-patches, being informed that when the absent members of the tribes returned to their homes in the autumn, compensation for the lands taken up by the settlers would be made at the same rate established— amounting in the aggregate to the value of a pair of blankets to each Indian—the chiefs, of course, coming in for the lion's share of the potlatch. The Indians, one and all, expressed themselves as perfectly content with the proposed arrangement, and even appeared anxious that settlers should come among them.[81]

Acting on Garrett's allegations of Catholic influence in hwulmuhw opposition to hwunitum settlement, Douglas invited the resident priest to dinner. This invitation, according to Garrett, "also had its uses as His Excellency was anxious to know all that could be told of that part of the country. When the repast was nearly over, the Governor spoke in this wise: "I hope, sir, that you will lend all the assistance which your acquaintance with the natives and the nature of the country may enable you to give, and should I find, sir, that at any time you excite the minds of the natives against any of her Majesty's subjects now making settlements here, it will be my painful duty to deal harshly with you."[82]

Verney and the gunboat *Grappler* arrived on Thursday, August 28th, only to find that "most of the settlers had returned to Victoria for implements." After exploring the area in more detail, his initial pessimism about the prospects of the settlers began to disappear. "There is certainly more good land here than I had expected to find," he wrote, "and land that can be cleared with comparatively little trouble, and now some of the settlers have brought up their wives and children which looks as if they were in earnest." Verney's mission was to protect the settlers in the event of trouble with Cowichan returning from the Fraser River fishing grounds: "I have instructed them to communicate with me frequently, and to let me know how I can be of use to them."[83] The *Grappler* remained at anchor in Cowichan Bay until September 15th, returning on several occasions over the following months to check on the condition of the settlers.

An incident, preserved in the oral history of the Penelakut, occurred in the late summer months of 1862 which prevented Douglas from returning to the Cowichan Valley and negotiating a proper land sale agreement. Its significance was revealed by the Reverend Garrett in an letter written in 1865. According to Garrett, Douglas' plan to negotiate a proper land sale agreement with the Cowichan in the fall of 1862 was disrupted by people from Lamalcha who "became troublesome ... and the Governor did not think it would be expedient then to carry out his original intention."[84]

The "trouble" alluded to by Garrett appears not to have been the infamous attack on Frederick Marks and his daughter Caroline Harvey the following spring, but an earlier incident involving Lamalcha warriors and the massacre of the crew of a coastal trading vessel that took place late in the summer of 1862, after Douglas' occupation of the Cowichan Valley. According to Mary Rice, the granddaughter of the Penelakut si'em Hulkalatkstun, the incident involved a hwunitum trader who "came to our land very often."[85] Mary Rice describes the trading relationship between the hwunitum and the people of Kuper Island and how it ended in drunken violence on a Gulf Island beach:

> ... the men brought presents of beads, bright and shining, blankets, and strange food. In return, the [Penelakut] gave meat, fish, and skins, and always there was great friendship between the White Chief and my grandfather. But one summer a bad, bad thing happened ... Well, that white chief and his men on the strange canoe were always good friends of Hul-ka-latkstun and the [Penelakut]. But on the other side of the Kuper Island there lived a tribe—the Lamalchas—they were a bad cruel people and they did not like these white men coming.
>
> Every Summer the Lamalchas went to another island to hunt and fish, and always they made their camp on the beach. One year they were in this camp and the white men came along in their great canoe and, seeing the Lamalcha's camp, they landed, bringing with them presents as they had to the [Penelakut]. The Lamalchas, with wickedness in their hearts, made friends, and that night they gave a feast for the white chief, and he and his men brought their food and a drink which was hot and strange, for it made the braves feel good and big, and brought great courage to their hearts. Later this courage grew to a madness, until they did not know what things they were doing, and they killed the white chief and his men.
>
> In the morning they went out to the canoe and brought it ashore, took out all the food and more of the drink, and all the bright and shining things that the white men gave to our people for skins; and they took down the wings [sails] from the trees [masts], for they thought these things would be good to put on their houses. Then they made a great fire and burned it; and as it burned they feasted and danced and sang in their madness.
>
> Well, some of the [Penelakut] were out fishing and they saw the sky all red and bright and, not knowing what it could be, they went to look. There on the beach they found the Lamalchas dancing and making strange noises as though evil spirits were in them. Softly they paddled nearer, and there

where the flames leaped high they saw the white men lying dead, and their canoe all broken and burning, with no trees, no wings, all one big fire.

When my people saw this they hurried back to Penelekhut, where they told Hul-ka-latkstun their story. "Let us go and punish these Lamalchas," they said, "for they have killed our good friends and have burned the canoe with wings!"

But as I have told you, my grandfather was a wise man. "No," he told them, "keep away from the Lamalchas, for well I know that there will be trouble for any who have done harm to this white tribe." [86]

Little documented by hwunitum historians, the incident and its aftermath resonated amongst hwulmuhw elders into the 1930s. Khul-Stae-nun, "one of the oldest Indians in Chemainus," recalled:

That fire-water made my people mad and they wanted to kill all they saw; then, when they had killed, the white man came and put ropes around their necks and hanged them. [87]

When the Cowichan people returned from the Fraser River fisheries to their homes in the fall of 1862 there was surprise and anger among those whose land was now occupied by hwunitum without permission or compensation. People returned to find their winter village sites and the immediate area secure, but large tracts of land used for communal hunting or owned in part by individual families for a variety of resources were taken over by hwunitum settlers. The impact on local game and fisheries was immediate as the newcomers began to indiscriminately harvest resources without, it is assumed, the permission of the owners. The *British Colonist* reported that "the harbour fairly teemed with salmon, and the streams swarm with trout and other kinds of fish. Anyone with a small seine could in a single night, secure a sufficient quantity of salmon for the winter's supply." [88] "Deer shooting" was said to be the Cowichan settlers' "favourite amusement." [89]

Some hwulmuhw families saw benefits in the hwunitum presence and welcomed the newcomers. The *British Colonist* reported that:

Doubtless one reason for their friendliness is that they find a ready market for their potatoes, fish, etc. which they were formerly obliged to take all the way to Victoria, but which they now dispose of to the settlers at Victoria prices. [90]

The lucrative potato trade was, however, soon endangered by hwunitum pigs and cattle which, unconfined by fences, wrought havoc on hwulmuhw potato patches and root cellars. William Smithe, a new settler in the Somenos District, wrote that the Cowichan farmers "are inconvenienced by cattle, and especially hogs of settlers near their camps roving at large over their potato patches ... I heard of one case that annoyed me very much. An Indian procured a stock of seed potatoes, and it being rather too early for planting them, he placed them in a pit, where a few days after, they were all dug up and destroyed by a settler's hogs. When the Indian complained to the owner of the pigs, all the satisfaction he received was a growled 'get out!' accompanied by an ocular demonstration of what it meant by being kicked to the door. With such treatment no wonder they become angry and retaliate." [91]

A good portion of the settlers aboard the August 18th expedition to Cowichan were speculators who returned to Victoria and sold their claims for a quick profit. Other settlers found the lifestyle too difficult. By November only some thirty to forty hwunitum remained on their claims, but they were busy clearing the forest, erecting "good substantial buildings with shingled roofs" and "splitting rails and making other preparations for enclosing part of their lands, intending to commence cultivating as early as possible next season." It was reported that "this new Settlement is progressing most favourably, and bids fair to become an important portion of the colony." [92]

A source of growing concern to Hul'qumi'num First Nations was the completion of the road into their territories from Victoria. In late October, Attorney-General Cary announced that the road would soon be suitable for cattle drives and within a few weeks the *British Colonist* announced that the road was navigable by horse as far as Nanaimo. [93]

In the Chemainus Valley north of Cowichan, a few hwunitum, including William Alexander Scott, James Habart and Robert Cunlan, had taken over the claims of earlier settlers, despite the animosity of local hwulmuhw. These men brought in cattle and numerous pigs for the dual purpose of raising stock and clearing the land. In the late fall of 1862, Scott drove a small herd of cattle over the recently completed road from Victoria through the Cowichan Valley to his claim on the Chemainus River. Scott received a hostile reception by local hwulmuhw regarding his occupation of their land and the damage to their potato fields by his unfenced stock:

> As soon as I got to Chemainis the Indians threatened to kill my stock, and here they act in such a manner that it is highly dangerous to live among them. [94]

Across Stuart Channel, the hwunitum settlements on Salt Spring Island numbered some sixty persons, less than the population of the second largest village on Kuper Island. [95] The four or five stone-cutters on the shore of Houston Passage and those hwunitum at the "Salt Spring Settlement" and in the Burgoyne Valley maintained good relations with hwulmuhw through ties of trade and marriage. At the Ganges Harbour settlement, however, relations with hwunitum and qihuye' were less cordial, based in part on the mismanagement of local food resources. Referring to those days, the daughter of a qihuye' settler recalled:

> That was the time the local natives themselves were quite hostile. They held meetings with much skookum wawa (Chinook for "strong talk") as they saw their beaches and hunting grounds usurped by the incoming settlers, and the sight of carcasses of animals lying on the beaches, their hides taken and the meat left to spoil. When an Indian came to one of such he made a clucking noise with his tongue (i.e. indicated disgust.) It only served as fuel to an already heated situation. [96]

A December editorial in the *British Colonist* on the "New Settlements" called on the colonial government to deliver on its promise to negotiate the alienation of land in the Cowichan Valley:

> The question of Indian claims resolves itself into this: The Indians have a right to be paid for their lands. If the Government has made any agreement with them they should in honour fulfill it; if not, it is high time that they should come to a fair and definite arrangement and have it carried out to the letter. They will thus avoid the troubles that the question has given rise to in the territories of the United States. [97]

Hwulmuhw such as Chealthluc of the Songees, a signatory to the one of the land sale agreements signed at Victoria in 1850, visited the area at Douglas' request, presumably to assuage Cowichan concerns, but his mission was unsuccessful. [98]

The isolation and insecurity of the Cowichan Valley settlers was magnified in December 1862, by an inter-family feud that threatened to erupt into "a regular Indian war." [99]

> Sometime in December a chief of the Quamichan tribe killed an Indian belonging to the Comiakens. A wholesome fear of British law not being before their eyes—more particularly as the various tribes in Cowichan say that Gov. Douglas has no objection to their killing Indians so long as they leave white men alone—there was a prospect of a regular Indian war. Fearing that a war would break out, Jean Baptiste, a renowned brave, and a very old chief of the Comiakens, visited the city to secure the mediation of Bishop Demers as a peacemaker. To save the effusion of blood among the children of the forest the Bishop about a week ago, went up to the Indian Mission at Cowichan. The Quamichans were asked to visit the mission; so they came down with a force of sixty or seventy braves, all armed to the teeth. About a dozen were sent into the mission whilst the others watched the progress of negotiations from a hill [Comiaken Hill], ready for a fight if necessary. After a long "wa-wa" [talk] the Bishop succeeded in making a treaty of peace. The Quamichan agreed to give

forty blankets to Jean Baptiste as an atonement for killing one of his people. Bishop Demers then ratified the treaty; and by doing so has no doubt saved the effusion of blood. The Indians in Cowichan seem to think that if the authorities were to imprison some of the bad Indians occasionally it would create a wholesome fear of British law. As it is, the only fear they entertain is of the men-o'-war's men, in case they should kill a white person. [100]

The situation was closely monitored by Douglas who, in his speech at the re-opening of the House of Assembly on January 2nd, 1863, pledged that the Government would "extend its fostering care to the recently formed settlements of Cowichan and Comox to provide for their protection and security." [101]

The hwunitum settlers in the Cowichan Valley were isolated, unwelcome and plagued with alcoholism as winter wore on. [102] In early March 1863, one wrote:

We have now in our neighbourhood upwards of 100 settlers, and many more would doubtedless have been here with their families, if there was a semblance of security and law. Previous to our settling here and taking up land, we were promised everything, all we could wish, and now we are left almost isolated and forgotten ... We have not even a constable now, and the Indians know it. [103]

The failure of the colonial government to conclude land sale agreements with Hul'qumi'num First Nations following the occupation of the Cowichan Valley led inevitably to violence. In February 1863, a group of warriors, apparently from the village of Quamichan, initiated a wave of violence by killing two hwunitum men "on one of the Islands in Haro Strait," taking "a Colt's revolver, a double-barrelled gun, and some other property." [104] In a little over a month, two more assaults on hwunitum transients would lead to military intervention, the elimination of active hwulmuhw resistance and the imposition of British imperial rule over the territories of Hul'qumi'num First Nations.

Chapter Six

Another Atrocious Murder

IN STARK CONTRAST to the bitter winter of the previous year, the winter of 1862-63 had been unusually mild, except for a severe three week "cold snap" in February. With the early onset of milder weather, small groups of Hul'qumi'num First Nations ventured from their winter villages to visit family-owned fishing and hunting territories to supplement the dwindling supplies of stored food.

In early April, two separate parties of hwulmuhw, one from Lamalcha on Kuper Island, the other from Quamichan on the Cowichan River, came into contact with hwunitum transients in the southern Gulf Islands and killed them. Although both attacks occurred within two days of each other in the same general area, they were unrelated. Robbery was said to be the motive behind the attacks, but in reality they were further examples of a clash in jurisdiction. These two violent incidents would, however, set into motion the end of Hul'qumi'num First Nations sovereignty and jurisdiction over their territories on the east coast of Vancouver Island and the Gulf Islands.

In late March of 1863, two canoes left the village of Lamalcha for Kulman, the hwulmuhw name for the northwest portion of Saturna Island, an important food-gathering area for Penelakut and Lamalcha families.[1] One of the canoes carried the warrior Palluk and his Lamalcha wife Semallee. The occupants of the other canoe were Allwhenuk and his wife Koltenaht, both from Penelakut but who now lived at Lamalcha. Another Lamalcha man, Shacutsus, joined them three days later but soon left for Victoria. Within a few days, Shacutsus returned to Lamalcha where Palluk and Semallee told him and others how they, along with Allwhenuk and Koltenaht, had killed a hwunitum man and a girl at Kulman.

The victims were forty-year-old Frederick Marks and his fifteen-year-old married daughter Caroline Harvey,[2] who occupied one of two boats en route from Waldron Island to Miner's Bay on Mayne Island when a sudden squall forced them to separate from their companions and seek temporary shelter on Saturna Island.

Frederick Marks was a German immigrant who, with his family, had lived in the Washington Territory for a number of years. Interracial conflict forced the family to flee north, where they took up residence on Waldron Island and established a small farm. An acquaintance and fellow countryman of Christian Mayer, who occupied 100 acres behind the old Saanich village of Elelen (Miner's Bay), Marks made an agreement with Mayer in 1863 "to join him in working his land." [3]

To assist in moving his family and their possessions, Marks borrowed Mayer's flat-bottomed boat which may have been, according to some descriptions, a large dugout canoe. Marks also hired another boat, the *Bella Coola*, owned by a man named Henry who lived on S'tayus (Pender Island), to assist in moving the family to Mayne Island. [4]

On Thursday, April 2nd, the Marks family, with Henry's assistance, loaded their possessions aboard the two boats and set sail from Waldron Island. Most of the freight, which included a heavy cast-iron stove and a large trunk containing the family's clothes, linen and other household goods, was loaded on Mayer's boat. This boat also carried Frederick Marks, his daughter Caroline Harvey, and their two dogs. Marks' pregnant wife, also named Caroline, and their other five children, who ranged in age from one to seven years, went with Henry in the *Bella Coola*.

The two boats left Waldron Island together and crossed Boundary Pass, then known as Ship's Channel, when, opposite Stuart Island, they "got becalmed." [5] Within a short time a southeasterly squall sprang up, the "wind blowing very fresh." [6] Caroline Marks recalled that "the weather was heavy, stormy." [7] The change was particularly dangerous for Frederick Marks and his daughter in Mayer's heavily-loaded, flat-bottomed boat. By three o'clock in the afternoon the boats had reached an anchorage protected from southeast winds, somewhere on the south shore of Saturna Island. [8] There Frederick Marks anchored to wait out the squall. The wind died down a little and it was decided that the less-encumbered *Bella Coola* would continue to Henry's place on Pender Island with Mrs. Marks and the small children. Caroline Marks watched her husband and daughter land on the beach and build a campfire. The *Bella Coola* left and it was the last the occupants ever saw of Frederick Marks and Caroline Harvey. Palluk, Semallee, Allwhenuk, and Koltenaht were nearby, watched the Marks arrive and set up camp, and decided to kill them. Palluk was the instigator of the attack, encouraged by Semallee who, it was alleged, desired the large trunk and other items of wealth stowed on board the boat. [9] The following lurid account, said to originate "from Indian sources," describes what happened:

> The father and daughter, after landing, made a fire, and some Indians came down to talk to the travellers, and subsequently, under pretense of bringing some fish to sell, brought their fire-arms and shot the unfortunate man through the back as he was sitting unsuspectingly by his

fire. The affrighted girl, startled by the report and the sight of her parent weltering in his blood, fled to the neighbouring rocks; her frantic efforts to escape were useless—the men pursued her and with devilish cruelty overpowered her struggles, while one of her own sex stabbed her to death." [10]

All accounts agree that Palluk was the one who shot Marks but there is less agreement on who killed Caroline Harvey. [11]

After Marks and Harvey were killed, Palluk and Allwhenuk brought the boat ashore and unloaded its cargo.

The two men carried the stove and the linen trunk onto the beach. Using rocks or the back end of an axe, they broke up the stove. They looted the trunk of its contents and then used an axe to chop it to pieces. They chopped holes in the bottom of the boat in order to sink it. The boat, however, on account of its flat bottom, did not sink and washed ashore where it was later discovered. Finally, rocks and portions of the broken stove were tied to the bodies of Frederick Marks and Caroline Harvey, which were then thrown into the sea. [12] Palluk, Semallee, Allwhenuk and Koltenaht then left Saturna Island and returned to Lamalcha, where they told others about what they had done.

Meanwhile, Henry, Caroline Marks, and her five children "waited all night and all the next day at Henry's place on Pender Island" for Frederick Marks and Caroline Harvey to show up. [13] On Saturday morning, April 4th, the group sailed from Pender Island to Christian Mayer's ranch at Miner's Bay in hopes of finding the missing family members there, but arrived to find that there was no sign of the other boat. [14]

The following day, Easter Sunday, Mayer decided to go in search of the missing party. "Taking a Cowichan Indian in his employ with him, he set off in a canoe to ascertain the cause of detention." [15] Finally, after two days of searching, they discovered Mayer's boat "on the beach at Saturna Island," with its bottom chopped out with a sharp axe. Mayer and his companion found Marks' two dogs "alive and uninjured" near the boat, but everything else, with the exception of the heavy iron stove and portions of a large trunk, was missing. [16] Mayer's Cowichan companion picked up a blue leather belt belonging to Caroline Harvey and exclaimed in Chinook: "The Cowichans have murdered them." [17] The two men returned to Miner's Bay on Mayne island, where Mayer made preparations to leave for Victoria to report the disappearance of the Marks.

The day before Christian Mayer set out to search for the whereabouts of Frederick Marks and Caroline Harvey, two other hwunitum travellers, William Brady and John Henley, were attacked in a small cove at the head of Bedwell Harbour on Pender Island. This attack was carried out by three young men, a young woman and an elder woman from the village of Quamichan on the Cowichan River.

In late March of 1863, 16-year-old Thalaston organized an expedition which left Quamichan in a single dugout canoe. Thalaston was accompanied by his wife, Thostinah, his half-brother Stalehum, Stalehum's mother Thask, and another teenage male named Oalatza.[18] They may have been on a food gathering expedition, but the exact purpose of their voyage is uncertain.

On the afternoon of Saturday, April 4th, the day the *Bella Coola* left Pender Island with Mrs. Marks and her children, the Quamichan party paddled towards S'tayus, the Saanich name given to the Bedwell Harbour area and, in a general way, North and South Pender Island, which at that time were joined together by a land bridge.[19] There they met William Brady who was visiting the area with his companion, another American named John Henley. Thalaston knew Brady and Henley from their visits to Cowichan and Salt Spring Island, and was with them when they purchased their whaleboat in Victoria.[20] Based on their previous relationship, the rendezvous between Thalaston's party and that of Brady and Henley may have been prearranged.

William Brady was "raised in the States," and came to the Colony of Vancouver Island in 1858 to take part in the Fraser River gold rush.[21] He was unsuccessful and, like many others, returned to Victoria. There, unable through lack of money to return to his place of origin, Brady looked for other ways to make a living in preparation for another attempt at the goldfields further north in the Cariboo. He became a professional hunter, a lucrative occupation supplying the restaurants and individuals in Victoria with fresh venison and elk. He soon formed a partnership with another American named John Henley.

Variously described as an "Indian" or a "colored man," Henley was born and raised in Texas of hwunitum and Cherokee parents.[22] Following the gold rush of 1858, there were "quite a lot of Cherokee Indians here who came from their native land to the coast of British Columbia for work."[23] Henley was a relative newcomer to the Colony of Vancouver Island, having arrived in the fall of 1862, attracted to the colony by the recent discoveries in the goldfields of the Cariboo.

Early in 1863, Brady and Henley began to make preparations for a mining expedition to the Colony of British Columbia. They purchased a whaleboat in Victoria and used it during the winter for hunting expeditions. In late March they left Victoria "for a short sojourn among the islands of the Gulf of Georgia, until the time should come for them to start for Cariboo."[24]

On April 4th they landed on Pender Island and made their camp "in a little cove" at the head of Bedwell Harbour, on the south side of the land bridge joining the two Pender Islands. [25] While Brady set up camp and prepared their supper, Henley went to hunt "about three in the afternoon."[26]

When Henley returned "about half an hour after dark," he found that Brady had been joined by Thalaston and his four companions. There is no mention of their arrival by canoe which suggests that the hwulmuhw party had approached the camp overland. Henley recognized Thalaston and he noticed that the face of the older woman Thask was "painted up."[27] The visitors "seemed very friendly, and were hospitably entertained."[28] "We had supper," Henley recalled, "then Brady cooked some bacon and made some tea for the Indians, he gave them two cakes of bread, and about half a cup of sugar."[29] Sitting around the campfire they "had some conversation with them about the places where we expected to get Hay."[30] After supper, Brady and Henley retired to their tent. "We then went to sleep," Henley recalled. "The Indians also lay down close to our tent."[31]

After eating the food which Brady had prepared for them, Stalehum complained to his companions that he had a sore throat. The group concluded that Brady had tried to poison them. [32] Thalaston and Thostinah decided that they would kill Brady and Henley after the latter went to sleep. Oalataza later recalled what happened:

> I was not the instigator of the firing. I did not wish to kill the man. I had laid down and gone to sleep with Kaisue [Thalaston] and Stealhum. Kaisue's klootchman came and woke me, telling me not to go to sleep. I then saw her go and wake Stealhum and tell him to get his musket. I was against taking my musket but when I saw the other two take theirs, I got mine and we all fired. [33]

The hwunitum had been asleep for about an hour when the hwulmuhw arranged themselves around the tent in preparation for the attack. Stalehum and Oalatza loaded their muskets with ball shot and fired into the tent while Thalaston, with his double-barrelled shotgun loaded with buckshot, reserved his fire. Inside the tent, Brady "had his thigh shattered by one shot" and was instantly immobilized. [34] Henley was also hit in the thigh but his wound was less serious: "When I heard the first shots I jumped up and asked Brady what it was. He said he was shot and I then rushed out of the tent."[35] Henley saw Thalaston "about two or three steps away from me when I came out of the tent after the first two shots were fired."[36] Thalaston fired one barrel from his gun which hit Henley in the arm. Henley recalled the ensuing fight for his life:

> When I got out of the tent I saw them all squatted round in the bushes watching. Thalaston I saw with a gun pointed at me. I jumped at it and threw it down and in doing this it went off and wounded me in the abdomen. I got hold of the gun and there was a struggle for it and I was

thrown over. They were all upon me. The woman then stabbed me in the temple with a small knife. [37]

Henley was a powerful man. [38] Though badly wounded he fought his assailants with his uninjured right fist, knocking two of them down. He later stated that his female assailants were more difficult to overcome than the men. After "two severe cuts on the head from a squaw who attacked him with a knife ... he finally succeeded by dint of hardened well dealt blows, in making his antagonists run." [39] He pursued his attackers some distance. "I got my rifle Gun," he said, "and fired several Shots, perhaps half a dozen, I don't remember how many, I was so much excited." [40] On guard against their return, Henley retreated to the camp where he found that "Brady had crawled out of the tent. I covered him up with blankets." [41]

Thalaston's guardian spirit had told him to kill the hwunitum, but his power was not strong enough. He and his companions decided to leave. The following day Henley "saw a party which I suppose to be the same leave the Island ... We did not leave because it rained so hard." [42]

The Quamichan paddled through the pouring rain to Salt Spring Island, where they ransacked one or more cabins built by hwunitum. Their participation in these events was confirmed by other Cowichan people who later identified them as "guilty of the robberies that occurred sometime since on Salt Spring Island." [43] One of their targets may have been the house of Edward Mallandaine whose place near Walker's Hook on the northeast side of Salt Spring Island "was burglariously entered during his temporary absence by breaking down a chimney and a lot of clothing, provisions, cooking utensils etc. carried away." [44] Hwunitum saw these depredations as criminal assaults on private property, without realizing that the buildings occupied family-owned properties such as food-gathering sites, graves, etc.; the Quamichan may have been simply exercising their rights as beneficial owners.

At Bedwell Harbour, the two badly-wounded men remained in their camp throughout Easter Sunday, tending their wounds as best they could, partially sheltered from the rain by the spreading branches of a large cedar, no doubt fearful of another assault. Brady "lingered in great pain" until three o'clock on Tuesday afternoon, when he died. [45]

The rain finally stopped and on Wednesday morning, April 8th, Henley "left the corpse on the island, together with two bags of flour," and manoeuvred himself into the whaleboat. Travelling with the tide, by two o'clock in the afternoon he reached Oak Bay, north of Victoria, where he was given assistance by former Hudson's Bay Company Chief Trader John Tod, who had built a house there after retiring from his position at Kamloops. Tod immediately sent word to Victoria and a police officer was dispatched with a light wagon to convey Henley "to the Royal Hospital where he received every attention."[46]

The following morning, April 9th, Henley was interviewed in the hospital by the Superintendent of Police, Horace Smith, who made the following statement of information under oath before Police Commissioner Augustus Pemberton :

> On Saturday night last a white man is reported to have been murdered and a half breed Cherokee was seriously wounded by being fired at while in bed on an Island near Mount Tuam. The party who attacked them consisted of as I am informed, three Indian men and two Indian women whose names I believe to be as follows—
>
> Sil-quayn
> Taw-cumsut   } men
> Tehk-wah
>
> Quilt-latz
> Woos-harlt   } women.
>
> The man who was murdered was named Bill Brady and the wounded man was named John Henle [Henley].[47]

None of the names given to Smith by Henley correspond to the those involved in the attack, which suggest either the use of aliases by the hwulmuhw themselves or perhaps an inability on the part of hwunitum to pronounce or recall hwulmuhw names.

Meanwhile, on Mayne Island, Christian Mayer made preparations to go to Victoria to report the disappearance of Frederick Marks and his daughter. On Thursday morning, well-armed and with a companion, he left by canoe. Another man stayed behind to watch over Caroline Marks and her children who were "in much distress and terror." Mayer and his companion arrived in Victoria in the evening, where they learned of the attack on Brady and Henley which had been reported in the *British Colonist* that day under the headline, "HORRIBLE MURDER BY INDIANS." Word of the Marks' disappearance spread quickly and Mayer was interviewed that evening by the *British Colonist,* which ran the story the following morning (April 10th), under the headline, "ANOTHER ATROCIOUS MURDER!"[48]

The Victoria newspapers, mostly on the evidence of Mayer, believed that robbery was the sole motivation for both of the attacks in the southern Gulf Islands. In the case of the assault on the Marks, because their boat had been loaded with household goods, including a large trunk packed full of clothes and linen, valuable items in any household, the motive for the assault appeared to be robbery. Mayer himself stated that "he has no doubt that Mr. Marks and his daughter have been murdered that they might be robbed of their effects."[49] This view is supported by the statements of hwulmuhw informants, including some of the participants.

Upon their return to Lamalcha, Palluk and Semallee boasted about their role in the affair. Palluk told a Lamalcha man named Sayah that "he saw a whiteman and took his musket and killed him because he wanted to have the man's property." Semallee also told Sayah "that she was of the same mind as her husband about killing the man for his property" and that "her husband had shot the man because she wanted the property and that her husband did kill the man and she had his things." Another Lamalcha man, Talleyok, later recalled that Semallee "had told him that she had asked her husband to kill a white man because she wanted his property. He had frequently heard her say that she would like to kill a white man because she got so much property by it." Palluk also informed Talleyok that Allwhenuk "had stabbed a young white girl ... because they wanted her clothing."[50]

While the desire for material goods may appear to have been a primary motive in the attack on the Marks, there is another possibility consistent with hwulmuhw custom regarding land tenure and ownership which suggests that robbery may have been a peripheral consideration. In the unceded territories of the aboriginal people, there was no bay, landing or tract of forest that was not owned, at least nominally, by some family. The possibility exists that Palluk, Allwhenuk and their wives, who had travelled directly to Kulman from Lamalcha only a few days before, were beneficial owners of the resources along the northwest shore of Saturna Island and that during their stay they executed their prerogatives as owners by killing the Marks, strangers whom they did not know, as trespassers. Palluk had a reputation among hwulmuhw as a warrior who, as his wife later declared, "always wished to kill white men."[51] The aboriginal title of Saturna Island had not been extinguished and hwunitum had no right to be there. As the Cowichan people informed John Humphreys, a hwunitum man who lived among them at Cowichan Bay, "If one Indian found another man poaching on his land he immediately shot and killed him as it was within the law to do so."[52] This law, of course, applied equally to hwunitum.

The Quamichan attack on Brady and Henley on Pender Island was also believed by the Victoria newspapers to have had robbery as its motive. When it first reported the attack, the *British Colonist* claimed that it had "all the appearance of having been an attempt to murder for the sake of robbing the victims of their guns and whatever other effects they possessed."[53] Subsequent action on the part of Thalaston and his band, such as the plunder of hwunitum cabins on Salt Spring Island, would also seem to support the robbery motive.

During their trial, however, there was no mention by the prosecution of robbery as a motive in the assault on Brady and Henley. In fact, the judge, Chief Justice David Cameron, declared:

It was impossible to penetrate the motives of the unfortunate prisoners. They believed that killing a man was a great piece of heroism and their sole motive in murdering Brady appeared to be that they might be accounted great chiefs among their people. [54]

Cameron was probably just repeating what he had been told by Governor Douglas, who was much more intimate with hwulmuhw culture, but their reasoning would not be inconsistent with some aspects of nineteenth-century hwulmuhw warfare:

> The initial act was often a foray by some warrior who wanted to prove his prowess at taking heads or slaves. In the south (Nanaimo, Cowichan, Sanetch, Squamish, Maskwiam), the origin was very frequently a desire on the part of a novice warrior to try his newly acquired spirit powers. The young man simply constituted himself the leader of a war party and mustered enough men to accompany him. Usually these were relatives and older warriors, but there were always a number of disagreeable and socially worthless individuals who were glad of an opportunity to kill and loot. Whether every southern war raid (except, of course, retaliatory raids motivated by revenge) had its inception or sanction in a dream-spirit demand, could not be determined. [55]

Thalaston and his companions were young men, approximately sixteen years of age, possibly with newly-acquired warrior spirits obtained in the winter of 1862-63, which they were eager to test. This aspect of hwulmuhw culture might seem to fit the scenario of the Quamichan and their attack on Brady, were it not for the evidence regarding their own motive for the assault preserved in the newspaper accounts of the trial. In reply to a question from one of the jurors "designed to elicit the motive for the perpetration of the crime," Stalehum stated "that the food which was given to them by Brady and Henley they thought was poisoned, because it gave them a sore throat." [56] The simple fact of the matter is that the Quamichan attacked Brady and Henley because they believed that the two men had tried to poison them.

The idea seemed far-fetched to hwunitum sensibilities, but the practice of witch-craft and sorcery was widespread among hwulmuhw, and their reaction to what they had good reason to believe was an attempt to poison them was justified in terms of their own cultural experience. Nor was their reaction without precedent on the Northwest Coast. Discussing hwulmuhw sorcery in the early 1860s, an early observer wrote that they:

> ... charge the cause of all physical ailments, and frequently death, upon the secret agency of malevolence. Should the victim of some machination be a man of distinction in his clan, and die—especially in a sudden manner—the friends of the deceased arbitrarily pitch upon some slave, stranger just arrived in the camp, or other individual with whom the

departed may have been recently at variance, as accessory to the deed; and nothing short of the life of the imagined culprit will satisfy the demands of the bereaved. It is believed that the sorceror effects his purpose either by magic, or the stealthy introduction of poison into the system of the sick man." [57]

The Easter attacks by hwulmuhw on the members of the Marks family at Saturna Island and against Brady and Henley on Pender Island, viewed in the context of hwulmuhw culture, can be seen as more than random acts of violence or robbery. They were part of a long established effective pattern of jurisdiction which predated the hwunitum and constituted hwulmuhw justice enacted to uphold hwulmuhw law.

Unlike previous killings of hwunitum transients in the Gulf Islands, word of which only surfaced as rumours months or even years later, the Easter killings of 1863 became widely known within a week of their occurrence. The killings shocked the hwunitum population of Victoria and the outlying districts and there was an immediate demand by the Victoria press and the public for retribution.

Of primary concern was the perceived threat to the safety of hwunitum settlers on unceded hwulmuhw territories. After reporting the Pender Island attack on Brady and Henley, Amor De Cosmos, the editor of the *British Colonist*, called on the authorities "for the institution of active measures for bringing the offenders to justice, as it is a subject that seriously affects the security of settlers in the outlying districts." [58]

The next day, following the arrival in Victoria of Christian Mayer, and his account of the disappearance of Marks and his daughter, the anxiety was further heightened and the threat to hwunitum interests made explicit:

> There will ... be an end to all settlement if effective measures are not promptly taken for giving the necessary protection to isolated residents, and terminating the 'reign of terror' which seems to have been inaugurated. [59]

The situation was made even more urgent by the absence of Royal Navy gunboats and men-of-war at the naval station in Esquimalt. "It happens most unfortunately," observed the April 10th *British Colonist*, "that no ships of war of a suitable character are available for sending in search of the perpetrators of the late outrage near Salt Spring Island. H.M.S *Devastation* is away on a cruise, the gunboat *Forward* is at San Juan Island and the machinery of the *Grappler* (lying at Esquimalt) is deranged, so that she cannot be got ready for sail." Only HMS *Topaze*, flagship of the North Pacific fleet, and too big to be of practical value in negotiating the twisting channels and rocky shallows of the Gulf Islands, was available at Esquimalt. Its commander, Captain the Honourable John Wellbore

Sunderland Spencer, the senior naval officer in the colony, could only wait for the imminent return of the gunboat *Forward*.[60]

On Friday, April 10th, both Christian Mayer and John Henley made sworn statements before the Police Commissioner Augustus Pemberton in his offices at the Police Barracks, detailing what they knew of the circumstances surrounding the two attacks.

In an article published on the same day in the *British Colonist*, Mayer gave more specific information on the motives and the identity of those responsible for the attack. Mayer singled out one man, as yet unidentified by name, whom he felt was responsible for the attack. Mayers described him as follows:

> ... a certain bad Indian, who has been in the constant habit of boasting of exploits of this nature, and how little he cares for Gov. Douglas and the men-of-war. His own Indian has told him that this ruffian, in company with several others, murdered three white men at Plumpers Pass, in 1858, and sunk their canoe.[61]

The bodies of the victims were said to have been weighted with stones and sunk in deep water and Mayer suggested that the bodies of Marks and his daughter were also "disposed of in the manner described." Mayer was told that "these pirates" scuttled the vessels of their victims "to avoid their crime being found and punished. The [Marks'] boat being found as described is attributed by Mr. Mayer to the fact of her having been flat bottomed, and therefore awkward for the assassins to sink."[62]

After alluding to the rumours of previous "murders," "the certain bad Indian," and the methods used by the attackers to hide the evidence, the *British Colonist* made the following observation:

> In contemplating the circumstances now brought to light, the terrible question suggests itself—Are these the only murders that have been perpetrated by these savages?[63]

Christian Mayer, it appears, did not return to Mayne Island for fear of being "a victim in the next tragedy."[64] In light of the situation he was determined not to return to his Mayne Island "ranch" until the present danger was over.

John Henley's sworn statement detailed the events leading up to and including the night attack of April 4th on Pender Island. He gave physical descriptions of the attackers and declared that they had told him "they came from Cowitchan." In contrast to his interview the day before with Smith, Henley did not provide any names. Perhaps in response to a suspicion on the part of Pemberton as to why Brady and Henley were in the area and whether or not they had intended to sell liquor, Henley insisted that he and Brady "had intended to have cut hay on the

Island, on which we landed ... Brady was not a Whiskey seller to Indians. We had no spirits with us, and were not in the habit of carrying spirits with us."[65] Cowichan informants later backed up his claim by declaring that "Brady and his mate were not whiskey sellers."[66]

With the information contained in the statements by Mayer and Henley, Pemberton met with Governor Douglas later in the day to discuss the situation and to plan an appropriate response. They had little information concerning those responsible for the assaults, other than the dubious names provided by Henley and statements that those responsible were "Cowichans." The arrival of the gunboat *Forward* in Victoria harbour that afternoon, on a return trip from the Royal Marine camp at Garrison Bay, San Juan Island, provided much-needed naval assistance. After remaining a short time in the harbour, the *Forward* "steamed round to Esquimalt" and the Royal Navy depot to await further orders.[67]

On April 11th, the *British Colonist*, reporting the arrival of the *Forward* the previous day, announced "Retribution at Hand" even though "the course decided upon by the authorities however had not transpired up to the hour of our going to press." Several days marked by below normal temperatures, rain and snow flurries were to pass before the *Forward* would leave to investigate the killings, much to the annoyance of the press. Governor Douglas, however, had already initiated information gathering among his network of hwulmuhw spies and allies resident in the colony and the outlying districts.

On Monday, April 13th, Douglas made a formal request for naval assistance to Commodore Spencer. Included were copies of the sworn statements of Christian Mayer and John Henley. "I have therefore to request that you will be good enough to despatch one of the Gun Boats to visit the settlements along the Coast as far as Comox to give confidence to the settlers and to allay any feelings of alarm that may at present exist amongst them, the Gun Boat remaining a few days at each place."[68]

Bearing in mind his experience in colonial warfare on the coast, Douglas explained the need for the Royal Navy to proceed with caution. He asked Spencer that the officer in command should meet with him to discuss strategy.

> It is very desirable that the guilty Indians should be apprehended but this can only be done by strategy, and not by force, as they would immediately flee and secrete themselves beyond the reach of capture, did the Gun Boat make any decided attempt to arrest them. The Officer in Command may however be able to gain information concerning the guilty parties from other Indians, and the well disposed amongst the tribe may be inclined to point them out and permit them to be taken quietly. I have already set on foot enquiries amongst the Indians here, and would wish to see the Officer you may detach in order to explain to him the bearing to be adopted

towards, and the most desirable mode of proceeding with the Indians of the Coast. [69]

Douglas knew that there was division among the hwulmuhw people, not only by family, but also by religion. Douglas' suggested strategy was identical to that used successfully by him during similar circumstances in 1853 at Cowichan and Nanaimo and again at Cowichan in 1856, when Hwulmuhw had killed or wounded hwunitum settlers. In each campaign, Douglas used both gifts and intimidation to gain information and co-operation from "the well-disposed amongst the tribe."

Douglas also requested that the *Forward* convey "several settlers belonging to Comox now in Victoria, awaiting an opportunity to forward their seed." [70] The planting season was well under way, and Douglas knew the importance of getting the seed to the recently-established farming settlement at Comox. But, to accommodate the settlers' needs, it meant further delays in the gunboat's departure.

Informed that they would set sail on the 15th, to begin inquiries as to those responsible for the recent attacks and to give confidence to hwunitum settlers in the Gulf Islands and along the east coast of Vancouver Island to Comox, the officers and crew of the *Forward* spent the next two days in preparation, which included cleaning "guns and arms, … drawing gunners stores from the Naval Store at Esquimalt, … drawing powder from Magazine," and stowing these items aboard the gunboat. [71]

On the morning of the following day, Tuesday, April 14th, the *British Colonist*, unable to comprehend what it saw as inexcusable delays to investigate the recent killings, ran a scathing editorial, penned by Amor De Cosmos:

> It is incomprehensible how the government can allow day by day to pass, without sending one of the gunboats to arrest the murderers. Both the *Forward* and the *Grappler* might have been dispatched on such a service; and before the blood of their victims was dry; whilst their hands were reeking with human gore, and gloating over their fiendish deeds, the murderers might have been lodged in our prisons.

Douglas directed Horace Smith, the Chief Constable and Superintendent of Police, who had been with the force since its inception in 1858, to accompany the expedition. As it had not been ascertained whether or not the Marks had in fact been killed, Pemberton issued a Memorandum of Instructions "for the guidance of the Superintendent of Police in executing Warrants to apprehend certain Indians charged with having murdered a man named Bill Brady." The instructions were as follows:

> 1. Mr. Smith will be ready to go on board HMS *"Forward"* tomorrow [April 15] at 12 o'Clock noon. He will make diligent search for the

supposed murderers, and if he requires assistance he will apply to the Officer in Command of the Ship.

2. He must take care not unnecessarily to endanger the lives of the men under his charge by straying too far from the Ship.

3. He will make inquiry as to the fate of Mr. Marks and his daughter, and if any outrage has been committed he will exercise his authority as a constable in arresting the perpetrators of the outrage if they be found.

William Young, the Colonial Secretary, sent a copy of the instructions to Lieutenant Commander Horace Lascelles of the *Forward,* along with the request "that you will be good enough to afford Mr. Smith such assistance as may be requisite to enable the object of capturing and bringing to justice the offending Indians to be fully carried out."[72]

Confident that matters were well under control, William Young, and his father-in-law the Governor, made preparations for a month long trip to the Colony of British Columbia to inspect work being done on the Cariboo Road in the Fraser Canyon.

Quamichan, Cowichan River. Young warriors from this village opposed hwunitum encroachment on their lands. The Quamichan party under Thalaston left this village in late March 1863 for Pender Island where they killed William Brady and wounded John Henley.
British Columbia Archives and Recortds Service, Photo HP 57606.

North end of Bedwell Harbour, 1934 (formerly known as Shark Cove prior to the removal of the land bridge which once connected the two islands of North and South Pender.) In this vicinity William Brady and John Henley were attacked on April 4th, 1863 by Thalaston and his companions.
Royal British Columbia Museum, Photo PN 1434.

Hwulmuhw settlement on Helen Point on Active Pass, Mayne Island (Sqthaq). People from this village were the first to identify Lamalcha involvement in homicides of hwunitum settlers. A village headman by the name of Jack assisted British forces in the campaign against the Lamalcha warriors. Royal British Columbia Museum, Photo 5734.

HMG Forward. *Commanded by Lieutenant Commander the Hon. Horace Lascelles, the gunboat played a prominent role in the war against the Lamalcha warriors. On April 20th, 1863 the gunboat was beaten at Lamalcha, Kuper Island by warriors under Squa'cum in the only pitched battle of the war.* British Columbia Archives and Records Service, Photo HP 27404.

Chapter Seven

The Terror of the Coast

O N APRIL 15TH AT 9:20 A.M., Her Majesty's Gunboat *Forward* left Esquimalt and proceeded to Victoria, where Lieutenant Commander the Honourable Horace Lascelles placed himself "under the orders of His Excellency the Governor."[1] Lascelles, the 26-year-old son of the third Earl of Harewood, had arrived in the colony in 1860 as a lieutenant on HMS *Topaze* and assumed command of the *Forward* after the accidental death of its commander, Charles Robson, in 1861. Described by his contemporaries as a member of "the horse-racing, fast set," Lascelles "never made any virtuous pretensions, nor posed as a moral man."[2] As commander of the *Forward*, Lascelles was much influenced by his predecessor Robson, a close friend who led the *Forward* in two pitched battles against native militants and used the lash freely on hwulmuhw taken aboard as prisoners—a tradition continued by Lascelles.[3]

During their meeting on the morning of April 15th, Douglas repeated to Lascelles what he had already outlined to Commodore Spencer: that those responsible for the killings would only be taken by strategy and not by force. The hwulmuhw were to be regarded "always as British subjects," and Lascelles was asked "not to visit them with undue severity." However, Douglas also instructed Commander Lascelles that "upon the refusal of any tribe to deliver up the assassins to seize upon their canoes and other property, and destroy their villages."[4]

Having taken on board the Superintendent of Police, Horace Smith, the *Forward* fired a blank round from one of its twenty-four-pound howitzers, a "signal for sea," weighed anchor and steamed out of Victoria Harbour at 3:20 p.m., bound for the Royal Marine camp at Garrison Bay, San Juan Island, where she arrived at 6:50 p.m. and anchored for the night.[5]

There was relief in Victoria that the *Forward* was finally under way even though, as one newspaper sarcastically suggested, "she will probably get there in time to hear of a few more massacres."[6]

De Cosmos' editorial in the *British Colonist* prayed "that success may crown the efforts now made, late though they may be, to secure the ruthless assassins ... The peace and security of the whole of our out-lying population depends upon the decisive action of the authorities at the present juncture, and if such a blow is not struck as will strike terror into the hearts of the natives we may look for the immediate return of many of the settlers who have within the past few months cast their lot in the fertile districts of the north."[7]

The *Forward* weighed anchor Thursday morning, April 16th, and proceeded from San Juan Island to Miner's Bay on Mayne Island. Arriving "in Active Pass off the Settlement," the *Forward* "fired a gun to call attention of settlers."[8] The British no doubt sent a party ashore to interview Caroline Marks, and to look into the welfare of her children.

Lascelles received "on board one half breed Indian as an Interpreter."[9] The identity of this man is not known, but he may have been Mayer's employee, Jack, who offered to guide the British to the site where the alleged attack on the Marks had occurred.[10] By mid-afternoon, the *Forward* weighed anchor "and proceeded under steam from the settlement in Active Pass."[11] "From information there received," wrote Lascelles, "[we] searched the shore of Saturna Island for the scene of the supposed murder of Mr. Marks and found the remains of the Boat with the stove, and several portions of the young women's dress."[12]

A "gentleman who accompanied the *Forward*" reported that they "succeeded in finding a boat, a mast, and a stove on the beach. The boat was chopped and the stove broken."[13] Mayer's boat "bore marks of having been chopped to pieces to cause it to sink."[14]

Smith investigated the site. "There was at this place," he later recalled, "a high ridge that shot out into the water. Marks' fire was on one side and on the other the surface bore marks of fingers as if some persons had crawled up that way to over-look him."[15] Smith followed the "marks of footsteps" to "a ledge of rocks jutting out into very deep water," about twelve feet above high water mark. Upon the ledge he found a single shoe and a pair of garters. Using a boat hook, Smith probed underneath the ledge and recovered "the skirt of a petticoat much torn and stained with blood" in a fathom below water.[16] "On this spot the murderers had evidently stripped the poor girl ... No trace of the bodies of either father or daughter were discovered."[17]

The effect that these discoveries had on the imagination of the British crew of the *Forward* must have been significant. The discovery of the garters and shoe on the rock ledge and the torn, bloodstained petticoat in the water was enough to convince the British that the young woman had been stripped, and possibly raped, before she was killed. After taking on board Mayer's wrecked boat, the *Forward* proceeded to the British camp on San Juan Island where she anchored for the night. [18]

The British spent the following morning, April 17th, in Garrison Bay, cleaning "guns and arms" and doing maintenance work on the rigging. In the afternoon, under gloomy, overcast skies, the *Forward* began the search for the body of William Brady. [19] Their only source of information was Henley's statement that Brady's body was "on a little island about three or four miles from Salt Spring Island" and that it was "a long narrow island with high mountains in the middle." [20] Although it barely fit the description, a party "boarded a schooner, and canoe" to search the shoreline of Sqoqote, a low elevation island (known today as Piers) one mile south of Salt Spring Island. The *Forward* then steamed through Satellite Channel, between Vancouver Island and the southern shoreline of Salt Spring Island, to Cowichan Bay where the gunboat arrived at 4:30 p.m. and anchored for the night. [21]

Saturday dawned "fine and warm but gloomy" with the approach of rain. [22] The *Forward* remained at anchor in Cowichan Bay while Lascelles went about enlisting the services of Tomo Antoine, whom Governor Douglas had recommended as an interpreter for the expedition. Passionately loyal to his former employer, the fifty-year-old Antoine was still "high in the favour of Governor Douglas whose constant factotum he was in every expedition." [23] A skilled interpreter and knowledgeable guide was crucial to the success of the expedition, and Antoine's service to Lascelles and the other British officers would prove invaluable in the upcoming weeks. Among the Cowichan, "few understood Chinook or English while Tomo spoke English without an accent besides understanding nearly every Indian language on the island." [24] Even Lascelles, who had a profound disdain for native people, and was ignorant of Tomo's Chinook/Iroquois ancestry, called him "a very valuable halfbreed Cherokee Indian." [25] By this time, Antoine was also a violent drunk—"a madman in liquor," according to a description by a contemporary. [26] Lascelles located him at his residence outside the entrance to Cowichan Bay where, since 1861, Antoine and his wife Seenatoah (Jane Anthony), lived in a cabin on land granted to him "by special order of Governor Douglas." [27]

There is no official record, but the British at this stage probably made contact with the Roman Catholic bishop, Modeste Demers, and other priests then present at the mission of St. Anne's at Comiaken. As Lascelles later recorded, Demers "volunteered his services to persuade the Cowichan Indians to give up the suspected men." [28] Bishop Demers was instrumental in facilitating the eventual surrender of the Quamichan who killed Brady, but for the moment the priests or others evidently only gave the British the names of those involved. It appears that the attack on Brady and Henley at Bedwell Harbour was not a secret among the Cowichan or the hwunitum settlers. Thalaston, Stalehum and the rest apparently boasted of their deed. Samuel Harris wrote of the "murderers going about and boasting what they have done." [29] The British were informed that two of the youths were "in the mountains ... the blind man is named Swane-ahya [Oalatza], the other now at large with him is named Kaisuk [Thalaston]—the two women are named Thask and Thostinah." [30]

The British were informed that Stalehum was with his father, an elder si'em, attending a stlun'uq (potlatch) at Chemainus and that they would be returning on Sunday to their village of Quamichan on the Cowichan River.

The clouds piled up and the rain began Sunday morning, April 19th, as the *Forward* weighed anchor and proceeded under steam out of Cowichan Bay. [31] By 10 a.m. Lascelles positioned the *Forward* at the entrance to Sansum Narrows, between Separation Point on Vancouver Island and Salt Spring Island, "to intercept the canoes returning from a Blanket feast at Chemainus having received information that Indians suspected of the murder were among them whose names the Superintendent of Police had." [32] Sighting a number of canoes coming towards them Lascelles "fired the Howitzer to Bring [the] canoes to." For the next two hours the British were "employed searching canoes," and as a result took two prisoners. [33] The "gentleman who accompanied the *Forward*" described what happened:

> Mr. Smith saw a number of canoes coming down the coast from a potlatch at Chemainus. Went off to them in a gig, when one of the young fellows jumped ashore and disappeared among the rocks. A Chief was taken from the canoe and detained for one hour as a hostage, at the end of which time a party of Indians, who had gone in search of the runaway, returned bringing him in custody. [34]

The young man was Stalehum, "and he proved to be the old man's son and one of the principal movers in the murder of Brady." [35]

Shortly afterwards, the British took another prisoner from one of the canoes, a Lamalcha man named Whisk who was said "to have been with the Lamalchas at the time Marks and his daughter were murdered and is thought to have had a hand in that bloody affair." [36] Whisk, however, had not taken part. Only the fact that Whisk was from Lamalcha gave the British grounds to detain him "on suspicion." [37] Stalehum and Whisk were put in irons and confined below deck, exposed to the constant din of the gunboat's steam-powered machinery and to the verbal and physical abuse of the crew who resented sharing their limited space with hwulmuhw "murderers."

The rain continued to fall as the *Forward* proceeded up Sansum Narrows and "with some trouble" stopped and searched every canoe returning from the Chemainus potlatch. [38] Lascelles' interpreters were told to order the canoes to stop. When some of the canoes ignored the demand, the gunboat forced them to comply with cannon fire. As Lascelles later explained, "being obliged to fire some blank Guns to bring them to, we searched them all." [39] Not all the shots were blanks. As Lascelle's log shows, at least one twenty-four-pound hollow shell was fired. [40] Further searching brought no results. Even though the gunboat "frightened some of them considerably by firing an occasional shot to bring them to. We found nothing as they had taken the alarm." [41]

By 4 o'clock in the afternoon the *Forward* steamed into Hwtlupnets (Maple Bay) and anchored for the night in Bird's Eye Cove. Perhaps it was in this anchorage that Stalehum "confessed that his father and mother and others assisted in the murder [of Brady]." [42] The British would also have interrogated Whisk about his fellow Lamalcha and he may have provided them, under threat of punishment, with information to substantiate rumours regarding Lamalcha participation in the recent killings. Up until Whisk's capture, there was nothing to directly implicate Lamalcha persons in the attacks on Brady or the Marks, but Whisk had his own reasons for sending the British in the direction of Lamalcha. Some time ago his uncle had been killed by Allwhenuk, the Penelakut warrior who now lived among the Lamalcha. [43] Allwhenuk had accompanied Palluk when the latter killed Marks and his daughter but Whisk and the British, at the time, were unaware of this.

At the anchorage in Bird's Eye Cove, the British pondered their next move. Four days of cruising had revealed some physical evidence of the attack on the Marks, but the whereabouts of Brady's body remained a mystery. They had captured one man definitely involved in the death of Brady and another on suspicion of his involvement in the attack on the Marks, but the others eluded their grasp. Perhaps it was Smith, the Superintendent of Police, who was familiar with the reputation of Lamalcha as a centre of hwulmuhw resistance, that led the British to Kuper Island. In any event, with little else to go on, the British suspected Lamalcha involvement in the late killings.

> Something happened out on those islands, some people were murdered, some people were killed and robbed and somebody in the village of wle-malce [Lamalcha] got blamed for it. The authorities at the time decided to teach the Indians a lesson. They sent up a Man-of-War from Victoria. They brought this ship up, cannons sticking out all over it. This ship was ordered up there to teach those Indians a lesson. [44]

The rain stopped by the morning of Monday, April 20th, and the day broke with clear skies and sunshine as the British prepared for battle. The *Forward*'s upper deck was scrubbed and washed, the guns and small arms cleaned, and at 9:50 a.m. the gunboat weighed anchor and steamed out of Maple Bay towards Stuart Channel and Kuper Island. [45]

En route, the British "boarded several canoes and searched them" before arriving in Lamalcha Bay at 11:35 where the *Forward* anchored in front of the village. [46] Seven or eight large houses stood along the beach inside a small crescent-shaped bay enclosed on both sides by thickly-forested points of land. At the centre of the village, in front of the lodges, was the Lamalcha fort, a blockhouse with walls eight feet high "strongly constructed of logs, properly morticed and loopholed on three sides for musketry." [47] Built with "squared timbers," in imitation of hwunitum blockhouses on the San Juan Islands, the fortification was designed to defend the village against attack by musket-armed hwulmuhw. [48] Recently, it had been further modified with the addition of anti-artillery bunkers in the shape of "regular rifle-pits constructed inside the Block House, covered over with thick plank." In addition, the blockhouse was protected "with numerous rifle-pits and trenches sunk around it." [49]

Forewarned of the approach of the *Forward*, with its billowing smokestack and steam exhaust visible a long way down Stuart Channel, the village headmen under the guidance of Squ'acum, the "war man," planned their strategy in case of attack. [50] The large-scale migrations to procure food resources had yet to begin and most, if not all, of the families were present. As a result, the village had its full complement of warriors. Although they occupied "a position naturally strong," the Lamalcha warriors were significantly outgunned and outnumbered by the British gunboat with its three cannon and rifle-armed crew of forty officers and men. The Lamalcha mustered, according to various estimates, between eight and twenty-two warriors armed with muskets, pistols and possibly a few rifles. [51]

To better utilize what little fire-power they had, Squ'acum had the warriors abandon their fortifications and divide into two groups which took up position on either side of the entrance to the bay "a quarter of a mile from the village." [52] In concealed "lookout" positions among the trees and brush above the sandstone rock of the shoreline, Squ'acum placed his men in the best possible positions to bring their musket fire within effective range of the gunboat when it anchored in the bay. [53] They were instructed to fire only upon a pre-arranged signal, such as the hoot of an owl or some other animal call. [54] Squ'acum's plan was an elaboration of Tzouhalem's tactics at the Battle of Hwtlupnets a quarter century before, when a hwulmuhw army caught the invading Kwakwaka'wakw and their allies in a similar cross-fire known in military parlance as "crossing the "T."" [55] Squ'acum's plan followed conventional hwulmuhw tactics, whereby musket-armed warriors waited in concealment until the enemy had approached within close range, at which time a deadly volley would be unleashed. As was customary among the hwulmuhw, shamans did not accompany active war parties, which may explain why Acheewun and his brother took their muskets and stationed themselves "in the bushes alone, a short distance from the main ambush." [56]

Superintendent Smith later claimed that he "could see with glasses the men leaving for the ambuscade," but there is no indication that the British were, at the time, aware of any such movement as they approached Lamalcha Bay.[57] Lascelles, in his official report, mentions only that "on arriving at the place, I found they had a strong log house, in the centre of the village, loopholed."[58] Confident that the guns of the *Forward* would make short work of such opposition, the British became less cautious and the gunboat was "run in as close as possible to the shore," where it anchored parallel to the village "between two points of land ... at the mouth of the harbour" directly across the Lamalcha line of fire.[59] The British kept a watchful eye on the blockhouse and its surrounding earthworks where they assumed that the Lamalcha warriors were concealed in their positions. To provide additional cover on board the gunboat, Lascelles "had the rifle plates up, and the men's bags put in the intervening places."[60]

No men were visible on the shore, and the British "could see only women and children," some of whom, fearful of impending attack, were "carrying goods away on their backs into the woods."[61] At noon, Smith called on the services of one of the interpreters to order the "chiefs" to come on board for questioning. "The interpreter called to them," a volunteer recalled, "and two boys came off in a boat."[62] Lascelles directed his interpreter to tell the two boys, one of whom was Shacutsus, that he "wished to speak with to the Chief."[63] The two youths returned to shore with the message.

"After waiting an hour we hailed them again and were told they would have nothing to do with us," recalled the "gentleman" volunteer.[64] Sayah, a Lamalcha youth who was present on the beach, corroborates: "I saw the gunboat come to Lamalcha; all the Indians [the women and children] came out of their houses to look at her; they were asked to send their chiefs on board, but the chiefs refused to go."[65] Lascelles claimed that the "chief" "returned an answer that he would not come nor would he give up the murderers."[66] The Lamalcha had no intention of boarding the *Forward* as they were well aware of what had taken place the previous spring when Lascelles had seized hwulmuhw people at Shiyahwt (Ganges Harbour) and taken them on board the *Forward* where they received "three dozen lashes each."[67]

After a further "two or three ineffectual attempts to converse with them," Smith, in frustration, "then had an interview with Lieut. Lascelles and asked him to render assistance."[68] Lascelles ordered a red flag to be raised and told one of the interpreters to inform the Lamalcha "that if the Chief was not on board before the flag which we hoisted was hauled down giving them a quarter of an hour I would fire on the village."[69] Since no one on board the gunboat spoke Hul'qumi'num, except Jack and Tomo Antoine, there is no certainty as to what he actually said to the Lamalcha or their reply. It was later learned that the interpreter did not "appear to have translated the message with which he was charged at all, but only warned the people to run out of the reach of the guns; and made known that the flag was a signal of grace while it was flying."[70]

The "gentleman" volunteer later claimed that the two Lamalcha youths were about to return to the gunboat with a reply when "the chief came out of the woods with his musket and stopped them. An old squaw was heard to say: "Don't go, they have come after the murderers, but they won't get them.""[71]

This account, which may have originated from Superintendent Smith, is suspicious for several reasons. It is unlikely that the elder used the word "murderer," it being at best a rather free translation of her actual words by the interpreter, if they were in fact ever uttered. The story may also have been made up to criminalize the Lamalcha and justify firing on the village by inferring that the Lamalcha were the ones who broke off negotiations.

On the other hand, Lamalcha oral history confirms the literal meaning of what the elderly woman shouted. She called out that the British may "have come after the murderers, but they won't get them" for the simple reason that they weren't there. The only Lamalcha directly involved in the attack on Marks and Harvey were Palluk and Semallee and there is no evidence that they were present at Lamalcha on April 20th.

> They told those Indians they have to give this man up who was blamed for the murders out on the island. His name was TIOC [Palluk?] They went ashore and they spoke to the Indians and they told them, "We're here to get this man, this man was responsible for those murders out on those islands." They said to this naval officer, "We can't give him up because he's not here, he hasn't been here for a long time and we don't know where he is." But the officer insisted anyway, "You either give that man up or we're going to blow your village all to pieces. There will be nothing left of it." They said, "How can we give this man up if he's not here?"[72]

In his official report, Lascelles states that "the Chief answered that he would not come, and was not afraid of us."[73] The British claimed that the Lamalcha broke off negotiations, but the warrior Shacutsus later stated that it was the British who refused to negotiate. During the time-period of the ultimatum, Shacutsus and his companion once again approached the gunboat in their canoe, but they were turned away, not by their "chief" but by the British. According to Shacutsus, "I and another Indian went off in a canoe to speak to the gunboat, and we were ordered off."[74] Which suggests that the British at this point, frustrated by their inability to contact the Lamalcha leaders, broke off negotiations and committed themselves to more intimidating tactics.

Taking heed of the interpreter's warning, the women and children began to flee the village with bags of provisions and this caused Lascelles to act. "At the end of the appointed time," Lascelles reported, "I hauled down the flag and fired into the Village which they deserted immediately." [75] It was approximately 1 p.m. [76] As soon as the gunboat fired a shell at the village the hidden Lamalcha riflemen, at Squ'acum's command, "opened a very sharp fire of musketry ... from the two points of land at the entrance of the Bay." [77] The Lamalcha "fired simultaneously, raking the gunboat bow and stern"—their shots "ploughing up the deck." The *Forward* lay lengthwise along the line of fire, and the crew were unprotected by the rifle plates which were only placed along the sides of the ship. As a result, one or more sailors were wounded and the powderman of the thirty-two-pound pivot gun, a sixteen-year-old sailor named Charles F. Gliddon, was hit "in the first raking fire" by a shot which "came over the stern" and "struck him on the temple and passed nearly through, killing him on the spot." [78] It was claimed that the fatal shot came from the gun of the Penelakut warrior Allwhenuk. [79] Gliddon became the first and last British serviceman killed in action in British Columbia.

Stunned by the sudden turn of events, Lascelles, "while the Indians were firing, got the anchor up and stood off a little" before he "warped his vessel around and commenced firing grape, cannister and shell upon the ranch." [80] In their new position, "distant about two hundred yards from the shore," out of effective small arms range, the British first "turned all our attention to the ambush, and shelled the Indians out of it." [81] "Firing now commenced on both sides," a British participant reported, "they fired from behind rocks and trees, and we then shelled the stockade as well as the wood—fired solid shot, shell, and grape, and applied rifles pretty freely for about an hour and a half." [82] The sailors and marines on board the *Forward* emptied 550 rounds from their rifles and Colt revolvers into the woods. [83] Despite the fact that he had only one arm, Tomo Antoine's handicap would not have prevented his participation in the fire-fight. As a contemporary observed: "In his one hand, which is naturally powerful, he holds a full-size firearm like a pistol, and shoots with tolerable accuracy." [84]

With no visible targets, the *Forward*'s thirty-two-pound cannon mounted amidships on its revolving carriage, fired twenty-seven rounds of exploding shrapnel shell, solid shot and grape-shot into the woods, while the twenty-four pounder fired some thirty-two rounds of the same projectiles as well as hollow shot and canister at the blockhouse and its surrounding trenches. [85] One round from the howitzer scored a direct hit on the blockhouse, but the twenty-four-pound solid shot only passed through one log wall into the blockhouse where it rebounded off an adjacent wall and landed on the floor. [86] The British fire against the houses of Lamalcha was equally ineffective.

In their concealed positions, Squ'acum "urged the firing" and the warriors, according to custom, shouted the cries of their guardian spirits as they replied to the cannon and rifle fire with their muskets.[87] According to one account, the "fire from the shore ceased soon after the gunboat commenced to fire vigorously" but Smith states that it was "after about an hour and a half heavy firing [that] they fell back through the thick woods."[88]

Most of the Lamalcha warriors left their positions near the shoreline and retreated further into the forest once the gunboat had moved out of effective rifle range. Lascelles, however, ordered his crew to continue firing at the unseen enemy. Some of the warriors later told a hwunitum trader that "while the gunboat was firing they were lying in the woods looking at her and laughing at the tenass [little] warship for wasting her powder and shot."[89] One Lamalcha rifleman, however, continued to fire upon the gunboat with some effect from his position up a tall tree:

> During the bombardment of the Lamalcha village by the gunboat, an Indian was observed perched on the limb of a large tree engaged in firing a rifle upon the blue-jackets. Several rifles from on board were brought to bear upon him but, somehow or another, the best shots on board seemed at fault. None could hit the fellow. Superintendent Smith, himself a "crack" shot, also made several attempts to dislodge the troublesome fellow, but his best efforts proved of no avail. Every minute or two, a puff from among the thick leaves would be seen and then "bang" would go the rifle of the redskin. At length one of the mortars was loaded with a large shell and brought to bear on him. When it was touched off there was a loud report, a "whiz," and a great crash! The huge monarch of the forest was struck in the trunk about twenty feet from the ground and blown into a thousand pieces. As the Indian was not seen again it is supposed that he felt tired and lay down.[90]

Shortly before 4 p.m. the British ceased firing and tried one more time, through the efforts of the interpreters, to communicate with the Lamalcha leaders.[91]

"We then quieted them," a participant reported, "and tried to get an interview with them but could not."[92] The British were fearful of landing and fighting an enemy of unknown numbers in the forest on their own ground. Lascelles "would not permit anyone to land" and was forced to retire after a furious fire-fight with an aboriginal force half his strength.[93] At 4 p.m. the *Forward* weighed anchor and steamed across Stuart Channel towards the village of Halalt on Willy Island, directly across from Lamalcha, where at 5 p.m. she "anchored for the night."[94]

Through his arrogance, Lascelles had ignored Governor Douglas' recommendations not to use force against the hwulmuhw "as they would immediately flee and secrete themselves beyond the reach of capture."[95] But the Lamalcha did not flee.

Lamalcha Bay, 1992. Taken from the site of the blockhouse in the centre of Lamalcha village, this photograph shows the north point of the bay occupied by Lamalcha warriors during Battle of Lamalcha on April 20th, 1863. Photo by Paul Schmid.

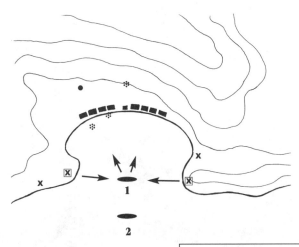

Battle of Lamalcha
April 20th, 1863

☐	Lamalcha Warriors
x	Lookouts
⬤	HMG *Forward*: 1. First position, 12:00-1:00 p.m.
	2. Second postion, 1:00-4:00 p.m.
❄	Grapeshot found
●	24 lb. cannonball found

Lamalcha Bay, 1983. View from the Lamalcha position at the north entrance of the bay. From this point and the opposite headland, Lamalcha warriors fired on the HMG Forward *which lay between.* Photo by Chris Arnett.

Despite the overwhelming military superiority of Her Majesty's Gunboat *Forward*, the Lamalcha achieved a victory in what was to be the only tactical defeat ever inflicted by a tribal people on the Royal Navy.

A characteristic of the Victorian military establishment was "the enormously powerful British expectation of victory" whenever its forces came into contact with aboriginal forces.[96] However, "the expectation of victory also meant that when defeats were recognized, they created a massive shock."[97] The British made every effort to deny their defeat. Lascelles delayed sending word of the fight to Victoria and Esquimalt for several days and, when he did, he claimed victory, asserting that the village of Lamalcha had been destroyed with many Lamalchas killed and wounded. Based on his information, the first newspaper reports of the battle claimed that six to eight Lamalcha were killed and "a large number" wounded.[98] These figures stand in sharp contrast to estimates from other hwunitum and hwulmuhw sources. One report claimed that "the Lamalchas acknowledge a loss of three women and a man by the bombardment, but their loss is believed to have been much greater."[99] The Lamalcha themselves informed Jonathan Begg of Salt Spring Island that although the *Forward*'s cannon had knocked down many trees, "all her efforts had failed to kill one klutchman [woman]."[100]

Hand in hand with magnifying enemy casualties was the impetus to diminish one's own. With the notable exception of Charles Gliddon, "Boy Second Class" who was "killed ... by a musket ball through the head,"[101] Lascelles did not acknowledge any other casualties: "Though the Gun Boat was hit in several places," he wrote, "we sustained no other injury."[102]

There were, however, rumours of one or more sailors being wounded. This information may have been deliberately suppressed to downplay the extent of the Lamalcha success. The first reports of the battle sent to Victoria by Lascelles himself reported that the Lamalcha had "killed a young seaman ... and severely wounded another."[103] As well, the first published account of the engagement to appear in a general history of the colony written by an Anglican minister who was in Victoria at the time, described the fight as "resulting in the death of one seaman and the wounding of others."[104]

The most effective palliative used by the British to suppress the Lamalcha victory and draw attention away from it was to criminalize the Lamalcha and portray them not as a sovereign people defending their homes and families, but as a "nest of pirates" and "murderers" who "had the villainy to fire on the *Forward*."[105]

For the aristocratic Lascelles, the seventh son of the third Earl of Harewood, the ignominy of defeat at the hands of an enemy he despised was a severe blow to his prestige. The unexpected outcome of the battle clearly traumatized him and was reflected to some degree by his indecisive behaviour and the meandering movements of the *Forward* over the next two weeks. Lascelles' handling of the affair would soon make him the object of derision by factions of the colonial press, and his single minded desire for vengeance would not disappear until the men responsible for his defeat were killed or captured.

Once they determined that the *Forward* had not left the vicinity, the people of Lamalcha made plans to temporarily abandon their village. Despite their military success, they realized that further open warfare at Lamalcha would have less favourable results. Sometime during the night of April 20th "they made their escape by means of their boats and canoes, carrying everything they had with them." [106] According to Henry Edwards, "When they shelled Lamalcha, the people ran away. They all scattered. They paddled across to Salt Spring [Island], moved to Salt Spring to escape the attack." [107] Some of the families then left for other places where they had relations or owned places of refuge. In the following weeks, most of them would be constantly pursued by the Royal Navy and other colonial forces.

On Tuesday, April 21st, the *Forward* weighed anchor at 8:15 a.m., off the village of Halalt on Willy Island and steamed back across Stuart Channel to Lamalcha. [108] Upon their arrival the British observed that "most of the Indians had left in the night." [109] Still wary of an ambush, they made no attempt to land and instead spent half an hour firing "into [the] Village to destroy it." [110] Lascelles later wrote that he "completed the destruction of the place with a few shot and shell and returned to Cowitchen." [111] Despite this claim, as well as second-hand statements attributed to Lamalcha informants that "their houses were destroyed," the seven or eight large dwellings and the blockhouse of Lamalcha stood more or less intact until May 2nd, when the structures were examined and then burned by a British shore party. [112]

Lascelles' terse description of events on April 21st, stands in sharp contrast to his actions as described by others. A sailor from HMS *Topaze* who served on board the *Forward* said nothing about the village being destroyed, only that the gunboat "returned and traversed the Island firing into every part of it in the hopes of dislodging the Indians from the bush." [113] The futility of randomly firing into the woods of Kuper Island, with no visible target, illustrates the level of frustration felt by Lascelles at his inability to come to grips with an elusive enemy. By 9 a.m. the gunboat "ceased firing," after which she "proceeded under steam from Village Bay [and] committed the Body of Chas. F. Gliddon to the deep" in the waters of Stuart Channel. [114]

Realizing that the enemy had dispersed to parts unknown, Lascelles "returned again to Cowichan to make inquiries about the murder of Brady." [115] Lascelles spent the day trying to figure out his next move while the crew spent the afternoon inspecting the powder magazine where it was discovered that "a leek" in the magazine had damaged several charges of gunpowder used in the twenty-four-pound howitzers, possibly as a result of the action on the 20th. [116]

Wednesday, April 22nd, dawned a warm, spring day as the frustrated British commander, determined to apprehend Brady's killers, resumed his tactics of intimidation against the Cowichan people of Comiaken and Clemclemalits, two of the largest villages on Cowichan Bay. He directed his attention first to the village of Comiaken, which, clustered below the Roman Catholic mission of St. Ann's on Comiaken Hill, was close to the shoreline. Once again, no "official" mention is made of the following events which were witnessed and described by "a highly intelligent settler from Cowichan."

> The Commander of the *Forward* sent Tomo, the interpreter, to an Indian village at Comiaken, to demand the surrender of one of the murderers, who was known to be there. This demand was refused, when the Commander replied that at the expiration of a certain time, if the party were not delivered up, he would fire into the rancherie. The result of this communication was that the Indians, with houses, bag, and baggage, migrated inland out of the way before the commander could do anything to bring them to their senses. [117]

Once again, the British were demanding the surrender of an individual who was not in the village. This time, however, Lascelles did not order an attack on Comiaken and "the gunboat went off without doing anything further." [118] Probably acting under the advice of Smith and Tomo Antoine, who would have informed him that firing on one of the main Cowichan villages would considerably widen the conflict, Lascelles realized the futility of such tactics. Instead, he issued an ultimatum to the Cowichan to surrender the three suspects in the killing of William Brady. Through the interpreter Tomo Antoine, "Lascelles told the Indians before leaving that he would return in six days for the other rascals and if not forthcoming he would finish his work." [119]

The people fleeing Comiaken carried his message as they passed the village of Clemclemalits to the west. As a result, the people of Clemclemalits quickly abandoned their village as the *Forward* steamed out of Cowichan Bay.

> At a rancherie at Clemclemlets ... where upwards of 100 Indians were located, some kind of panic seized the inhabitants after the gunboat went off and they all, with two or three exceptions, left the place and have gone up the Cowichan river after the other tribes. [120]

That day Smith penned a hasty letter on a piece of *Topaze* stationary to Augustus Pemberton, the Commissioner of Police, to inform him of the status of the expedition including the first news of the fight at Lamalcha. The letter was apparently conveyed to Victoria by Jean Lemon, a former "French voyageur" of the Hudson's Bay Company who was married to a Cowichan woman and operated the

"Cowichan Hotel," a rough log shanty near the village of Clemclemalits.[121] Smith wrote:

> We have captured two Indians one of them assisted to murder Brady the other was in some way connected with both murders—Two others are in the mountains, we shall call here for them on our return the blind man is named Swan-ahya the other now at large with him is named Kaisuk—the two women are named Thask and Thostinah—The old woman Thask is in Victoria and can be taken by the police. She is the mother of one of the murderers—We found the Lamalchas fully prepared for us. They took most of their women and children and property into the woods. They were in a position naturally strong and had a large block house built of square logs and loop holed. After about an hour and a half heavy firing they fell back through the thick woods—We did not land as their marksmen could have killed nearly every man & we had one killed. We shall try to get the murderers ... We hear of other murders around these islands too—We have not yet found Brady's body—if you could point out the place on the map to Johny Lemion he will assist us on our return—At Saturna we found the boat and the garters one boot and a petticoat belonging to the girl—We hear the Lemalchas have another place stockaded.[122]

When the letter reached Victoria, Pemberton had it "forwarded for the information of His Excellency," who was by now in the Colony of British Columbia.[123] The letter contained the first news of the fight at Lamalcha, but it is interesting to note that there is no reference to Lamalcha involvement in the attacks on the Marks, only a reference to Gliddon's death with the comment "we shall try to get the murderers," in other words, the ones who shot the sailor. The contents of the letter were not shared with the press, which would not learn of the Battle of Lamalcha for four more days.

Lascelles postponed the *Forward*'s departure for Comox in order to spend one more day searching the small islands south of Salt Spring Island for the body of William Brady. On the morning of April 23rd the *Forward* proceeded from Cowichan Bay down Satellite Channel to Sxecoten (Portland Island), where shore-parties "landed and overhauled" the island for an hour, finding nothing.[124] The *Forward* then proceeded to Lo'le'cen (Moresby Island), where the British conducted a similar search without success.[125] They also searched "some smaller [islands] for the body of Brady but found no trace of it."[126]

The *Forward* was running low on coal, the prisoner Stalehum would not cooperate and Henley's written deposition on the location of Brady's body was "so very vague" that Lascelles decided to give up the search and proceed to Nanaimo for coal.[127] He was also mindful of his orders from the Governor to proceed to Comox "to give confidence to the settlers" and deliver their seed cargo. The *Forward* went to Mayne Island where Jack, the "Indian Interpreter" whose services were no longer required, was "discharged ... to the shore" at the hwulmuhw settlement inside Helen Point. The *Forward* continued into Miners' Bay and "communicated with [the] settlers." [128] The British checked to ensure the safety of the Marks family and unloaded the remnants of Christian Mayer's wrecked boat which had been on board the gunboat for almost three weeks. [129]

While the *Forward* lay at anchor, a hwulmuhw man, on the basis of secondhand information, identified Acheewun as the man responsible for the deaths of Marks and Harvey on Saturna Island, thus confirming British suspicions concerning Lamalcha involvement in the Marks killings. According to Smith, "an Indian in Plumper's Pass ... told me he had seen one Lamalcha Indian who was present at the murder of Mark's and his daughter. He said the Lamalcha Indian told him that a brave named Oh-chee-wan [Acheewun] shot Marks; the daughter then fled to some rocks close by where she was caught by another Indian of the same tribe who killed her while a squaw stabbed her—they stripped her—tied a piece of a stove to her hair and sank her in deep water." [130] Two days later, when Smith wrote to Pemberton from Nanaimo, he claimed that this information was verified by "an Indian belonging to the Penalcut [Penelakut] tribe some days after [who] gave me a description of the affair exactly corresponding with the above." [131]

Why the Cowichan at Miner's Bay and the Penelakut man at Nanaimo identified Acheewun and not Palluck as Mark's killer is not known, but it may have had something to do with inter-family feuds or, in the case of the people at Miner's Bay, anger directed at the Lamalcha in general for killing hwunitum and driving away Christian Mayer, their employer and source of trading goods, from his farm on Mayne Island. At any rate, the information gave belated justification for the British attack on Lamalcha.

Lascelles found Mrs. Marks living on Mayer's homestead "in great distress at the loss of her husband and daughter." [132] He promised her that upon his return he would take her and her children to Victoria. Leaving Active Pass, the *Forward* sighted the old Hudson's Bay Company steamer *Beaver,* which had been recently commissioned by the Royal Navy as a surveying vessel under the command of Lieutenant David Pender. After communicating, the two vessels proceeded together to Nanaimo." [133]

The two ships arrived in Nanaimo in the early evening of the 23rd, where the *Forward* remained for two days to coal and clean the ship.

On Saturday, the 25th of April, Smith wrote the following letter to Pemberton, his superior officer, containing the information from the hwulmuhw of Miner's Bay which alleged Lamalcha involvement in the death of Marks and Harvey. This letter contained the first reference to the man who killed Marks, whom the British believed was Acheewun, as having killed eleven hwunitum men. Smith connected the killing of Marks and Harvey with the Lamalcha resistance at Kuper Island, and underlined the threat that Acheewun posed to hwunitum settlement in the unceded territories.

> Since my last we have discovered that Marks was shot by Lamalcha Indians—the Chief who shot him is the terror of all the Indians around, he boasts that Marks is the eleventh white man he has murdered—The girl when her father was shot ran on to a higher rock and was there caught by an Indian and held while a squaw stabbed her—They then stripped her and after tying a piece of the stove to her hair they sank her in deep water—When the news went to Victoria it was reported that a gunboat would come up, and the Indians immediately made preparation. They intended to get a boat crew on shore if possible and then to kill every man, which they would certainly have done, had a boat been sent ashore—They are still there and boast they will fight again. Their place is very strong and they can only be dislodged by landing a strong force and driving them through the woods—We are now going to Comox and I trust on my return here to receive further instructions as to how I am to proceed—I shall be happy to do any kind of duty that may be required of me and I think there will [be] no safety for any one around these Islands unless that chief is taken dead or alive. [134]

The story about the Lamalcha planning an ambush for the boat's crew is suspicious, and suggests that Smith and Lascelles were already concocting an explanation for the tactics which took them by surprise at Lamalcha on April 20th.

Lascelles, on the same day, wrote a letter to his superior officer, Commodore Spencer, giving a brief account of events. He made no mention of his actions at Cowichan Bay, but devoted half the letter to the April 20th fight, where he did his best to downplay his defeat by masking both the duration and the extent of the battle. He wrote that "the firing lasted about half an hour when having thrown a few shells into the woods, and knocked the village down as much as possible I went over to Chemainos Bay for the night." Lascelles described the "very sharp fire of musketry on us ... by which I regret to say that one Boy Charles F. Gliddon was killed," then hastened to add that "we sustained no other injury" and, the following day "completed the destruction of the place." [135] But even in this positive light, the fact that there was no mention of the British taking the Lamalcha position, only that they "knocked the Village down, as much as possible," carried between the lines the admission of failure. As if to justify opening fire on the village without cause, Lascelles drew his superior officer's attention to the nature of the enemy, clearly drawn from the intelligence gathered by Smith: "This tribe called the Le Malcha [Lamalcha]," he wrote, "are the terror of the Coast, both to Indians and white men, and make a boast of the number of white men they have killed." [136]

Lascelles concluded with a brief outline of his plans for vengeance: "I propose starting to visit the Comox settlement tomorrow [Sunday, April 26th], and on my way back to Esquimalt to call again on Kuper Island and Cowitchan." [137]

Although he made no mention of it to Spencer, Lascelles was hoping to intercept reinforcements in the shape of the six-gun paddle-wheel sloop, HMS *Devastation*, under the command of Captain John Pike who had been engaged on a difficult campaign in the north against the illicit alcohol trade, and whose return to the south was imminent. [138]

Rumours of conflict in the unceded territories began to surface in Victoria by April 24th, when "a canoe filled with Indians from Comox" reported "that a squad of men from the gunboat *Forward* had landed at Cowichan and destroyed the Indian village." Another canoe "in which were several whitemen" arrived from Salt Spring Island and reported "that while encamped on a small island near Salt Spring ... they heard about 20 reports from cannon apparently about three miles distant." [139] News confirming the fight at Lamalcha reached the naval headquarters at Esquimalt that evening when "letters arrived from the *Forward*," but the information was not immediately shared with the press. [140]

Finally, on April 26th, the *Victoria Daily Chronicle* broke the news that "intelligence confirmatory of a paragraph published by us yesterday has reached town from Lieutenant Lascelles, commanding HM Gunboat *Forward*. The gunboat has had an engagement with a tribe of Indians inhabiting Kuper's Island off Somenos district, during which one marine was killed and another wounded." The report implied that the Lamalcha had fired first, whereupon "the *Forward* then opened fire with grape and canister on the village, killing six or seven natives and wounding a large number and completely destroying the buildings."

> No particulars can be given, but it is confidently believed that so terrible a lesson will be taught the redskinned rascals who have recently dyed their hands with the blood of white men, that the survivors will henceforth be less disposed to give rein to their blood thirsty propensities. [141]

Commenting on this information, Lieutenant Verney of the gunboat *Grappler* at Esquimalt wrote that "we have not yet heard all particulars; in the mean time I think it not improbable that I may be sent up to that neighbourhood: opinion is divided here as to whether this little brush will prove a wholesome lesson to these wretched savages, or whether it will lead to a general row and desire for retaliation ... With the very scanty information that has reached me, I do not know what view to take of the matter: I hear that the commodore thinks more lightly of it than the colonial government: it is not said that Lascelles acted either hastily or injudiciously." [142]

Nevertheless, Verney noted that "at any rate if this little affair leads to further hostilities I cannot but be thankful that the responsibility of firing the first shot has not fallen to me." [143]

The following day, April 27th, the *British Colonist* "received direct information from several sources of the circumstances attending the collision between the *Forward* and the Indians in the neighbourhood of Cowichan." [144] Under the bold headline, "BOMBARDMENT OF THE SAMALCHAS' RANCHERIA BY GUNBOAT FORWARD! SEVEN INDIANS AND A MAN-O-WARMAN KILLED!" The paper ran five versions of the fight in the order that they were received.

The fact that the Lamalcha families, according to custom, banded together only in self-defence to repel an unprovoked attack on their village was not recognized by the press until months later. As far as hwunitum were concerned, all Lamalcha were responsible for the attack on the Marks' family and, as evident by their armed resistance to the *Forward*, the press was quick to brand them all as "outlaws."

The views of the press were, of course, shared, and possibly to some degree influenced, by the colonial government. Governor Douglas, familiar with their reputation as fierce, proud sovereignists opposed to British rule, described the Lamalcha as a "nest of pirates and murderers" who "bear a very bad character." [145]

Statements by hwunitum settlers served to further criminalize the Lamalcha. A "highly intelligent settler" from the "Cowichan District" informed the *Evening Express* that:

> The band of desparadoes inhabiting the island, referred to, were the outcasts of all the various tribes along the coast, and were distinguished for their depraved habits and murdering propensities. They were leagued together on this spot for the purposes of plunder, and it is supposed they have been very successful in preying upon the property of persons with whom they were strong enough to cope. They were in possession of a large whaleboat and a plunger, sails and everything complete, which it is believed was taken by them in some piratical acts along our coast. [146]

Hwunitum were not alone in their desire to see Lamalcha individuals punished. As revealed in the following account from the *Victoria Daily Chronicle*, hwulmuhw factions had their own grievances against Lamalcha families and were eager to see the colonial government wage war on them.

> It is said that the Indians who have lately committed murders in this vicinity are men and women who have been expelled from their own tribes on account of bad conduct and who have banded together and rendezvous on Kuper Island for the purpose of committing depredations upon the property of whites and Indians alike. The chiefs of the Cowichan, Comox

and other tribes repudiate all responsibility for the recent outrages—say that the perpetrators are "none of theirs" and express the desire that the gunboat will "clean 'em out"—a desire that is re-echoed by more than one civilized person in this colony. [147]

Overlooked by the press was a brief report communicated to the *British Colonist* by a "French Canadian," which contained a revealing statement regarding the motives of the Lamalcha in their resistance to the *Forward*. The "French Canadian" stated "that the enraged Indians are vowing destruction to the Boston men for the nefarious liquor traffic carried on them among their tribes." [148] This brief statement suggests that the Lamalcha may have believed that the *Forward* had come to their village not because of the attack on the Marks, but to punish them for their attack on the liquor trading vessel the previous summer.

A day after news of the battle hit the Victoria papers, the steamer *Enterprise* "arrived from Nanaimo" and "brought confirmatory news of the bombardment of an Indian village on Kuper Island by the gunboat *Forward*." [149] The report stated that the Lamalcha fired first, that their village was destroyed and that eight of them were killed, contrary to fact. The information was very similar to the "letters" sent by Lascelles which arrived in Victoria on the 24th, and presumably originated from naval personnel onboard the *Forward* which was in Nanaimo at the same time as the *Enterprise*.

The report also contained the first graphic description of the death of Frederick Marks and his daughter Caroline, which confirmed the worst fears of the Hwunitum in Victoria concerning their disappearance. [150]

As well, the crew of the *Enterprise* identified the man who led the attack on the Marks, who by all accounts was the warrior Palluk, as "having killed eleven white persons within the past 4 years." Smith claimed that his sources identified the man as Acheewun. Even when it was discovered later that Palluk was the one who killed Marks and possibly Harvey and other hwunitum as well, Acheewun would continue to have the deaths of eleven hwunitum attributed to him. The confusing statements make it unclear who exactly was responsible for the high tally of hwunitum victims.

Following their flight to Salt Spring Island after the battle at Lamalcha, the seven or eight extended families dispersed to various other locations where they owned campsites or had relatives with whom they might seek refuge. According to one report, some of the families were "known to have landed to the north of Cowichan, and have gone up the river of that name. Others are scattered over the islands of the coast." [151] Some accompanied the si'em, Squ'acum, to an undisclosed location, possibly on the east coast of Vancouver Island. Acheewun, with his brother Shenasuluk, their mother, and four or more warriors and their families, may have been the party which one newspaper reported "fled to Galiano Island after the bombardment."[152] Acheewun owned a cave of refuge at Sumnuw (Montague Harbour) on Galiano, but if he did leave for the island he remained there only a short time before seeking shelter among the people of the Chemainus River, to whom he was related by marriage.

A man named Sarguck and his wife, Quolastenaht, sought refuge with relations at Penelakut on the northeast corner of Kuper Island, where they were joined by others in the ensuing weeks. The warrior, Tishtan, fled to Hwuy' (North Cove), a long narrow inlet at the north end of Thetis Island, where he dragged his two canoes ashore and hid them above a cliff.[153]

Others sought refuge at greater distances. One Lamalcha man hid amongst the Songhees people at Victoria, while three others, Sayeh, his wife Cheemulswaht, and their son Talleyok canoed across the Strait of Georgia to stay with relations at Musqueam on the the mouth of the Fraser River.[154] Other individuals sought safety with relatives in the Washington Territory.[155]

For some of the Lamalcha warriors, the dispersal was only temporary. A few days after the fight at Lamalcha, "several Indians came into Nanaimo in canoes" and boasted of their victory over the gunboat. They "asserted that the Cowichan tribe expressed themselves eager and willing to fight the tenass" [little] man of war, and "were quite confident of their own powers of resistance."[156] As Smith pointed out in his April 25th letter to Pemberton, some of them had already returned to Lamalcha, "and boast that they will fight again."[157]

At Cowichan, news of Squ'acum's victory over the gunboat at Lamalcha and reaction to Lascelles' threat of military retaliation fueled anger over the hwunitum occupation of Cowichan territory the previous summer. For a brief time the situation endangered the lives of hwunitum settlers, especially those living in the vicinity of the Cowichan villages of Somenos and Quamichan.

James Miller, "a settler at Cowichan" who left the area the week of April 26th, reported:

> ... that the Indians are in a great state of excitement swearing vengeance against the settlers and their families, five of whom are residing close to each other near his farm, combining together for mutual protection, men, women, and children. The settlement is about six miles inland ... and within 3/4 of a mile from them is one of the Indian rancheries, the wild yells from which strike terror into the hearts of all around the settlement.[158]

Cowichan anger was directed at certain hwunitum in the vicinity of Somenos (present-day Duncan), who were forced to flee their homesteads by canoeing down the Cowichan river.

Some settlers coming from the Somenos district were attacked with stones by the Indians, on their way down the river, and the men had to draw their revolvers to protect themselves. The Indians seeing this determination evinced, prudently retired. [159]

Despite this confrontation, and the fact that "the settlers in the outlying quarter have drawn together for mutual protection and defence should they be attacked," Miller felt that a general assault on hwunitum in the Cowichan Valley "was not likely to be the case at present." [160]

As it turned out, Cowichan response to the recent events was not uniform and varied from hostility to apathy, a reflection of the degree to which individual families and their relations were affected by events. [161]

The Cowichan informed the settlers that the unrest was the result of unresolved matters of jurisdiction and sovereignty. Hwunitum law did not apply until hwulmuhw land was sold by mutual agreement—a pledge made to the Cowichan by Douglas himself. According to information supplied by Miller:

> The settlers are told that the principal cause of the difficulty arises from the Government having broken its promises in regard to the payment for the land, and the belief is general that until they are paid the settlers can have no feeling of security. [162]

These reports raised fears among the hwunitum population of Victoria that the conflict would escalate without prompt action by the government. The *Daily Evening Express* called on the colonial regime to uphold its promise: "At present the urgent necessity of stationing an armed force at every rancherie for the protection of the lives and property of the settlers is undoubtedly called for. Now is the time to show the settlers that the government will protect them at all hazards." [163]

Governor Douglas was away in the Colony of British Columbia, and his temporary absence from Victoria made the situation seem particularly urgent, as an editorial in the *Daily Evening Express* revealed:

> The position in which the settlers at Cowichan are placed by the difficulties just now existing between the authorities and the Indians, is already assuming an appearance calculated to cause no slight anxiety to those who have friends in that section of the country. We have no desire to alarm, unnecessarily, our fellow-citizens, but we feel the necessity of pointing out the great importance that attaches itself to the next step taken by the Government towards enforcing the law against the tribe which has, by the recent resistance offered to the demands of the *Forward*, abetted the murderers whose crimes the Commander went to investigate. It is to

be much regretted that the Governor is temporarily absent from the Island in the present state of affairs, as a few days inaction for want of instructions may prove no small obstacle to the prompt suppression of the rebellion. [164]

Both the naval and civil authorities in Victoria ensured that Douglas was made aware of the crisis. Commodore Spencer informed the Admiralty that "copies of the correspondence received from this office as also from Lieutenant Lascelles have been forwarded for the information of His Excellency Governor Douglas who has been absent on an official visit to British Columbia and with whom I have been unable to communicate personally." [165] Pemberton, the Commissioner of Police, also forwarded Smith's correspondence "for the information of His Excellency the Governor." [166] When word of the crisis reached Douglas, he cut short his visit just north of Spuzzum, returning to Victoria on the evening of May 6th. [167]

In light of reports that the settlers in the Cowichan Valley were "combining together for mutual protection," the *Daily Evening Express* called on the colonial government to see whether or not they were supplied with proper arms and ammunition. The paper drew attention to an unused stand of fire-arms sent from England some years previous to equip a rifle company. Referring to these weapons:

> ... if the means of defence are not found to exist, let them at once place in the hands of the squatters some of the rifles and ammunition sent some time since from England for the use of the volunteer forces of the Colony. [168]

The newspaper suggested that the government issue "a proclamation calling for the enlistment of volunteers," arguing that "the very fact of an efficient armed force being concentrated at a place so near the district now troubled, would operate in a most favourable manner in making the Indian respect the superior prowess of the white man and form a most useful auxiliary to the navy should war become inevitable." [169] Governor Douglas, within a short time, acted upon this advice.

In Esquimalt, Commodore John Spencer forwarded Lascelles' report of hostilities to the Lord Commissioners of the Admiralty in London:

> ... by which it will be seen that he has succeeded in capturing two of the Indians suspected of being concerned in the outrage and that he had considered it necessary to fire into a Village belonging to the Lamalcha tribe, who it appears returned the fire, occasioning I regret to say, the loss of a first class Boy of the *Forward*. [170]

Spencer, following the "smear campaign" levelled against the Lamalcha by the colonial government and the press, informed the Admiralty that:

From all information that I have been able to gather respecting the above named Indians, they appear to consist of all the outcasts of all the different tribes on the Coast, and are in fact little better than a nest of Pirates. Kuper Island on which they have located themselves being admirably adapted from its situation for the purpose of capturing the numerous small Trading Vessels which are in the habit of passing through the inner passage up the Coast. [171]

Lieutenant Commander Charles Rufus Robson (left) and Lieutenant Commander the Hon. Horace Douglas Lascelles (right). Robson commanded the gunboat Forward *until his accidental death in 1861 after which Lascelles took command. Both officers flogged aboriginal captives aboard their vessels.* British Archives and Records Service, Photo HP 3819.

Lieutenant Edmund H. Verney commanded the gunboat Grappler *during the war against the Lamalcha. A prolific letter writer, Verney left detailed eyewitness accounts of episodes during the campaign, although he was noticeably silent regarding the physical abuse of Lamalcha captives.* British Columbia Archives and Records Service, Photo HP 71122.

Chapter Eight

Much Indebted to the Roman Catholic Bishop

A fter waiting in Nanaimo for over two days, far in excess of the time it took to coal, the *Forward* finally left on Sunday morning, April 26th, for Comox where she arrived in the late afternoon. [1] The British found all of the forty or so hwunitum settlers in the Comox Valley safe and hard at work ploughing, cultivating gardens and felling trees on the lands they occupied. The seed shipment was delivered. The gunboat then sat in Comox Harbour for three days, as one volunteer acerbically put it, "without affecting anything." [2] Evidently Lascelles was waiting to intercept the *Devastation*, under the command of John William Pike, which was on its way down from the north, thereby gaining reinforcements as well as direction from a senior officer. On the 27th, 28th and 29th, the men were employed at routine tasks and drilling for combat. [3] Alternatively there were other reasons for the gunboat commander's three-day layover at Comox, which may have had more to do with his state of mind. In contrast to previous situations, in which Lascelles acted on his own initiative quickly and decisively against hwulmuhw opponents, his indecisive behaviour following the fight of April 20th suggests that he was partially traumatized at being beaten by an aboriginal enemy, and unsure of what further action to take.

At Esquimalt, upon receipt of Lascelles' April 25th "Letter of Proceedings," Commodore Spencer "immediately directed Lieutenant Commander E.H. Verney to proceed with the *Grappler* to place himself under the orders of Lieutenant Lascelles." Spencer included "further instructions for *Forward* not to employ force with the other Tribes if it could possibly be avoided." [4] The Commodore, committed now to hostilities with the Lamalcha, and possibly aware of Lascelles' ultimatum to the Cowichan, did not wish his impetuous subordinate to broaden the conflict.

Spencer displayed typical Victorian military arrogance and disdain for the fighting capabilities of the aboriginal people, seeing little reason to be concerned with the military threat posed by "a nest of pirates." [5] "From what the Commodore says," wrote Verney, "he evidently expects that there will be no more fighting." Nevertheless, the *Grappler* "filled up with ammunition," and Spencer sent along

"Dr. Turnbull, Assistant Surgeon of Her Majesty's ship *Topaze,* in the event of any medical assistance being required."[6]

The *Grappler* had been scheduled to have new boilers installed, and Verney was worried that this would "be a reason for my being kept in the background." He convinced himself and Spencer that "the old boilers however are not so bad but what they could be made to work for another six months."[7] Commenting on the imminent departure of the *Grappler* "for the seat of war," the *Victoria Daily Chronicle* reported that "the authorities express an intention to mete out a terrible punishment to the redskins."[8]

The *Grappler* left Esquimalt on the morning of April 28th, "well supplied with ammunition," and arrived at Cowichan Bay by mid-morning.[9] Reporting on its departure, the *Daily Evening Express* commented that "it was probable, however, that offensive operations will not be resumed until the *Devastation* has arrived, from which vessel the requisite force of sailors and marines, to act with advantage ashore, might be landed."[10]

The arrival of the *Grappler* in Cowichan Bay calmed the fears of hwunitum settlers and helped subdue overt hostility towards them by Cowichan factions. The schooner *Victoria Packet* left Salt Spring Island the same day and, upon its arrival in Victoria, reported that "the *Grappler* was lying off Cowichan but no further fighting had taken place."[10] The schooner's master, Edward Walker, added that on Salt Spring Island "relations existing between the Indians and the settlers were peaceable with the exception of some threats which the former were making of, there was nothing occurring to excite any very serious apprehensions of further outrage by them."[11]

Despite this reassurance, continuing reports of unrest among the hwulmuhw population, further details of the fight at Lamalcha, and the unexplained departure of the *Forward* from the "theatre of war" prompted the first public criticism of Lieutenant Commander Lascelles. The *Daily Evening Express*, unaware of Lascelles' orders to proceed to Comox, viewed the departure of the *Forward* from Cowichan as abandoning the settlers and leaving them vulnerable to attack. The editors began to question what they perceived to be the inexplicable actions of the gunboat and its commander.

> There is some cause for gratulation in the thought that long ere this [April 30th] the *Grappler* has been at hand to afford protection to the settlers in the district above mentioned, and, if found necessary, to remove them to a place of security. We can hardly, however, understand the policy of the commander of the *Forward* in leaving the settlers unprotected to the mercy of a race, characteristic for their vindictive malignity and smarting under the loss of their houses and property. It may be that the *Forward*

has gone in search of HMS *Devastation*, but this excuse can hardly palliate the act of deserting the settlers when such danger was at hand." [12]

The paper continued its criticism of Lascelles when an unidentified settler from Cowichan accused Lascelles of making a strategic error when he failed to confiscate or destroy the canoes and boats belonging to the Lamalcha which enabled them to make their escape:

> It is thought very strange and unaccountable that the Commander of the *Forward* left the Island after the suspension of hostilities, without taking the boats and canoes with him or sinking them before he took his departure. So far as we can judge, the failure of the whole expedition up to the present time is the result of this important omission. Upon this island were concentrated all the most desperate characters, as we have stated, of the Indian tribes, and the murderers, as it is believed, of our settlers. What an opportunity one would have imagined, for bringing them to justice, and punishing them with a heavy hand their deeds of blood! But the opportunity, once lost, will be hard to repair; and the services of large detachments of troops will be required to follow up the fugitives who, after the gunboat left, made their escape by means of their boats and canoes, carrying everything they had with them. [13]

These criticisms, and more to follow, were not to go unnoticed by Lascelles who, at the earliest opportunity, would exact a bizarre revenge on the editors of the *Daily Evening Express*.

The *Grappler* remained at Cowichan for only an hour before continuing to Nanaimo where "we found the *Devastation* with the bishop on board." [14] Perhaps on account of low-lying fog the HMS *Devastation*, after a month-long policing action against the alcohol trade on the north coast, had steamed down the Strait of Georgia past Comox Harbour where the *Forward* sat waiting to intercept her.

The following day, April 29th, the *Grappler* "started at six for Port Augusta [Comox], where we arrived at about two and found the *Forward*." [15] In accordance with Commodore Spencer's orders, Verney reluctantly placed himself under Lascelles' command, and both gunboats left Comox at 8:10 a.m. the following day. [16] The *Grappler*, plagued by defective boilers, soon fell behind the *Forward* which reached Nanaimo to rendezvous at last with the *Devastation*. [17] An hour later, the *Grappler* limped into the anchorage.

Having "completed coal," the *Devastation* left Nanaimo on May 1st for Esquimalt. [18] Reporting its arrival, the *Daily Evening Express* noted that:

> There had been no further hostilities between the naval forces and the red-skinned warriors, but it was not improbable a combined attack would

soon be made on the settlements of the tribe which has offered such resistance to the laws of the country.[19]

The "combined attack" alluded to by the newspaper report was a plan by Lieutenant Lascelles for a pre-dawn assault on Lamalcha by the *Forward* and the *Grappler*. Commander Pike of the *Devastation* reported that both gunboats had "anchored at Nanaimo to complete coal, and from whence Lieut. Lascelles informed me they will proceed at once to Kuper Island."[20]

Before they left for Comox on the 26th, Lascelles and Smith had been informed that the Lamalcha had re-occupied their fortified village, and were boasting that "they will fight again."[21] Lascelles anticipated avenging his recent defeat as the *Forward* took on board another eight tons of coal. He planned to leave Nanaimo early in the morning of May 2nd "with the intention of surprising the Lamalcha Indians by daylight" and attacking them with the combined firepower of the *Forward* and the *Grappler*.[22]

Leaving Nanaimo at 1:30 a.m. under "a bright moon," the gunboats "reached Kuper Island at about five." Verney describes the pre-dawn assault of May 2nd:

> We steamed into the little bay in front of the village in the morning, at quarters with all our hammocks and bags stowed round the gunwales as protection against musketry, fully expecting that the Indians would have made some resistance.[23]

To their disappointment, or relief, the British discovered "that the Indians had abandoned their village taking with them all their traps."[24] Lamalcha, "the lookout place," was aptly named. If any Lamalcha were present at the village, they knew of the approaching steam-driven gunboats long in advance, especially on a moonlit night over the calm waters of the Gulf Islands.

The British were fortunate that the Lamalcha were not present in force. Upon entering the shallow bay, "the *Forward* got on shore, and did not get off until about 2 p.m." with the incoming tide.[25] Had the Lamalcha warriors made plans to resist, the crew of the *Forward*, stranded close to shore on their vessel, would have made easy targets and the British might well have suffered a second defeat.

Seeing that the village was deserted except for "a large number of dogs," Lascelles allowed a small landing party, consisting of Smith, Captain Bazalgette of the Royal Marines, Tomo Antoine, and four other men, to go ashore and "set fire to [the] Indian Village."[26] For the first time, the British were able to examine closely the nature of the Lamalcha defences. "We found on landing," Lascelles noted, "everything prepared for resisting an armed force."[27]

> The village, which consisted of seven large lodges, contained a population of about 100, and was strongly fortified. In front of the lodges was a block-

house, about eight feet in height, constructed of morticed logs with loopholes fronting on two sides with numerous rifle pits and trenches sunk around it. A solid shot, which had been fired from the gunboat during the bombardment, was picked up inside the blockhouse. It had passed through one wall, but had rebounded on striking the second.[28]

After they examined the fortifications, "the lodges were fired and burned."[29] The shore-party also found and burned "a few canoes."[30] Lascelles could now truthfully report that "the place is completely destroyed."[31] Some Lamalcha families may have watched from the surrounding forest as the British destroyed their houses and canoes. When the gunboats left, the people once more re-occupied their ground.

With the houses of Lamalcha burning behind them, the *Forward* and the *Grappler* left Lamalcha Bay in the early afternoon and proceeded to Ganges Harbour on Salt Spring Island. Lascelles "communicated with [the] settlers," and both gunboats anchored for the night.[32] The *Grappler*, always prone to mechanical failures, "required some slight repair to her boilers."[33]

The following morning, Sunday, May 3rd, the *Forward* left the *Grappler*, which was still under repair, and proceeded to Bedwell Harbour, Pender Island, "to find the body of the man Brady which one of the prisoners volunteered to show us."[34] Stalehum, after two weeks of captivity in the cramped hold of the *Forward* in which he was subjected to the verbal and physical abuse of the crew, was finally compelled to "volunteer" his assistance.

That same morning, the *Devastation* left Esquimalt with orders from Commodore Spencer "to proceed to Cowichan with a view of displaying more force in order to give confidence to the Settlers in the neighbourhood, who appear to be greatly alarmed by the warlike attitude of the Indians, and at the same time endeavour by peaceable means to induce the Chief to give up the other suspected Indians."[35] It is unclear which "Chief" Spencer was referring to—the father of the prisoner Stalehum, whose other son was Thalaston, both of whom took part in the Brady killing, or Jean Baptiste Glasetatum, the si'em recognized as the paramount chief by the Catholic Mission. Regardless, Pike, "a most vigilant, active, prudent, zealous officer," was eager to comply with the Commodore's orders.[36]

The *Forward*, after leaving the anchorage at Ganges Harbour, passed the south end of Salt Spring Island, where shortly after 10:00 a.m. she sighted the *Devastation* approaching from the south across a broad expanse of water.[37] According to Pike:

Off Pender Island I fell in with HMS *Forward*, and hearing from Lieutenant and Commander Lascelles that he was in search of the body of one of the men murdered by Indians on the 4th of April last I accompanied him into Bedwell Harbour. [38]

The two vessels arrived at the mouth of Bedwell Harbour where the *Devastation* stopped and Pike went on board the *Forward*. The *Forward* then steamed into Bedwell Harbour and at noon a shore party was detached to begin the search for Brady's body. The *Forward* dropped anchor a half hour later. [39]

Boats were lowered and "the Indian 'Stealum' [Stalehum] directed us to the spot where the murder had been committed." [40] As Pike later wrote, "there at the head of the harbour in a spot marked Shark Cove was found the body of Brady laying in the position in which he died." [41] Verney, who accompanied the landing party, was struck by the contrast between the physical beauty of the place and the horror of Brady's corpse which, after a month of exposure, was in "a sickening state of decomposition." [42]

> In the most retired, secluded, romantic spot, under a spreading cedar lay the putrefied body of poor Brady: it was a sight to make the most careless look grave: nothing had been touched since Henlee had left: the corpse was covered over with blankets, the caps of two Indians were lying near, where they dropped them in their hurry to escape, and it was the sort of lovely retired spot that one would select for quiet meditation and never suspect would be the scene of violence. [43]

Another eye-witness made the point that "no whiskey was found in the camp," which suggests that the British were still suspicious of Brady and Henley's activities up to April 4th. [44]

The identity of the body had to be established, but it was so "very much decomposed" that the Assistant Surgeon Turnbull "could scarcely tell where the ball took effect but that the trousers showed a hole in the thigh, and from paper and other things found on the spot there was no doubt that it was the body of Brady." [45] The British took what they deemed necessary to identify the body: a boot, a coat, and two caps which belonged to the assailants. Finally, "Lieutenant Lascelles caused the remains to be interred." [46]

All the officers from the two naval vessels "landed and inspected the place." [47] Making a short reconnaissance of the area, they discovered a refuge "where the Indians had concealed themselves nearby." [48]

The shore-party returned to the *Forward* by 1:15 p.m., and within half an hour Pike was back on board the *Devastation*. [49] As senior officer, Pike decided that the force would go to Cowichan Bay to apprehend the other Quamichan people involved in the attack on Brady and Henley. Pike directed the two gunboats to rendezvous with the *Devastation* at Cowichan Bay, whereupon he left for that destination.[50] The *Forward* proceeded to Salt Spring Island to return Lieutenant Verney to his ship, which was still under repair at Ganges Harbour. The *Forward* then continued on to Cowichan Bay, where Lascelles placed himself under the orders of Commander Pike.[51] Back at Ganges Harbour, repairs to the *Grappler's* boilers were soon complete and Verney planned to rendezvous with the other vessels early the next morning.

Earlier that day, while the British searched for Brady's corpse, the Roman Catholic Bishop Modeste Demers celebrated Mass in the log church of St. Anne's. Bishop Demers had made plans to leave Cowichan for Victoria the week of April 26th, "but the Indians were so alarmed at the presence of the gunboats that they refused to allow him to leave actually taking his canoe out of the water to prevent his leaving."[52] Because of his success in resolving the feud between the Comiaken and Quamichan during the winter, the people now called upon him to negotiate a similar resolution between the Quamichan and the hwunitum.

Demers had already "volunteered his services to persuade the Cowitchin Indians to give up the suspected men," and during his sermon to the packed congregation, acted upon that offer.[53] Everyone was aware of the ultimatum, given by the Commander of the *Forward* twelve days previously, to deliver the persons responsible for the killing of William Brady or suffer the destruction of their homes and property. Bishop Demers, "when addressing the assembled Indians at Public worship on Sunday ... pointed out to them that in order the innocent might not suffer with the guilty, it was their duty to aid the authorities in handing over the culprits to the officers of the law."[54] The Bishop made a convincing argument— "few were they who could remain insensible to his forceful eloquence and burning zeal."[55]

The arrival of the *Devastation* with its churning paddle-wheels, accompanied by the *Forward*, in Cowichan Bay late that afternoon, added substance to the Bishop's sermon. Towards evening, Lascelles gave Tomo Antoine an important task and "sent his interpreter up the river to demand the surrender of two murderers."[56]

The following morning, Monday, May 4th, the *Devastation* and the *Forward* were joined by the *Grappler* which arrived from Salt Spring Island.[57] The three vessels, manned by three hundred sailors and marines and carrying twenty-four cannon, made up the most powerful naval force ever seen in Cowichan Bay.

That same morning, following Antoine's preliminary negotiations of the night before, Superintendent Smith and Tomo Antoine left the flotilla in a gig with a crew of four sailors and proceeded up the Cowichan River to the village of Quamichan:

> ... where [they] found the Indians encamped in large numbers. They did not attempt to deny that the murders had been committed by their relations: acknowledged the propriety of bringing them to justice, and

offered to surrender the guilty parties after having a talk with Bishop Demers.

> The chiefs then brought four prisoners down the river to Bishop Demers, but at the last moment, with characteristic vacillation, did not like to let them go. [58]

One reason for the last minute reluctance to surrender Thalaston, Oalatza, and Stalehum's mother Thask, was that the si'em had been under the impression that only one individual would be surrendered—according to hwulmuhw law. The British, after all, had acknowledged this law in 1853 and 1856 during similar disputes where hwunitum had been killed or seriously wounded.The si'em:

> ... had previously been willing to give up one of the murderers, arguing that as only one white man had been killed by them, it was fair to kill only one Indian in return. Mr. Smith told them that if three white men killed one Indian, we would hang all three, and therefore required the same from them. [59]

Smith and his shore party returned to the *Devastation* while the Cowichan conferred with the Bishop. According to Verney, "all the morning was spent in saying masses for them, and it was agreed that a flag should be hoisted as soon as the two men were ready, that a boat might be sent for them." The British commander grew impatient at the delay and "about two o'clock, Captain Pike pulled away towards the river in his boat, with the inspector of police." Verney describes what happened next:

> ... shortly afterwards the flag was hoisted, and Lascelles and I started off in my gig: when we reached the priest's house, we found a large body of Indians assembled, perhaps a couple of hundred: through the interpreter they asked all sorts of questions, and seemed desirous of prolonging the discussion as much as possible: what particularly puzzled them was that they could not understand why four Indians were to be hung when only one white man had been killed: the oldest men said that ever since they could remember it had been considered fair and just that if they killed a man of another tribe, one of their own must suffer, but we were not content with that. At last Captain Pike was tired of waiting: the Indians wanted to deliver up the prisoners the next day, so he walked down to his boat ... telling the Indians that as they would not give up the murderers they would bring trouble on the whole tribe.

> Lascelles remained behind with the inspector of police, two of the *Devastation*'s men with revolvers under their frocks, and myself, and my boat's crew armed with stretchers, waiting behind some bushes at the foot of the hill, in case I called them.

In the mean time we explained to the chiefs that we must have the murderers at once, and while we were making hasty arrangements to take them by force, of a sudden the assembly opened, and down a lane formed in their midst, marched the two villains, with every possible sign of majestic, dignified, self-importance, charmed at the sensation and excitement they were producing.

First they adjoined to their lodge where each was fitted out with a new blanket, and a new pair of socks, and many of their friends emptied out their little collections of treasures to give them parting presents. [60]

At this point, according to another witness, "Superintendent Smith stepped forward and arrested them, and was permitted to hand them over to the custody of the blue-jackets without resistance." [61]

Verney records the departure of Thalaston, Oalatza and Thask from Comiaken: "At last amid the howling of the women, the sobbing of their friends, and the farewell salutations of the whole tribe they embarked in my boat and we took them on board the *Forward*." [62]

Commander Pike claimed that the prisoners "were delivered over to Mr. Smith's custody without any coercive measures having been necessary." [63] Pike "was not prepared to take offensive measures for lack of orders," but the presence of three naval vessels in Cowichan Bay, and his statement to the Cowichan that if they did not surrender the "murderers" it "would bring trouble on the whole tribe," at the very least implied the threat of violence. [64] While negotiations for the surrender of the hwulmuhw were under way, Pike, on board the *Devastation*, exercised the ship's marine contingent "at Rifle drill firing at a target" as well as exercising the "First and Second Captains of Guns at shot practice with 6 [pounder]." The thirty-two-pound Armstrong gun also fired two live rounds at unspecified targets. [65]

While the military threat posed by the British was not insignificant, according to all accounts it was Bishop Modeste Demers who effected the surrender. As Verney noted: "We are very much indebted to the Roman Catholic Bishop for his efforts to persuade the Indians to give up the culprits. I do not think we should have got them but for him." [66]

After the Quamichan were surrendered to the British, there was one final misunderstanding which caused "great commotion and talking among the tribes." [67] A major condition of the surrender was that Thalaston and Oalatsa be hanged in the presence of the people as was done to Tathlasut in 1856. According to Verney, "their chief request was that they might be hung on the marshes at the river's mouth, in presence of all the neighbouring tribes, and not at Victoria." [68] It was rumoured that during the negotiations, Bishop Demers had secured this condition and "stipulated that they were to be taken up to Cowichan to be hanged." [69]

Not all the suspects in the attack on William Brady and John Henley were surrendered that day. Thostinah, "a girl they call the good looking squaw" who was the wife of Thalaston, was "somewhere up the river at Quamichan." [70] Thostinah later surrendered to the hwunitum settler, John Humphreys, and confined herself to his house but she was never taken into custody by the colonial authorities.

Cowichan people were questioned concerning the motive for the attack on Brady and Henley and whether or not the two men were involved in the liquor trade. They replied that "Brady and his mate were not whiskey sellers," and stressed that he "was a hunter and did not deal in whiskey." Their remarks left the British "uncertain whether the murderers perpetrated their crimes for the sake of plunder exclusively, or with the view of obtaining the reputation of 'braves.'" [71] The British, of course, would refuse to believe that Brady was killed because of his cooking.

Early Tuesday morning, on May 5th, the *Forward,* "having been directed by Commander Pike to proceed to Victoria with the persons captured in charge of the Superintendent of Police," left Cowichan Bay. [72] Bishop Demers was also on board. The *Forward* proceeded first to Miner's Bay on Mayne Island, where they took aboard Caroline Marks and her five children who were "nearly destitute of food and clothing." [73] Leaving Miner's Bay, the *Forward* arrived in Victoria Harbour in the afternoon, where the Marks family was landed under the care of Bishop Demers. [74] The gunboat also "landed the five prisoners and turned them over to the Civil power." [75] The *Forward* then proceeded to Esquimalt where she arrived at six o'clock.

The prisoners were marched to the Police Barracks "situated inconveniently near the main street." [76] The castle-like brick building housed "the Court rooms and offices of the Police Commissioner, chamber of the Government Assessor and Sheriff, rooms belonging to the police force, the cells of prisoners and a prison yard." [77] Hwulmuhw, using the Chinook jargon, called it the "Skookum House." [78] The names and the charges against the prisoners were entered in the Gaolers' charge book: "Kaisue alias Thalaston, Swane a hya alias Oalatze, Stalehum" and "Thask, a woman" were "charged with the murder of William Brady on Pender Island" and "with shooting at John Henley with intent to kill him." Whisk, the Lamalcha man, was not charged but held "on suspicion of being concerned in the murder of Christian [sic] Marks and his daughter on Saturna Island." [79] All five prisoners were remanded by Pemberton until the following Monday, after which they were "lodged in jail." [80]

That evening, at Esquimalt, Lascelles wrote up his letter of proceedings, reporting the movements of HM Gunboat *Forward* since leaving Nanaimo on April

26th, praising Superintendent Horace Smith and Bishop Modeste Demers for their part in the success of the recent expedition: "Before concluding," he wrote, "I beg to inform you of the great service Mr. Smith the Superintendent of Police has been to me during the whole time we have been employed in this service, and also of the great assistance that was given by Bishop Demers who volunteered his services to persuade the Cowitchen Indians to give up the suspected men, and owing to the great influence he has, I am convinced was mainly influential in enabling us to arrest them."[81]

His comments regarding the role of the Roman Catholic Bishop were echoed the following day in the pages of the *British Colonist*:

> All the accounts received give confirmation to the fact that it was mainly owing to the spiritual and moral influence which the worthy Bishop exercises over the tribes in that neighbourhood, amongst whom he is held in universal respect, that the Indian murderers were surrendered, and further disturbance happily averted.[82]

For the next few days the Victoria newspapers reported to the public, for the first time, eye-witness accounts of the discovery of the site where the Marks had been killed, the allegations by the Cowichan people of Mayne Island that Lamalcha people were responsible for their deaths, the battle of Lamalcha, the destruction of the village, the discovery of Brady's body and the capture of his killers.

A comparison of the information in the newspaper accounts with the log of the *Forward* and the letters written by the Superintendent of Police during the expedition reveals that whoever relayed the account to the press deliberately distorted the sequence of events leading up to the battle of Lamalcha by claiming that the British learned of Lamalcha complicity in the attack on Marks and Harvey prior to the attack on the village, thereby exonerating their action. For example, the article in the *Victoria Daily Chronicle* began with a description of the discovery of the "crime site" on the beach at Saturna Island on April 16th, followed by the subsequent information:

> After leaving Saturna Island the gunboat proceeded to Plumper Pass, where they were told that the Lamalchas Indians had boasted that they crawled over the ledge and fired upon Marks and Mrs. Harvey while they were seated at the campfire.[83]

In fact, as the April 16th entry in the log of the *Forward* shows, the gunboat did not proceed to Plumper Pass (Active Pass) on that date at all, but continued on to the British camp on San Juan Island. A hwulmuhw man from Plumper Pass eventually did furnish the British with allegations of Lamalcha involvement in the attack, but this information was provided on April 23rd, when the *Forward* returned to Miner's Bay, three days after the battle of Lamalcha.[84]

As the newspapers pointed out, there was unfinished business: "There are supposed to be one more concerned in Brady's murder, and six or eight more in the murder of Mr. Marks and his daughter, including the woman who stabbed the girl. Great hopes are entertained of securing more of the guilty parties." [85] The *British Colonist* reminded its readers that "the 'Great Lamalcha Brave,' who has not yet been caught, boasts that Mr. Marks is the eleventh white man he has killed." [86]

On May 8th, Pemberton asked Horace Smith to clarify the information alleging Lamalcha involvement in the deaths of Harvey and Marks in his April 25th letter from Nanaimo in order that it might be forwarded to the Colonial Executive. Smith wrote: "In reference to my former report wherein I stated 'it was rumoured that the Lamalcha Indians murdered Marks and his daughter' I beg to say: That information I received first from an Indian in Plumper Pass, who told me he had seen one Lamalcha Indian who was present at the murder of Marks and his daughter." Smith then related the information already quoted regarding the alleged manner in which Marks and his daughter were killed and concluded by stating that "an Indian belonging to the Penalicut tribe some days after gave me a description of the affair exactly corresponding with the above." [87]

Although some of his actions had been criticized by one newspaper, the successful capture of those responsible for the death of William Brady made heroes of Lieutenant Commander Horace Lascelles and the other naval officers. Governor Douglas communicated to Commodore Spencer that he was "much gratified that the capture of the murderers of William Brady has been affected without bloodshed and I request you will be good enough to convey to Commander Pike and Lieutenant Lascelles my best thanks for the judicious manner in which they executed the service entrusted to them, and for the effective assistance they afforded the Civil Power." [88]

On May 6th, the day after the *Forward* arrived in Victoria with the Quamichan prisoners, Commodore Spencer instructed Lascelles to proceed "to San Juan Island to convey Clothing and Provisions to the Detachment of Marines landed there, and then to Cowitchin to relieve the *Devastation*." [89] The following morning, when the *Forward* steamed out of Esquimalt towards Victoria Harbour, there was an exceptionally low tide which left the channel between Hospital [Songhees] Point and St. Ours Wharf "fordable for a considerable distance." Trying to negotiate the shallow passage, "the *Forward* ran aground in the Outer Harbour while endevouring to enter but floated off soon after," finally departing for San Juan by 1 p.m. Commenting on this slight mishap, the *British Colonist* hoped that "upon her return … she will be ordered immediately to resume the search for Indian murderers." [90]

At Cowichan Bay, Captain Pike impatiently awaited the return of the *Forward* with seine fishing, shore reconnaissance, and rifle and gunnery practice. The daily racket of rifle-fire and the roar of the cannon echoed throughout the district as an intimidating reminder of British naval power. [91]

The villages of Clemclemalits, Comiaken, Khinepsen and other Cowichan settlements near the coast were, for the most part, deserted. According to information supplied by one of the settlers, "the Indians who were all located in the immediate vicinity of the coast when the gunboats visited the district have since all made their way into the bush." [92] Samuel Harris, the self-appointed constable, reported that most of the Cowichan "were absent fishing and planting potatoes." As an indication of hwulmuhw belief in his authority, Harris had "in his possession one hundred pairs of blankets deposited with him by the chiefs as security for the good behaviour of the tribe." [93]

Taking advantage of the absence of the majority of the Cowichan, and to ensure the safety of the hwunitum settlers, Pike made a short reconnaissance up the Cowichan River in a ship's boat: "I took the opportunity," he wrote, "to visit the settlements up the Cowitchin River. The settlers appear to be free from uneasiness or fear of the Indians, all of whom as far as I could judge seem very well-desposed." [94]

Verney made his own reconnaissance and found the Cowichan "on the whole, very peaceable, and well-desposed towards the settlers, who treat them with every kindness." [95] Both officers commented in their official dispatches on Cowichan grievances that promises made the previous summer by Governor Douglas had not been kept. Pike detected that "some soreness of feeling seems to have arisen among them from the fact of the compensation promised them, for certain lands not having yet been paid them." [96]

Verney repeated the concerns of his senior officer in stronger language, which drew the ire of the Commodore. Verney found a "general contentment of the settlers" but they complained to Verney that the colonial government had not dealt fairly with the Cowichan people over the question of land title extinguishment.

> The only cause of complaint, and it appears to be a just one, is that the Governor has not yet paid the Indians for the land according to his promise; when they are hindered by the farmers from cutting down trees, or establishing themselves on new potato patches they plead the non-fulfillment of the Governor's promise and an affair of this nature might at any time lead to a serious disturbance. [97]

Pike had expected the *Forward* to return to Cowichan Bay by May 6th, and he grew increasingly impatient. Unaware that Commodore Spencer had ordered the gunboat to San Juan, Pike saw no reason to remain in the district. The British naval occupation of Cowichan Bay had succeeded in stopping threats of violence against hwunitum settlers, who now occupied their chosen plots of land with the aid of Britain's Royal Navy. Pike found it impossible to keep up with the whereabouts of the different Lamalcha families, and no hwulmuhw allies had volunteered to assist the British in locating them. Pike found himself unsure of what further action to take. He wrote:

> Lieutenant Lascelles had before my arrival destroyed the village of the piratical tribe who perpetrated the murder on Saturna Island, and since that they have been wandering about the Islands and I have been unable to ascertain their whereabouts, and I have abstained from undertaking any measures, being of opinion that none but the strongest will have any effect or produce any result. [98]

"Feeling our presence at Cowichen not being any longer necessary for the protection of the settlers" and "tired of waiting for the *Forward*" the *Devastation* left Cowichan Bay on the morning of May 8th for Esquimalt. [99]

Before leaving Cowichan Bay, Pike instructed Lieutenant Commander Verney of the *Grappler* to "remain for the three ensuing days, at the anchorage for the protection of the settlers, and at daylight on Monday morning next (should you receive no contrary orders from the Commodore & Senior Officer) proceed to New Westminster to replace the Buoys displaced from the Channel at the entrance of Frazer River." After performing this task, the *Grappler* was to return to Esquimalt after "visiting the Eastern Settlements on your way back." [100]

When the *Devastation* returned to Esquimalt, the *British Colonist* reported that, in light of the capture of the Quamichan "murderers" and the naval occupation of Cowichan Bay, "the Indians generally appear greatly cowed and manifest a decided disposition to give the gunboats a wide berth." [101] This was confirmed the following day when the sloop *Louise*, under Captain Thorne, arrived from Cowichan with information that:

> Affairs are quiet in the district. The Indians, overawed by the presence of the gunboats, have subsided into a state of quiescence. The *Grappler* lies at anchor in the bay, ready for action at a moment's notice. [102]

Despite the apparent pacification of the Cowichan, reports of Lamalcha defiance and threats against hwunitum settlers continued in the "Chemainus District," north of Cowichan. At least one hwunitum settler was of the opinion:

> ... that the government must follow up this matter until the murderers are handed over, and the punishment which they deserve meted out to them, otherwise there will be an end to the progress in improvement which the various settlements give good evidence of. [103]

In contrast to the extensive coverage of the inter-racial conflict by the Vancouver Island newspapers, the New Westminster press in the neighbouring Colony of British Columbia paid little attention to the events taking place across the Gulf of Georgia. Far removed from first-hand accounts of the incident, the New Westminster newspapers relied on the reports as they appeared in the Victoria newspapers. This situation changed when John Robson, the editor of The *British Columbian* and no friend of Governor Douglas, published a scathing editorial against the policies of Douglas and his administration. The *British Columbian* admonished the Victoria press for frightening away potential immigrants through what it believed to be sensationalized coverage of the "Indian War." Robson went so far as to suggest that the Victoria press was exaggerating the nature of the conflict in an attempt to enhance the prestige of the Governor in the offices of the Colonial Secretary in London. Robson blamed the current trouble on the failure of the Douglas administration to address hwulmuhw grievances relating to the alienation of their traditional territories and the illegal trade in alcohol.

> The murders recently committed by a few kultus (bad) Indians in the Gulf, and the circumstances connected with subsequent proceedings, have been invested with all the importance of an "INDIAN WAR" by Victoria sensation journals. We are treated to voluminous accounts of a terrible engagement between H.M. Gunboat and a number of Indians, who, having erected a regular stockade, fought like "devils." We have column after column containing "thrilling accounts" of these proceedings in which many Indians are killed and wounded. Indeed some of these accounts read very much like a chapter of the American war news vamped up to suit the occasion. And, strikingly like the sensational accounts we are sickened with from the States, when the smoke and clamour have subsided it turns out that nobody was killed —nobody hurt, at least on the side of the red-skinned enemy.

> Whatever motive has impelled the Victoria press to adopt such a course it is a most unwise one, and admirably calculated to injure the country abroad and deter immigrants from coming to these Colonies. People from the older countries are not very likely to seek a home in a Colony where such "thrilling" scenes are being enacted. We could understand a journalist depicting such incidents in as moderate language as would at all consist with truth. But what could induce an opposite course, to such an extreme, too, as to display the most wanton disregard of truth, is a puzzler indeed.

> There is just one motive we can suggest as being the possible cause of all this insane ado about nothing; and that is a desire to perpetuate if possible the rule of Mr. Douglas. It is very well known that his supposed

control over the aborigines of these Colonies had much to do with his appointment as well as with his retention in office till now. He and his personal friends succeeded to a charm in making the impression at home that he possessed a most extraordinary influence over the various tribes which inhabit these Colonies. The "fogies" in the Colonial office were made to believe that at a wag of his finger he could raise 80,000 red-skin warriors, and with as little difficulty could reduce them to quiet and inoffensive citizens; and with their terrible East India experience yet fresh, it was little wonder that a Government at all times most solicitous to avoid Indian difficulties should overlook every other objection in view of so important a recommendation as this.

Let us examine for a moment how far the subsequent administration of Mr. Douglas has justified the expectations entertained at home respecting his peculiar qualifications to manage the Indian tribes, and how true the representations were which gave rise to such expectations.

What has been done in order to secure to the Indians those patches of land which have been cultivated from time immemorial; and, handed down from generation to generation, are almost held sacred to the poor Indian? Absolutely nothing. The white man has taken the most unceremonious possession of a country which the red man has been accustomed to look upon as his own. The pale-faced intruder has greedily grasped at the fertile patches under cultivation by the natives, and, in many instances, debauched their wives and daughters, desecrated their burial grounds, and introduced amongst them the blighting curse of intemperance. The villainous compound smuggled to our coast and palmed off upon the poor savages as whiskey, and their valuable furs taken in exchange for it, has led them to see that the white man is their worst foe. Conscious that the drug dealt out to them is making their "heart sick," and leading to bloody feuds amongst families and friends, yet destitute of the moral fortitude to resist the tempting cup; they appeal to the "King George" Government to put a stop to the traffic, and not allow "the bad schooners to come amongst them with firewater."

This traffic in spirits is, we are convinced, the most fruitful source of trouble amongst the Indians; and what has the Governor done to stop it? Has he not rather consented to become a patron of it? He granted all possible facility to coast smuggling when in 1862 he instituted a "bogus" clearance system at Victoria, whereby vessels trading upon the coast of this Colony could clear in another, and, at the same time, intimated to the Collector of Customs for this Colony that he should deal leniently with the smugglers. He has been lolling about his home, his thumbs in luxury at indolence, caring only how he might enhance the value of his enormous property there, as oblivious of the welfare of the country and the Indians as though no responsibility rested upon his shoulders. Strutting about in silver lace and childish gew-gaws, more suited to a siwash than an English gentleman, he foolishly reckoned upon the veneration and respect of the native tribes. But, heathens as they are, they are shrewd enough to distinguish between mere tinsel and the sterling metal. "Biscuit and molasses" are all very well in their place, and palatable enough to the Indian; but he is not to be cheated out of his rights or bamboozled into unceasing and unconditional friendship through any such trifles.

Governor Douglas has proved himself just about as incompetent to manage the Indians as to govern the whites. And although the difficulties and depredations to which we have alluded have been most outrageously exaggerated, yet they are sufficiently important to prove that unless a thorough Indian policy be soon introduced we may very likely have our hands full enough of trouble with them. The Indian, as a general rule, only seeks to molest and injure the whites in retaliation for some wrong, real or imaginary. That wrongs have been and are every day committed by the so-called Christian race which have come in upon their "hunting grounds" there can be no doubt at all. The first step will be to remove the cause and then the effect will soon cease.

We have more than once pointed out the necessity as well as justice of seeing that the Indians were properly protected in the possession of their property, or, when it is desirable to remove them, suitably compensated for the same, and we have repeatedly warned Government against the danger of permitting matters to continue as at present, a course which could hardly fail to lead to fatal and sanguinary results. It is always much easier to prevent an Indian war than to quell one. But admonition and warning seem alike thrown away upon our indolent and obtuse Government. [104]

Comiaken and the Roman Catholic Mission of St. Ann's. Comiaken Hill, behind the village, was used as a strategic strong-point by British colonial forces in 1853 and 1856. On May 4th, 1863, Thalaston and three others were handed over to Captain Pike in the vicinity of the Catholic Mission of St. Ann's. Taken around 1869, this photo shows the construction of the stone church of St. Ann's which still stands.   Royal British Columbia Museum, Photo 6481.

Tomo Antoine. Born of a Chinook mother and an Iroquois father, Antoine served the Hudson's Bay Company for 40 years before marrying the daughter of the Taitka si'em, Thosieten. As a guide and interpreter for British military expeditions to the Vancouver Island and the Gulf Islands area, Antoine was unparalleled. Drawing by L.R. Ryan.
Courtesy of Ladysmith Chronicle.

The Police Barracks. Situated on the site of present-day Bastion Square in Victoria, the Police Barracks, visible at upper left, was the site of the Police Court and contained the cells where hwulmuhw prisoners were incarcerated. The public executions of May 23rd and July 4th, 1863 took place in the picket-fenced yard beside the barracks to the left. Hundreds of people filled the area to witness the events. British Columbia Archives and Records Service, Photo HP 3766.

David Cameron was the brother-in-law of Governor James Douglas and first Chief Justice of the Supreme Court of the Colony of Vancouver Island. In May and June of 1863 he sentenced seven Cowichan and "Chemainus" warriors to hang in Bastion Square.
British Columbia Archives and Records Service, Photo HP 2414.

Chapter Nine

Suspended Between Heaven and Earth

O n the morning of Thursday, May 7th, the Police Commissioner and Magistrate Augustus Pemberton presided over a preliminary hearing at the Police Court where John Henley confronted the five hwulmuhw prisoners who were "fully identified as the murderers with but one exception." [1] Henley "was conveyed from the Hospital in a buggy" to the Police Barracks where, "although suffering much, [he] was just able to walk into the court." [2] To one observer, Henley "presented a deplorable spectacle." [3] Thalaston, Stalehum, Oalatza, Thask and the Lamalcha man,Whisk, were brought into the court. The only translator mentioned as present was Sergeant Blake, and it seems that the entire proceeding was conducted in English and Chinook. Once the hwulmuhw were "placed in the dock," they were asked to state their names. Two caps, a boot, and a coat found at the site where William Brady died were placed on a table as Henley's April 10th deposition was read aloud in the court.

> The Information and complaint of John Henley of Victoria in the Colony aforesaid taken this tenth day of April in the year of our Lord One thousand, eight hundred and sixty three, before me Augustus Frederick Pemberton Esquire, one of Her Majesty's Justices of the Peace for the said Colony of Vancouver Island and its dependencies, who being sworn upon his Oath, saith:

> Last Saturday about two o'Clock in the Afternoon I encamped on a little Island about three or four miles from Salt Spring Island, it is a long narrow Island, with high mountains in the middle, I was accompanied by a man named Bill Brady, I went to Hunt and returned, about an hour and a half after dark. In the meantime five Indians had arrived, three men and two women. We had supper, then Brady cooked some bacon and made tea for the Indians, he gave them two cakes of bread, and about half a cup of sugar.

> We then went to sleep. The Indians also lay down close to our tent. About an hour after we had been asleep, I was awakened by shots fired.

173

There were four shots fired. Three at me and one at Brady. The first shot hit me in the thigh, the second shot hit me in the Arm, a third shot hit me in the private parts. Brady had his thigh shattered by one shot, and he was not able to move afterwards. He lived until the third day and died about three o'Clock in the afternoon. After I was wounded I got my rifle Gun, and fired several Shots, perhaps half a dozen, I don't remember how many, I was so much excited. The Indians retreated and I saw a party which I suppose to be the same leave the Island, the second day after this occurred. We did not leave because it rained so hard, I started the morning of the fourth day on a boat by myself and I reached Oak Bay about two o'Clock the same day, travelling with the tide. A policeman fetched me from Mr. Tod's House at Oak Bay to the Hospital. One of the Indians had a glass eye, that is the ball of the eye was white, he was about sixteen years of age. One had large projecting lips, the third one is well looking but his teeth are a little undershot, none of these men were older than sixteen years. I have seen the undershot Boy at Cowitchin, he was present when Brady and I went to buy a whaleboat at Victoria. This boy was one who shot at me. One of the women was an old woman full of wrinkles, she might be forty years of age, the other woman was a well looking girl about sixteen years of age, with long black hair reaching down to her waist, and thin small lips with good pretty teeth. Brady was raised in the States he had been here since fifty-eight. He has been hunting this winter with me. We had intended to have cut hay on the Island, on which we landed. The Indians told us they came from Cowichan. Brady was not a Whiskey seller to Indians. We had no spirits with us, and were not in the habit of carrying spirits with us. I am half bred Cherokee, born and raised in Texas. I came to Victoria last fall.

Sworn before me the day and date above written. A.F. Pemberton.[4]

After his deposition was read, Henley was sworn and made the following additional statement:

I have heard my information read. It is true. I hear one man present call himself Thalaston alias Kaisue. I saw him not three steps away from me after the first two shots were fired. I called him the one with undershot teeth. I hear another prisoner call himself Oalatza, alias Swane-a-hya, he is the one with the glass eye. I saw him during the firing. I hear another prisoner call himself Stale-hum; I saw him there during the firing—I called him the man with thick lips. I hear the female prisoner call herself Thask—I saw her during the firing. There was another squaw present; I know the prisoner Whisk, he was not there at the time. The four prisoners I have mentioned were present at the murder of Brady as described in my information of the tenth of April last. The coat and boot produced belonged to Brady. When I left, two caps, corresponding to the ones produced were lying in the camp—they belonged to the Indians. [5]

The reporter for the *British Colonist* wrote that the four Quamichan "made no remark and appeared quite unconcerned," possibly because Henley's deposition and statement were not translated into either Chinook or Hul'qumi'num. The hearing was the last order of business for the day and the "case was postponed till Monday next." [6]

After further delay the Quamichan prisoners were brought before Pemberton at 1:30 p.m. on Tuesday, May 12th. Once again, Henley's April 10th deposition "was read in court" but this time "its purport [was] interpreted to the prisoners by Police-Sergeant Blake." [7] Blake tried to translate Henley's deposition using the Chinook trade jargon, effective for basic communication, but of limited value in a court proceeding. At the trial, which took place two days later, a Hul'qumi'num-speaker, a hwulmuhw man named Kappia, assisted the court as an interpreter but he is not mentioned as being present at the Police Court hearing. The content of Blake's Chinook "translation" of Henley's deposition to the four accused Quamichan will never be known, but its effect was immediate.

> Oalatza, having been duly cautioned that whatever he says will be taken down in writing, and may be used in evidence against him upon his trial says, through Sergeant Blake who is duly sworn to interpret:
>
> Thalaston alias Kaisue was the instigator of the firing—it was not my wish—I had laid down and gone to sleep with the two other male prisoners when Kaisue's wife awoke me—and I saw her go to Stalehum and awake him and tell him to get his musket. I saw Stalehum and the other male prisoner get their muskets—so I got mine, and then we all fired. [8]

Oalatza's confession was followed by a statement by Thalaston who, "upon being interrogated admitted that he had instigated the murder." [9] He boldly declared: "If there had only been myself the men could not have been killed, but there being three of us we felt sure of killing the two men." [10]

The third youth, Stealhum, made no statement. Thask stated "that she hid her face and cried while the crime was being committed." [11] The Chinook statements of Thalaston and Oalatza were written down in English by Blake and each made a cross next to his name at the bottom. [12] After hearing their statements Pemberton had all four "fully committed to trial." [13] Whisk, the Lamalcha arrested on suspicion of being concerned in the murder of Marks and his daughter, "was remanded for one week for further inquiry." [14]

The *British Colonist*, shocked at the reaction of the three youths to the charges made against them, published the following comment under the heading "Light Value Attached To Life":

> The Indian boys who, according to their own confessions, were the murderers of Brady, appear to be utterly regardless of the awful fate which in all probability awaits them. Fully aware that conviction of the crime laid to their charge would subject them to sentence of death, they nevertheless volunteered yesterday in the Police Court, after due caution, to implicate themselves by describing the manner in which the cold-blooded murder was effected. [15]

Two days later, proceedings shifted from the Police Court to the unfinished complex of government buildings known as the "birdcages." Separated from "downtown" Victoria by James Bay, the government offices were accessed by a long wooden causeway, a continuation of Victoria's main thoroughfare, Government Street. Only one of the buildings in the complex was completed and, as a result, the Supreme Court and the Legislature were forced to share the same space for four years "with court sittings being choreographed to fit between those of the Assembly." [16]

The four Quamichan charged with the murder of William Brady and the attempted murder of John Henley were to be tried at a Special Assize commissioned by Governor Douglas, and presided over by Chief Justice David Cameron. Cameron's decade-long career as Chief Justice of the Supreme Court of Civil Justice was plagued by controversy, not the least of which was the fact that he was the brother-in-law of Governor James Douglas and had no legal training.

Born in 1804 in Perth, Scotland, Cameron left in 1830 following an unsuccessful career as a cloth merchant. He emigrated to Demerara, in British Guiana, where he began a new career as the overseer of a sugar plantation. Eventually he acquired his own small plantation on the Essequibo River. As owner and manager of a sugar plantation built on the labour of black and mullato workers, Cameron, for over a decade, "enjoyed a good income and every comfort consistent with the position." [17] As fortune would have it, he married Cecilia Douglas Cowan, James Douglas' sister.

Cameron probably would have flourished in this environment were it not for the crumbling colonial economy. The recent abolition of slavery in the West Indian colony made it less easy to exploit manual labour which in turn created a climate of economic instability for the sugar plantations. "Serious losses fell upon many," including Cameron who, in January 1851, declared bankruptcy. [18]

Cameron came to the Colony of Vancouver Island in July 1853, at the invitation of Andrew Colvile, the Governor of the Hudson's Bay Company, who offered him a position as superintendent of the coal mines recently opened at Nanaimo. He spent little if any time in that position, for shortly after his arrival in the colony, Douglas appointed Cameron to the position of Chief Justice of "the first Supreme Court west of the Rockies." [19] His appointment, paid for by an increased tax on liquor sold at licenced establishments, outraged segments of the hwunitum population who protested both his "improperly close family connexion," and his complete lack of legal training. [20]

For the Hudson's Bay Company, which equated the practice of law with the management of people, Cameron's experience as a plantation overseer more than qualified him for the position. [21] With Cameron as Chief Justice, the Hudson's Bay Company, which already enjoyed an economic monopoly in the new colony, found its political monopoly strengthened. Cameron happily carried out the wishes of the Colonial Executive, which to all intents and purposes were those of Douglas himself. For hwunitum and hwulmuhw who found themselves in his court, "each time Cameron took the bench his presence was a symbolic contradiction of the very notion of impartial justice." [22]

Throughout his twelve-year career, David Cameron's court room behaviour was often criticized by other colonists, who claimed that he had "exhibited notorious and gross partiality, acrimony, malice and indecorum" in his role as Chief Justice. Others described him as having "a want of moral weight or legal knowledge." [23] During one court session, Cameron "conducted himself in so disgraceful a manner that the other three magistrates passed a resolution censuring him in the strongest measures ... [His] conduct was so gross that the whole of those in Court soon actually hissed him." [24] Public criticism of Cameron continued throughout his career, and by 1863 his behaviour was the subject of investigation by a committee of the British Parliament in London. [25]

An indication of the low esteem in which Cameron was regarded by his contemporaries is revealed by the naval officer Verney, who characterized the Supreme Justice as "an inane booby" who "generally wears a benign vacant smile on his countenance." [26]

Cameron's notorious behaviour was particularly evident in cases involving hwulmuhw defendants, where the uneven application of justice had fatal results. During his tenure as Chief Justice, Cameron presided over several cases of hwunitum men charged with murder, but none were ever sentenced to death. By contrast, cases involving hwulmuhw charged with murder were "the only occasions on which the extreme penalty of the law has been put in force since the advent of the whites in Vancouver Island." [27]

In August 1860, Cameron presided over the trial of a young Tsimshian man named Allache, who was charged with the drunken killing of a qihuye' man who made repeated sexual advances towards his wife. The Supreme Court had only recently been granted jurisdiction over criminal cases and this trial set the pattern for criminal court proceedings against hwulmuhw defendants for the next four years.

Allache and other hwulmuhw defendants faced Cameron without the benefit of legal counsel or adequate translating services. For trials involving hwulmuhw defendants, no matter which language they spoke, Cameron's courtroom relied on the Chinook trade jargon, a vocabulary of five hundred or so words invented over the years by hwunitum unable or unwilling to master the indigenous languages of the Pacific Northwest.[28] It included many Nuuchahnulth and Chinook words borrowed from those peoples with whom hwunitum traders had the most contact and was taught to native people to facilitate communication between the races. The Chinook trade jargon, despite whatever facility it had in rudimentary business transactions, was incapable of communicating the finer points of nineteenth-century English law. Its limitations were well known to hwunitum missionaries such as Thomas Crosby, a Methodist minister who arrived in the colony in 1862. Crosby referred to Chinook as "a wretched means of communication, poor in expression and almost destitute of grammatical form."[29] Allache, who spoke only Tsimshian, would be on trial for his life without benefit of counsel and "with a Chenook Interpreter by his side, who neither knows good English nor Tsimsean Indian."[30] Alfred Waddington, a Victoria businessman, described the proceedings:

> And questions are being put on every fact which is sure to condemn him, but not on one which would exculpate him; a lonely, helpless victim, surrounded by judges the more inhuman because the more educated. Nor does a single lawyer present have the heart or the humanity to offer to defend him. And it is in an English Court of Law and a Christian Court of Justice withal, that such deeds take place, and that an Attorney-General complacently looks on and authorizes them by his presence! And the Chief Justice too looks quietly on in that same Court, where every one seems to have forgotten the common feelings of justice, and forgetting his duty also, does not even assign a counsel for the defence, or remind one single lawyer of what he owes to himself and his profession.[31]

Allache was convicted and sentenced to hang on the gallows in the courtyard of the Police Barracks. After the execution, Waddington, who was familiar with the details of the case and disgusted at the proceedings of the trial and its outcome, wrote and published a pamphlet at his own expense entitled "Judicial Murder."

Waddington contrasted the proceedings of Allache's trial with that of a hwunitum man the day before:

> ... who had been accused of cowardly murdering a helpless drunkard on the highway—a man who could barely lift up his arms to implore for

mercy ... and the foul deed was proved before that same tribunal, clear as daylight ... But his well-paid lawyer was eloquent, the Chief Justice too spoke in his favour, the feelings of the Jury were worked upon, and the cowardly, dastardly assassin escaped with four years imprisonment. Not so with Allache. [32]

Waddington called Allache's death "the first judicial execution in Victoria." He hoped that his pamphlet, "this feeble exposure of a great inequity be the means, under Divine Providence, of hindering the recurrence of any such judicial atrocities." [33] But Alfred Waddington's wish was not to be fulfilled. David Cameron is overshadowed in the history of British Columbia by his more colourful mainland contemporary Matthew Begbie, Chief Justice of the Supreme Court of Civil Justice of the Colony of British Columbia whose nickname, the "Hanging Judge," might just as well be shared by his Vancouver Island colleague.

On the morning of Thursday, May 14th, a Special Court of Assize, *Regina vs. Thalaston, Oalitza [Oalatza], Stalehum and Thask,* was convened at the Supreme Court with Chief Justice David Cameron at the Bench.

A Grand Jury was empanelled and included James C. Carswell, C.C. Curtain, J.P. Davies, R.D. Dunn, Alfred Fellows, Lumley Franklin, John Gastineau, C.N. Nicholson, Thomas C. Nuttall, J.T. Pidwell, Daniel Scott, S. Siffkin, William B. Smith, and Robert Williams. James C. Carswell was chosen foreman. [34]

Chief Justice Cameron opened the proceedings by addressing the Grand Jury:

... stating that his Excellency the Governor deemed it necessary to issue a Special Commission to try the prisoners for the sake of the settlers on the East Coast of the Island who were in the neighbourhood of the late Indian outrages and that a speedy punishment might be inflicted as a warning to other natives. His Lordship said that the depositions taken before the Police Magistrate would be laid before the jury and he believed that the evidence against the prisoners was so strong as to cause but little doubt of their guilt. [35]

Cameron handed a copy of the indictments to the foreman, James Carswell, who, with the rest of the Grand Jury, "retired for half an hour" during which time they endorsed the indictments as warranting prosecution of the accused. They "re-entered the court, having found true bills against the prisoners. His Lordship thanked the gentlemen of the jury and they were then discharged." [36]

The Sheriff then "called out the list of Common jurors," who were sworn and empanelled as a special jury to hear the first arraignment on the charge against "Thalaston for murdering one William Brady and against the others for feloniously aiding and abetting him in the same." The jurors were Edward Coker, Archibald

Dods, Abraham Belarco, Charles J. Palin, Edward Dickinson, John Eyre, Rowland Fawcett, W.H. Forsythe, John P. Foord, Walter Miles, Solomon Shamur, and George Stevens. Edward Coker was selected as foreman. [37]

The prosecution would have been undertaken by George Cary, the colony's Attorney-General since 1858, but on the day the trial took place he was being examined by Dr. J.S. Helmcken, who issued a medical certificate advising that Cary suffered "from general nervous disability and that change of air and scene is necessary for his restoration." [38] As well, he had been thrown out of a horse-drawn buggy the previous Sunday, all of which made him unable to perform his duties. [39] His place as Crown Counsel was taken by David Babington Ring who, as the senior barrister of the colony, was appointed by Douglas "to act as Attorney-General during the absence of Mr. Cary," to whom Douglas granted a three months leave of absence. [40] Ring, a fellow native of Ireland, came to the Colony of Vancouver Island in 1858, and sat in the Legislative Assembly in Nanaimo. Disappointed both with the climate and expectations of financial recompense he was, according to an acquaintance, "the first grumbler we have seen." [41] In Victoria he "always walked about with a dog-whip in hand and several dogs after him." [42]

Thalaston, Oalatza, Stealhum, and Thask were not represented by counsel, and Ring "suggested that the court should appoint counsel for the defence, the prisoners being too poor to retain legal assistance." His request was denied. Cameron stated that "it was not customary now to do this, and moreover no counsel happened to be present. The Court would, however, watch the case more particularly, to ensure that the prisoners obtained ample justice." [43] It is doubtful that Cameron's statement would have reassured the Quamichan defendants, if indeed they understood what he was saying.

Mindful of criticism regarding the absence of adequate interpreters during previous trials of hwulmuhw defendants, in the present case a Hul'qumi'num speaker named Kappia was engaged by the court to serve as interpreter. [44] But if the court felt that this would alleviate misunderstanding, they were mistaken. Kappia did not speak English and the court testimony was, once again, forced to rely on Chinook which, among the Cowichan, "few understood." [45] Nevertheless Police Sergeant George Blake and "an Indian—Cappia, were sworn in, the former to interpret Chinook into English; the latter, the Cowichan language into Chinook." [46]

The interpreters proceeded to explain the charges against the accused and asked them how they pled—a procedure that was not understood by the Quamichan prisoners. Cameron intervened: "On the prisoner Thalaston being asked if he was guilty, his Lordship thought better and directed that a plea of not guilty be entered." [47]

David Ring then addressed the jury:

> I have the honour to appear on behalf of the Crown, to lay before you the
> facts of a murder alleged to have been committed by the prisoners at the
> bar, for it is indifferent to the law whether the act of of one of them alone
> has deprived the deceased of life, those aiding and abetting such a crime
> being held equally guilty. As it is not customary for Crown Counsel to
> enlarge upon the circumstances of a crime imputed to an undefended
> prisoner, I will proceed to lay before you the evidence. There is, however,
> one point to which I must allude, viz., that the murder, if you believe it to
> have been such, was committed with cold-blooded deliberation. The
> atrocity of the crime was enhanced by the fact that the victim was
> murdered after administering to the wants and comforts of these men. It
> is for you to say whether they are guilty or not guilty. [48]

The Crown Counsel then called upon three witnesses to give evidence. The first
witness was John Henley who, after arriving in a buggy from the Hospital, was
sworn, and "gave a clear and succinct account of the circumstances attending the
death of Brady." [49]

> A short time ago I was encamped on an Island near Salt Spring Island. It
> was on a Saturday over a month ago. I had a companion with me named
> Bill Brady. We went to see if we could find a place to cut Hay. I went
> hunting. Brady remained in the Camp. I went about three in the afternoon
> and returned about half an hour after dark. I found the four prisoners
> there and another squaw. I see the first prisoner Thalaston. He was there.
> I knew him before. I saw him in Town on the day we left and I also saw
> him at Salt Spring Island. I see the second. I don't know that I saw him
> before that night. I know him again by his eye (Oalitza has a glassy looking
> eye.) The third Stalehum I know by his mouth (Stalehum's lips were a
> prominent feature of his face.) I saw the woman Thask also there. I saw
> their faces clearly by the light of the fire. There were three men and two
> women. After I got there Brady called me to supper. We sat down to
> supper and the Indians also had some. Brady gave them some Bacon, half
> a cupful of Sugar and about two loaves of Bread. We had conversation with
> them about the places where we expected to get Hay. We went to sleep.
> The prisoners also lay down on the outside of the tent. Right at the door.
> I was awakened by the sound of shots. The first took effect on Brady's
> thigh. I was also shot first in the thigh, second in the arm and third in the
> abdomen. I received the shot in the arm when I was fighting. When I heard
> the first shot I jumped up and asked Brady what it was. He said he was
> shot and I then rushed out of the tent. I saw two guns in the hands of the
> prisoners before we went to sleep. They were carried away. After I was

wounded I got my Rifle and fired several shots. I was on my guard against their return. On returning to camp I found Brady had crawled out of the tent. I covered him up with blankets. He died on the third day. I left the Island on the fourth day. When I got out of the tent I saw them all squatted down in the bushes watching. Thalaston I saw with a gun pointed at me. I jumped at it and threw it down and in doing this it went off and wounded me in the abdomen. I got hold of the gun and there was a struggle for it and I was thrown over. They were all upon me. The woman then stabbed me in the temple with a small knife. I don't know how I escaped except that it was by the interposition of God. I can't swear which of the women it was that stabbed me. [50]

From the outset, there were difficulties in communicating the testimony which the interpreters translated "as it was given at short intervals." [51] According to one observer, "the translation of the evidence into Chinook by Sergeant Blake, and the Chinook into Cowichan by [the] Indian interpreter, occupied a long time." One can imagine Blake trying to grapple with the detail of Henley's long statement, given the limitations of Chinook. The accused, however, made replies "that they understood." [52] At the conclusion of Henley's testimony, "the prisoners were again made to understand the nature of it. Thalaston and Oalatsa seemed somewhat affected. Thask, the old woman and her son Stalehum once or twice smiled, and looked not much concerned. On being asked if they had anything to say they replied that they had nothing to say, but that the evidence before given was true." [53]

The next witness for the Crown was Horace Smith, Chief Constable and Superintendent of Police who, after being sworn, "deposed to the circumstances of the arrest of the prisoners, and the finding of the body of the murdered man." [54]

I am Superintendent of Police. In consequence of information I received I went to the Island mentioned by the witness Henley. I was with Commander Pike and Dr. Turnbull. We found the body of Brady. I had not seen him before but I knew it was his body by the papers that were in his pocket. It was so much decomposed that it could not be examined by the Doctor as to the wound. There was a hole in the Trousers as if a Bullet had gone thro them into the thigh. The description of the Bay given by Henley led us to the spot and we found the body and everything else as he described. One boot was on the body and the other was off.

The boot was produced and shown to Smith who said, "this is the boot I brought away." Henley "identified the boot produced as having belonged to Brady."

Smith's evidence "was translated to the prisoners as before. They had no questions to ask."

The final Crown witness was Police Sergeant Blake who, upon being sworn, said:

I was present at the examination of the prisoners before the Magistrate. They were warned that they could not say anything to the charge but if they did it would be taken down and might be read again at them as evidence at the trial. [55]

Ring then "put in the examination of the Witnesses and declaration of Thalaston and Oalitza before the Magistrate as evidence against the prisoners." The acting Clerk of Arraigns then read the declarations made by the two youths on May 12th in the Police Court to the jury. [56]

Sergeant Blake was recalled "and on being asked by the judge—said 'the prisoner Thask is the prisoner Stalehum's mother.'" After this clarification Ring announced that this closed the case for the prosecution.

Once the prosecution was over, "the court desired the Interpreters to ask each prisoner what they had to say in their defence." Thalaston and Oalatsa "declined making any defence," Thalaston saying only "that he had nothing further to state but what was given at the Police Court." Thask said "that she was frightened when she heard Henley's voice and ran away and hid in the bushes." [57] Stalehum seemed to be the most remorseful and declared that Thalaston "was to blame, having taken the lead; he added that [the] deceased was a kindhearted man, who had given them both bread and sugar. Finally, in reply to a query from the jury designed to elicit the motive for the perpetration of the crime, Stalehum said that he got a sore throat after the food was given them and they did not know but that it was poisoned." [58]

Chief Justice Cameron did not comment on the Quamichan motive for killing Brady, but instead addressed the jury.

He considered the evidence conclusive against the prisoners that they were the parties who killed Brady. The circumstances were certainly very atrocious and it was difficult to assign any reason for such a murder. It was impossible to penetrate the motives of the unfortunate prisoners. They believed that killing a man was a great piece of heroism and their sole motive in murdering Brady appeared to be that they might be accounted great chiefs among their people. His Lordship said that during the whole of his experience he had invariably noticed that it was the young boys who were imbued with this fierce thirst for blood. It was essentially necessary that they should be made to feel how heavy a punishment will fall on the perpetrators of similar deeds. From the facts adduced in evidence, corroborated by the confessions of the prisoners, the jury could but come to one conclusion. He then read over the evidence and instructed the jury with regard to the woman Thask, that if they thought she did run away they must find her not guilty; but if they believed she was engaged in the fight she was guilty.[59]

The jury retired, but was soon recalled "for a slight correction in the charge of the bench."[60] Finally, after deliberating for ten minutes, the jurors "returned a verdict of guilty against all prisoners, but recommended to mercy the woman Thask."[61] Chief Justice Cameron thanked the jury and stated that he "entirely concurred in their verdict, and would see that the recommendation to mercy be attended to." He added that "the other indictments, which were five in number, could not be got into." The jury was discharged, the prisoners were escorted back to prison and the court was adjourned to 11 a.m. the following day "when the prisoners were to be brought up for sentence."[62]

The next day, Friday morning, May 15th, Thalaston, Oalatza, Stalehum and Thask were brought before Chief Justice Cameron for the last time to receive sentence. "A large number of persons were in attendance," reported the *Victoria Daily Chronicle*, "and watched the proceedings with much apparent interest. The prisoners (especially Stalehum) appeared dejected and awfully conscious of the dread abyss which yawns at their very feet. No appearance of contrition was visible, but in the face of each we plainly read a sullen resolve to meet a richly-merited fate unflinchingly. Sergeant Blake acted as interpreter. When asked if they had anything to say why sentence of death should not be pronounced, the prisoners replied, "halu," (nothing.) His Lordship proceeded to pass sentence, addressing each prisoner by name:[63]

> You Thalaston, are convicted of being a principal in the murder of William Brady. You, Oalatza, you, Stalehum, and you Thask, are convicted of aiding and abetting in the deed. The punishment for accessories is the same as for principals. The law makes no distinction between murderers and abettors in murders. The recommendation to mercy for the woman Thask shall be laid before the Governor; and to him the decision of her fate must be left. For the other three I can hold out no hope of mitigation. The offence was accompanied with circumstances of peculiar atrocity. You found Brady and his friend harmlessly encamped on a lonely island—you shared their hospitality—you lay down with them to sleep, and in the dead of night you rose up to murder your entertainers. It is a frightful offence, and it is necessary for the protection of residents in our outlying settlements that it should be punished by the heaviest penalty the law can award. The judgement of the court is that the prisoners be taken from the Court to the place whence they came, and that on Saturday, the 23rd of this month, between the hours of six and eight o'clock a.m., you be hanged by the neck until you are dead—and may God have mercy on your souls.[64]

The condemned would be hanged as a prelude to the weekend festivities surrounding the celebration of the Queen's birthday.

According to the *British Colonist*, the Quamichan "received the explanation of their doom with perfect indifference. Stalehum alone appeared a little more nervous than on the day of the trial. The squaw Thask was quite apathetic. As soon as the sentence had been interpreted to them they were taken back to the jail."[65] As the prisoners began to leave the court room, someone noticed that William Brady's coat and boot had been left on one of the tables and it was suggested "that the clothing of the murdered man which had been produced in court might be taken away." Sergeant Blake then "handed the coat to one of the prisoners to carry, who forthwith with utmost nonchalance, put it on." The condemned prisoners, "surrounded and followed by a crowd of persons, were then reconducted to prison."[66]

During the journey back into town, to the jail in the Police Barracks, a conversation between Oalatza and Sergeant George Blake revealed his fatalism and disbelief in hwunitum justice:

> On the way into town, Oalatza asked the sergeant whether he had said that they were to be hanged "tomorrow." He was told "tomorrow week," when Oalatza remarked, "What is the use of keeping us all that time? They might just as well hang us at once. He further expressed himself as not appreciating the justice of three Cowichans being hanged to expiate the offence of killing one white man ... In subsequent conversation, as to the probability of Thask, the old woman, being pardoned, Oalatza said they might as well hang her as the rest while they were about it.[67]

The hwulmuhw population of Victoria protested the outcome of the trial, once word of the verdict against the four Quamichan became known. The editor of the *British Colonist* noted that:

> A good deal of excitement has been caused amongst the Indian part of our population by the sentence recorded against the Cowichan murderers ... and several were heard to say that their people would have vengeance on the whites for hanging their friends. One man even went so far as to say that they had laid a plot to burn down the town. There may be little or no real meaning in all this vaporing, but we must remember that on the occasion of a former execution it was judged necessary to swear in a number of special constables some days previous to the events.[68]

In a similar vein, the *Chronicle* reported that "a Cowichan Indian told a Johnson Street storekeeper, on Thursday, that should the authorities hang the murderers of Brady the Cowichan tribe would burn Victoria."[69]

Governor Douglas commuted the sentence against the woman Thask from the death penalty to "imprisonment for life."[70] As Cameron informed his brother-in-law: "The Trial Jury you will observe have recommended the woman Thask to mercy and I have now to submit that recommendation for His Excellency's consideration and to say that I join with the Jury in it as I think her declaration may be true that she was not an acting party in the Offence and that justice will be sufficiently satisfied by the infliction of the full penalty on the other three offenders."[71]

Word of the fate of the three Quamichan youths soon reached the Cowichan people. On the day they were sentenced to death, Thostinah, "the girl alluded to by the three youths ... as having taken a conspicuous part in he foul crime," surrendered herself to John Humphreys who lived near Quamichan village. Thostinah "stated her willingness to come to Victoria whenever she was wanted. She did not appear to entertain any fears of the consequence, and was only anxious to see her spouse Kaisue [Thalaston] before he underwent the penalty of the law."[72] When Humphreys left for Victoria a few days later, "she remained at his house."[73] Despite Thostinah's apparent willingness to share the fate of her husband, there was no attempt by the colonial authorities to apprehend her.

Among certain Cowichan factions, most likely those influenced by the Roman Catholic clergy, there was said to be enthusiastic support for the court's verdict and the upcoming execution. Humphreys described them as "well-affected and satisfied as to the justice of the sentence meted out the murderers of Brady. A rumour to the effect that the Governor would pardon Thask, the old squaw, had reached the tribe, and they declared that if this was the case, they would themselves shoot her."[74]

According to information supplied by Father Rondeault of the "Cowichan mission":

> The natives themselves think the punishment just, and they have even gone so far as for a deputation of the Chiefs of the various tribes to wait upon Bishop Demers to ask him to convey a message to the Governor, to request him to have the murderers hanged from the yard arm of one of the ships of war in the vicinity of the place where the murders were committed. This voluntary request we believe the Bishop has laid before his Excellency with what result we have not learned.[75]

Some evidence suggests, however, that not all Cowichan were pleased with the state of affairs. There was controversy generated over rumours concerning the role of the Roman Catholic Bishop in the surrender of the Quamichan warriors and the woman, Thask. Father Rondeault informed the press that:

> ... many of the reports which have passed current for facts with respect to the part Bishop Demers took in relation to the detection of the

murderers, are entirely without foundation. The statements are calculated to do the Bishop much harm among the Indians. One especially to the effect that he dictated the terms upon which the murderers were to be given up, and stipulated that they were to be taken up to Cowichan to be hanged, is false from beginning to end. [76]

As the day of execution drew near, the families of the condemned men began arriving in Victoria by canoe to witness their deaths. The day before the hanging, the *Victoria Daily Chronicle* reported the arrival of some of these people and allayed fears among the hwunitum population that this foreshadowed a rescue attempt:

Three canoes, filled with Cowichan Indians, arrived yesterday morning. They report that several other canoes with Indians will arrive today. The tribe, generally, are anxious to see their tilicums [friends] hanged tomorrow. No trouble is anticipated—the natives having become too much cowed, by recent events which have transpired in their neighbourhood, to attempt a rescue. [77]

During the night before the execution, the condemned men listened as hwunitum carpenters built a gallows inside the picket-fenced yard adjacent to the Police Barracks where they would be hanged. The three youths were visited by the Oblate priest Father Charles Pandosy, founder of the Oblate's Okanagan Mission, who had recently been brought to Esquimalt. Pandosy comforted the men during their final hours as friends and family arrived in Victoria to witness their deaths.

Reporters from the *Victoria Daily Chronicle,* the *British Colonist* and the *Daily Evening Express* were present to document "the solemn and painful episode."

All through the night preceding the morning of the execution small groups of Indians, men and women, were gathered in the vicinity of the Barracks and as day broke their numbers rapidly increased. About daylight the whites began to make their appearance, until, at the hour of execution there could not have been less than 400 persons who had gathered to witness the solemn spectacle ... A company of forty sailors from the *Topaze* armed with muskets, were stationed within the Barrack yard, ready for action in the event of an attempt at rescue being made by the Indians present.

The morning was raw and sombre-looking. At precisely twenty minutes to seven o'clock the three prisoners (who had been attended during the night by the Reverend Father Panzas [Pandosy]) ascended the scaffold. All looked pale and care-worn, especially Oalatza, who, as he reached the platform, uttered a low wail, which was instantly responded to by several Indian women who stood upon the outside of the enclosure. Among them were the mother and sister of Stalem [Stalehum]. The poor creatures stood pressing their forms against the picket fence, and gazing with streaming eyes upon their misguided son and brother, uttered heart-rending cries and sobs.

The prisoners bore their fate firmly; they were offered some brandy by the officers in attendance, but Oalatza declined to partake of any until he had appealed to the Priest to know if he were right in doing so, and upon receiving the permission of the Rev. gentlemen, he asked a blessing and took some.

Kaas-sic [Kaisue/Thalaston] appeared to be very weak when the rope was placed about his neck; but a few words from the priest seemed to reassure him. While the executioner [whose face was half-masked] was busied in arranging the rope about the neck of each, and pinioning their legs, the good father moved rapidly from one to the other—breathing words of comfort into their ears and exhorting them to be calm.

All the preliminaries having been arranged, the black caps were drawn over the face of each—the light of day was shut out forever from their eyes—the priest stepped back from the drop—the executioner quickly cut a cord which passed under the platform—a signal was made to some person within the Barrack-yard, the drop was sprung, and the murderers were suspended between heaven and earth.

Oalatza and Stalum [Stalehum] suffered for several minutes, to judge from the convulsive movements of their bodies and limbs. Kaa-sic [Kaisue/Thalaston] lived about two minutes and seemed to die easily.

When the bodies fell, the sobbing and wailing of the women became louder and more painful. The male natives preserved a dignified silence and viewed the scene with that stoicism which is noted as a feature in aboriginal character. The whites present were very orderly in their demeanor, and not a single incident transpired to mar the solemnity of the scene.

After hanging an hour life was found to be extinct and the bodies were cut down, placed in coffins, and handed to their friends for interment."[78]

The hanging was marked by an incident on the Songhees Reserve, when John Yale, a Metis also known by the name Nisqually Jack, was arrested and charged by Sergeant Blake "with having incited the Indians at the Reserve to rebel against the Government."[79] While nothing in the newspaper accounts linked the incident directly to the hanging, the fact that it happened either the night before, or on the day of the execution, strongly suggests that the disturbance on the Songhees Reserve was motivated by the public execution of May 23rd.

A hwunitum witness, Mr. Sealy, claimed that he saw John Yale deliver a speech in Chinook and English. According to Sealy, John Yale had been:

> ... talking to Indians at Solton's ship yard on the Indian Reserve. There were about a dozen Indians sitting down and paying great attention to what he was saying. He told them that he was Sir Geo. Simpson's son. He told them he was a tyhee, and that all the land in Victoria belonged to the Indians; and a great deal more that he did not understand. He said "King George was hyas klauche; Sir George Simpson, hyas klauche. Halo kumtux Victoria, kanoway Victoria." I understood him to mean that they did not know Victoria and Victoria might go away. They did not recognize her as Queen. I told him he had better mind what he was saying to the Indians or he might be locked up. He said he would see that the Indians had their rights, if they listened to him. He told me if I informed on him he would stop me. I then left and informed Mr. Holton. I forgot to state that he said the "Skookum House" [Police Barracks] and the tyhee houses [large stores] belonged to the Indians. I believe the prisoner was the worse for liquor but not so drunk that he did not know what he was about. [80]

After Sealy fetched him to hear what Yale was saying, William Holton arrived in time to hear Yale urge his hwulmuhw audience:

> ... to set fire to the town and kill every white man they came across. He told them he had been in jail and wanted to have revenge and wished them to assist him. [81]

John Yale was arrested and incarcerated in the "Skookum House," and eventually deported to the Washington Territory.

The coffins containing the bodies of of Thalaston, Stalehum and Oalatza were taken by canoe to Comiaken where they were publicly displayed by the si'em Jean Baptiste Glasetatum in a funeral which combined hwulmuhw and Catholic rites:

> Jean Baptiste, the Comiaken Chief who received the bodies of the three murderers executed on the 23rd, conveyed them to his rancherie, and sent messages to all the camps directing his people to assemble at a given time. When the people were collected the coffins were laid out before them, and the old chief made a funeral oration deprecating the iniquitous acts for which the offenders had been brought to justice. He also addressed himself fervently to the women and made an allusion to the escape of the old woman Thayk [Thask] from punishment. The young men of the tribe are said to have felt sensibly the degradation entailed

upon them by their kinsmen and a feeling of regret was manifested that Thayk [Thask] had not been permitted to suffer with the others.[82]

Following Glasetatum's oration, a ritual was administered to the bodies in front of the assembly by an "old medicine woman," probably a professional undertaker (shushkwuyath.)[83] According to a hwunitum witness:

> ... when the coffins containing the bodies of the three boys ... were exposed to view by the Chief Jean Baptiste, there was a great lamentation among the Indians assembled; during the excitement which resulted, an old medicine woman lifted the heads of the corpses and commenced a vigorous application of restoratives, under the apparent persuasion that her arts would avail in restoring animation.[84]

The rites recall those performed on the body of the Somenos warrior Tathlasut, when he was hanged by the British in 1856, after which his mother breathed into his nostrils and fed him "with salmon."[85] The treatment given to men hanged by hwunitum differed from the usual practice, whereby food and drink were offered to the deceased five days to three months after the funeral and then burned in a fire.[86]

Following this ritual treatment, the bodies of the three youths were buried. Masses "were daily chanted by the Indians at the Rancherie for the departed souls of their comrades."[87]

Not all Cowichan people agreed with the justice meted out to the three Quamichan youths and there were renewed threats against hwunitum settlers. According to information received by the *Victoria Daily Chronicle,* some of the Cowichan:

> ... have lately threatened some white settlers with extermination because of the execution of the three murderers a few days since. The Cowichan say that had but one Indian been hanged for the murder of Brady they would have said nothing; but the act of taking the lives of three Indians to avenge the death of a single white man is monstrous.[88]

In Victoria, Stalehum's mother Thask was reported to be "very sick. For the last week she seemed to be pining away under her great grief."[89] How much longer she lived is unknown. There were no other women imprisoned in the Police Barracks, and her confinement amongst the male population of the jail presented a problem. The Songhees si'em Chee'althluc, called "King Freezy" by the hwunitum on account of the wavy hair inherited by his Hawaiian father, offered a solution which seemed to amuse the Victoria press:

> King Freezy here Chief of the Songish tribe of Indians, has been considering for some days the dilemma in which the authorities are placed by the commutation of the sentence of death recorded against

Thask, the Quamichan murderess. In consideration of the inconvenience attending the keeping in jail of one of the gentler sex, this public spirited individual has actually suggested that the old woman be handed over to him as a slave. [90]

It is not known how the colonial authorities responded to Chee'althluc's suggestion, but it is just possible that they agreed, viewing her fate as a slave to be commensurate with life in prison while at the same time resolving their predicament of confining a female inmate in a male population. Whatever her fate, Thask's name does not appear on a list of prisoners in the Victoria gaol compiled at the end of the year. [91]

Then, as now, capital punishment was the subject of impassioned debate. The public execution of May 23rd sparked a comment from the editorial pages of the *British Columbian,* questioning the value of hanging as a deterrent to hwulmuhw assaults on the hwunitum population of the colonies.

The "death punishment" is doubtless just and right, especially where it operates as a deterrent. And no one who has read the details of the murder of poor Brady can be otherwise impressed than that his cowardly, treacherous murderers have met their just deserts. In cool blood they took the life of a fellow creature, and their own lives thereby became the legal forfeit.

But the infliction of capital punishment even for the crime of murder is a most serious measure; and whenever it is conclusively proved that it has not the effect of lessening capital offenses it becomes a question whether it ought to be continued.

This leads to a question which has been much discussed, and has occupied the minds of learned and experienced Jurists for many years, a discussion which has settled down in the conviction that capital punishment does operate as a deterrent, as a rule, especially when applied to civilized and Christian communities. In its application, however, to mankind in a pagan state, holding such a diversity of views as to a future state and the final destiny of man, there is still room for argument.

Those who have carefully noted the manner in which the natives of this country have submitted themselves to the executioner, and have heard their expressed feelings and sentiments regarding the ordeal, strikingly confirmed in many instances by their deportment upon the scaffold, must entertain considerable doubt as to the *utility* of capital punishment in its application to the Indian tribes of these Colonies. The stolid indifference with which the Indian listens to his sentence, the impatient eagerness with

THE TERROR OF THE COAST

which he awaits the fatal hour, and the heroic calmness and fortitude with which he demeans himself upon the scaffold, even joyfully chanting his death song, all tend to show that he views the terrible ordeal to which he is about to submit with neither fear or dislike. Indeed it would appear from the manner in which both the victim and his relatives and people seem to regard an execution that they hold it to be a sort of honourable and heroic martyrdom. [92]

In light of this overtly subjective view of how the hwulmuhw viewed death by hanging, the *British Columbian* asked "whether some other mode of punishment should not be devised; something which would be regarded as at once a dishonour and a terror." In the meantime, the paper observed that it was "the duty of the various branches of the Christian Church to double their diligence" in converting the hwulmuhw to Christianity. Once "brought under the healthful and benign influences of Christianity," the hwulmuhw could be "influenced by an intelligent belief in a future state, and their personal responsibility to their Creator" and regard the gallows with the same dread as other good Christians.

Chapter Ten

The Seat of War

The colonial government expedited the trial and execution of the Quamichan youths who killed Brady, as Chief Justice Cameron explained in court, "for the sake of the settlers on the East Coast of the island who were in the neighbourhood of the Late Indian outrages and that a speedy punishment might be inflicted as a warning to the other natives."[1] Despite claims that the Cowichan were now "overawed by the presence of the gunboats" and in "a state of quiescence,"[2] ongoing reports of hwulmuhw defiance continued in those territories of Hul'qumi'num First Nations, referred to by hwunitum as the "Chemainus District." In the Chemainus Valley, hwunitum settlers and their livestock bore the brunt of hwulmuhw anger. According to one report "stock had been shot and settlers threatened by Indians in the district."[3] In another case, where a hwunitum had been building a fence, hwulmuhw owners "fired the woods, burnt a portion of his rails [and] destroyed part of the fence he has put up."[4]

A party of hwunitum hunters was reminded of hwulmuhw jurisdiction during an excursion along the east coast of Vancouver Island. Upon their return to Victoria the hwunitum informed the *Daily Evening Express*:

> ... that the behaviour of the Indians to them was extremely insolent, and that they boasted of their ability to take schooners, etc. if they pleased. A white man living a few miles north of Cowichan Bay told them that while absent fishing one day his cabin had been robbed of every valuable he possessed.[5]

It would appear these incidents were based on organized attempts by Hul'qumi'num First Nations, including the Lamalcha, to drive hwunitum settlers from lands which they had taken, without agreement, in the Chemainus Valley and on Salt Spring Island.

> There is a considerable amount of excitement among the Indians in the different districts north of this growing, it is said, out of the delay of the Government in fulfilling their agreements. If they are allowed to procure

powder and ball freely as they are reported to have been doing lately, they may be tempted to follow the example set them by their red-skinned brethren in Oregon and Washington Territory, and attempt to get rid of the whites.[6]

Hwulmuhw tactics stopped just short of killing, but settlers were harassed and their property and stock destroyed.

Reports of threats to hwunitum settlers could not compare with a rumour that Caroline Harvey had been raped by six men before she was killed. The allegation, according to the press, was made by unidentified "Cowichan Indians" and was communicated to the editors of the *Daily Evening Express* on the morning of May 9th. The following volatile editorial appeared in the evening edition of the same day:

> The Death of Mr. Mark's Daughter.—The information which we have received this morning respecting the death of the unfortunate girl, poor Mr. Marks' daughter, is so revolting that it makes the blood curdle to relate the story. We would not excite the feelings of the community by alluding again to it, if we had no other end to serve than to satisfy a prurient curiosity. We have every reason to believe that before the savages took her life, some six of the miscreants, rivalling the Sepoys of Cawnpore in their infamous cruelty, violated her, and that death itself became a welcome relief from agony and shame. God forbid then that the story be true! but on further inquiry it should be found to be as the Cowichan Indians say, we trust that the Governor in person will see that every rancherie and canoe belonging to the tribes that shelter the murderers are destroyed unless they are given up. Let us not be just, even in our anger, and make sure that we do not punish innocent persons; but the wretches themselves ought to swing from the yard-arms of the gunboats, in sight of the whole tribe. Wholesome severity now is the greatest mercy to both races. We have to prevent further massacre of the whites, as well as to punish the Indians; and it is hardly too much to say that the life of every settler out of Victoria and Esquimalt is in jeopardy. Any temporizing with the traitors, like Anson's policy in India, may lead to most disastrous consequences.[7]

The *Daily Evening Express* was the only Victoria newspaper to publish this information and there was no further evidence to substantiate the allegations. None of this, of course, mattered at the time, and the sensationalized account further shocked and enraged a prejudiced hwunitum population, which included the men and officers of the Royal Navy.

It was possibly no coincidence that on the same day this story made its circulation among the hwunitum population of Victoria, Governor Douglas decided to launch a major military expedition against the Lamalcha of Kuper Island. In a letter to Commodore Spencer, Douglas acknowledged receipt of the reports of Pike and Lascelles, "detailing their proceedings on the South East Coast of this Colony in connection with the recent Indian Outrages and Murders." Those responsible for the death of Brady had been caught, but the Battle of Lamalcha, which Douglas clearly recognized as a military success on the part of the Lamalcha, was a direct challenge to the authority and jurisdiction of the government of the Colony of Vancouver Island. For Douglas, it was a situation that could not be ignored. The military capability of the Lamalcha warriors worried Douglas, and he suggested to Spencer the following course of action:

> With respect to the encounter with the Lamalcha Indians to which tribe the murderers of Marks and his daughter are believed to belong it will be necessary that decisive and vigorous measures should at once be adopted otherwise these Indians will continue their murderous and piratical practices, and the lives of the white settlers will be in constant danger. As they have no doubt fled to a stronghold from which they can only be successfully dislodged without great risk of bloodshed by those who are accustomed to their haunts and mode of warfare I propose to raise a small voltigeur corps composed of halfbreeds and Indians and as soon as that plan is matured I will further communicate with you. [8]

In his sixtieth year, and already notified by the Colonial Office of his impending retirement, Douglas' proposed campaign against the Lamalcha was an opportunity for him to regain some of his former glory by leading one last military expedition, a crowning achievement to his years as governor.

Wise in the ways of colonial war, Douglas did not underestimate Lamalcha military capabilities. He recognized them as well-led, skilled marksmen capable of "a sustained and well-directed fire." [9] They had proven their ability against a fully armed gunboat, and Douglas knew that they possessed a network of refuge caves and defensive positions throughout the Gulf Islands. Having made the decision to personally accompany the expedition, Douglas needed experienced men accustomed as he was to the tactics of guerrilla warfare on the Northwest Coast. He gave authority to the Superintendent of Police, Horace Smith, to raise a small force of men along the lines of the Victoria Voltigeurs, the militia unit used in previous expeditions led by Douglas against the Cowichan in 1853 and 1856. The press was quick to applaud his decision:

> It is generally believed that the Governor will himself proceed to visit the various settlements on the east coast where disturbances have arisen, and that the *Devastation* will be ordered to convey His Excellency on this tour.

Such a step would no doubt be productive of highly beneficial results. Governor Douglas is well and favorably known throughout the various tribes on the coast and from his long experience thoroughly understands the native character. His presence therefore might be the means of securing the surrender of all guilty parties without difficulty or bloodshed; and ensuring the safety of the settlers residing in and about the different settlements, who have lately had just cause to feel in a state of alarm. Mr. Superintendent Smith has been directed by His Excellency to raise a number of half-breed and other volunteers to accompany the Expedition to Galiano Island where it is pretty well known that some of the Lamalcha murderers have secreted themselves. Mr. Smith is now actively engaged in the enlistment. [10]

Smith made inquiries in the City of Victoria, seeking out former members of the Victoria Voltigeurs or other suitable recruits. Some approached Smith to volunteer their services, including Chee'althluc, ("King Freezy"), the half-Hawaiian Songhees si'em. The Governor's emphasis on the recruitment of former Hudson's Bay Company employees of Metis and Hawaiian ancestry led the editors of the *Victoria Daily Chronicle* to offer a stinging commentary on the whereabouts of the one hundred and thirty hwunitum men who, two years previous, in response to a speech from the throne by Governor Douglas calling for the creation of a local militia, enthusiastically took it upon themselves to form a "rifle company."

What has become of the patriotic "Vancouver Island Rifle Volunteers"? The country stands in need of their services—they are wanted to quell the Cowichan insurrection. Where are the loud-mouthed cannon, the muskets, the bayonets, the lace-bedizened uniforms, the officers, the money? The country bleeds for volunteers to aid in the punishment of the red man for the commission of horrid crimes; but not a single member of that "war like host" has up to writing made application for enrollment, and the Superintendent of Police has been compelled to appeal to the heterogenous denizens of Kanaka Row to fill up the ranks, and even the renowned "King Freezy" has presented himself as a candidate. Alas! Alas! for the degeneracy of the times—that the "right arm(s) of the country's defence" is only to be found in the possession of Hudson Bay half-breeds and renegade descendants of the cannibals of the South Sea Islands. [11]

Similar sentiments were echoed two days later by the editors of the *Daily Evening Express*. While acknowledging the personal courage and experience of Governor Douglas, the newspaper also questioned his preference for Metis and Hawaiian troops to accompany him on the upcoming expedition, and warned of potential treachery.

A posse of half breeds and Kanakas are not a fitting escort for Her Majesty's representative. We well remember to have read of the consternation that spread throughout South Africa when the Cape Corps Rifles, a mounted regiment of 1000 strong, composed of half-breeds and Hottentots, went over to the Caffres with their horses and ammunition. Let the Governor be on his guard against similar treachery, if he has to trust natives for his personal protection. [12]

Spurred by these editorials in the colonial press, Smith soon received "a number of offers from volunteers to serve on the expedition to Galiano Island, not only from half breeds and Kanakas *et hoc graus omne* but also from enterprising sons of Albion." [13]

On May 11th "about thirty trappers and hunters" including "half-breeds, Kanakas and Englishmen," arrived at the government offices overlooking James Bay, "to be enrolled as volunteers for the Indian war." [14] Once they were assembled, Douglas "gave authority to two hunters to pick twenty volunteers." Those chosen "consisted principally of half-breeds" who "were preferred to act as guides against the Lamalchas." [15] Unfortunately for Douglas, his hopes of enlisting a bodyguard, along the lines of his beloved Victoria Voltigeurs, were dashed when the enthusiasm of the recruits was tempered by their demand for higher pay.

His Excellency offered them each a suit of clothes, and to equip, feed and pay them each a dollar a day, but they refused to go under three dollars a day each. His Excellency thereupon decided upon having an additional number of bluejackets and marines instead. [16]

Commenting on his failure to raise a volunteer force, the colonial press gave up the opportunity of further embarrassing the colony's Commander-in-Chief. The *British Colonist* reported that "the volunteer system was abandoned as impracticable and expensive besides its unlikelihood to lead to any decisive result." [17]

On that day, more information reached Victoria that Lamalcha warriors had re-organized and taken the offensive. An unknown number of them re-occupied the site of their village and made threats against hwunitum at the north end of Salt Spring Island. Since the beginning of the conflict, work had continued in the quarries of the Salt Spring Island Sandstone Company without interference by the Lamalcha, who regarded themselves as owners of the area and its resources but permitted the quarrying activities under an unspecified arrangement. [18] But now the situation had changed. Having been attacked by the hwunitum of the Royal Navy, the Lamalcha served notice to other hwunitum that their presence in the family territories would no longer be tolerated. According to information supplied by Captain Elder of the schooner *Royal Charlie* which arrived in Victoria "with a load of freestone" from the Salt Spring Island quarries:

> The Lamalchas Indians who engaged the *Forward* at Kuper Island had returned and occupied the same camping ground they held on the occasion of the fight. They were very insolent and said while the gunboat was firing they were lying in the woods looking at her and laughing at the tenass [little] war ship for wasting her powder and shot.

> They notified the stonecutters on Salt Spring by special messenger that they would give them one week more to live and at the expiration of that time they would cut all their throats. [19]

The Lamalcha warriors threatened other hwunitum and qihuye' settlers on Salt Spring Island both directly and indirectly. George Richardson, a qihuye' settler at Ganges Harbour, reported "that Indians told him and other settlers that the Lamalchas would come and secret themselves in the bush and shoot them while they were at work." [20] Similar threats were recorded by Jonathan Begg, who left his pre-emption in the Salt Spring Settlement. Upon his arrival in Victoria he reported "that the settlers feel much apprehension in consequence of the recent threats of the Lemalchoes to come and kill them." [21]

The re-occupation of Lamalcha, and the threats, raised fears that an all out offensive by Lamalcha warriors on the hwunitum settlements of Salt Spring Island and the Chemainus Valley was imminent. The colonial authorities, with the assistance of the Royal Navy, planned to strike back at the Lamalcha and their allies with an overwhelming display of military force that would turn their territories into a "Seat of War."

Ongoing reports of hwulmuhw defiance of British sovereignty over the unceded lands of the "Chemainus District" and Salt Spring Island led the editors of the *Daily Evening Express* to compare the situation with recent events in the British colonies of India, South Africa and New Zealand, where indigenous people had taken large-scale military action against the British colonists.

> It is not improbable that the Indians, led away by evil councillors of their own nation, are inclined to try one final struggle with the settlers for supremacy. We can not tell what wild hopes they are indulging, nor what bloody measures they are scheming. The slumbering fire of which we see the evidences in every district, may be nothing worse than the vindictiveness of a few bad men—or it may be the temper of the whole race. Possibly we are slumbering unconsciously on the edge of a volcano, which sooner or later will break into an explosion or bloodshed and flame from one end of the Island to the other. We are no alarmists, but wish to rouse the Government and residents to immediate action. Our

safety lies in being prepared for every chance—not in denying the presence of danger. All these savage tribes are more or less treacherous. No one expected any serious difference with the Maories until a bloody war broke out. Sir Harry Smith scorned the idea of danger in 1851, until he found himself surrounded by twenty thousand Caffres [Kaffirs] under Sandili and Heromanus. General Anson refused to listen to tales of disaffection amongst the Sepoys, until the bloody massacre of Cawnpore and revolt of Delhi destroyed his fatal confidence. Let us take a lesson from the mistakes and sufferings of other Colonies, and happily we may escape similar troubles here. [22]

There were calls for the colonial government to pass legislation to stop the sale of gunpowder to First Nations, but the suggestion was ignored. As the settler William Smithe of Somenos explained, "a law of this sort ... would be impractible so long as the Indians are at liberty to trade with each other." [23] Smithe described the failure of a similar attempt to stop the sale of firearms and ammunition during recent inter-racial conflict in Oregon:

If we glance at the history of the last Indian war in Oregon we find that although the States have prohibited the sale of both arms and ammunition to the natives, it was found when the war broke out they were as well, in many instances better, armed than the whites themselves, and that until the war was finished their supply of ammunition failed not, even when their opponents, the "Bostons," had become hard up for that important article. Now, if we reason from analogy, we must conclude that any law similar ... would be useless. [24]

The *British Colonist*, which had previously suggested banning the sale of "munitions of war" to hwulmuhw "during periods of excitement," ignored the current debate to focus on what the editor, Amor De Cosmos, saw as the root cause of the present conflict—the lack of compensation promised them for land occupied by hwunitum in the Cowichan and Chemainus Valleys and on Salt Spring Island.

While on all sides at present there prevails an earnest desire to see the strong arm of the law make itself to be felt upon the savage wretches who have given vent to their blood-thirsty instincts in the murder of so many of our white population along the coast north of this, very little stress is placed upon the necessity of giving the Indians no cause for entertaining ill feelings against the whites. While we insist that they shall observe the obvious dictates of natural law, we should at the same time take care that nothing but the most equitable course of conduct shall characterize our dealings with them ... Now, while we are given to understand that some at least of the recent outrages have been committed by some very bad members of tribes generally conducting themselves peaceably towards the whites, yet we have heard upon very good authority that there prevails among all the members of the tribes whose lands have been taken by the Government, a great amount of ill feeling towards the dominant race. The cause of this animosity is simply the neglect of the Executive to make the natives compensation for the property we have appropriated belonging to them. ... In the present instance there is no excuse. Government have been authorised to expend some $9000 in satisfaction of Indian claims at Cowichan—so that they only are to blame for any trouble that may arise out of the non-payment to the natives of what is fair and just under the circumstances. [25]

The ongoing occupation of their lands over the past five years, and the recent aggression of the Royal Navy, raised the level of frustration and anger the hwulmuhw felt at the loss of control over their traditional lands for which government representatives, including Douglas himself, had repeatedly promised them treaties and compensation. The military success of the Lamalcha warriors over the gunboat *Forward* proved that the hwunitum were not invincible, and encouraged other hwulmuhw to openly challenge the rights hwunitum settlers felt that they had to the land. [26]

The Reverend Alexander Garrett visited the settlers at Cowichan, and upon his return to Victoria presented a petition to Governor Douglas "drawing the attention of the Governor to the encroachment of Indians, in several instances, on their lands, and asking that a gunboat might remain for some time in the vicinity." Douglas, planning the military expedition to the area, gave "their prayer his favorable considerations."[27]

As a token effort to reassure the hwunitum settlers, Douglas appointed Major John Peter Mouat Biggs, a retired East India Company officer who had recently pre-empted land on the "Chemainus Prairie," as Justice of the Peace for the "Chemainus district" and Salt Spring Island. The *British Colonist* welcomed this development without mentioning that Major Biggs would be powerless without the armed backing of the Royal Navy:

> The existence of a gentleman armed with magisterial powers has of late been rendered doubly imperative and such an appointment we feel sure will be joyfully hailed by the adjoining settlers. [28]

Regarding the issue of hwulmuhw ownership, a settler on the Chemainus River claimed that Major Biggs told him "that the Government was going to pay them for their land." [29]

In Victoria the police were busy preparing information, such as it was, and warrants for the arrest of Lamalcha men alleged to be involved in the slaying of

Marks and Harvey. Acheewun was the primary suspect, based on the information Smith received in the last week of April, and the police had the names of six others, including Squ'acum, the si'em who led the warriors in their battle against the *Forward* on April 20th. The other names contained in the information may have been members of Acheewun's "small band" of retainers and/or relatives. On May 11th the Superintendent of Police, Horace Smith, swore the following "information and complaint" before Police Magistrate Pemberton:

> On or about the fourth day of April last a man named Marks and his daughter were barbarously murdered while camping on Saturna Island, and from information I have received from various Indians, I believe the murders were perpetrated by Indians belonging to the Lamalcha tribe and the following men I believe to have been principally concerned in the murders: Shah-cutch-us; Ah chee wun; She mal-tum; Sqin aas un; Tishtan; Squaw-a-cum; and Oalassa—All belonging to the Lamalcha tribe.
>
> I pray that warrants may be issued for the arrest of each of the above named men. [Signed] Horace Smith. [30]

Pemberton immediately issued warrants for their arrests and on May 12th he forwarded Smith's statement to the Colonial Secretary, William Young, along with the following letter:

> I beg leave to forward the copy of an Information laid by the Superintendent of Police charging certain Indians with the murder of a man named Marks and his daughter about the fourth of April last at Saturna Island, and I have issued warrants for the apprehension of the offenders. As it is probable that these men can not be arrested except a strong guard be sent to protect the officer in the execution of his duty, I respectfully apply for such a naval or military force as His Excellency the Governor may deem necessary. [31]

On the day he received Pemberton's communication, Douglas made a formal request to Commodore Spencer for naval assistance. He informed Spencer that he "had been disappointed in effecting an efficient organization of a small body of Voltigeurs to accompany any regular force dispatched to secure the apprehension of the Lamalchas." The rest of his letter stressed the importance of punishing the Lamalcha to ensure the safety of hwunitum settlers. Douglas outlined the strategy by which this might be accomplished, suggesting that an overwhelming naval force be employed and that alliances be made with other hwulmuhw factions "acquainted with the ground and the haunts of the Lamalchas."

> I therefore propose to despatch Mr. Smith the Superintendent of Police with the hope that he may be able to obtain a parley with the Tribe, and to effect the arrest of the Chief, and the offending parties, but failing this by

peaceable measures, there is no alternative consistent with our dignity, and with the safety of other men's lives than to resort to coercive measures. I would therefore ask you to provide for the conveyance of Mr. Smith to the encampment of the Lamalcha's and afford him such support and aid, as may be requisite to carry out the desired object. [32]

Upon receipt of Douglas' letter, Commodore Spencer made immediate plans to comply with the request to assist Superintendent Smith in "arresting the Chief of the Tribe and the offending parties." Spencer informed the Secretary of the Admiralty in London that he:

... directed Commander Pike to proceed in search of them with the *Devastation* conveying Mr. Smith and taking under his orders the *Forward* and the *Grappler* Gun Boats with the two launches of Her Majesty's Ship *Topaze* and their Guns, and Seventy Officers, Seamen and Marines under the Command of Lieutenant Geneste, Lieutenant Pusey and Lieutenant Symons R.M. respectively and to use every means in his power to carry out his Excellency's wishes, if possible without bloodshed. [33]

Acting on Douglas' suggestion "that a large force be employed," Spencer assembled the largest naval expedition ever used against aboriginal people in what is now British Columbia. In addition to the firepower and the crews of the paddle-wheel sloop *Devastation* and the two gunboats *Forward* and *Grappler*, the force included the above-mentioned amphibious unit made up of two twenty-four foot launches from HMS *Topaze* each with a twenty-four-pound cannon mounted in the bow. This special unit was designed to ensure the rapid employment of landing parties along the often shallow, rocky shorelines of the Gulf Islands. The two launches carried seventy men, including twenty-four Royal Marines under Lieutenant Symons from the *Devastation*, the balance being "bluejackets" from the *Topaze*. The launches would be towed by the *Devastation* "to the scene of operations against the rebellious Indians." [34]

Tomo Antoine was once again enlisted as an interpreter and Superintendent Smith, with Douglas' help, recruited a number of "voltigeurs" including James Gowdie, Orin Gates, L.P. Lewis, and Peter Legacy "as guides in the expedition." [35] These men joined the crew of the *Forward*.

In addition to the naval forces mentioned above, Spencer had at his disposal the screw sloop HMS *Cameleon*, which had arrived on May 8th from Guaymas, Mexico. The 952 ton *Cameleon*, launched in 1860, was commanded by Captain Edward Hardinge and carried a crew of one hundred and sixty-five men. It was a state-of-the-art warship armed with the latest in military hardware including twelve thirty-two-pound six-inch cannon, four forty-pound eight-inch Armstrong rifled cannon, and a single forty-pound ten-inch Armstrong rifled cannon on a revolving (pivot) carriage.[36] She was "considered by all nautical judges to be a beautiful specimen of her class."[37] In all, the British force mustered two men-of-war, two gunboats, two armed launches and approximately five hundred men.

Against this armada, the Lamalcha warriors would have no hope of success in a pitched battle. They had defeated the *Forward* with their full complement of warriors, but now the various families had "scattered about the islands of the coast" in small groups of no more than seven warriors accompanied by women and children. Yet in a guerrilla war, small bands of six or seven well-armed warriors, intimately familiar with the rugged terrain, could attack isolated cabins and prove effective against small naval landing parties. Some had already made preliminary movements against hwunitum settlers in the Chemainus Valley by threatening them and shooting their stock. Hwunitum on Salt Spring had also been threatened with violence. The gunboats were shown not to be invincible, and carefully planned tactics, such as those used by Squ'acum at Lamalcha, could prove successful. As the following letter by the Somenos settler William Smithe illustrates, the Lamalcha and their allies "were quite confident of their own powers of resistance." Smithe was particularly concerned over hwulmuhw contempt for the Royal Navy.

> Although I still think that we have little to fear from our aboriginal neighbours, as they seem to be pretty peaceably disposed, we have no reason to thank those whom we have been taught to look upon as our protectors. The gunboats have lost all the prestige that they formerly held over the minds of the Indians. A short time ago they were, as a rule, as much afraid of a gunboat as superstitious people are of the supernatural; now they see that man-o'-wars-men are like themselves fallible, and far from being shrewd to boot. A party of Indians passing our way a day or two ago informed us that two war vessels had proceeded to the "seat of war," adding, with roughish leers, that although there were very few of the "rebels" they expected they would (in familiar parlance) clear the Jacks out, inasmuch as they were braves and not afraid.[38]

Despite their bravery and willingness to fight against great odds, there was a greater obstacle than the Royal Navy to any Lamalcha hope of victory. Even if they had the numbers, the Lamalcha warriors could not fight a prolonged war simply because their economy could not sustain it. Each warrior was also a hunter or a fisherman whose contribution during designated periods of resource extraction was crucial to the support and survival of the family. Unlike the professional armies of the hwunitum, aboriginal forces were not supplied with a commissary. They could only wage war at certain times of the year, and then only briefly. Prolonged conflict and the neglect of food-gathering cycles would eventually cause the collapse of the aboriginal economy, and starvation.

Douglas was hopeful that hwulmuhw allies could be induced to assist the naval expedition. He directed Smith to enlist the support of Sewholatza of Taitka (Valdez Island) whose father, Ashutstun, had been killed some years before by Acheewun. As an unprecedented financial incentive, Douglas authorized Pemberton to offer "a Reward for $500 for the apprehension of the murderers of Frederick Marks and his daughter Caroline Harvey at Saturna Island on the 4th ult. or $100 for every person convicted as an accessory." [39]

Up until the last minute, it was believed that Douglas himself would lead the military against the Lamalcha, as he had against the Clemclemalits in 1853 and the Somenos in 1856. "As far as we can ascertain," reported the May 14th morning edition of the *British Colonist*, "it is still his Excellency's intention to accompany the expedition." [40] But following the lackluster response to his attempt to raise a unit of colonial troops the disillusioned governor would not be going to "the seat of war."

On May 14th Captain John Pike, who was to command the naval expedition, received his orders from Commodore Spencer. On the same day, Pemberton issued the following Memorandum of Instructions "for the guidance of the Superintendent of Police in executing Warrants to apprehend certain Indians charged with the murder of Frederick Marks and his daughter Caroline Harvey":

1. Mr. Smith will be ready to go on board H.M.S. "Forward" tomorrow morning. He will make due search for the supposed murderers; and if he requires assistance he will apply to the officer in command.

2. He must take care to guard against treachery on the part of the Indians and avoid unnecessarily exposing the lives of the men under his charge.

3. Mr. Smith must remember that he is a peace officer, and he will endeavour to make the arrests without bloodshed if possible. [41]

The last instruction was a not-so-gentle reminder for Smith to avoid, if at all possible, a situation similar to what happened on April 20th at Lamalcha.

Since the 9th of May, when Douglas announced his intention to send an expedition against the Lamalcha, Lieutenant Lascelles made "every preparation for hot work." [42] In addition to the usual routine of ship maintenance and loading provisions, a portion of each day was spent exercising the "small arms men" and the crew of the pivot gun while the "watches" were employed "at cutlass drill." [43]

On Friday morning, May 15th, the *Forward* and *Devastation*, with the launches of HMS *Topaze* in tow, set out from Esquimalt for Otter Bay on Pender Island. Later in the day Captain Edward Hardinge with HMS *Cameleon* left Esquimalt for Nanaimo to take on coal "and await further orders." [44]

James Douglas, 1863. Governor, Commander-in-Chief and Vice-Admiral of the Colony of Vancouver Island.   British Columbia Archives and Records Service, Photo HP 57606.

Sewholatsa, preeminent si'em of Taitka (Lyacksen), Valdez Island, joined forces with the British expeditionary force under Captain Pike on May 15th, 1863 to avenge the death of his father, Ashutstun. Sewholatsa's assistance was instrumental in the eventual subjagation of the Lamalcha warriors.   *Royal British Columbia Museum, Photo 5919.*

Pike's first priority was to contact hwulmuhw allies at Miner's Bay, Taitka and Penelakut to assist in the campaign against the Lamalcha. The *Devastation* arrived at Otter Bay where it met with the *Forward* and dropped anchor. [45] Pike boarded the *Forward*, which then proceeded to Miner's Bay on Mayne Island, arriving there shortly after 1 p.m. [46] Tomo Antoine went ashore and enlisted the services of Jack, who had sailed with the *Forward* in April as a Voltigeur for a dollar a day. [47] Described in one newspaper account as "the servant of the murdered Mr. Marks," Jack was in fact the employee of Christian Mayer and had assisted him in the search for the Marks when they disappeared. [48] Jack "volunteered to assist our search," wrote Pike, "but he could give no information of the whereabouts of the Lamalchas." [49]

With the first hwulmuhw recruit on board, the *Forward* proceeded under steam out of Active Pass and then under sail for Valdez Island to enlist the services of other hwulmuhw allies recommended by Douglas. Leaving the narrow entrance to Active Pass, the *Forward* sailed beneath the steep rocky terrain at the south end of Galiano Island and entered Sumnuw (Montague Harbour), probably on the recommendation of Jack, since the place was frequented by Lamalcha and Penelakut people, including Acheewun. [50] The *Forward* sailed in one end of Sumnuw and out the other through the narrow passage created by Kwi'kwens (Parker Island), which lies across the front of the harbour. [51] Proceeding up Trincomalee Channel, the *Forward* investigated another Lamalcha locality, Hath'akem (Retreat Cove.) [52] Both Montague Harbour and Retreat Cove "were found to have been deserted for a considerable time." [53]

The *Forward* continued towards the village of Taitka at Lyacksen on Valdez Island where, Douglas had informed the expedition, they could expect help from the si'em Sewholatza. "We then went to Cowitchen Gap," wrote Pike, "under the supposition that Indians could be found there, who, under promise of a reward, would render some assistance. We found however only one lodge with some 8 or 10 men and double the number of women and children." [54] Sewholatza, the si'em of the house, proved to be a valuable ally. Sewholatza saw the British proposal to join forces with them against the Lamalcha as an opportunity to avenge the death of his father, Ashutstun, who was killed by Acheewun in 1858. [55] The mustachioed si'em, in accordance with his status, was provided with a naval lieutenant's uniform. As Pike later noted in his letter of proceedings, "The Chief whose father had been killed by the Lamalchas volunteered his assistance and was very useful during the cruise as a guide through the bush." [56]

Unaware of the new expedition, Lieutenant Verney and the *Grappler* had left New Westminster that morning and passed through Porlier Pass about 1 p.m. en route to Nanaimo to coal before proceeding, according to Pike's previous orders, to "visit the Eastern Settlements of Vancouver Island." [57] Hwulmuhw informed the

British that they had seen the *Grappler* and before he left, Pike dispatched a canoe to Nanaimo with a message for Verney, no doubt to inform him of the current situation. [58] The message apparently did not reach Verney, who sailed early the next day for Port Augusta (Comox) where he stayed for four days. [59]

The *Forward* left Taitka in the late afternoon and steamed down Trincomalee Channel to Otter Bay to rejoin the *Devastation* at its anchorage for the night. [60] Possibly acting on the advice of Sewholatza, the expedition made plans to proceed the next morning to the village of Penelakut on Kuper Island where many of the Lamalcha, including Acheewun, had relations and owned property.

On Saturday morning, May 16th, the *Devastation*, with the *Topaze* launches and the ship's pinnace in tow, proceeded with the *Forward* "up Trincomalee Channel, inside Governor Rock, carefully examining the Coast on both sides," including the east shoreline of Salt Spring Island, the west side of Wallace (then called Narrow) Island and the Secretary Islands. [61]

The expeditionary force continued towards the village of Penelakut on the northeast corner of Kuper Island, anchoring off the fifteen or so large houses which lined the beach along the south end of the hook-shaped sand and gravel spit. [62] A boat was lowered and a landing party with Superintendent Smith and Tomo Antoine went ashore. With Antoine interpreting, Smith "communicated with [the] Indian chief concerning the murder of Mr. Marks and daughter." The people refused to be intimidated by the presence of the naval vessels and "at first denied any knowledge of where the Lamalchas were encamped." However, upon further questioning, "a woman informed the interpreter that they [the Lamalcha] had gone towards Dodds' Narrows, and two Indians offered to conduct the vessels to the spot." [63]

The Lamalcha had dispersed in several groups, and it is unclear which group, if any, was at Dodds' Narrows, or Kwhwuyt, a narrow passage between Mudge Island and Vancouver Island used on a seasonal basis from March through August, by Hul'qumi'num First Nations for fishing and sea mammal hunting. [64] The place was also famous for its "whirlpool-like eddies that could suck down a canoe." [65] The Penelakut informants either referred to a specific party or they deliberately deceived the British. Acheewun's people were south at Halalt, at the mouth of the Chemainus River, and this information may have been known to the Penelakut but the British were sent north in the opposite direction. There are ambiguous statements about the willingness of the Penelakut to assist the British at this point. Pike states that two Penelakut men "offered to conduct the vessels to the spot," but another source states that the two were "brought away ... as hostages." [66] In any event, the subsequent search was unsuccessful.

The *Forward* and *Devastation* left Penelakut for the south end of Kuper Island to the deserted site of Lamalcha, "but after searching for some time, could find no human beings left on the Island."[67] The *Forward* log mentions that the gunboat was "employed ... overhauling canoes."[68]

In his official report, Pike declined to mention a chase down Stuart Channel, which demonstrated to the British the speed of a hwulmuhw dugout canoe. Leaving Lamalcha the naval expedition "chased a canoe full of Indians a considerable distance but they ultimately escaped close to Chemainos [Kulleet] Bay."[69] It is not known who the occupants of the canoe were, but one of them may have included Acheewun himself, whose canoe, on account of its crew of "picked men," was "supposed to outstrip all others in speed."[70]

The *Devastation* and the *Forward* continued towards Dodds' Narrows where they sighted a group of hwulmuhw on the Vancouver Island shore.[71] The *Forward* "stopt and sent [a] boat on shore & brought off [an] Indian woman and canoe supposed to be a Lemalcha."[72] The *Devastation* also stopped and Pike boarded the *Forward*, presumably to interrogate the woman.[73] The *Forward* then proceeded to the entrance of the narrows, dropped anchor and "sent [a] boat on shore."[74] Pike returned to his own ship as the shore party "examined several encampments which were found to be Nanaimo Indians." After the shore party returned the *Forward* "proceeded under steam through Dodd's Narrows" in both directions. The expedition then headed south where, "after an unsuccessful search we anchored for the night in Horse-shoe Bay [present day Chemainus Harbour]."[75]

Acheewun's people had been staying with relations a mile south, at the village of Halalt, on Willy Island. Alerted to the British presence, they made their escape during the night by canoeing north past where the naval vessels lay anchored, towards the village of Chemainus on Kulleet Bay.

Early Sunday morning, May 17th, the British weighed anchor and "proceeded to the village at the entrance of Chemainus River, having been informed that some of the Lamalchas had been, if they were not then, living with the Indians up the river."[76] The arrival of the expedition in the area proved timely for at least one hwunitum settler who had "been threatened by the Indians that his cattle would be shot for damaging their crops, and but for the appearance of the gunboats the next day the threat would possibly have been carried out."[77]

The *Devastation* and the *Forward* anchored in front of the five or six large houses of Halalt and Pike "sent [the] Launches and Pinnace away" to land and "reconoitre."[78] Lascelles also sent a party ashore in the *Forward*'s gig. In the excitement, one of the men dropped his Colt revolver overboard, which Pike dutifully recorded in the ship's log.[79]

Throughout the morning the British were "employed overhauling the Indian Ranches."[80] Later in the morning Pike took time out from the search to return to the *Devastation* where he "mustered the crew by divisions and performed Divine Service."[81] At Halalt, through the interrogative efforts of the British officers, with Tomo Antoine as interpreter, the expedition learned from the villagers that Acheewun had been there the night before. "Divine Service" over, Pike, following the usual British tactic, seized "the Chiefs of the Village" as hostages.

> I took on board two Chemanus Chiefs, as it was found to be quite true that the tribe had been harbouring the principal murderer amongst them, and that he had only gone away the night before, hearing that we were at anchor close at hand.

> This measure brought about the arrest of the father-in-law, Uncle, wife and child of Ot-chee-wun, the principle murderer, and chief of the Lamalchas, upon which the Chemanus chiefs were landed.[82]

Acheewun's people had left, and faced with the seizure of their si'em and the probability that they would be flogged, the families of the hostages turned over people related to Sally, Acheewun's wife. Her relation, Klee'saluk, who was living at Halalt and said to be the "uncle" or "brother-in-law" of Acheewun, was the first to be taken into custody. The British were then "informed at this place that the father-in-law of Marks' murderer was up the river. The volunteers were accordingly sent up and the man was captured."[83] Sally's father, Statumish, described as "the hunchback," was seized at the village on the Chemainus River referred to by the British as the "Upper Settlement," but Sally remained hidden.[84] The volunteers then returned to Willy Island with their captive. Statumish and Klee'saluk, who were important relations (sk'wilu) to Acheewun, were interrogated by the British.[85] It is not known how the British elicited information from their captives but there is the possibility, given the fact that Lascelles was in charge of the interrogation, that flogging or the threat of flogging was involved. As a result, "from further information received Superintendent Smith went up in his gig the same afternoon and took the wife and child of the murderer."[86]

During the day the British used cannon fire to further intimidate the people of Halalt and the Chemainus River. The crew of the trading vessel *Emily Harris* reported that "having passed the *Devastation* and *Forward* near Kuper Island on Monday ... she saw the latter, which had steam up, fire several shots."[87]

Towards dusk, the *Devastation*, with the first launch in tow, left for the anchorage at Horseshoe Bay while the *Forward* remained off Halalt with the captives on board.[88]

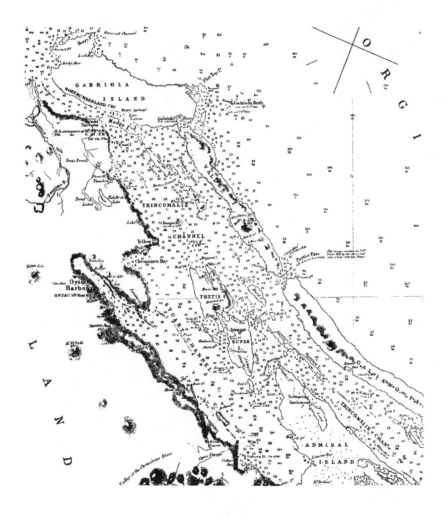

Admiralty map c. 1865, showing the main theatre of British naval operations against the
Lamalcha warriors.   *Courtesy of Surveyors General Branch, Victoria.*

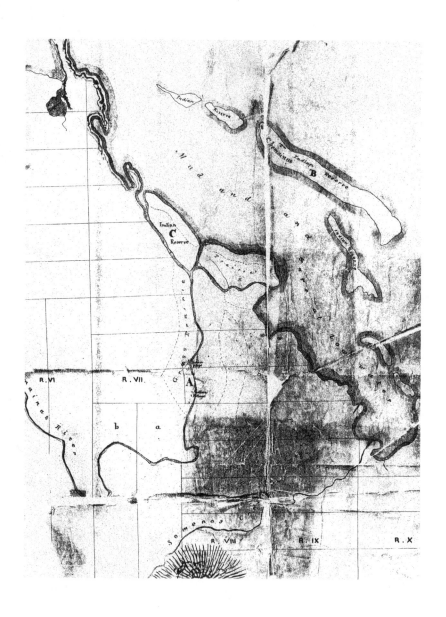

Map of the Chemainus River c. 1863-1864, showing village of Halalt (called Chemainus on the map) and the village known as the "Upper Settlement."
British Columbia Archives and Records Service, CAA30.71, C42.1.

From these people we had detained, Lieutenant Lascelles at length obtained information that a party of Lemalchas were encamped in Chemanus [Kulleet] Bay, about nine miles north of Chemanus River.[89]

The wording of Pike's brief description of Lascelles' interrogation of Statumish, Klee'saluk, and Sally during the night of May 17th suggests that the information they provided was not given freely. Realizing that Acheewun was doomed, and to protect his daughter and grandchild, Statumish agreed to cooperate with the British who enlisted him as a "voltigeur." Statumish served twenty-two days at a dollar a day and proved to be "very active in the capture" of his son-in-law.[90]

Early the next morning, Monday, May 18th, Lascelles headed straight to Kulleet Bay with the second launch and the *Devastation*'s pinnace in tow. Passing Horseshoe Bay the pinnace was detached to inform Pike of the *Forward*'s destination.[91] At 6:50 a.m. the *Forward* anchored in front of the eight large houses of Chemainus which stood along a crescent-shaped sand spit that jutted out from the shore. The village "was totally deserted," the people having recently left either to plant potatoes or to procure seasonal resources.[92]

The Lamalcha who had left Halalt for Chemainus the night before included Acheewun, his brother Shenasaluk, Palluk, Semallee, Shacutsus, and Sheemaltun. At least two elderly women, whose names are not recorded, but one of whom was Acheewun's mother, also accompanied them. They occupied a camouflaged, temporary camp of woven mats inland on the far side of the small estuary, or "lagoon," behind the Chemainus village. They had hidden their canoes in the bush. The Lamalcha watched the arrival of the *Forward* and the accompanying launch, waiting for an opportunity to shoot any hwunitum who came near their hideout. A heavy rain reduced visibility and washed out any noise, increasing the potential for a successful ambush.

After the *Forward* anchored Statumish "told them where the Lamalchas had been encamped when he last saw them."[93] Upon receipt of this information, "the boats were ordered away and a vigorous search instituted" along the shore-line of crushed shell beach and eroded sandstone, backed by thick forest.[94] Wary of a surprise attack Smith took Statumish and Sally, Acheewun's wife, with her baby, along in the *Forward*'s gig as human shields. The hwulmuhw and hwunitum scouts landed and began to carefully search the shoreline. Lieutenant Lascelles and Lieutenant Pusey closely followed their progress just off-shore in the launch to provide support in case of attack. "We searched for some hours," recalled a member of the expedition, "and destroyed a quantity of provisions, mats, etc., belonging to the Lamalchas, but failed to discover them or their canoes. As it poured with rain all the morning we returned to the gunboat at 8 o'clock to put on dry clothes."[95]

The *Devastation* in the meantime, had left Horseshoe Bay for Oyster Bay, apparently confused by the directions left by Lascelles. By the time the ship arrived off Chemainus, Smith, Lascelles and their men had resumed their search. Pike, as soon as his ship anchored, "sent [the] Pinnace, Cutter, & *Topaze's* launch away manned and armed … to cover Mr. Smith's party while searching." [96]

The Lamalcha remained in their hiding place throughout the rain-soaked morning, waiting for an opportunity to ambush the shore-party under Smith, an opportunity made more difficult by the fact that Smith had forced Acheewun's wife, child and father-in-law to accompany his men, which effectively prevented the Lamalcha warriors from opening fire.

About 11 o'clock the Lamalcha hiding place was discovered by Smith and his men who "at last came upon a party of Lemalchas encamped in the bush on the opposite side of the lagoon at the back of the Chemanus winter village." [97]

Details of this brief encounter between Smith's scouts and the Lamalcha are extremely vague. It was only barely mentioned in one of the newspaper accounts of the expedition, which suggests that the shore party under Smith did not distinguish themselves. Commander Pike, who gives the most detailed account in his "Letter of Proceedings," states only that upon being discovered the Lamalcha "immediately ran into the bush." There is no mention of Smith's reaction, only that "Commander Pike immediately ordered Lieut. Geneste to land his men and search the wood, which he did. At the same time Lt. Pusey landed his men and ranged them along the skirt of the wood." Eager to engage the enemy, the thirty-five sailors and marines under Geneste advanced into the old growth forest and "tracked them for nearly a mile but could not come up with them." [98] As for Smith and his Voltigeurs, one can only conclude that upon discovery of the Lamalcha position, Smith's party, anticipating an ambush, fled. By the time the marines and bluejackets of the *Topaze* launches landed ashore, the Lamalcha warriors had made their escape into the forest.

Despite this setback, the British managed to take two prisoners—Acheewun's mother and another elderly woman, who had been "deserted in an abandoned ranch." [99] "In their flight," Pike reported, "they left behind two decrepit old women one of them the mother of Ot-chee-wun, from whom we heard that the party consisted of Ot-chee-wun and five others … but we could get no further information from her of the remainder of the tribe." [100]

The British soon discovered seven canoes "carefully secreted in the bush" and the contents of the camp. [101] The canoes "were destroyed and the mats, provisions, and property, all burnt." [102]

Pike reasoned that with their canoes destroyed the Lamalcha would go across the peninsula separating Kulleet Bay and Oyster Bay to seize canoes from the

Chemainus Village, Kulleet Bay, c. 1930. Acheewun's followers sought refuge in the deserted village during the night of May 16th, 1863.   *Royal British Columbia Museum, PN 5962.*

Rear view of Chemainus Village showing lagoon and shoreline where Lamalcha warriors hid. Royal British Columbia Museum, PN 6048.

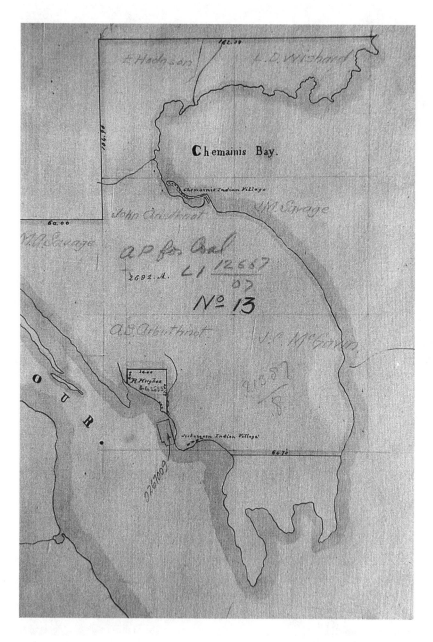

Detail from an Indian Reserve Commission map of 1877, showing Siccameen and Chemainus villages.   Courtesy of Surveyors General Branch, Victoria.

people of Siccameen, a village on the east side of Oyster Bay. In the late afternoon, Pike boarded the *Forward* which proceeded to Oyster Bay with the *Topaze* launches in tow. They arrived off Siccameen village where the first launch under Lieutenant Geneste went ashore with orders to watch the village, "it being most probable," Pike wrote, "that during the night some of the Lamalchas would make their way across to try to get a canoe." [103] At Siccameen, where a number of villagers were present in the five large cedar houses along the white shell beach, "the officers in command made the Chemainos tribe haul up all their own canoes upon the beach and also give their word not to render assistance to the Lamalchas in any way." [104] The Siccameen canoes "were all stowed in one spot on the beach" and Lieutenant Geneste's launch, with its complement of Royal Marines under Lieutenant Symons remained close by "in the bay to see that these orders were carried out." [105]

Acting on information that "two or three" Lamalcha warriors had slipped through the blockade and were now on Kuper Island, Pike directed Lascelles to take the *Forward*, with the second launch, to investigate. Upon their arrival the "2nd Launch with [the] volunteers" went ashore and "searched the island." The "volunteers" scrambled along the east shoreline of Kuper Island looking for signs while the launch moved with them keeping watch from the water. Further offshore, the *Forward* followed their progress, "steaming along Kuper island keeping [the] Boat in sight." [106] The British "did not succeed in finding them," and with the failing light, the shore parties returned to the *Forward* which proceeded to Kulleet Bay, and rejoined the *Devastation* at its anchorage. [107]

Pike then directed a party to go ashore to the Chemainus village:

> ... to watch in one of the huts in case they [the Lamalcha] should return
> to the spot in which we found them that morning. [108]

Acheewun's mother and the other elderly woman were confined in one of the houses as hostages, possibly with the hope that her son would return to look for her. During the night "some of them did return as the old woman [Acheewun's mother] stated next morning that she had heard them, but they were not near enough for the watch to see them." [109]

During the night of Monday, May 18th, just as Pike predicted, the Lamalcha warriors "struck across as expected to the Tsu-meen [Siccameen] village & Shah-kutch-sus, one of the principal murderers was captured & sent on board the *Devastation*." [110] Pike does not specify who captured him. An account in the *British Colonist* stated that "the Indians in Oyster Bay captured one man, and said they thought the others were in the woods near the camp we had just destroyed." [111] A later report of Shacutsus' capture stated that he gave himself up to the British. According to this account he:

217

... went to the village in Chemainos Bay for food he being nearly starved. The Chemainos tribe refused to give him anything and he surrendered himself to the *Topaze*'s launch. [112]

In the latter version the place-name is incorrect; Shacutsus was not taken at Chemainos Bay (Kulleet Bay) but at neighbouring Oyster Bay (Ladysmith Harbour), where Lieutenant Geneste's launch was stationed off Siccameen. In any event, the various accounts indicate that Shacutsus received no assistance from the Siccameen people. Faced with their indifference to his plight, which may have had something to do with inter-group rivalry or British intimidation, Shacutsus was left with no choice but to surrender.

As soon as he was in the hands of the British, Shacutsus was taken in the first launch to the *Devastation* where he was brought on board, "tied to a gun and flogged to extract confessions and information as to the whereabouts of [his] confederates." [113] According to Pike, Shacutsus "confessed to having been an accomplice in the murder & that his brother and his brother's wife had killed Marks' daughter, the man holding her while the woman struck her with an axe." [114] Lascelles, on the other hand, claimed that during an interrogation Tuesday night Shacutsus confessed that it was he, and not his brother, who "held the girl by the belt while a squaw stabbed her to the heart." [115]

The discrepancies in the accounts given by the two officers indicate that flogging was a poor method of extracting truthful confessions. Having finally caught one of the men named in the arrest warrant, the British wanted confirmation of what they had already been told by hwulmuhw informants concerning the death of Caroline Harvey—that "an Indian caught her by the waist while an Indian woman stabbed her to the heart." Shacutsus, unless he was telling the truth, may have told the British what they wanted to hear to stop the flogging. The British certainly would have questioned him about Acheewun's role in the killings, but Shacutsus said nothing to implicate him. At this point the British must have come to the realization that Acheewun was not "the principal murderer" of Marks and his daughter and in fact had nothing to do with the incident.

Running low on coal, the *Forward* left Kulleet Bay the next morning, May 19th, for Nanaimo, while Pike continued to search for the other Lamalcha warriors. At 9 a.m. Pike ordered the second launch and the ship's cutter to escort a landing party under Superintendent Smith to Siccameen in Oyster Bay, where Geneste's men of the first launch guarded the village. [116] Acting on information supplied by Siccameen villagers that the Lamalcha "were in the woods, near the camp we had just destroyed," "Mr. Smith took his voltigeurs, a party of marines and some Indians and marched them through the woods from Oyster Bay to Chemainos Bay, and convinced himself that the Indians had left." [117]

While Smith's men combed the peninsula Pike, possibly acting on information extracted from Shacutsus, decided to search on Thetis Island. With the second launch, the *Devastation* proceeded towards Hwuy' (North Cove) at the north end of the island. [118] The *Devastation* steamed into the bay and out again, anchoring near the entrance where Pike could keep an eye on any movements in Kulleet Bay. Pike sent the "Launch, Pinnace & 1st Cutter away manned and armed" and the island was "thoroughly searched by a party which traversed it through the bush, and the boats pulling around and examining the creeks." The shore parties located "two canoes recognized as belonging to one of the murderers named 'Tishtan,' found hidden on the top of a high cliff." [119] After breaking up Tishtan's cedar canoes the sailors and marines returned to the *Devastation*.

When the *Forward* arrived in Nanaimo that morning to coal, its crew learned of a mass desertion from HMS *Cameleon* the previous day. After a long voyage including a recent layover in the heat and mosquito-infested port of Guaymas, Mexico, the temptations of the spring climate and new discoveries in the gold fields of the Cariboo were enough incentive for thirteen sailors to plan "a bold attempt at desertion." The *Cameleon*, too large to take on coal at the dock, had to be loaded through a laborious process in which "lighters" brought the coal to the ship where it was then transferred to the man-of-war. Shortly after mid-day, the ship's cutter "was ordered off to bring a lighter filled with coal alongside." An eye-witness, the Captain of the *Emily Harris*, reported that as soon as the boat was lowered, "eighteen [sic] men jumped into her carrying with them their revolvers and cutlasses, and pulled off, but not before some confederates on board threw them in some provisions. For some minutes the utmost confusion prevailed, but finally two shots were fired without effect." [120]

The deserters ignored the firing "and succeeded in getting clear off," only to be captured the following day when the *Forward* sighted them "hauling across the Gulf of Georgia." [121] Thirteen prisoners were taken on board the *Forward* and Hardinge ordered Lascelles to Esquimalt with them.

When the *Forward* arrived at Kulleet Bay Pike ordered Lascelles "to lay that night in Chemainos [Kulleet] Bay" to watch the Chemainus village while the *Devastation* blockaded Oyster Bay.

The *Forward* left the next morning, May 20th, for Esquimalt, where she arrived in the afternoon, and transferred the thirteen deserters from the *Cameleon* to the *Topaze* "to await Court Martial." [122] There was a brief layover as the *Forward* received fresh provisions.

Two days before the *Forward* returned to Esquimalt the *Daily Evening Express* published information from Jonathan Begg of the Salt Spring Settlement who had left his home to wait out the war in Victoria. Begg had disturbing news:

From Mr. Begg, who arrived from Salt Spring Island yesterday morning [May 17th] we learn that the settlers feel much apprehension in consequence of the recent threats of the Lemalchoes to come and kill them. The Indians told them that the gunboat was "very good to cut down timber, but no use for catching them, and that all her efforts had failed to kill one klutchman." Small doubt can be felt that the adoption of the motto "He that fights and runs, etc." by the *Forward* has excited in the minds of the Indians a supreme contempt for the powers of the gunboat. [123]

Shortly after his arrival in Esquimalt, someone showed Lascelles the article from the *Daily Evening Express* which, with its implied accusation of cowardice, infuriated him. At 3 p.m. the *Forward* steamed to Victoria, where the press was eager for an update on the naval operations. When the gunboat arrived in Victoria Harbour a sailor went ashore to fetch Charles Allen, one of the proprietors of the *Daily Evening Express*, on the pretext of giving him some news about the expedition, but D.W. Higgins of the *Victoria Daily Chronicle* went aboard first. To get rid of him before Allen arrived, Lascelles gave false information that a battle had taken place between the forces of the naval expedition and Lamalcha warriors. Higgins rushed back to his office where the paper printed an extra edition that afternoon with the headline, "Latest From the Seat of War—The *Forward* bombards the Lamalchas—Thirteen Whites Wounded." [124] When Allen came aboard, he was confined below deck as the *Forward* left the harbour. He escaped his confinement and confronted Lascelles who was standing atop one of the guns. Lascelles kicked him in the chest. Allen jumped overboard, was pursued, and roughly taken back on board. Finally, "after being falsely imprisoned for some hours, ill-used, half-drowned and kicked," Allen was "landed on the beach to find his way to Victoria, bruised and fatigued, as best he might." [125]

The "Lascelles' Outrage," as the press quickly dubbed the incident, was the beginning of the end of Lascelles' naval career. "Lieutenant Lascelles' commission to H.M. Gunboat *Forward* is the last command in which he will have an opportunity of tarnishing the reputation of the British Navy," the *Victoria Daily Chronicle* predicted. [126] Charles Allen took him to court, where Lascelles was ordered to pay $1,000 in damages. He received no further promotions and "retired from the Navy" within two years. [127]

Allen's experience of Lascelles' volatile personality, and his confinement in the *Forward*'s brig where he was subjected for two hours "to the jeers of the men, and their conversation regarding the treatment of their Indian prisoners," gave him an insight into the war which was reflected in the editorial content of the *Daily Evening Express* and the *Victoria Daily Chronicle*. [128] Both papers ceased to glorify the actions of the navy, and occasionally showed some empathy with the Lamalcha people as they were captured one by one.

Allen, of the *Daily Evening Express*, was particularly concerned about what sailors on board the *Forward* told him regarding the treatment of Shacutsus and other prisoners who were "by the orders of British officers, tied to a gun and flogged" to extract confessions and information. "We hope, for the honour and sake of Her Majestey's navy, that such barbarity has not been perpetrated in defiance of the Governor's express injunction that all captives be treated as British subjects."[129]

> Since when has torture become a rule in the examination of prisoners according to English law? By whose orders are the ships of Her Most Gracious Majesty Queen Victoria turned into dens of cruelty? How long have the techniques of the Inquisition been restored in British Dominions? ... We sometimes pride ourselves on our superiority to our American neighbours in the justice and humanity with which we treat the coloured races. But what shall we say if the allegation is true, that under the Union Jack, in the nineteenth century, the boasted civilization of England has returned to the iniquitous system of question by torture, and that the lash has been apllied to extract evidence from Indians to be used in our own law courts to incriminate themselves and their friends. It cannot be true—unless Pandemonium is come back upon us and made falsehood truth, might right, and lawless cruelty justice. Two weeks ago we saw ignorant Indians tried for their lives without counsel. Now we are asked to believe that we have descended to cross-examining prisoners against themselves, and using the cat-o'-nine-tails to enforce the questions.[130]

Other news began to arrive in Victoria regarding the naval expedition, as hwunitum left their pre-emptions to wait out the conflict in the safety of Victoria. Major John Peter Mouat Biggs, the newly appointed Justice of the Peace for "Chemainos" and Salt Spring Island, had arrived on the 19th to report that "collectively the tribes around are peaceable, but that individually there is some uneasiness in consequence of the parties concerned in the late outrages having so many relations, connections and friends living in the neighbourhood." Biggs claimed that he had "handed over to the naval authorities a man who had harboured one of the murderers."[131]

George Mitchell, a hwunitum settler at Burgoyne Bay on Salt Spring Island, reported that:

> ... everything was quiet, though the settlers feel some uneasiness on account of the present troubles with the Indians ... The Cowichan and Chemainus Indians were perfectly quiet, and he heard of no firing or disturbances. If there had been any bombarding in the neighbourhood he must have heard it as the last firing was very audible.[132]

Back at the "Seat of War," the British blockade of Chemainus and Siccameen was joined on the morning of May 20th by the *Grappler* and Lieutenant Verney, who placed himself under Pike's command. [133]

Suspecting that some of the Lamalcha warriors were back on Kuper Island, Pike ordered another search, focusing on the island's three villages. During the course of the day, as Pike reported, "the Island was thoroughly searched by Mr. Smith's party, & the Marines under Lieut. Symons, & by the boats pulling around." [134] Pike boarded the *Grappler* which proceeded with the second launch, the pinnace and another boat from the *Devastation* in tow, to the village of Yuhwula'us in Telegraph Harbour. The *Grappler* anchored and "landed a small arm party and sent boats to cover their landing." [135] After two and a half hours of searching the vicinity of Yuhwula'us the landing party returned to the *Grappler*. The search "shifted to Village Bay" [Lamalcha] where the British force followed the same procedure, with the gunboat, launch and boats watching from the water while a landing party conducted a search ashore. Landing at Lamalcha "at the head of a strong party of marines, scouts, and some Indians," Superintendent Smith conducted a two hour reconnaissance. The British found "no Indians or canoes ... though there were traces of them having recently been there." At Lamalcha, the British discovered "a considerable quantity of property and provisions and two large stacks of plank" which were destroyed. [136] As a bonus, the British seized "almost 25 bushels of potatoes." [137]

After the destruction and looting at Lamalcha, the expedition returned to the *Grappler* and proceeded around to the east side of the Island to Penelakut, where the *Grappler* anchored off the village while the shore party landed, under the protection of the launch and small boats. [138] Using the services of Tomo Antoine, Pike warned the Penelakut villagers "against harbouring any of the Lemalchas should they make their way there." [139] After a two hour search of the village and the surrounding terrain, the boats and landing party returned to the *Grappler*, whereupon the force returned to Kulleet Bay by evening. [140]

On Thursday morning, May 21st, rain fell as Pike sent another landing party to Siccameen village and overland to Chemainus to convince himself that the Lamalcha had indeed left the area. The shore party "landed in Oyster Bay, walked through the bush & came out in rear of the place where the party of Lemalchas had encamped but without finding any fresh traces of them." [141] The *Devastation* returned to Kulleet Bay to await the results of the reconnaissance. When the landing party emerged from the woods at Chemainus village they were joined by a party of Penelakut warriors. With their assistance, the shoreline of Kulleet Bay "was again searched." The British and Penelakut succeeded in finding "more of the Lemalchas property and food," all of which was destroyed. [142]

With Siccameen and Penelakut factions now assisting the British effort, Pike assumed that the Lamalcha warriors would return to the Chemainus River. "This seemed very probable," he wrote, "as they were the only tribe among whom they had relations and who had not compromised themselves to hostilities with the Lemalchas by assisting our search for them." [143] Pike conceived a plan whereby two columns of troops would converge on the "Upper Settlement of the Chemainos River," the village where Acheewun's wife, son and father-in-law had been seized, in the hope of capturing any Lamalcha who might be there. Just after midnight, the *Grappler* with the second launch in tow, left Kulleet Bay to carry out the manoeuvre. At Sunuwnets (Horseshoe Bay) the *Grappler* detached the first group, "a party of five marines, four scouts, and about twelve Indians," under the command of Superintendent Smith. [144] Smith was to lead his troops "from Horseshoe Bay to the Upper Settlement of Chemainos River, and then down the river." After disembarking Smith's men the *Grappler* continued to the mouth of the Chemainus River where Verney "went up the river with another party" in one of the *Grappler*'s boats. [145]

Smith's men "walked through the trail, came out in rear of the villages up the Chemainos River" and rendezvoused with Verney's contingent. [146] After "an unsuccessful search," both parties returned to the *Grappler*. [147] The British, however, took one prisoner. According to an entry in the *Grappler*'s log, the "party succeeded in capturing an Indian Woman." [148]

Earlier in the day, at Kulleet Bay, unidentified Penelakut allies delivered three Lamalcha prisoners, two men and one woman, to the *Devastation*. The prisoners were Sayeh, his wife, Cheemalswaht, and a fourteen-year-old named Talleyok (possibly their son) who, upon their return to Kuper Island, were captured by Penelakut factions eager for a reward. According to Pike's report, which may have been based on what their Penelakut captors told him, the captives "had all been present at the murder [of the Marks] and had taken refuge with the Mus-quee-won tribe at the entrance of Frazer River." [149] None of the captives, however, had anything to do with the Mark's death and their captors received no compensation for their efforts even though the family was taken into custody.

In the early afternoon of May 21st a canoe arrived with a message from the Reverend John B. Goode of the Anglican Mission at Nanaimo, requesting the assistance of the navy in rescuing a Nanaimo woman who had recently been kidnapped by Penelakut people. [150] Pike weighed anchor and the *Devastation* visited Siccameen and Halalt before reaching Penelakut in the gathering dusk. Pike "demanded the restoration of a woman who had been kidnapped by that tribe ... The demand was at once complied with." [151]

Rain fell throughout the night and into the morning of the 22nd when a Penelakut canoe arrived alongside the *Devastation* with a female prisoner, "a woman of the Lemalcha tribe name of Tsuk-see-mich," who was "the sister of

Ot-chee-wun." She was "brought on board by the chief of the Pennellacuts" and confined below deck with the other prisoners.[152]

The *Devastation* returned to the mouth of the Chemainus River where the *Forward* had just returned from Victoria, via San Juan Island, and joined the *Grappler*. Pike learned that "information had been brought that Ot-chee-wun [Acheewun] & his party had retreated in-land towards Mount Prevost [Swuqus], being assisted by the Indians of the Chemainus River." Once again, Pike conceived a plan to send troops upon the Lamalcha position from different directions "to arrest them."[153] Smith and a "party of marines, scouts and Indians" would approach from the Chemainus River "to endeavour to get in their rear under Mount Prevost."[154] Another party of marines and bluejackets under Verney's command was ordered to approach Mount Prevost from Cowichan Bay with the hope of catching the Lamalcha in a pincer movement.

While some "Chemainus Indians" were employed to take Smith's party up the river by canoe, another contingent of twenty-six "Chemanus Indians" arrived to assist the British in their efforts.[155] Some of these warriors were from Penelakut. As for the others, they were evidently not related to, and obviously did not share common cause with, the Lamalcha who were being pursued.

The *Forward* remained off Halalt while the *Grappler* and the second launch proceeded to Cowichan Bay, followed by the *Devastation*.[156] At Cowichan Bay Verney commanded a landing party of fifty men made up of "a party of blue-jackets" from the *Grappler* and the second launch, and Symons' "strong party of marines" from the *Devastation*. These troops disembarked and "bivouaced Friday night."[157]

The next morning, May 23rd, Verney's command was guided through the bush "to meet Mr. Smith under Mount Prevost," by "Sam a Cowichan" who served three days "as a guide & Voltigeur."[158]

Meanwhile, Smith's men had "searched all the country to Mount Prevost, and encamped there, posting sentries up to the trail, so as not to allow any one to pass during the night."[159] Smith "offered $100 to any Indian who would lead on to Otcheewan's camp."[160] No one accepted his offer and "on the following morning he marched to Somenos, and met Commander Verney."[161]

Once again, Acheewun and his followers eluded the British and their hwulmuhw allies. As the marines and voltigeurs under Smith's command proceeded up the Chemainus River towards Mount Prevost, the Lamalcha fell back onto the slopes of Pulumutsun (Mount Brenton) which they ascended to seek refuge in a cave near the summit. From this position, Acheewun and his people may have watched the progress of the British forces as they made their way below to the Somenos rendezvous, only to discover that they had been outmanoeuvred. At Somenos, "information was brought from the different settlers and Indians in that locality that this party of Semalchas [Lamalchas] had taken refuge in a cave up a mountain lying between Chemanus River and Horseshoe Bay."[162] Smith "took his men back" and made an exhaustive search of the Chemainus River and the surrounding mountain sides including Pulumutsun. According to the description in Pike's report:

> Mr Smith's party had crossed from Mount Prevost to the Chemanus River, had ascended and searched the river and then searched the bush as far as the mountains at the back of Horseshoe Bay.[163]

Verney's sailors and marines left Somenos and returned to Cowichan Bay with instructions to meet Smith's men at the Chemainus River.

While the British sought Acheewun's party in the steep terrain above the Chemainus River, the Lamalcha si'em Squ'acum "with about 4 followers and some squaws" landed at Sthihum (Osborne Bay) where they set up camp.[164] Around 1 p.m., at its anchorage off the village of Halalt, the *Forward* received on board the "26 Indians who had been in search of the Lamalchas during the night."[165] They informed Lascelles "that a party of Lamalchas with their canoes had been seen in Osborn Bay."[166] Although Osborne Bay was but a short distance from the *Forward*'s anchorage, Lascelles did not proceed there directly, either for fear of meeting strong resistance or for lack of orders. Consequently, the *Forward*, with the twenty-six "Chemanus" allies, weighed anchor and proceeded past Osborne Bay to Cowichan Bay to confer with Pike. Pike ordered the *Forward* and the *Grappler* back to Osborne Bay.[167] As they approached, Verney "observed the *Forward* lowering and manning and arming boats" and likewise "lowered and armed [the] 2nd Gig to chase Indian murderers."[168] Before they could make contact, Squ'acum and his people "decamped into the bush," leaving five canoes, of which three were taken on board the *Forward*.[169] As reported by Commander Pike, who put the incident at Sthihum in as positive a light as possible:

> [Lascelles] landed and seized five canoes & destroyed everything in the encampment, in which their fire was quite warm. The Indians escaped into the bush which was searched by Lieutenant Pusey & his launch's crew accompanied by twenty-three Chemanus Indians who soon however, gave up the search, but none of the Lemalchas could be met with.[170]

While the two gunboats launched their aborted attack on Squ'acum's party, Smith's marines, voltigeurs and hwulmuhw warriors "encamped at the foot of the mountains high up the Chemainos River." From his camp, the Superintendent of Police "sent scouts down the river during the night and found that all the Indians had left the river." Smith was informed that "among others, it was believed that Otcheewun [Acheewun], the Pirate Chief, who seemed to be the terror of all the Indian tribes, had stolen a canoe and left the river."[171] On Sunday morning, May

24th, "Mr. Smith broke up his camp," reached Horseshoe Bay and found the *Grappler*, which arrived there the previous evening following the raid at Osborne Bay.[172]

Pike and the *Devastation* remained for two days in Cowichan Bay to ensure the safety of hwunitum settlers and seek information on the whereabouts of the Lamalcha:

> At Cowitchin everything had been quiet since our last visit, and in answer to enquiries I made, I could not hear that the settlers had either experienced or apprehended any annoyance from the Indians, from whom however, I was unable to obtain any assistance towards the capture of these pirates.[173]

The uncooperative mood of the Cowichan was due to the May 23rd public execution of Thalaston, Stalehum and Oalatza in Victoria which angered many Cowichan people, some of whom "threatened some white settlers with extermination."[174]

On Sunday morning, May 24th, the *Devastation*, with the first launch and pinnace in tow, proceeded to Osborne Bay where she rendezvoused with the *Forward*.[175] There had been some undisclosed disturbance in the early morning hours and Lascelles had "Landed Boats in search of [the] Indians."[176] Four hours later they returned to the *Forward* with nothing to show for their efforts. Later that morning the *Grappler* arrived from Horseshoe Bay with Smith's voltigeurs, and all three ships lay at anchor in the bay.[177]

Word was received that Acheewun and his people had gone to Montague Harbour on Galiano Island where they owned resources and had refuge caves among the rocks north of the harbour and on Mount Sutil. Anticipating a fight, the *Forward* and *Grappler*, with the two *Topaze* launches and the *Devastation* pinnace, left Osborne Bay for Galiano Island via Houston Passage and Trincomalee Channel.[178] The force arrived off the north end of Parker Island and the boats were sent ashore "to examine the Rocks on Galiano Island, where [the] Lamalcha Indians were supposed to have hidden." Sewholatza, or another hwulmuhw ally, led the British to "a cave in the face of the Cliff which was pointed out as the retreat of some of the Lemalchas."[179] The cave, which may have been one of Acheewun's "hiding places," "was visited by all the officers" who noted that it "was capable of holding a number of people, and the floor was perfectly smooth and level."[180] Evidently the British had been led to believe that the cave would contain evidence of Lamalcha "crimes." Verney recorded that "today we have discovered a cave which we thought would have contained their plunder, but it was empty."[181]

The gunboats entered Sumnuw (Montague Harbour) where the small boats were again sent ashore, "overhauling canoes and bush for the Lamalchas."[182]

Acheewun, Palluk and the other Lamalcha, if they were present, were far away from the shoreline in another refuge cave on the mountain (Mount Sutil) above the harbour. The British concluded that "the information which induced us to go there, turned out to be false; beyond one small canoe no trace of Indians could be found." [183] The landing parties returned, and the gunboats left to rejoin the *Devastation* at anchor in Osborne Bay.

During the night, possibly lured by the promise of a cash reward, "a Penellicut Indian came on board the *Forward* and informed them that two Lamalchas were in the Penellicut village." The informants were Tahwayah and Silseleum who, it seems, offered to accompany the British back to Penelakut. Upon receipt of this information, Pike ordered the *Forward* to proceed in the dark to the village. Shortly before midnight, with the first launch in tow, the *Forward* "got up steam immediately and went to Kuper Island." [184]

In order to surprise the Penelakut, the *Forward* eased steam as it approached the village. At 1:20 a.m. Superintendent Smith, Tomo Antoine, and the "volunteers" embarked with Lascelles in the *Forward*'s gig which, to reduce any noise, "was propelled by paddles instead of oars." The first launch "followed some distance off with muffled oars." [185]

The boats probably landed at the north end of Penelakut Spit and approached the sleeping village on foot led by Tomo Antoine and one of the Penelakut informants who knew exactly which house sheltered their quarry. The night-time action was briefly described by a member of the expedition:

> They landed 300 to 400 yards from the village, which they silently entered, preceded by the interpreter Tomo and an Indian. The party succeeded in capturing two men and one woman, and returned to the gunboat. [186]

One of the prisoners was Qualataltun who was described as "a half-Chamainus & Lamalchee Indian." [187] His wife, Quolastenaht, was also seized. The other prisoner was a Lamalcha man named Sarguck (also called Scloom). None of them were named in Smith's warrant but Tahwayah and Silseleum informed Pike that the captives "were of the party who murdered Marks & his daughter." [188]

The night-time raid took only an hour and the *Forward* left the vicinity under steam to rejoin the other naval vessels at Osborne Bay with no losses except for two Colt revolvers accidentally dropped overboard by members of the landing party. [189]

The following morning, May 25th, the *Devastation* steamed from Osborne Bay for Penelakut. [190] Near the south end of Kuper Island, two canoes piloted by Slelum and Cawley from Penelakut approached the warship with three more prisoners, two men and a woman. [191] Their prisoners included two Penelakut, Allwhenuk and his wife Koltenaht, as well as the Nanaimo elder, Skilloweet, all of whom lived at

Lamalcha. As before, none of the captives' names appeared on Smith's warrant but their captors insisted that they were implicated in the deaths of Frederick Marks and his daughter Caroline. According to information Pike received from Slelum and Cawley, Allwhenuk "was stated to have held Marks' daughter while his wife Kol-ten-aut, killed her."[192] Skilloweet was "the man stated to have shot Marks."[193]

After the prisoners were taken on board, the *Devastation* continued through Houston Passage towards Penelakut, stopping "between Indian and Kuper Islands" for two hours while the crew "mustered at quarters," after which the ship returned to Osborne Bay. During this time Pike, with the assistance of Smith and his interpreters, interrogated the prisoners who were defiant and unrepentant. Pike found that they "undisguisedly avow that several murders of white men have been committed by their tribe."[194] Allwhenuk boasted "that it was he who shot the seaman on board the *Forward*."[195]

The Nanaimo elder Skilloweet, "alarmed at the prospect of punishment," confessed to the British about his participation in the previously unknown killing of the hwunitum at S'tayus (Pender Island) in 1860:

> The Man Skullowayt [Skilloweet] declares that he & and another Indian named Pallak & a woman named Sheemalliett [Semallee] committed their first murder of a white man as much as six years ago; describing in the most fiendish manner how they fired at him, & the flint missed fire, how he fought them until the woman disabled him by a blow across the back with an axe when they stabbed him, & then went and shot his companion.[196]

In general, Pike found that "on questioning the men & women I have detained, I can elicit no reliable information."[197] Significantly, none of the prisoners admitted taking part in the attack on the Marks and none of them implicated Acheewun. Instead, it "was generally admitted by the Indians" that "the man Palluk ... and his wife Se-mallie [Semallee], helped to murder Marks."[198]

At this time, Palluk and Semallee were at Montague Harbour on Galiano Island with the remnants of Acheewun's band. Towards evening Palluk, Semallee and Sheemultun left the group and canoed towards the Chemainus River, where they encountered the hwulmuhw allies of the British. The Lamalcha "came into the Chemanus Camp during the night" but "at daybreak" there was a sharp skirmish during which Palluk was killed and his wife, Semallee, captured.[199] According to information received by Pike, "the Chemanus made an attempt to capture them, but Sheemaltum escaped & stealing a canoe crossed over to Retreat Cove, Pallak was shot by an Indian in self defence."[200] Smith claimed that "Palluck" was shot "through the head while he was attempting to escape up Chemainus River."[201] The man who fired the fatal shot is not known but it was probably either Samellan or Swayahalt, both of whom split a one hundred dollar reward, significantly less than

Site of the "upper Settlement" on the Chemainus River (Chemainus Indian Reserve No. 10).
Abeewun's wife, child and father-in-law, Statumish, were captured here by colonial troops on
May 17th, 1863. In this vicinity, on May 26th, 1863, the warrior Palluk was shot by
"Chemainus" warriors.   *Photo by Chris Arnett.*

Halalt, Willy Island. On May 17th, 1863 British forces under Captain John Pike seized the
leading si'em of this village as hostages to force the people to turn over relations of Acheewun.
                                      Royal British Columbia Museum, PN 891.

Penelakut, Kuper Island. Taken many years after 1863 this photograph shows the original village along the beach and newer houses on the heights above.

Royal British Columbia Museum, PN 4578.

Site of Lamalcha, 1983. On May 2nd, 1863, the village and its fortifications were burned by British forces. The village site is indicated by the low mound visible in the middle foreground behind the beach.

Photo by Chris Arnett.

the reward of five hundred dollars originally posted by Commissioner of Police Pemberton "for the apprehension of the murderers of Frederick Marks and his daughter Caroline Harvey."[202]

On Tuesday morning, May 26th, Semallee was taken by her captors by canoe to the *Devastation*. She treated the British with contempt and boldly admitted her role in the deaths of hwunitum. She "confessed to having assisted her husband and others in the murder of white men" and, unlike the other prisoners, when questioned about the murder of the Marks, "made no contension of the crime."[203]

Nevertheless, Semallee was somehow coerced into providing the British with other important information and "offered to point out the spot where Ot-chee-wun & three others are encamped with four canoes."[204] The fact that she divulged such information after being so defiant suggests that she was either forced to cooperate through threats of physical violence from the British, or she did so as an initiative on her own part to secure her release. Semallee's boldness, plus the fact that she was physically attractive, led the British to treat her with some deference. Accordingly, Commander Pike "directed Lieut. Lascelles on his way to Victoria to examine Retreat Cove & see if this information is correct."[205]

A message was sent to the *Forward*, which was anchored off the mouth of the Chemainus River, to proceed with the two *Topaze* launches to Osborne Bay. Upon their arrival, Pike transferred nineteen hwulmuhw prisoners to the *Forward* for transportation to Victoria.[206] Before departing for Victoria Lascelles was ordered to proceed "under steam to Galiano Island in search of Lamalchas."[207] With various members of the families of Acheewun and his brother, Shenasaluk, on board the British hoped to put extra pressure on them to surrender. As the gunboat approached Montague Harbour, Acheewun and his companions hid their canoes and climbed up the rocky heights above the shoreline. According to a member of the British search party:

> The woman, Semalile [Semallee], informed us that she had left a party of the Lamalchas the night before on Galiano Island, just at the entrance of Montague Harbour. Under her directions we landed a party of scouts and found two canoes. The Indians had evidently been there lately as we found the remains of their camp, and several articles concealed in the bushes. We also found a deerskin, perfectly fresh, but the Indians had fled into the woods, probably at our approach. As we had orders not to delay in getting to Victoria with the prisoners, there was not time for a satisfactory search of the Island.[208]

The "volunteers" fired some thirty rounds into the bush in a fruitless attempt to flush out their adversaries, but by 1 p.m. the expedition left Galiano for Victoria.[209]

The destruction of their canoes effectively marooned the remnants of Acheewun's band, which had been reduced to his brother Shenasaluk, Sheemaltun and Sheemaltun's wife and child, on Galiano Island.

At Osborne Bay, where the *Devastation* lay at anchor, "three Indian Canoes arrived from Chemanos River bringing the body of an Indian named Paillak [Palluk]." After viewing it, the British "committed the body of [the] deceased to the deep."[210]

Palluk, the acknowledged "murderer of Marks," was dead and Pike may have found himself in a quandary with regards to the continued pursuit of Acheewun and the others named in the original arrest warrant. The British now knew that Palluk, his wife Semallee, and possibly others they had captured were the ones actually responsible for the deaths of Marks and Harvey, not those named in the warrant—and Palluk was now dead. The expedition had met its goal in locating the man who killed the Marks, even though Palluk was not one of those originally "charged with the murder of Frederick Marks and his daughter Caroline Harvey." As for the death of Charles Gliddon at Lamalcha on April 20th, one of the captives, Allwhenuk, claimed to have fired the fatal shot. On the other hand, the additional objective of the expedition, which was to negotiate with, or capture, the Lamalcha "chiefs" Squ'acum and Acheewun, who were alleged to have been involved in the killings, had not been achieved. Despite some close calls, the Lamalcha leaders had successfully eluded intense and persistent pursuit.

After twelve days of campaigning, British resources had been stretched to the limit as the navy, police and hwulmuhw allies pursued the Lamalcha back and forth across the Gulf Islands and along the east coast of Vancouver Island. Verney, of the *Grappler*, found "the continual work ... rather harassing and fatiguing."[211] The British had in their custody ten men, nine women and several infants but only one of them, Shacutsus, had been named in the original arrest warrant issued by the Victoria Police. The British had also seized or destroyed a significant amount of Lamalcha property, including canoes, house-planks, and bushels of potatoes. As Pike noted:

> With the exception of one or two canoes believed to have gone towards Frazer River all belonging to them in this locality to the number (including three burnt by Lieut. Lascelles on a previous occasion) of seventeen, and a large quantity of property have been destroyed.[212]

Pike felt that he had achieved as much as was possible and, as he informed Douglas, he decided to return to Esquimalt "that I may hear from yourself what further measures you may order to be taken to prove to this piratical tribe that the authority they refuse to acknowledge, must be respected."[213] Pike's reasons for calling off the search carried an underlying tone of defeat.

During the whole of the cruize, we have found it impossible to obtain any parley, or to enter into any communication with the Lamalchas, and two parties of five each have now retreated into places so inaccessible to the means we possess of tracking them, that I feel compelled to desist for the present from further search."[214]

Several members of the families of Acheewun and Shenasaluk were held in custody, including their wives and children, and Pike trusted that their confinement would mitigate any retaliation by Lamalcha warriors. As if to include a positive note in his official report to Douglas, Pike wrote:

I doubt that any further outrage will be committed by them unless under direction of their Chief—Ot-chee-wun [Acheewun] for whose being quiet for the present, I believe there is sufficient surety in the hostages I have detained.[215]

On the following day, May 27th, the *Devastation* joined with *Grappler* and both ships proceeded together down Sansum Narrows en route to Esquimalt.[216] Along the way each ship exercised its crew "at General Quarters," firing several rounds of solid shot and grape-shot as a farewell to the "Seat of War."[217]

Recalling the 1853 and 1856 British military expeditions into the territories of Hul'qumi'num First Nations, the Chemainus and the Penelakut si'em who allied themselves with the British, hoped that by turning over or killing those responsible for the attack on the Marks, the British would be satisfied and not return. With the possible exception of one man "who had harboured one of the murderers" and was "handed over to the naval authorities" by the Chemainus District constable Major Biggs, and Shacutsus, who may have given himself up, all of the captives had been taken by hwulmuhw allies. Through promise of reward or motivated by inter-family feud hwulmuhw allies surrendered nineteen persons whom they accused of having some part in the Marks' killings. Palluk, the warrior who "always wished to kill white men," and openly boasted of shooting Marks, had been shot. But the war was not over. The Royal Navy, eager to avenge the death of the sailor Gliddon at the Battle of Lamalcha and to punish those who had tarnished their reputation by eluding their grasp, would not be satisfied until Squ'acum and Acheewun either were in their custody or dead. Sewholatza, who served on condition that his father's death be avenged, was also dissatisfied. For its part, the colonial regime of James Douglas was determined to put an end to any further activity on the part of the Lamalcha and Penelakut warriors to resist hwunitum colonization of their territories.

Hulkalatkstun, preemiment si'em of Penelakut, Kuper Island, was an important ally of the British. He played a key role in the capture of Acheewun at Montague Harbour on June 2nd, 1863. This photo, taken many years later, shows the venerable warrior in old age.
Private Collection.

Officers and crew of HMS Cameleon *circa 1863.*
British Columbia Archives and Records Service, Photo 29825.

HMS Cameleon. *Commanded by Captain Edward Hardinge, the* Cameleon *took part in the third expedition of May 31st-June 8th, 1863 against the Lamalcha warriors during which Acheewun, his brother Shenasaluk, and Sheemultun were captured.*
British Columbia Archives and Records Service, Photo HP 446.

Chapter Eleven

Come! I, Hulkalatkstun go to kill um!

Following the unsuccessful search for Acheewun and his people at Montague Harbour, the *Forward* and the two *Topaze* launches left Galiano Island for Victoria where they arrived on the evening of May 26th. Imprisoned on board the *Forward* were a quarter of the adult population of Lamalcha with an unknown number of children. [1] As the gunboat and launches made their way into Victoria Harbour, a large crowd gathered at the St. Our's dock to watch the prisoners disembark. The onlookers included three correspondents from the city's newspapers who came to record their impressions as the prisoners were landed. The *Daily Evening Express* reported that:

> On landing, the prisoners were all ranged between two files of marines, and marched to the gaol. They did not betray in their countenances any appearance of terror or dismay as they marched off, although we could not help thinking that when they landed and saw the crowd gazing at them, a feeling which we can only describe as one of resignation, crept over their faces. The large crowd of persons who assembled to see them land behaved well, and many felt a pang of pity for the little babes who were suspended to their mother's backs. [2]

The newspapers praised the members of the expedition such as Horace Smith, the Superintendent of Police, for being "energetic and unceasing in his exertions to bring the fugitives to justice." The naval officers, Lieutenants Pusey and Geneste, and Lieutenant Symons of the Royal Marines, and the officers and men under their command, were commended for their "admirable zeal" and for performing "their arduous and often trying duties ably and efficiently." [3]

The *Daily Evening Express* and the *Victoria Daily Chronicle* made no mention of Lieutenant Horace Lascelles and waited to hear what he had to say in regard to his kidnapping of Charles Allen and the subsequent charges brought against him. [4] The *British Colonist*, however, was unequivocal in its praise of the Royal Navy:

Upon the service rendered by the navy in the affair, which has of late occupied the public attention, too much value cannot be placed. In order to judge of the full extent of our indebtedness, we have only to ask ourselves how, with our limited means, we could well have got on without them? They have had a trying and disagreeable duty to perform; one from which little glory could be gained, and where failure would meet with no sympathy. To Captain Pike and Commanders Verney and Lascelles with their commands, therefore, much credit is due for the part they have taken in bringing matters to a satisfactory termination. They so far have succeeded well in checking the insolence of the native miscreants, and inspiring a wholesome dread of the consequences of transgression. Nor must we forget the active and able part taken also by Superintendent Smith in assisting the navy to bring the perpetrators of the recent murders to the justice they deserve.[5]

As details of the recent expedition became available, particularly in regard to the assistance given the Royal Navy by hwulmuhw allies, Amor De Cosmos expressed relief that "the dread of an Indian war, though perhaps reasonably enough entertained in some parts of America need not, however, disturb the nerves of settlers along these coasts."

Murders may occur ocassionally, as the results of individual passion; but a regular combination of more than one tribe for purposes hostile to the whites is scarcely within the bounds of probability. The fact of their always being more or less enmity between the different bodies of natives themselves, their faithlessness towards all who deal with them, be they friends or foe, and their knowledge of the white man's power, will always make them distrustful of the success of any attempt at union.[6]

Nevertheless, de Cosmos again suggested that the ongoing reluctance of the colonial government to settle the question of land title extinguishment could create future conflict.[7]

The colonial press acknowledged the important role played by hwulmuhw allies in the late expedition: "Taking all things into consideration," noted the *British Colonist*, "they have, we think, shown as great a desire to have the murderers of Marks and Brady brought to justice, as is often to be met with among the whites, and so far they deserve credit ... The Indians were at first very shy about aiding the expedition in the search for the known culprits. They preferred working with the party to working by themselves. Latterly some of them behaved very well and rendered valuable assistance."[8]

Douglas, on May 28th, hosted a special reception to honour the hwulmuhw warriors who accompanied the *Forward* and *Devastation* to Victoria to collect their rewards:

> His Excellency had a "talk" yesterday with the Chemainus Indians who aided in the capture of the Lamalchas. The Indians expressed themselves as loyal subjects and were feasted on rice, molasses and bread, and we believe received each pecuniary compensation for their valuable service. [9]

Douglas distributed $220 to six men; Samellan and Swayahalt each received $50 as "1/2 reward for capture of Palluck," Sleleum and Cawley were paid $80 "for capture of Ull-whe-nuck," while Tah-wayah and Silselum were given $40 for the capture of "Qualahilton and Scloom." [10] In addition to food and money, the hwulmuhw allies may have also received naval caps and uniforms to wear in recognition of their service with the Royal Navy. In later years, hwunitum settlers recalled that Sewholatza always "wore a naval cap" and when he greeted them he "gave the naval salute—with gravity and dignity as if to the manner born." [11]

Not all were happy with the reward for their services. According to the *Victoria Daily Chronicle*:

> The Chemainus Indians who assisted in the capture of the Lamalchas have gone away quite dissatisfied. They understood, while engaged in the hunt, that they were to have $100 for every Siwash taken by them; instead of which only one of their number was paid $100 for killing Polluck. They declare that they will assist in the war no longer unless an advance be paid them. [12]

On the same day that Douglas had his celebration, the Lamalcha prisoners were marched into the Police Court for a preliminary hearing to determine charges. Continuing the campaign of misinformation, the press referred to the Lamalcha and Penelakut captives as "the sixteen Indian prisoners charged with murder." [13] A reporter from the *Victoria Daily Chronicle* described the scene:

> The prisoners are eight men and six women. Three of the latter have babies at the breast, and one of the male prisoners is a bright-eyed boy of about fourteen years of age. Another of the males is fully 80 years old and scarcely able, because of his decrepitude to stand erect. All appeared very much downcast, and without exchanging a word with each other, watched with painful interest every movement which took place.

> Before going into court, three of the number were identified by an intelligent looking Cowichan as having fired at the gunboat at the time that the sailor was killed. One of those identified appeared to be about fifty years old, and when pointed out, trembled like an aspen leaf. The

remaining two gazed defiantly upon their accuser and the policemen. The Chief of Police asked for further time in which to produce evidence, and the Magistrate remanded the prisoners for one day. [14]

The colonial authorities soon realized that, despite the number of prisoners in their custody, only three admitted complicity in the deaths of hwunitum. Semallee, by her own admission, was a participant in the deaths of Marks and Harvey. Allwhenuk admitted that it was he who shot the sailor Gliddon in the fight at Lamalcha. The Nanaimo elder Skiloweet confessed to another killing of which the authorities had not been aware. The police needed more time and more coercion. The colonial government was mindful that the Lamalcha leaders, the real opposition and threat to the stability of the frontier, had to be apprehended before a Court of Assize could take place. The following morning, when prisoners were again brought into the Police Court, Smith "applied for a further remand of a week or ten days stating that he had received orders to proceed forthwith to Cowichan, to continue his search for the members of the gang who are still at large." [15]

Following the return of the *Forward*, the colonial press was finally able to report the events of the previous two weeks without relying on rumour. The *British Colonist* was favoured with the most detailed accounts possibly because its proprietor, Amor De Cosmos, had seen fit not to publish any copy critical of the naval forces or any of its officers.

For the first time in the crisis, the Lamalcha si'em were referred to by name in the newspaper accounts. Squ'acum, the military leader, was described as "the chief of the Lamalchas." Acheewun was labelled "the Pirate Chief" and blamed for the deaths of hwulmuhw and hwunitum. The *British Colonist* concluded that Acheewun:

> ... who glories in having killed 11 white men, two or three chiefs and numerous Indians, is a perfect fiend and is the terror of all the tribes. They believe an aim from his gun to be certain death, and that whoever he threatens is doomed. His canoe is also supposed to outstrip all others in speed, but the truth is that A-chee-wun is a cunning villain and employs picked men to paddle his canoe. Some of the Indians informed officers of the Expedition that one night when closely pursued he had eluded them by putting to sea in a raft. He has a number of retreats and hiding places on Galiano and other islands. There was one cave high up in the rocks near Montague Harbour, which was visited by all the officers. [16]

Acheewun's reputation as a killer outweighed hard evidence and these rumours are suggestive of the continuing "smear" campaign perpetrated by the police against the Lamalcha in general and Acheewun in particular. Acheewun was originally identified by Smith, according to hearsay, as the man who killed Marks.

Smith's letter of April 25th stated that "the chief who shot him [Marks] is the terror of all the Indians around, he boasts that Marks is the eleventh white man he has murdered."[17] But it was Palluk, not Acheewun, who killed Marks. Palluk, according to his own wife, "always wished to kill white men," and it is possible that the tally of hwunitum victims attributed to Acheewun by the press and subsequent hwunitum writers was more applicable to the late warrior killed by his enemies on the Chemainus River.

In any event, Douglas was adamant that Squ'acum, Acheewun and the others named in the arrest warrant of May 11th be apprehended, not so much because they were responsible for any specific "crime," but because they symbolized hwulmuhw resistance to hwunitum jurisdiction and sovereignty. The colonial authorities had in their custody the individuals responsible for the death of Marks and the sailor Charles Gliddon, but the leaders responsible for the defeat of the British at Lamalcha on April 20th and rumours of other killings and demonstrations of hwulmuhw jurisdiction could not be ignored. As well, Douglas was obliged to capture Acheewun and try him for the killing of Sewholatza's father Ashutstun, which was the major reason Sewholatza, and probably others, had assisted the colonial government in the recent campaign.

On the morning of May 29th Douglas met with Commodore Spencer to discuss the importance of pursuing the Lamalcha leaders and the others named in the May 11th warrant. Following their conversation, Douglas penned two letters requesting that another naval expedition be dispatched "at the earliest possible moment."

> Referring to the recent proceedings against the Lamalcha Tribe of Indians, I consider it very desireable that our offensive measures should not be discontinued until every effort has been made to capture the remaining Indians of that Tribe charged with murder. The guilty Tribe has now been pursued from place to place, the services or sympathies of nearly all the Indians of the Coast are now enlisted against the Tribe, and if measures be speedily taken, I doubt not that the remaining men will be captured without much further difficulty. A delay in the proceedings would probably cause us much trouble hereafter, and require us to do a second time what has now been done. I would therefore beg that you would again detach a force upon this service at the very earliest possible moment to follow up the work so well begun.[18]

Douglas may have already made contact with Acheewun's estranged relation, Hulkalatkstun of Penelakut, of whom Douglas was "such a good friend."[19] Douglas was so confident of success that he wrote a second letter, requesting that once the naval forces apprehended the remaining Lamalcha, they continue up the coast to investigate other attacks against hwunitum in Johnstone Straits and Bentink Arm.[20]

Word of another expedition soon reached the press where it was reported that "Mr. Smith will proceed to Cowichan in the *Forward* and make search for the evil-doers who have thus far eluded capture." [21] Additional help was expected from hwulmuhw allies who shared a desire to capture Acheewun. As the *British Colonist* put it:

> ... every hope is entertained of the eventual capture of this notorious character. The Indians consider that they have now compromised themselves with him, and are bent on having him. [22]

Two of the hwunitum "voltigeurs" would again accompany the naval forces in spite of a drunken escapade on the eve of the expedition which garnered them a place in the May 30th edition of the *Daily Evening Express* under the headline "Hors de Combat." [23]

Upon receipt of Douglas' request for further naval assistance, Commodore Spencer called on the services of Captain Edward Hardinge and the seventeen-gun sloop *Cameleon* which had recently returned from Nanaimo. The *Cameleon* had sat out the late campaign in Nanaimo and suffered the Royal Navy's second fatality of the war when "a seamen in a state of intoxication fell from the bridge [in town] and died the next day in consequence of injuries." [24]

On May 30th Hardinge received orders from Commodore Spencer to proceed to Cowichan Bay with the two launches of the *Topaze*, where he would rendezvous with the *Forward* before searching for the remaining Lamalcha fugitives.

Sunday, May 31st dawned "fine and warm" as the *Forward* made ready, following "Divine Service," to leave Esquimalt. [25] The *Forward* proceeded to Victoria Harbour and received "on board Mr. Smith, Inspector of Police, 2 Volunteers and 2 Indian Searchers." [26] The interpreter Tomo Antoine, for some reason, would not accompany this last expedition against the Lamalcha.

At 3:15 p.m. the *Forward* proceeded under steam from Victoria Harbour and soon "made all plain sail" under threatening skies. [27] That evening, shortly after the *Forward* secured anchorage in Cowichan Bay, the storm broke and "blew quite a gale ... between nine and twelve o'clock from the westward accompanied with rain, thunder and flashes of lightning." [28] The storm continued throughout the night.

On the following morning, Monday, June 1st, "it rained incessantly" as the *Cameleon,* with the two launches of the *Topaze* in tow, left Esquimalt and "proceeded to the anchorage off Cowichan." [29] Once there, Hardinge communicated with the *Forward* and abruptly left. [30] As Captain Thorne of the schooner *Louisa* observed:

[The *Cameleon*] arrived in Cowichan Bay, where the gunboat *Forward* was lying ... and steamed away, without anchoring, to Chemainos [Halalt], leaving orders for Lieutenant Commander Lascelles to follow and continue the search for the uncaptured Lamalchoes. As soon as the *Forward* could get up steam she weighed and proceeded after the *Cameleon*.[31]

Hardinge had an option "to stop at Cowitchin to secure the apprehension of two men implicated in the murder of a man named 'Roe' at North Saanich two years before, (whom Superintendent Smith had heard of in the neighbourhood), but directed the force solely upon the apprehension of the Lamalchas."[32] Accordingly, Hardinge ordered the *Forward* "to Osborne Bay, directing Lieutenant Lascelles to proceed to the Chemainos River, in order, if possible to obtain information relative to the remaining Lamalchas at large."[33]

There was a rumour that "several of the Lamalchas" had "recently made an appearance in a half-starved condition and after having supplied themselves with dried fish, left again for the woods."[34]

In the late afternoon the *Forward* weighed anchor and proceeded towards the mouth of the Chemainus River, passing the *Cameleon* which was anchored in Osborne Bay.[35] The *Forward* continued towards the village of Halalt, where a party was landed. But, as Hardinge later reported, "at Chemainos River (from the village at its mouth) no information had been obtained, and no disposition shown to assist us."[36]

By the morning of Tuesday, June 2nd the rain had passed and the day dawned with clear skies as the *Forward* proceeded from Halalt for Penelakut where Hardinge "had directed Lieutenant Lascelles to meet me." The *Cameleon* also made ready to sail early in the morning, but Hardinge's plans were disrupted shortly after weighing anchor at 4 a.m. when the man-of-war approached too close to the east side of Osborne Bay and ran aground. Hardinge was undeterred by this incident as is evident in his report.

Unfortunately in turning the ship took the ground on a sand bank, and as the tide was falling after making an ineffectual effort to get her off, and seeing that she was in no way in a dangerous position, I proceeded with the *Topaze*'s two launches to the Pennelikut village and went on board the *Forward*.[37]

Hardinge found, in contrast to the negative response of the Halalt to British requests for assistance, that "in the Pennelikut Village the reverse was happily the case, and from there Mr. Smith obtained six scouts, but with no further information than that Ah-chee-wun with two others of his tribe were on Galiano Island."[38]

The six Penelakut scouts included Hulkalatkstun, Whulumthat, and Quolaquoi. Hulkalatkstun acknowledged that Acheewun was "of my house" but the relationship did not interfere with his decision to help the British. [39]

There may have been several reasons why these men helped the British in their search for Acheewun. Hulkalatkstun was Roman Catholic, and influenced by the priests from the Catholic mission at Comiaken, especially Father Rondeault, with whom he had a close relationship. These men may have have helped convince him to aid the hwunitum against "a bad and cruel man" who had killed the si'em Ashutstun and possibly several hwunitum. But the primary motive for helping the British, according to the account by his granddaughter, Mary Rice, was their anger at Acheewun over his participation in the attack on the men of the hwunitum trading schooner the previous summer. The deaths of the crew and the burning of the vessel may have disrupted a lucrative trading agreement which existed between their families and the hwunitum. Hulkalatkstun referred to the slaughtered hwunitum as "his good friends." [40] The Penelakut may have assumed that this incident was the reason the British wanted Acheewun. The British, apparently, knew nothing about it; there may have been rumours, as well as material evidence found at Lamalcha, but there was no official acknowledgement.

Mary Rice recalled the story of Hulkalatkstun's meeting with the British on June 2nd on the beach at Penelakut:

> There came a great war ship "Man-o'-War" my grandfather called it— with many, many white men, and the white chief came to Hul-ka-latkstun and talked to him.
>
> "'Tell me," he said, "what do you know of those white men and their boat?' And Hul-ka-latkstun told him of his good friends the white men ... and he told them that there was great sadness in the village, for the [Penelakut] had seen the burning of the canoe and the white men lying dead.
>
> "Well," the white chief said to my grandfather, "we have been to the Lamalcha's village, and there we found food [flour] from the canoe, and on top of some of the houses were the wings [sails] from the boat. There we took seven men prisoner, but there is one more, and he is the chief of the village; he must be caught and punished with the others. You are chief here, and so you must come with us and help us find this man; and until you come back no person must leave the village—all must stay here."
>
> "I will come with you," said my grandfather, "for the Lamalcha chief is of my house, a man named Qha-och-ewan [Acheewun], and I know he is a bad and cruel man."

So the white men came off the ship and they carried the canoes far up to the beach, and on every canoe they put a mark (number) and on the back of every man, woman and child they made the same marks, so that they could tell if any left the village.

After this Hul-ka-latkstun said "good-bye" to my grandmother and their two boys and he was taken out to the war ship, and all the tribe, with those strange marks upon them, gathered on the beach and watched their great and wise chief go away to help the white men.

Now there were other men on the war ship—taken by the white chief until the Lamalcha chief should be found. These men were Chief Ce-who-latza [Sewholatza] from Valdez Island (who was later named O'Shea), and Whul-um-that, and Quola-quoi (who were called Jacob and Joe), and were from Kuper Island.[41]

At 8 a.m. the *Forward* left Penelakut with the *Topaze*'s first and second launches in tow and proceeded towards Montague Harbour, where it was believed that Acheewun and his party were still located.[42] As the gunboat passed through the north end of the harbour, the first launch was detached to begin the search for Acheewun and his small band. "I detached Lieutenant Genestes' launch," Hardinge later wrote, "with Mr. Smith and his party of Marines, scouts and Voltigeurs numbering fifteen and directed Lieutenant Geneste to support Mr. Smith with a part of his crew; before detaching them the [Penelakut] scouts were all armed."[43]

At the same time, a man and a woman from Penelakut were on their way to rescue Acheewun's band but the arrival of the British and their Penelakut allies thwarted the escape plans. Unable to help, the couple hid on Parker Island to await a better opportunity to save their friends.[44]

Leaving the first launch to land the shore-party and begin the search the *Forward,* with the second launch in tow, continued on "to Miner's Bay, in Plumper Pass ... to endeavour to obtain information from the settlers there."[45] At Miner's Bay Hardinge interviewed hwunitum settlers, presumably Christian Mayer and his partner, but "all that was known was that a party of three Lamalcha men had been a week before on Galiano Island."[46] These men, Acheewun, his brother Shenasuluk, and Sheemultun who was accompanied by his wife and child, sought refuge in a cave high above the shoreline.[47] On the heights of Mount Sutil above Montague Harbour, they watched as the British and their Penelakut allies disembarked from the first launch on the beach below.

Hulkalatkstun was familiar with the area and Smith's landing-party followed him along the shoreline as he searched for signs of the Lamalcha warriors. The launch followed their progress just offshore, with its twenty-four-pound cannon and the rifles of the sailors trained on the surrounding forest in case of attack. Finally, "at the foot of the mountains, Superintendent Smith's party discovered a fresh foot-print which satisfied them that one of the men of whom they were in search, was close at hand."[48] According to Mary Rice, the discovery was made by Hulkalatkstun who then guided the British up the mountain to Acheewun's hiding place.

He went along the beach, looking under trees and bushes for some tracks of the man; my grandfather found a canoe far back out of site!

Now Hul-ka-latkstun was a mighty hunter with eyes like those of an eagle, and very soon he found tracks in a clear place, and they were the tracks of a man, a woman and a child! Ah, how he shouted with joy, for he knew that Qha-och-ewan [Acheewun] had a wife and child with him. "Oheeeee!" he shouted, "Ah! Ah! Qha-och-ewan, I will get you! Why have you killed my friends and kept me like a prisoner from my people and my home all these days? Now I have you, ugh! Ughhhh!"

The white chief [Smith] heard his shouts and came hurrying up, and seeing the canoe and the tracks, he said to my grandfather, "Good, we will get him now," and he told his men to move out so and so [fan-wise], and in this way to climb up the mountainside. So they followed the tracks. Sometimes they were in soft mud and easy to find, then would come rock and no marks could be found. But my grandfather went first and his quick eyes found tracks now here, now there.

The white men soon got tired, for they had never climbed in this way before, and they said, "Let us rest for a time and have some food." But Hul-ka-latkstun waved his stick and shouted "Come! Come! I, Hul-ka-latkstun go to kill um!" and he would not wait.

"Listen," the white chief told him, "You must not kill this man; the white men will punish him. It is law!"

On and on they went, and now the men far away came closer, closer, until they had Qha-och-ewan [Acheewun] and his wife and child amongst them. Ah, but how tired and thin they were. Their hair hung over their faces and it was all hard and dirty, and they could scarcely walk. "Oh-aaaaa!" shouted Hul-ka-latkstun, "now we will kill you! Oheeeeee!" But Qha-och-ewan [Acheewun] threw himself on the ground and tears were running down his face.

"Ah, Hul-ka-latkstun," he cried, "do not kill me, for remember, I am of your house. Let the white men kill me, for, see, I am nearly dead now, and my child cannot walk for want of food!"

Again the white chief told my grandfather, "The man and his family must not be killed. If you kill these people, then you must be punished; it is the white man's law!" So they turned and went back down the mountain, Quola-quoi helping the woman, Whul-um-that, carrying the child, and Qha-och-ewan [Acheewun] going with the white men. [49]

Mary Rice's detailed description of Acheewun's capture, no doubt told to her by Hulkalatkstun himself, differs slightly from the more abbreviated accounts preserved in the British record. Of Hulkalatkstun's crucial role in locating Acheewun there can be little doubt. The substance of the hike up the mountain at the south end of Galiano Island appears to be factual and is corroborated by other accounts which credit the discovery of Acheewun and his party to the Penelakut scouts. Mary Rice's version, however, contains some obvious errors of fact—for example, Acheewun's wife and child were not present on Galiano Island but were held captive on board the *Forward*. Most notable, however, is the discrepancy between Hulkalatkstun's version and the British version regarding the manner in which the Acheewun was finally caught. Hulkalatkstun was telling a "war story" which raised the prestige of the narrator by exaggerating the capitulation and humiliation of the enemy. By contrast, in the British version of the events of June 2nd, Acheewun was only captured "with great difficulty."

According to one account, upon the discovery of the footprints on the beach, Smith's shore-party "proceeded round to join Lt. Geneste, with the first launch, when he and the greater part of his command, accompanied Superintendent Smith's party over the back of the mountain. On the summit the Indians discovered the three men who dropped some ammunition and fled. [The British and Penelakut] gave chase and drove them down the face of the mountain. Just as they were on the point of catching them, the gunboat and second launch were seen in the straits, and a volley fired to bring them in." [50]

While the British and the Penelakut scouts were pursuing the three warriors down the steep rocky slopes of Mount Sutil, Hardinge was returning from Miner's Bay in the *Forward* with the second launch of the *Topaze* in tow. After interviewing hwunitum at Miner's Bay, who confirmed that the three men he sought were still on Galiano, Hardinge decided that the entire island needed to be searched. He reasoned that the Lamalcha would not escape "as during the recent operations the canoes of these men were believed to have been destroyed." While the men of Lieutenant Genestes' launch searched the south end of the island, Hardinge "intended to station Lieutenant Pusey's Launch towards the North End of Galiano Island, communicating with both parties by the *Forward* until their adversaries were caught." [51]

The *Forward* was on its way to the north end of the island to station Pusey's launch when they heard the volley of rifle fire from the British and Penelakut in hot pursuit of Acheewun and his men. "On passing the land about Montague Harbour," recalled Hardinge, "at 1 P.M. our attention was attracted by musketry on shore, the *Forward* was immediately headed for the Harbour, and Lieutenant Pusey's launch detached as soon as the men on shore could be made out, the *Forward* anchoring in the south entrance of the Harbour." [52] It was approximately 2 p.m. [53]

With thirty or more men pursuing them down the mountain, and a similar number approaching from the water, Acheewun and his companions were trapped. Contrary to Hulkalatkstun's version of his capture, Acheewun did not give up without a fight. There was a brief struggle after "the braves (who had taken refuge in a mountain) were driven down to the water's edge. Ar-che-won when brought to bay raised his musket twice to shoot at one of the marines, but his gun missed fire, and ere he could re-cock it he was in irons." [54] Another account stated that "he offered great resistance when taken, and handled three or four sailors with perfect ease, and it was not until overpowered by numbers that he yielded." [55] Just as the men of the second launch "were on the point of landing, A-chee-wun and his two tillicums were caught and handed over to Lt. Pusey's command and conveyed to the gunboat." [56]

"Shortly afterwards," wrote Hardinge, "Ah-chee-wun (the chief pirate) with Shu-na-se-luk his brother, were brought on board to our great satisfaction their capture having been effected chiefly by the scouts tracking them closely, assisted by the Voltigeurs, and by the number of men at Mr. Smith's disposal, by which he was able to surround them and close all outlets of escape." [57]

Acheewun and Shenasuluk found that the hwunitum had their wives, sisters and infant children imprisoned on the gunboat, with what effect on the people involved can only be imagined. The warriors were interrogated:

> ... they stated in conversation that they were to have been taken off Galiano Island, about the time of our arrival by a Pennelikut man and a Lamalcha woman, who were with their canoe on Parker Island." [58]

Informed of this, Hardinge ordered the *Forward*'s gunner, William Clarke, to take a boat's crew in the gig and investigate. Searching the shoreline of Kwi'kwens (Parker Island), Clarke's men found the canoe which was brought on board; but they saw nothing of the people. [59]

The British shore-parties, led by the Penelakut scouts, continued to search for Sheemaltun, "the third man, known to be with Ah-chee-wun." Within an hour Sheemaltun, "together with his wife and two children," were taken prisoner by the Penelakut warrior, Whulumthat. [60]

By late afternoon, satisfied that the men they had been seeking for weeks had been apprehended, Hardinge ordered a gun fired "to recall [the] boats and searchers."[61] The *Forward* and the launches then proceeded to Penelakut where they landed "the scouts we had obtained there, Mr. Smith paying them the reward for their share in the capture of the prisoners."[62] One hundred dollars was paid to Quolaquoi for the capture of Shenasaluk, and Whulumthat collected a reward of fifty dollars for capturing Sheemultun. The hwunitum record shows that a man by the name of Qu-she-lum received one hundred dollars for his role in the "capture of Acheewan."[63]

After the Penelakut scouts disembarked, Hardinge went in the *Forward* to Chemainos River where "in consequence of his having been very active in the capture of the prisoners, landed Sha-tu-mish (father-in-law of Ah-chee-wun) Klee-sa-luk (uncle of Ah-chee-wun) and Ah-chee-wun's wife, Sally, who had been detained as hostages by Commander Pike."[64] The degree to which Statumish co-operated with the British of his own free will is not known. Regardless, he received twenty-two dollars for "22 days as a Voltigeur."[65]

At 8:20 p.m., with the setting sun streaking the sky red, the *Forward* approached Osborne Bay where Hardinge was relieved to find that his ship, the *Cameleon*, "had come off the high bank at high water, with the stream anchor laid out astern."[66]

During the night Acheewun, Shenasuluk and Sheemultun were interrogated by the British on the whereabouts of Squ'acum and other Lamalcha people. Details of the questioning are few, but allegations of the methods used to torture the prisoners to extract information eventually surfaced. The *Victoria Daily Chronicle* later accused the navy of subjecting the prisoners to "crimes of flogging, torture, and a hanging rehearsal which all but terminated fatally."[67] There is, as usual, no official mention of such brutality on the night of June 2nd, only the passing comment that "Mr. Smith having in conversation with the prisoners obtained a statement that the two remaining were hid [on Secretary Island]," northwest of Salt Spring Island and halfway between Kuper and Galiano Islands.[68]

Hul'qumi'num First Nations know the low-elevation Secretary Islands and the inter-tidal zone between them as Shumutsun, a descriptive name which means "beach [between] goes dry."[69] At Shumutsun were clam beds, sea urchin and sea cucumber gathering areas owned by Chemainus, Penelakut and Lamalcha families.[70] Nearby was Shmumukwela, "isle of coffins," a rocky islet used as a burial ground.[71]

On account of "the navigation being intricate and uncertain" due to the numerous rocks and reefs around the Secretary Islands, Hardinge left the *Cameleon* at anchor in Osborne Bay and proceeded the next morning, June 3rd, in the *Forward*, with the armed launches of the *Topaze* in tow.[72] Upon their arrival Hardinge ordered the gunboat's two gigs to be lowered with an armed crew "to watch outlets" while the sailors and marines of the two launches with Smith and his men went ashore with the prisoner Sheemaltun. They "searched both parts of this large island and found traces of about two days old, also three baskets of potatoes and a masked spring of water. Mr. Smith in this search was guided by Wall-e-shuk [Sheemaltun] who was shackled to one of the men."[73]

Not finding anyone, Hardinge directed the first launch under Lieutenant Geneste "to search another island [Wallace] and watch the neighbourhood" while the rest of the force proceeded to Montague Harbour to look for the Penelakut man and woman who were to have rescued Acheewun and his party the day before.[74]

As the *Forward* neared Montague Harbour, Hardinge detached the second launch, instructing Lieutenant Pusey and his men to search Parker Island. "Mr. Smith with the Voltigeurs" also landed. The *Forward* anchored in Montague Harbour and Lascelles went ashore in the ship's gig to search "the shore of the harbour on Galiano Island."[75]

On Parker "very recent traces were found on the island, so Lieutenant Pusey was left for the night to watch the island with his launch." The *Forward* then proceeded to Osborne Bay, stopping en route to pick up Lieutenant Geneste's launch. Geneste informed Hardinge that he "had found very late traces [on Wallace Island] and from the behaviour of the men in a canoe, which had followed them, suspected that they had been aiding the fugitives." By this time it was dark, the *Forward* required coal, and Hardinge "deferred enquiries until the next day."[76]

Frustrated at the difficulty in locating Squ'acum and the remaining Lamalcha refugees, Hardinge decided that a greater show of force was required. On the morning of June 4th both the *Forward* and the *Cameleon* left Osborne Bay for Penelakut where the appearance of the *Cameleon*, the biggest man-of-war seen by the Penelakut, caused a great deal of consternation. Superintendent Smith landed "to make inquiries" about the whereabouts of Squ'acum and "found a spirit of opposition amongst many of them—he therefore cautioned them against the ill-effects of not assisting us." To underline this threat, Hardinge anchored the *Cameleon*, with its seventeen rifled cannon, "off the village by way of intimidating them."[77] The Penelakut were angry that the British continued to harass them after they had already captured so many of the Lamalcha.

Hardinge left Penelakut in the *Forward* with the first launch in tow for Montague Harbour "to pick up Lieutenant Pusey's launch, and to examine Julia Island," a small island at the south entrance. They met the second launch and came to off Parker Island where the *Forward* anchored and the two launches went ashore to search both Parker and Julia Islands.[78] On Julia Island, Sewholatza and other hwulmuhw scouts discovered very recent signs. As Hardinge noted:

... upon this island their tracks were not many hours old, as the Indians assured us, besides which tubs of spring water were found filled near a small encampment. This appeared very like their being assisted by Indians with canoes, as there was no spring found on the island. [79]

The Royal Navy suffered its third fatality in the war as the second launch pulled away from Julia Island at the conclusion of the search. Robert Newson, "a young gunner's mate of the *Topaze,*" was mortally wounded "by the accidental discharge of a rifle." [80] The sailor was "leaving hurriedly from one of the launches" when "a musket belonging to one of Newson's comrades, accidentally went off; the ball entered the former's hip, and passed through his intestines." [81] Another sailor, Richard Whitehouse, was wounded in the hand by the same shot. [82] Dr. Charles Forbes, surgeon of the *Topaze*, was present "and did all he could but his efforts were unavailing and the poor lad died in a few hours." [83]

The *Forward* and the two launches left Galiano Island to rejoin the *Cameleon* which lay at anchor off Penelakut. Smith went ashore, with John Lemon as interpreter, to remind the people that there was a reward for the capture of Squ'acum and that they were to be confined to their village. Smith, wrote Hardinge:

> ... had placed a reward of $50 on the head of each of the two men, and the villagers were informed no canoe could leave the village without our written permission, as Ah-chee-wun had stated some of his property was still in the village and the hiding places of these fugitives had been found by us on islands not a mile distant from the village. [84]

Hardinge, however, did not wish to alienate those who had already given valuable assistance. As he acknowledged, "a party of them had assisted us [and] it seemed desireable to put no further pressure upon them, as it was believed that the reward offered would soon bring them round." [85]

That evening, certain si'em decided that Squ'acum, who was camped near by, should be captured and turned over to the British. Six warriors undertook to search the woods. Informed of their plans in the early morning of June 5th, Hardinge ordered Lieutenant Geneste's launch to be stationed "off the village, so as effectually to guard the village." [86] Shortly afterward, as Hardinge recalled:

> ... the chief then communicated with Mr. Smith, and took a party from the village to bring in Squ-a-cum who, it now transpired was on the island and not far from the village. [87]

Hardinge ordered the second launch under Lieutenant Pusey "to the Saltspring Settlement and the Quarry to make inquiries" while he himself "went in the *Forward* with Mr. Smith taking one of the *Cameleon*'s cutters to Chemainos River." The *Forward* anchored off Halalt and Hardinge took the cutter, "and went up with one of the *Forward*'s boats in addition to the village of Ah-chee-wun's father-in-law to try for intelligence and at the same time to show that we were still prosecuting the search." Hardinge's foray proved uneventful and the British returned to Halalt. Pusey's reconnaissance to the two hwunitum settlements at the north end of Salt Spring Island was equally unsuccessful.[88]

Upon his return to Penelakut Hardinge heard the disappointing results of the Penelakut foray against Squ'acum on Kuper Island. He wrote that the six Penelakut warriors "on their return in the evening ... stated that they had come upon him, but wishing to take him alive had not fired upon him, but that he had escaped carrying with him two paddles."[89]

When Hardinge received this report he ordered "Lieutenant Pusey's Launch to the other side of the island to watch about Telegraph Harbour" (to watch the village of Yuhwala'us) in case Squ'acum should try to leave the island.[90]

The following morning, June 6th, Hardinge ordered the *Forward* to watch Penelakut while the *Cameleon* and the first launch proceeded around the south end of Kuper Island to search for Squ'acum. Hardinge rendezvoused with Lieutenant Pusey's launch at Telegraph Harbour "off the village there." "Shortly after," reported Hardinge, "three Chemainos Indians came across from the river, and with their assistance I left Mr. Pusey to search the Southern part of Kuper Island, some of the tribe of the village in the bay assisting."[91]

Hardinge directed the first launch under Lieutenant Geneste to go "round Thetis Island to examine the coves and shore." The *Cameleon* returned to Penelakut to communicate with the *Forward* and then steamed back to Telegraph Harbour where Hardinge heard the results of Pusey's joint British/"Chemainos" search of the south end of Kuper Island:

> I learnt from Lieutenant Pusey that he had come upon very recent traces, and had found the spot where two canoes had been launched, and the foot marks of three men and a woman. As the three Chemainos guides stated that it was most unlikely they would cross to Vancouver Island, where the Chemainos tribes had already acted against them; Lieutenant Pusey searched this afternoon the south part of Thetis Island while one of this ship's boats visited the north, Lieutenant Geneste also searched Tent Island, while another of my boats searched the small islands which form the harbour.[92]

In Victoria, meanwhile, the first report of the capture of Acheewun made its appearance in the *British Colonist*:

> A gentlemen who has come down from Salt Spring Island informs us that he had met a canoe near Cowichan and the Indians stated that the

notorious A-chee-wun and two of his tillicums, [friends] had been taken by the men-of-war. From what our informant could gather from the Indians he supposes that the men were betrayed by their friends.

This information is important and we hope will soon be confirmed. The capture of A-chee-wun the recognized head of a band of pirates and murderers who openly exults in the number of white men he himself has butchered, will we hope serve to put an end to the atrocities which have been committed among the islands in the neighbourhood of Cowichan.[93]

Later that evening HM Surveying ship *Beaver* arrived in Esquimalt en route from Nanaimo with confirmation that "the blood-thirsty villain A-chee-wun" had indeed been captured and "was at present a close prisoner on board the gunboat *Forward* together with two of his followers."[94] As for the other "Lamalcha scoundrels who were known to be secreted in the woods. It was expected that the latter would either be taken or surrender from hunger before Saturday night, in which case the expedition will probably return on Monday."[95]

On Sunday morning, June 7th, "there was a fine commanding breeze" and the *Topaze* launches hoisted sail from Telegraph Harbour to resume the search for Squ'acum and his people. Lieutenant Pusey's launch "was detached to Chemainos River, and Lieutenant Geneste's to visit Horseshoe Bay, Oyster Bay, and the coast on that side."[96] The *Forward* arrived and Lascelles informed Hardinge "that the Pennelikuts had reported that the fugitives had left the island."[97] Upon receipt of this news, Hardinge gave the Penelakut allies "permission to take two large canoes for their further search." The *Forward* was ordered "to Chemainos River to determine if possible whether the fugitives had not crossed over to that part of the coast."[98]

Weighing anchor at noon, the *Forward* crossed Stuart Channel, arriving off the village of Halalt where she anchored. There, Superintendent Smith "instituted a search at Chemainos River."[99] Smith and his scouts paid five dollars to "four Indians" to convey them "up the Chemainus." They stopped briefly at the "Upper Settlement" to pay Acheewun's father-in-law, Statumish, his wages for "22 days as a Voltigeur" before continuing their ascent of the river.[100] Upon his return Smith reported:

> ... that recent traces of Indians had been found on the mountain at the head of the river, which the Indians assisting could not account for, but the rough nature of the country precluded our people from assisting in the search, and owing to the extent of the country the further search was left in the hands of the Indians.[101]

That day, at the suggestion of Superintendent Smith, Hardinge "released the wife and children of Wall-e-shuk [Sheemaltun], as there was no case against them."[102]

A contributing factor to their release may have been the fact that Sheemaltun by this time had agreed to be a Crown witness against Acheewun and Shenasaluk.

On the morning of Monday, June 8th, the *Forward* left Halalt for Telegraph Harbour to inform Hardinge of Smith's latest reconnaissance. [103] With Acheewun, Shenasaluk, and Sheemaltun in custody and satisfied that he had executed the search for Squ'acum to the best of his ability, Hardinge decided to call a halt to the current expedition. Both ships then proceeded to Penelakut where the people were urged under promise of reward to continue the search for Squ'acum and again warned not to aid the remaining Lamalcha fugitives. As Hardinge informed Douglas:

> Taking into consideration the unsuccessful nature of the search since Tuesday and having obtained the co-operation of the Pennelikuts and Chemainos, I have decided that the *"Forward"* and launches should leave today to rejoin your broad pendant; the Indians having directions to take the prisoners down to Victoria, in the event of capture, where they will be paid the reward. The different tribes are informed that the search is not abandoned, only postponed, and the request I have made to Lieutenant and Commander Lascelles to visit these villages on his way up to Nanaimo, will no doubt when acted upon, have a good effect. [104]

The "co-operation" of the "Chemainos" people and the Penelakut may not have been entirely voluntary. Hulkalatkstun complained that his service to the British "kept me like a prisoner from my people and my home." [105] The hwulmuhw were clearly intimidated by HMS *Cameleon*. According to information received by the *British Colonist*:

> The Indians, in general, are said to have behaved very well on this occasion and to have rendered valuable assistance. The *Cameleon* created quite a sensation among them—her appearance was far too formidable to be relished. [106]

When the ship first appeared at Cowichan Bay a hwunitum observed that the hwulmuhw, recalling the brutality and pyrotechnics of the previous expedition, were "all quiet" and "now possessed with a wholesome dread of the powers of the men-of-war." [107]

The *Forward*, with the two launches of the *Topaze* in tow, left Penelakut for Victoria where the British "discharged the Prisoners." [108] Anti-climactically, the *British Colonist* reported that "she brought Superintendent Smith, with his guides and three prisoners, amongst whom is the noted A-chee-wun." [109] Upon disembarking at the St. Our's wharf, the three men were "delivered to the civil authorities" and imprisoned in the Police Barracks. [110]

The *Cameleon* remained at Telegraph Harbour where Hardinge was informed by a group of Penelakut allies that Squ'acum was believed to be on Galiano Island and that they were on their way to find him. Hardinge had intended to proceed to Nanaimo but "having learnt the direction in which the Pennelikut Men intend to search I have decided to remain today in Montague Harbor in order to receive any information they may obtain, and if they are unsuccessful proceed to Nanaimo tomorrow."[111] As it turned out, Squ'acum, preeminent si'em of Lamalcha, was never captured.

Captain Edward Hardinge, Commander of HMS Cameleon.
British Columbia Archives and Records Service, Photo HP 24332.

Site of the Supreme Court, 1863. This building, one of the famous "bird-cages" which stood on the site of the present Legislature in Victoria, was the setting for the trials of May and June, 1863.   *British Columbia Archives and Records Service, Photo HP 28729.*

Protestan Irish Reverend Alexander Garrett served as "Chinook interpreter" at the June Court of Assizes. His lack of fluency in the Hul'qumi'num dialect ensured that the testimony of hwulmuhw witnesses and accused was misunderstood and manipulated.
British Columbia Archives and Records Service, Photo HP 03835.

David Babbington Ring, another Protestant Irish immigrant was the Acting Attorney-General and Crown prosecutor for the trials of May and June 1863.
British Columbia Archives and Records Service, Photo HP 04372.

Chapter Twelve

Judicial Murder

The Colony of Vancouver Island, having waged war against the Lamalcha, prepared to treat its prisoners of war as criminals. As soon as word of Acheewun's capture reached Victoria, Governor Douglas commissioned another Court of Assize for mid-June to prosecute those taken during the late naval operations who were to be charged with criminal acts.

Acheewun and his fellow companions were still en route to Victoria when the Lamalcha and Penelakut captives, captured during Pike's naval operations of May 14th to 28th, were given a preliminary hearing in the Police Court to determine charges against them. During this time, two of the Lamalcha men, Shacutsus and Sayeh, as well as Talleyok, "a Lamalcha boy, aged about 14 years," agreed to act as witnesses against those of their fellow prisoners who faced charges of killing the Marks, the sailor Gliddon and an unknown hwunitum hunter on Pender Island. Palluk, the warrior who had killed Marks and possibly his daughter as well, was dead but the British wanted someone amongst their seventeen hwulmuhw prisoners to pay for their deaths and justify the expensive naval expedition sent in search of the killers. Allwhenuk, although he admitted firing the shot that killed the sailor at Lamalcha, would, thanks to the collusion of hwulmuhw witnesses with the colonial authorities, be framed for the death of Caroline Harvey.

The degree of coercion used to convince these and other hwulmuhw to give evidence against their own people may never be known. Hwunitum advocates alleged that witnesses were "flogged to obtain confessions," some having been "tied to guns on board one of Her Britainic Majesty's vessels and then lashed with the cat of nine tails to compel them to give unwilling testimony." [1] Other witnesses, it was said, "gave their evidence to avoid flogging, choosing rather to give false evidence than to be beaten." [2] Despite their cooperation as witnesses for the Crown Shacutsus, Sayeh and Talleyok remained incarcerated along with their former comrades, according to hwunitum custom.

On Friday, the 5th of June, all of the prisoners captured during Pike's May expedition were taken from their cells to the office of the Police Court, where the

Police Magistrate, Augustus F. Pemberton, heard "the charges of murder, etc. preferred against the Lamalcha men and women recently captured by the gunboats."[3] Sergeant Blake of the Victoria Police served as Chinook interpreter. A Hul'qumi'num speaker who understood the "Chinook jargon" was also likely present, although there is no record of his name.

The first order of business was the presentation of evidence concerning Semallee's participation in the attack on the Marks. Semallee, "the wife of Palluk, the villain who was shot by the Indians," took her place in the dock and "was first charged with being concerned in the murder of Mr. Marks."[4]

The first witness called was Caroline Marks. Pemberton had met with her the previous day to obtain a statement and at his request she appeared at the preliminary hearing to give her testimony.[5] Caroline Marks, "attired in widow's weeds ... was first sworn, and confirmed the information which had been laid by her before Mr. Pemberton on the 4th June":

> On the 2nd day of April last I left Waldron Island in a boat. My husband and his daughter started in another boat at the same time. About 3 o'clock in the afternoon my husband, Frederick Marks, anchored his boat at Saturna Island. My daughter, Caroline Harvey, was with him. I parted company with them there, and have not seen them since and from information I have received I believe they have been murdered by Indians.
>
> I produce a belt which belonged to my daughter. It was given to me by Mr. Mayer. It was found at the place where I saw the camp fire on Saturna Island, and where I last saw my daughter.[6]

After hearing Caroline Marks' testimony the court called on Shacutsus, Sayah, and Talleyok as witnesses. All three testified that Semallee admitted to them that she was an accomplice in the attack on the Marks and that she had encouraged her husband Palluk to kill both Marks and his daughter for their property. Shacutsus was the first to speak. After being sworn he "stated that about a month before he was arrested Semallee the prisoner, returned to the camp and said that she and her husband Palluk had shot a white man with a musket. He did not hear her say she encouraged her husband to commit the murder. He heard Palluk also say that he had done it."[7]

After Shacutsus gave his testimony Sayah and Talleyok were sworn as witnesses. Their testimony further incriminated Semallee in the death of Marks. Sayah claimed that Semallee encouraged her husband to kill the Marks in order to gain wealth. Sayah said that he "heard Palluk say about a month and a half ago that he saw a white man and took his musket and killed him because he wanted to have the man's property. Semallee was with him (Palluk) at the time. He had heard Semallee say that she was of the same mind as her husband about killing the man for his property. Palluk said Semallee took the things. Semallee told him her husband had shot the man because she wanted the property and that her husband did kill the man and she had his things."[8]

Talleyok was then sworn. He directly accused Semallee of instigating the attack on Marks for the sake of wealth. Talleyok stated that "Semallee had told him that she had asked her husband to kill a white man, because she wanted his property. He had frequently heard her say that she would like to kill a white man, because she got so much property by it. It was a month and a half since he had heard Semallee say her husband had just killed a white man."[9]

At this point Pemberton, through the court interpreter(s), asked Semallee "if she wanted to put any questions to witness, but she thereupon commenced statements in self defence which the Magistrate stopped."[10] Semallee, however, was able to communicate the following statement before Pemberton silenced her. She said that

> Pol-luck (my husband) always wished to kill white men; I always told him if he did such thing that he would be hung; he killed the white man 3 years ago against my wish; he also killed Marks and his daughter; I am a good woman.[11]

Allwhenuk was then placed in the dock and "charged with killing the daughter of Mr. Marks, Caroline Harvey." The previous three witnesses were recalled and gave their testimony which, as before, was based on conversations they said they had with Palluk. But, as the reporter for the *British Colonist* observed, the witnesses "said nothing directly to criminate the prisoner."[12] Shacutsus stated:

> ... that Palluk told him Um-wha-nuk [Allwhenuk] had killed the girl on the same day and place Palluk killed the white man, by stabbing her with a knife. Prisoner was present when Palluk made the statement and acknowledged having done it.[13]

Allwhenuk, when he heard what Shacutsus said, "seemed very much amused at the statement, [and] denied that he was guilty as charged."[14] Allwhenuk insisted that "Palluck killed both Marks and his daughter."[15]

The next witness, Sayah, was recalled and stated that he "heard Palluk say that Um-wha-nuk [Allwhenuk] said he had killed the girl on the same day that Palluk killed the man. Prisoner [Allwhenuk] was not present when the statement was made. He had no conversation with Um-wha-nuk [Allwhenuk]."[16]

Talleyok was recalled and told the court "that about a moon and a half ago Palluk told him that Um-wha-nuk [Allwhenuk] had stabbed and killed a young white woman; Um-wha-nuk was not present when Palluk spoke to witness; Palluk said that Um-wha-nuk killed the girl because he wanted her clothing; the place where the murder happened was one days travel in canoe from the Lamalcha village; it is in Arris's land, known in Indian as Chul-le-man [Kulman] ... Prisoner belonged to the Penelicut [Penelakut] tribe." [17]

Another account of Talleyok's testimony stated that "Um-wha-nuk [Allwhenuk] killed the girl because they wanted her clothing," which seemed to implicate his wife Koltenaht in the killing. [18] After her capture on May 23rd she was, in fact, accused by other hwulmuhw of Harvey's death. [19] Initial reports of the attack also identified a woman, not a man, as the one who stabbed Caroline Harvey.

To clarify exactly who was present at the killings on Saturna Island, Pemberton recalled Shacutsus who made the following statement:

> I saw two canoes leave Lamalcha; in one of the canoes was Palluck and his wife Se-mal-lee; in the other was Al-whan-ock [Allwhenuk] and his wife Ker-nal-kutz [Koltenaht], and saw them go in the direction of Kulman Island; the third day afterwards I saw the same canoes at Kulman Island and saw all the occupants there; had no conversation with them; went to Victoria, and when I returned to Lamalcha Palluck told me all about the murder. [20]

Koltenaht was then questioned by Pemberton about her role in the attack. She admitted being present but stated "that Palluck killed both Marks and his daughter; I took none of the things because they were not worth taking." [21] Talleyok's testimony seemed to implicate Koltenaht and she "was then charged with being concerned in the murder of Caroline Harvey." [22] As she watched the proceedings, Koltenaht, "who bore in her arms a bright looking infant boy, passed the time between laughing immoderately, and nursing her babe, and commenting, in an undertone, upon the evidence as it was drawn out." All of the female prisoners, it was noted, "exhibited but little concern, and laughed and chuckled as chapter after chapter of the tale of blood was opened to the horrified gaze of the spectators." [23]

Although each of the accused "seemed to indicate Palluck as the guilty person," Pemberton accepted the hearsay evidence of Shacutsus, Sayah, and Talleyok and charged Allwhenuk, Koltenaht, and Semallee each with two counts; the first "with having murdered Frederick Marks on Saturna Island on or about the second day of April last," and the second "with having murdered Caroline Harvey daughter of Frederick Marks on Saturna Island about the second day of April last." [24] All were committed to trial.

Pemberton then focused the proceedings on the killing of the unknown hwunitum hunter around 1860 on Pender Island. Semallee was arraigned a second time, "and charged with the murder of a white man about three years ago, on an island near Cowichan, by cutting him down the back with an axe, while the victim was engaged in a death struggle with her husband Palluck." [25]

The first witness was Shacutsus, who recounted for the court what Palluk, Semallee, and Skiloweet had told him several years before. He testified the following:

> ... about three snows ago a white man came in a canoe to Sty-ish Island [Pender Island], some distance beyond the Lamalcha village; he had a musket, and came to hunt the deer; Se-mal-lee, Palluck and one of the old men prisoners, named Skul-onide [Skiloweet] murdered him; Palluck fired first and wounded him in the arm; the white man ran and caught Palluck and the old man by the hair and knocked their heads together, and while they were struggling, Skul-onide [Skiloweet] drew a knife and cut the white man across the abdomen, and Se-mal-lee chopped him on the back of his neck with a hatchet and killed him; the murderers told witness about the occurrence upon their return to the village. [26]

Sayah was also called to testify. He said that he heard what Shacutsus had just said about the attack on the Hwunitum on Pender Island and that it was "a common report amongst the Indians about three years ago." [27]

The next witness was Talleyok who stated that he "was present when Palluck and Semallee had a quarrel, and on that occasion Semallee accused Palluck of having killed a white man. This was about three years ago." [28]

Pemberton then called upon the Nanaimo man, Skiloweet, who first confessed to the killing, to hear what he had to say about it and the charges against him. In reply to the question put to him by the interpreters, Skiloweet said:

> I am an old man, and do not wish to die; I would be very happy to remain in jail forever; it was not my wish that the man was murdered; I tried to disuade Palluck from it, but the woman (Semallee) saw lots of things in his canoe; and wished that her husband should kill him; after he fell on the ground Palluck stuck a long knife into him; we left the body lying on the beach and took all the things. [29]

As a result of this testimony Pemberton charged Semallee and Skiloweet "with the murder of a white man whose name is unknown about two or three years ago" and committed both of them to trial. [30]

The final undertaking of the preliminary examination was to determine who among the prisoners had fired upon the gunboat *Forward* at Lamalcha on April 20th. The only newspaper references to this portion of the hearing are statements made by two of the crown witnesses, Shacutsus and Sayah. Sayah was called first and gave his version of what took place:

> I saw the gunboat come to Lamalcha; all the Indians came out of their houses to look at her; they were asked to send their chiefs on board, but the chiefs refused to go; they then fired upon the village and destroyed the

houses; after the houses were destroyed eight of the Indians fired on the gunboat; they are named Sha-cut-sus, Lee-mal-tem [Sheemaltun], Qual-la-tal-tun, Al-whan-ock [Allwhenuk], See-mack, Qu-sa-lut, Ot-chee-wuan [Acheewun], and Qual-kais. Three of those who fired are now in court.[31]

The three men present in the court who had taken part in the battle, were Shacutsus, Allwhenuk and Qualataltun. Shacutsus, during his testimony, spoke of his involvement in the negotiations that took place before the fighting and admitted that he had fired in the following brief statement: "I and another Indian went off in a canoe to speak to the gunboat, and we were ordered off, after the bombardment I fired on the gunboat."[32]

As a witness for the Crown Shacutsus was not charged. Allwhenuk, who admitted that it was he who shot Charles Gliddon, "was charged with firing at HM Gunboat *Forward* and killing one of the men on board." The third man, Qualataltun, the "half Chemainus & Lamalchee," was also "charged with firing on HMG *Forward* about six weeks ago."[33] Pemberton committed both of them to trial.

It was less than a month since the last Court of Assize tried and hanged the three Quamichan youths. With another trial imminent, the press began to question the ability of the courts to deal fairly with cases involving hwulmuhw defendants. Paramount among these concerns was the failure to provide any legal counsel for the accused. The *Daily Evening Express* cited the case of "the late trial of the murderers of Brady," and noted:

> ... we have already ventured to point out the disadvantage under which they laboured in being unprovided with legal aid. It is too late now to urge the matter on their behalf, but we feel it our duty to crave the boon for the unhappy captives now in the Victoria jail who are charged with being concerned in the second tragedy ... We observe that in the course of the proceedings in the Police Court last Friday, as reported, hearsay evidence, recriminations, and quasi confessions, (calculated seriously to compromise the witnesses) came constantly before the court.[34]

The *Daily Evening Express* argued that counsel for the accused was particularly urgent in light of rumours that the captives had been physically abused "to extract confessions" on board the gunboat *Forward* prior to their arrival in Victoria:

> There are strange rumours afloat as to the manner in which the captives ... have been treated ere they reached Victoria ... a medical examination of the persons of the accused should at once be instituted, ere the marks of their ill treatment disappear. We hold that the law should be vindicated in such a manner as that the native tribes may approve its purpose and respect its power; but are confident that not an Englishman who values the sacredness of his liberty would endorse acts of arbitrary violence upon an

unconvicted and helpless prisoner, for the purpose of extracting confessions that would lead to his own condemnation or to seek vengeance upon ignorant Indians for even the most heinous offence, without allowing them a fair trial.[35]

The sentiments expressed in the above editorial prompted more calls for a medical examination of the prisoners. One reader asked, "Is there no lawyer humane enough to volunteer on behalf of the prisoners? Or cannot the public subscribe to provide them counsel?"[36]

The allegations of physical abuse went unheeded, although they were to resurface in subsequent editorials by the *Daily Evening Express* and the *Victoria Daily Chronicle* as the trials progressed. The pages of the *British Colonist* were strangely silent on the matter. No medical examinations of the Lamalcha prisoners were forthcoming and "no humane lawyer," of the ten or so practicing in the colony, came forward to offer his services to the accused.[37]

On Tuesday morning, June 9th, the day after their arrival in Victoria, Acheewun, Shenasaluk and Sheemaltun were brought before Augustus Pemberton in the Police Court where they were "remanded for three days to await the production of evidence."[38] Following this brief appearance the three men were marched back to their cells. Having heard so much about "the cunning villain," Acheewun, the press was eager to see if his appearance lived up to his reputation as "a perfect fiend." The *British Colonist* correspondent seemed disappointed.

> The great pirate robber, who has not by any means a forbidding experience, if we except the villainy which lurks in his piercing wicked eye, was perfectly self-possessed and betrayed no concern whatever for his fearfully precarious position.[39]

The *Victoria Daily Chronicle* described Acheewun as "the noblest Flathead Indian we have ever seen. He has an aquiline nose, dark copper-coloured features, fine figure and piercing black eyes."[40]

Both morning newspapers featured news of the *Forward*'s arrival and brief anti-climactic accounts of the latest naval expedition. The *Victoria Daily Chronicle* reported:

> Ar-che-won [Acheewun], a noted brave, was among the prisoners, and it is stated that he acknowledges to having killed twelve white men, and regretted that the number was not larger. His brother is also in custody. Both are fine specimens of North American Indians, and were captured with great difficulty.[41]

The capture of Acheewun more than compensated for the fact that there were "still 2 or 3 of the Lamalchas hiding in the woods" who "could not be discovered." [42] As one newspaper put it, "The worst of the tribe have all been now apprehended." [43]

In the afternoon, on the other side of Victoria Harbour, there was a large naval funeral to bury the remains of Robert Newson, the *Topaze* sailor accidentally shot at Montague Harbour "during the recent hunt for the Lamalchas." [44]

Two days later, on Thursday morning, June 11th, Acheewun and Shenasaluk were "brought up on remand" before Augustus Pemberton in the Police Court, "upon charges of murder and piracy." In the interim, Sheemaltun, the third man captured on June 2nd, "had been accepted as Queen's evidence." Acheewun faced charges of having murdered Ashutstun of Valdez Island. Shenasaluk faced charges of being "an accessory to the murder." [45] Both brothers also faced charges of firing on the *Forward* at Lamalcha during the battle of April 20th.

The first business of the Police Court dealt with the killing of Ashutstun by Acheewun during the 1858 fight at "Swamuxum" on Porlier Pass. The chief witness against the two brothers was Sewholatza, the victim's son.

Sheemaltun also testified against his former comrades. There is no record of interpreters being present but, given the detail of the proceedings preserved in the newspaper accounts, it is likely that the usual Chinook and Hul'qumi'num interpreters were present.

Horace Smith, the Superintendent of Police, opened the proceedings with the following statement:

> From information I have received I have reason to believe that an Indian named A-shut-sun was murdered at Porlier Pass about 5 years ago and that A-chee-wun was the man who murdered him, and that She-nah-su-luk was an accessory to it. [46]

Following Smith's opening statements, Sewholatza was sworn and gave evidence of the feud between his father and Acheewun:

> About five years ago the prisoner, Otcheewun [Acheewun] became angry with me and my father. I do not know for what reason. He came to the camp one day. He was drunk. I saw him strike my father, who bled very much from the effect of the blow. Some of my friends carried my father to my house. As he was being carried in at the door of the house, Otcheewun fired at him with a musket. The ball wounded one of the men who was assisting my father to the house, and entered my father's right side, passed through him, and came out at the left side. After receiving the ball he staggered, fell and died.

I saw Otcheewun fire the musket. Two shot were fired into the house after my father died. The prisoner, Otcheewun, called to me to come out of the house and he would serve me the same way. My father's name was Ah-shuts-tun. [47]

Sewholatza added that Shenasaluk "was also there with his musket [but] could not state which of them fired into the house." [48]

Following Sewholatza's testimony Shacutsus was sworn and "confirmed the statement of the previous witness." [49]

Sheemaltun "was next sworn and after being duly cautioned also deposed to the same facts," adding that "he was standing about four yards off when A-chee-wun fired at A-shuts-tun." [50]

After these witnesses were heard Acheewun "was then cautioned by Mr. Pemberton and was asked if he wished to make a statement." [51] Acheewun did not deny that he killed Ashutstun but stated that he acted in self-defence.

Yes. I did kill A-shut-stun. He first got angry and struck me in the face with a knife; A-shut-stun had a long time before killed one of my friends who was making a canoe, and I killed A-shut-stun to be avenged. [52]

Shenasaluk declined to make a statement and "this closed the evidence adduced for the crown." [53] Pemberton then charged Acheewun "with having murdered Au-shut-stun an Indian" and committed him to trial. His brother Shenasaluk was "charged with being an accessory to the murder of Au-shut-stun, an Indian" but he was "remanded for one week." [54]

The next set of charges against the brothers concerned their participation in the Battle of Lamalcha on April 20th. Charges were brought against them by Superintendent Smith upon the following information:

On or about the 20th day of April last I was present on board H.M. Gunboat *Forward* at Village Bay, Kuper Island opposite the camp of the Lemaltsa [Lamalcha] Indians. A number of Indians fired upon the gunboat and killed a seaman whose name I do not know. I have reason to believe that A-chee-wun and She-nah-su-luk were two of those Indians who fired at the gunboat. [55]

The court called upon the two Lamalcha witnesses, Shacutsus and Sayah, to give their testimony. Shacutsus identified Shanasaluk as having taken part in the fire-fight but, to the surprise of the court, neither witness identified Acheewun as having fired on the gunboat. Shacutsus expressly stated that Acheewun did not fire. After being sworn he stated:

... that about a month and a half ago he saw the gunboat lying off the village; She-na-sa-luk was there and fired on her with others but A-chee-wun did not. [56]

Sayah was called to testify and, despite his previous detailed account of the engagement given in the Police Court on June 5th, on this occasion "his knowledge of the action was found to be hearsay." [57] Evidently he, as well, stated that Acheewun had not fired on the *Forward*.

The reporter for the *British Colonist* found this evidence difficult to accept and wrote that "an evident disposition was manifested by most of the Indian witnesses to shield the rascal A-chee-wun as much as possible." [58] But it may have been that Shacutsus and Sayah were simply telling the truth.

One of the witnesses, however, had identified Shenasaluk as having fired on the gunboat. Pemberton cautioned Shenasaluk "and asked if he had any statement to make." Possibly not understanding the question as it was translated, Shenasuluk only "replied that he did not want to be hung." [59]

Pemberton then addressed the court and "said that he did not consider the evidence at present adduced sufficient to commit She-nah-sa-luk he would therefore remand him for one week. Against A-chee-wun there was no evidence." [60] Nevertheless, Pemberton allowed the charges against the two brothers "with having fired upon H.M. Gunboat *Forward* about six weeks ago" to remain and remanded them for one week to gather further evidence. [61]

On the eve of the Court of Assize the proprietors of the *Victoria Daily Chronicle* published the following editorial, entitled "Even-handed Justice," which pleaded with the court to resolve what it saw as three major failings of the justice system regarding court cases involving hwulmuhw defendants in general, and the current legal proceedings in particular: failure to appoint adequate legal counsel, "confessions ... obtained by improper influence," and the use of "policeman as interpreters." Only by correcting these deficiencies, the *Chronicle* argued, would the upcoming trial proceed "according to law."

> Five of these men, though not aliens, are strangers to our laws, and cannot defend themselves in any way, either by challenging witnesses, or addressing the court in their own behalf. The spirit of English laws is full of tenderness and humanity to the prisoners; and to deny, or not to assign counsel to these wretches who are too poor or too ignorant to obtain for themselves this single safeguard, has an appearance of injustice which no one wishes to see repeated. [62]

The Court of Assizes opened Wednesday morning, June 17th, in the temporary offices of the Supreme Court, overlooking James Bay and the City of Victoria beyond. Chief Justice David Cameron took his seat at the bench and reviewed the "criminal calendar of prisoners to be brought up for trial." Seven persons were to be tried. In addition to the five Lamalcha and Penelakut prisoners, there was a hwunitum man named Robert Williamson charged with the murder of another itinerant hwunitum on the Saanich Road. There was also the case of the "half-breed" John Yale, alias Nisqually Jack, "for inciting Indians to rebel." [63]

The following hwunitum were empanelled to serve as Grand Jurors to consider the indictments against the accused: Alexander Munro, Robert Burrell, Joseph J. Cochrane, Joseph C. Ridge, William A. Cooper, William R. Meldrum, Julius L. Gumbinner, Alfred T. Elliott, R. Harvey, Augustus R. Green, Jesse Cooper, Elwood H. Jackson, Joseph C. Nicholson, Jason Lowe, Thomas Roper, William Jeffray and Charles Fellows. Joseph R. Ridge was chosen to be foreman. [64]

In his address to the Grand Jury, Cameron stated that "they were summoned upon a commission issued by His Excellency the Governor, for a Court of Assize and General Jail delivery of all prisoners. During the interval which had transpired since the last special Court of Assize, a number of Indian prisoners had been apprehended and it was expedient that the jail should be delivered of these prisoners." [65]

After a brief review of the cases against the hwunitum Williamson and Nisqually Jack, Cameron "described the nature of the various crimes charged against the Indian prisoners which it would be the duty of the Grand Jury to enquire into and return their bills accordingly." [66]

Cameron announced that the charges against the Lamalcha woman, Semallee, would be dropped: "In the case of Al-who-uck [Allwhenuk], for the murder of Caroline Harvey, an Indian woman, who had conived at the murder of Marks, would be used as a witness against Al-wha-nock." [67] His Honour "then drew the attention of the jury to the indictment preferred against an Indian woman named Semallie [Semallee], and informed them that the Attorney-General had decided upon introducing this prisoner as a witness for the Crown against the other prisoners implicated." [68]

Sometime after her June 8th appearance in the Police Court Semallee, who had been charged in connection with three counts of murder, made an arrangement with the prosecutor, David Ring, to be a witness for the crown against Allwhenuk for the death of Caroline Harvey, and against Skiloweet for the circa 1860 killing of the unknown hwunitum on Pender Island. The decision not to try Semallee was not unusual in light of nineteenth-century British legal practice. On the basis of gender and racial stereotypes "women of colour," even in the context of serious crimes, were considered "to be somewhat unpredictable and childlike—and ultimately not quite responsible" for their actions. [69] The fact that Semallee was "quite a young girl and by no means ill-looking," further disinclined the British to prosecute her for murders while others of the opposite sex could be found to pay for the crimes. [70]

The final indictments which the Grand Jury had to decide upon were those concerning "Otcheewun [Acheewun], the chief" who "was indicted for the murder of a Cowichan some five years ago; and Skiloweet, for the murder of an unknown white man, 3 years since." [71]

After the address by the Chief Justice, the Grand Jury was directed to retire to deliberate on the fate of the hwunitum prisoner and "after a few minutes deliberation they returned a 'true bill' against Robert Williamson." The Grand Jury retired a second time to consider the indictments of the hwulmuhw prisoners when, across James Bay, in the heart of Victoria "the fire bell began to ring vehemently." [72]

> Away went indictments, depositions, informations, slanders, &c; visions of blazing stores and dry goods being soused by the merciless engines, was more than mercantile human nature could be expected to stand; an immediate adjournment for half an hour was agreed to, and in the course of a few moments the Grand Jury were to be seen making good running over the bridge to town. [73]

The fire, if there was a fire, was not serious and by 1 p.m. the Grand Jury had reassembled in the courtroom to consider the indictments against the hwulmuhw accused. The evidence used to indict them was based solely on the testimony of hwulmuhw witnesses, and this caused some debate among some of the jurors who questioned the reliability of such information. Finally, after two hours of discussion, the Foreman "entered the court and presented true bills against Um-wha-nuck [Allwhenuk], for the murder of Caroline Harvey, and Skiloweet for the murder of a white man on an island five years ago." [74]

Incredibly, the Grand Jury did not feel that the indictment against Acheewun for killing Ashutstun warranted prosecution and the bill against him "was ignored." [75] Sewholatza's reaction to this turn of events is not known but he must have been dismayed at the inconsistencies of hwunitum justice. He had testified as an eyewitness to the fact that his father had been killed by Acheewun. Acheewun in turn did not deny it, and yet he would not be tried for Ashutstun's death.

When Joseph Ridge, the Foreman, "enquired whether any further business was required of the jurors," Cameron, displeased with the failure of the Grand Jury to indict Acheewun, informed him "that fresh indictments might be presented." The Chief Justice "then directed the Grand Jury to reassemble on Friday, and adjourned the court to 10 o'clock," Thursday. [76]

The Colonial Executive was clearly in a quandary. They had pinned their hopes on Acheewun and his brother being arraigned for the death of Ashutstun in what seemed to be a clear case against him, but the Grand Jury thought otherwise. It was therefore decided that even though Allwhenuk was acknowledged as the warrior who fired the shot which killed Charles Gliddon at Lamalcha on April 20th, the court would proceed with trumped up charges against him for the death of Caroline Harvey. In his place, Acheewun, Shenasaluk, and Qualaltaltun would be tried and hanged for the death of the seaman to satisfy both Sewholatsa and the Royal Navy, and to serve as an example of what befell those who opposed hwunitum colonization.

When the Court of Assize resumed Thursday morning, June 18th, the first business was a request by the prosecuting attorney to postpone the trial of Robert Williamson of "the Saanich Road Murder," pending the return of two important witnesses from the Cariboo. The court granted the application and moved quickly to the case of Allwhenuk "of the Lemaltsa [Lamalcha] tribe [who] was arraigned for feloniously killing and murdering Frederick Marks and his daughter Caroline during the month of April last upon an Island in Plumper's Pass." [77] Allwhenuk was placed in the dock and the trial of *Regina vs. Um-whan-uck [Allwhenuk]* commenced.

Two men were sworn as interpreters for the trial. Acting on the advice given the day before in the *Victoria Daily Chronicle*, the court dispensed with the services of Police Sergeant Blake and appointed Frederick Minie, "who was sworn to interpret English into Chinook, and vice versa." The other interpreter was Whisk, the Lamalcha man captured on April 19th in Sansum Narrows, who would interpret "from Chinook into Cowichan." [78] The choice of Whisk as interpreter for the trial of Allwhenuk appears to have been a deliberate move on the part of the authorities to ensure the conviction of the accused. Hwulmuhw informants later claimed that Whisk was the son of an Indian whose brother was killed by Allwhenuk in an unknown altercation. [79] It was further alleged that Whisk manipulated the testimony of hwulmuhw witnesses and "interpreted the very contrary to what the accused and witnesses deposed." [80]

It made little difference that the Reverend Alexander Garrett was "present to watch that the interpreters correctly performed their duties." [81] Despite his ability to speak "fluently in what is called the Chinook," Garrett possessed little if any knowledge of the Hul'qumi'num language. [82] He could not understand either the substance of the questions put to the witnesses and the accused, or their replies through the interpreter Whisk.

Despite the presence of a Hul'qumi'num interpreter, the translation of courtroom testimony continued to rely on the medium of Chinook which was, it seems, woefully inadequate to communicate the proceedings of an English court of law. This was made evident when the Chief Justice tried unsuccessfully to explain the meaning of the indictment to Allwhenuk through all three interpreters in order that the court might hear his plea. Finally, in exasperation:

> The explanation of the indictment was waived, and a plea of not guilty was entered on behalf of the prisoner. This was after a vain attempt to convey the meaning of the indictment to the prisoner. It was then explained to the accused that he might challenge any of the jurors that he pleased. The explanation of this simple notification occupied about twelve minutes, and at one time a satisfactory result appeared hopeless.[83]

During all this talk, Allwhenuk managed to communicate one statement through the interpreters stating, in reference to the charges against him, "that he saw the deed committed but that he took no part therein."[84]

It is almost certain that Allwhenuk did not understand what was happening as the jury was empanelled. Not represented by counsel, he did not challenge any of the jury which consisted of the following individuals: Henry Knapp, Thomas Wilson, John Martin, Alfred Green, Albert Frederick Hicks, John McLeigh, William Fearing, Joseph King, William R. Gibbon, Charles Gerow, Robert P. Whear, and William Beck, who was chosen as foreman.[85]

Dissatisfied with the translating services of the Chinook speaker Mr. Minie, Cameron dismissed him and "Mr. Garret assumed the duties of interpreter."[86]

Acting Attorney-General David Babbington Ring:

> ... opened the case for the prosecution, and in the course of his remarks touched upon the facts connected with the horrid crime. It appears that Marks and his family were moving to an Island in Plumper's Pass. Himself and daughter were in one canoe and his wife and the other children in another. Marks and his daughter were never seen after, but from articles found on Saturna Island, it is believed that they were both murdered by Indians.[87]

He added that "some of Caroline Harvey's clothing" would be presented in court "which Mrs. Marks, the widowed mother, would be called to identify."[88]

> The policy of the Government had been to impress upon the minds of the savages that punishment would be dealt out to the tribes for offences committed towards each other or towards colonists. They were given to understand that they were protected by and were amenable to English law, and he had no doubt that after a patient inquiry the jury would have no hesitation in finding a verdict against the prisoner.[89]

The first witness for the prosecution was Semallee who, "being questioned by the Reverend Mr. Garret upon her comprehension of the nature of an oath ... replied that she believed if she said what was untrue, when she died her soul would go to hell, but if she told the truth her soul might go to heaven."[90] After this she "was thereupon duly sworn" and gave the following testimony according to the Reverend Garrett's English translation of Whisk's Chinook:

> I know Alwhanock; [I] remember, about a moon and a half ago, a boat coming to Kulman (Saturna) Island, in which was a white man and a young woman; Alwhanock, Polluck (my dead husband), Alwhanock's wife and me were all on the island; my husband shot the man, and my husband was afterwards shot at Chemanis; Alwhanock took a knife and stabbed the young woman; Pollock shot the white man first; Alwhanock cut the girl across the stomach, and she fell dead; after she was killed the body was thrown in the water; the prisoner's wife did not assist in the murder; stones were tied to the bodies and the man and woman were thrown into the saltchuck [water].[91]

At the conclusion of Semallee's testimony, "though every effort was made to explain to him the object of cross-examination," Allwhenuk "said that he had no questions to ask the witness; that Semallee had told lies, and that as soon as all the witnesses had spoken, he would tell his heart (the truth.)"[92]

Allwhenuk's wife, Koltenaht, "a young woman with an infant at her breast," was next called.[93] Koltenaht, like Semallee, was originally charged with the murder of Caroline Harvey and, in exchange for immunity from prosecution, agreed to testify as a Crown Witness. It is unlikely that she realized all the consequences of her decision. In order that she could be used in the court to convict her husband "special pains were taken to establish that she was not 'legally' married to [Allwhenuck]. Otherwise crucial prosecution evidence would have been excluded because English law prohibited a wife from testifying against her husband."[94]

Koltenaht, "on being questioned by the Reverend Mr. Garrett upon the nature of an oath said she had heard that she was baptized in infancy and reluctantly stated her knowledge of an oath," and said that, "she knows if she tells a lie she will be punished after death in Hell."[95] Upon being sworn she said, according to Garrett's translation:

> I remember the white man and the white woman coming to Kulman Island in a canoe; it was about a moon and a half ago; I saw Pollock shoot the man, and I saw Alwhanock stab the girl; when the man was shot Alwhanock was near; [Polluck and the prisoner had counsel together before the man was shot]; the two bodies were tied together by Alwhanock and Pollock, weighted with stones and thrown into the salt chuck; the

bodies were not stripped; the girl wore shoes, and as far as she knew they went into the water with the body; (woman's shoe produced in court) did not recognize it as one worn by the girl [Koltenaht also claimed that "the shoes on the deceased girl were better than the one produced in court"]; saw a belt around the girl's waist (a blue leather belt shown witness); identified this as the belt which was worn around the girl's waist. [96]

Contrary to their statements at the Police Court on June 5th, where both Semallee and Koltenaht identified Palluk as the man who killed Marks and his daughter, they now identified Allwhenuk as an accomplice. Hwulmuhw observers claimed that Whisk, in his questioning of Koltenaht and Semallee, "interpreted the very contrary to what the accused and witnesses deposed or wished to say; that he made two of the witnesses [Semallee and Koltenaht] answer yes when they did not comprehend the substance of the question. He also told them that if they said yes they would be pardoned and at liberty." [97]

When asked if he had any questions to put to her, Allwhenuk, confused by his wife's testimony, declined, "averring her statement to be false and declaring that he was a good man and his heart was right." [98]

Semallee was recalled, and upon further questioning continued the sham and "corroborated the evidence of the last [witness] as to the circumstance of both bodies having been tied together were [then] sunk." Semallee testified that "Polluck and Prisoner took the bodies and tied them together head and foot and weighted the bodies with stones and threw them into the water. Prisoner was within a few yards of Polluck when he shot Marks." [99]

The next witness called for the prosecution was Shacutsus who, "on being examined as to his knowledge of the nature of an Oath," said "that he knows that if he tells lies habitually that his soul will go to Hell." [100] Shacutsus was then sworn and said:

Palluk said nothing to me about the white man and woman in presence of the prisoner. I did not say so before [in the Police Court]. I saw Palluk and the prisoner going to the island together about a moon and a half ago. I saw them return to Lemalcha together.

I saw them frequently conversing about the murder of the girl. Palluk told me not to say anything of the murder. The prisoner was not far away at the time. He also told me in the prisoner's hearing that he (the prisoner) had killed the girl with a knife. Prisoner said it is not too good to talk a great deal about it better keep it secret. [101]

Allwhenuk again asserted that the witness was not telling the truth. When asked if he wished to challenge Shacutsus' statement, Allwhenuk "said that Sha-cut-sus was a great liar and declined to ask him any questions." [102] Cameron's notes indicate that Allwhenuk also charged that, "He (the witness) was there and saw it." [103]

Caroline Marks, dressed in black "widow's weeds" was called as the next witness and, after being sworn, made the following statement:

> It was in the month of April last that myself and family started for Plumper's Pass. My Husband and daughter in one boat myself and children in another. We got to Kulman Island together. The weather was heavy, stormy. I saw them land on the Island and never saw them after. There was almost all my clothing and the clothing of my daughter in the boat with her. She had on a pair of new shoes and a pair of old ones were in the boat with her. (Shoes shown to witness) These are the old shoes. (A bundle of clothes were then shown witness) These clothes were my daughter's and were also in the boat. [104]

The testimony of Caroline Marks and her forlorn appearance seemed to have a debilitating effect on Allwhenuk as he realized the hopelessness of his situation. Reverend Garrett translated the statement of the bereaved widow into Chinook which was translated by Whisk into Hul'qumi'num: "The evidence of Mrs. Marks having been interpreted, Alwhanock said that he did not wish to put any questions—that it was good he should die." [105]

The final witness for the prosecution was Superintendent of Police Horace Smith who, after being sworn, stated:

> I am Superintendent of Police. In consequence of information which I had received I went to Kulman Island. Saturna is the name on the Chart. I went there about a week after receiving the information. I there saw the place where Marks and his daughter encamped. I know it by the things lying about and by finding the boat there with the bottom chopped to pieces. I found the shoe which I now produce on a ledge of rock jutting out into deep water. The petticoat was about a fathom under water. I fished it up with the Boathook. There was at this place a high ridge that shot out into the water. Mark's fire was on one side and on the other the surface bore marks of fingers as if some persons had crawled up that way to overlook him. [106]

Asked whether he wished to put any questions to the witness, Allwhenuk only said "that he had no doubt the articles were found at the spot indicated." [107]

Smith's testimony closed the case for the Crown. Ring, in summing up the case for the prosecution, "addressed a few words to the jury in explanation of the words 'aiding and abetting' in the indictment," reminding them "that the prisoner was indicted for the murder of Frederick Marks as well as for the murder of the girl." [108]

Cameron then "directed the Interpreters to tell the prisoner that if he had any witnesses to call in his defence the Court would hear them, or if not it would now hear what he had to say for himself." Cameron recorded Allwhenuk's reply which indicated that "he has no friends to speak for him and that he does not wish to die and that was all he has got to say." [109]

Chief Justice Cameron "summed up in his usual impartial manner" by addressing the jury: "He observed that it was the duty of the gentlemen of the jury, after having heard the evidence in support of the charge against the prisoner, to say whether he was guilty of the crime laid to his charge or not. The evidence brought before them had been given almost exclusively by the prisoner's own tribe. Some of the facts had been corroborated by Mrs. Marks and Mr. Smith. The fact that Mr. Marks and his daughter were killed had been established beyond a doubt by all the witnesses; but who committed the deed is proved alone by Indian witnesses." [110]

> His honor then proceeded to explain that it was not necessary to render evidence admissible that the witness should be a Christian; it was sufficient if the witnesses signified their belief in the responsibility of an oath and of future punishment in case of its willful abuse, to render the evidence legal; the credibility alone would rest with the jury. His Lordship then went over the evidence and explained the wording of the indictment. He concluded that it was clear, if they believed the evidence, that the prisoner had killed the girl, and was equally guilty of murder in aiding and abetting the man who killed her father. [111]

The jury retired to their room and returned to the courtroom after deliberating for "two or three minutes." When they returned to their box the foreman of the jury, William Beck, "pronounced the prisoner guilty." [112]

Cameron remarked "that no other verdict could have been arrived at from the character of the evidence ... The verdict was translated to Alwhanock, who shrugged his shoulders and moved gloomily away in the custody of an officer." [113] Cameron stated that he would reserve sentencing and adjourned the court.

After the trial, when she realized the consequences of the day's proceedings, Koltenaht approached Cameron to tell him that her court testimony had been altered by Whisk and that "she did not comprehend at the time what she was answering to." [114]

The court resumed Friday morning, June 19th, with the Grand Jury being presented with indictments against Acheewun, Shenasaluk and Qualatultun, charging them "with murder by firing on H.M.Gunboat *Forward* and shooting Charles Glyddon, and further with resisting the Queen's officers in the discharge of their duty." [115] Before they returned the indictments it seems that some of the jury needed more information from the primary witnesses, Shacutsus and/or

Sheemaltun. "After swearing some of the witnesses," the Grand Jury returned, "True Bills" against the three accused. [116]

The court then proceeded to the case of *Regina vs. Skiloweet*. The "aged Lamalcha," as he was termed by the press, who were unaware that he was from Nanaimo, entered the courtroom and "was arraigned upon an indictment which charged him with having murdered an unknown white man, on Stais Island [Pender Island] about five years ago." [117] The Reverend Alexander Garrett and Whisk were again sworn as interpreters.

In his opening remarks, Acting Attorney-General Ring stated that the accused assisted in the murder of an unknown hwunitum at Pender Island, where the victim:

> ... had landed upon the island for the purpose it is supposed of hunting game. While there Palluck, his wife Semalee, and the prisoner, set upon him and killed him. The murder did not come to light until a few weeks ago, when the gunboat *Forward* visited the [Penelakut] village, and the prisoner, alarmed at the prospect of punishment, confessed that he had been an accessory to the crime. But for the confession it is probable that the murder would never have been brought to light. [118]

Skiloweet, "when asked to plead, trembled excessively, and said that he did assist at the murder, but that another man told him to do it, [and] consequently did not consider that he was to blame." [119] A plea of not guilty "was entered by direction of the Chief Justice." [120]

Skiloweet was given in charge to the following jury: A.F. Hicks, A. Green, John McLeigh, James Malkin, Thomas Gleed, F.W. Clark, G. Bagnell, George Creighton, and A. Benoir with Edward Wilson as foreman. [121]

The first witness called by the Crown was Semallee who, after "being duly sworn," gave the following testimony through the interpreters Garrett and Whisk:

> Know the prisoner; he is a Lamalcha Indian; know an island called Stais [S'tayus]; remember being on the island with the prisoner and Polluck about three years ago; there was one white man on the island and my husband (Polluck) fired at him, and wounded him in the arm; the white man had given no offence but was sitting outside of his tent by a fire; it was morning when he was shot, and Palluck and Skiloweet were close by when the shot was fired; they had been conversing with the white man for some time. [122]

At this point Judge Cameron interrupted Semallee's testimony and Skiloweet was "asked if he understood what the witness said," and he replied, "Yes it is all true." [123]

Semallee continued her testimony: "When shot, the white man jumped up to get his gun; Palluck rushed upon him; before he got the gun the prisoner came to the assistance of Palluck; the white man caught both Skiloweet and Palluck by the hair of the head, and while struggling with them I seized an axe and cut him in the back; Skiloweet then cut him across the abdomen with a knife and he fell dead, his intestines falling out; the body was left unburied." [124]

Cameron again interrupted Semallee's testimony and asked Skiloweet if he had any questions to put to the witness. Skiloweet replied, "All Semallee says is true; she has told no lie." [125]

The final question put to Semallee by Crown Counsel Ring, was an attempt to determine whether or not the attack was premeditated. Semallee said, "Palluck and Skiloweet had a talk together previous to the commission of the deed, but I did not hear what they said." [126]

The next witness called was Shacutsus who "deposed that prisoner and Palluck together told the story to the Lamaltsas about killing the white man about five years ago." Ring then read Skiloweet's June 6th confession before Augustus Pemberton in the Police Court:

> Its substance was that Palluck was the originator. Prisoner tried to disuade him from the commission of the deed. Semallee saw a lot of things in the white man's boat, and persuaded her husband to kill him so that she might possess herself of the property. [127]

When Skiloweet was asked if the information was correct he replied, "Yes; I stabbed him three times in the stomach; Palluck was the originator of the crime, and mine was the result of a subsequent resolution; it happened five years since." [128]

This concluded the evidence for the crown, and Crown Counsel Ring briefly addressed the jury:

> ... observing that it rested with them to say whether there were any mitigating circumstances in connection with the offence charged against the prisoner. They should consider whether upon the impulse of the moment, finding his companion was getting worsted, he rushed to his assistance or whether they had previously combined together and if there were any mitigating facts in his favor it was their duty to give him, the prisoner, the benefit of them. If, however, they considered that prisoner was there aiding and abetting in the intention to kill, they must find him guilty of murder. The prisoner was accused of murder but it was in the power of the jury to bring in a verdict of manslaughter. [129]

Before they retired to deliberate, Cameron summed up the evidence in his charge to the jury. The Chief Justice:

> ... drew the attention of the jury to the wording of the indictment informing them that the time was not a material point; the essence of the offence was the murder and it remained for them to find whether murder had been committed by the prisoner or not. The law, in an offence of this nature, presumed a felonious intent, and it rested with the prisoner to show that there was no malice aforethought. The evidence was brief and the woman Semallie was herself an accomplice, but his Lordship had no doubt that her evidence was true and the prisoner himself said that she spoke the truth.
>
> His Lordship then instructed the jury that if they did not find the prisoner guilty of murder, it was competent to return a verdict of manslaughter.
>
> The crucial question was as to the degree of guilt; there could be no doubt whatever of the homicide. Had Palluck been brought before them, the evidence of murder would be conclusive as against him and in the eye of the law a person aiding and abetting the principal in the commission of a deed was equally guilty. They would therefore only have to take the circumstances into consideration and if they believed the prisoner's statement that Palluck was the instigator of the deed and that he did not draw his knife until in the grasp of the murdered man, the law always allowed the prisoner the benefit of such doubt. [130]

The jury retired to their room to deliberate the case but, "from the sounds which had proceeded from the room," wrote one court reporter, "it was evident that differences ran high among the jury." After an absence of twenty minutes "the jury returned to the Court and requested the Chief Justice to read over the evidence in detail and make a few more remarks on the case ... The jury asked whether the witness had ever said that the prisoner did try to persuade Palluck not to commit the deed?" [131] Judge Cameron replied, "No; the prisoner alone said he had ... The jury were told by the Chief Justice that the law instructed the jury to give the prisoner the benefit of any reasonable doubt in their minds." [132]

The jury then retired a second time, but after ten minutes "they were recalled again, least they should have misunderstood the Chief Justice, who said the jury, in his opinion, could not avoid returning a verdict of homicide. The only question upon which they could differ was the grade of the offence, whether, in short the prisoner had deliberately committed the murder. The judge himself evidently inclined to the lesser offence of manslaughter." [133]

Once more the jury returned to their room and "after nearly an hours deliberation were called into court and stated that they could not agree upon their verdict, two of the number were opposed to the other ten. One of the Jurors here rose and said he was one of the minority, and as the evidence showed that prisoner had cut the man's entrails out from the effects of which he fell dead, he as a Juror felt bound to find him guilty of murder." Judge Cameron "again explained the difference between murder and manslaughter, and the prisoner's right to the benefit of the doubt, and the jury retired for the [fourth] time."[134]

The court adjourned until 2:30 p.m. and the jury argued the case for another three hours. While sequestered in their room during the lunch hour, "an amusing occurrence here took place thro' the Original Pieman being caught in the act of supplying the jury with pies through a broken window, contrary to law. In the absence of Chief Justice Cameron, it was unanimously voted that he should be fined pies round, for the benefit of the officials and reporters, but after a severe reprimand he was mercifully allowed to go in peace."[135]

When the court reassembled the jury brought in a verdict of manslaughter. Judge Cameron "reserved judgement," and the court was adjourned until 10 o'clock on Monday morning.[136]

An editorial in the *Victoria Daily Chronicle* entitled "The Dark Side of Human Nature," looked at the trial in light of the saying, "murder will out."

> The Indian Palluck, Skillomeet [Skiloweet], and Semallee might have kept their own counsel, had it been possible to do so; years had rolled on, but the stain of blood was revealed against them and through their own restless admissions one has already perished violently by the hands of his own race; another waits the sentence of the law; the third—the worst, though screened from legal punishment, will meet perhaps a harder fate than either. Young, full of strength, she will be turned back upon the races who hate her—hate her for the sake of her husband's cruelty—hate her for her own crimes—hate her for the baseness which made her twice instigate her friends to commit them, and then without emotion and to save her own guiltier neck, gave evidence against them. The woman, when the police have done with her, will be turned loose, a wretched, solitary creature, shunned by all who know her, an outcast, a Pariah, a female Cain, "and it shall come to pass that every one that findeth her shall slay her."[137]

The final trial in the current Court of Assize was to have taken place Monday morning, June 22nd, but, "in consequence of the arrival of the mail steamer," with the latest news from around the world, "the Chief Justice adjourned the Assize Court until Wednesday at 10 a.m." On the following day, presented with testimony from some sailors from the *Topaze* regarding Acheewun's resistance to his capture on Galiano Island, "the Grand Jury found a true bill today against Ah-chee-wan for attempting to shoot some of Her Majesty's sailors (upon the day of his arrest.)"[138] One other indictment against John Yale(Nisqually Jack) "of attempting to incite Indians to rebel, by the use of seditious language, was thrown out."[139]

Of the three trials in the June, 1863, Court of Assizes, the final trial of the warriors Acheewun, Shenasaluk, and Qualaltaltun on Wednesday, June 24th, would be the most controversial, both in terms of its conduct and the verdict which followed. The colonial authorities knew they had only flimsy evidence on which to try Acheewun; the Grand Jury had already thrown out three bills of indictment against him which the authorities had felt sure would warrant prosecution. The jury barely admitted three more, mainly on account of the persistence of the judiciary.

On the day of the trial, the Wednesday morning edition of the *British Colonist* published an article that was clearly intended to influence the jury and the outcome of the trial. Supposedly "elicited from some of the prisoners," the information described "some criminal intentions of the Lamalcha prisoners when the *Forward* visited Kuper Island." It ran under the heading, "Treachery."

> The following plot laid by the Lemaltzas [Lamalchas] at the instigation of the notorious Achee-wun for the destruction of the gunboat *Forward* and all on board, has just come to light; the facts have been elicited from some of the prisoners who were present.
>
> Upon the arrival of the *Forward* at Kuper Island a council of war was held within the camp, and at the suggestion of Achee-wun it was decided that the major part of them should secrete themselves in the cover, while upon the pretext of a friendly wha-wha, they should inveigle as many as possible on shore. It was thought that the landing party would not consider it necessary to be fully armed.
>
> After conversing with them the opportunity should be watched, when their backs were turned for the purpose of returning to the boat, to fire into them and kill as many as possible. After disposing of the landing party it was believed that but a few would be left on board and that they could easily be picked off, this done, the gunboat would become an easy prey, and on falling into their hands she would be sunk.[140]

It is unlikely that the story originated from any of the Lamalcha captives. If, for one reason or another, one of the captives did reveal such a plot, it seems unbelievable that such important information would not be used in court.

The contents of this "news item" parallel too closely a letter written by the Superintendent of Police, Horace Smith, two months earlier to leave any doubt that he was the source behind the "information" given to the *British Colonist*.

Attempting to explain the events which overtook the British at Lamalcha on April 20th, Smith wrote to Pemberton that when the Lamalcha heard that a gunboat would be dispatched to apprehend the killers of the Marks, they "immediately made preparation. They intended to get a boat's crew on shore if possible and then to kill every man, which they would certainly have done, had a boat been sent ashore."[141] Invented as a palliative to explain what befell HMG *Forward* on April 20th, the story intended to offer a suitable alternative to any recognition of superior battlefield tactics on the part of the Lamalcha and to criminalize them.

The trial testimony of Horace Smith further reveals the connection to the planted story. As the major witness for the prosecution, Smith tailored his recollection of the events of April 20th to fit the details of the false story by repeating the story of the "ambush."

According to Smith's sworn testimony of June 24th, "As we neared the shore we saw Indians leaving the village with their Guns in the direction of the ambush."[142] Smith also testified that "they asked us to come on shore. We refused to go." His testimony was a deliberate manipulation of the truth. The Lamalcha never tried to inveigle as many as possible on shore, and no such manoeuvre was ever mentioned in any of the earlier eye-witness accounts.

The story's appearance in the *British Colonist,* and nowhere else, further indicates the dubious source of the information, especially when it is recalled that the newspaper, under the guidance of its editor, Amor De Cosmos, was the only publication to remain uncritical of the Royal Navy and unsympathetic to the plight of the Lamalcha captives.

As the *Victoria Daily Chronicle* correctly observed the following day under the same heading, "Treachery": "the statement was calculated to prejudice the jurors against the prisoners, and it was both heartless and improper in our opinion to insert such a paragraph on the morning of the trial. The intent of the paragraph was evident, and from the nature of the verdict rendered by the jury, it had its desired effect."[143]

Commenting on the *British Colonist* article, a reader noted that if it "had met the eye of Mr. Chief Justice Cameron, it would have been his duty to warn the jurors against allowing such inconsiderate statements to weigh on their minds. All good Judges in countries where the forms of law are better understood instruct the jury to set aside prejudices they might have formed, and give their verdict solely according to the evidence produced in court."[144] But if Chief Justice Cameron read the article, and it is likely he did, there was no mention of it during the day's proceedings.

When the court resumed Wednesday morning, June 24th, Acheewun, Shenasaluk, and Qualataltun:

... were arraigned upon an indictment charging them with the murder of Charles Glyddon [sic]; one of the sailors of the gunboat *Forward*, who was killed by a musket ball supposed to have been fired from a weapon in the hands of one of the prisoners during the bombardment of the Lamalcha village by the gunboat. A second count in the indictment charged them with manslaughter. [145]

The fact that Allwhenuk had already confessed to British naval officers that it was he who fired the shot that killed Gliddon was conveniently forgotten.

The Reverend Alexander Garrett was "duly sworn to interpret the English language into Chinook," but Whisk, the Lamalcha man who had assisted as a translator in the previous trials of Allwhenuk and Skiloweet, was not present. [146] In his place was "Sam a Comiakin Indian to interpret the Chinook language into Cowitchan and 'vice versa.'" [147]

As in the previous trials, the accused were not defended by counsel.

With the aid of the interpreters the indictments "were read over and explained to the prisoners." [148] Cognizant to some degree of the court proceedings, Acheewun and Shenasuluk "pleaded not guilty," but Qualataltun "pleaded guilty." Despite Qualataltun's answer, a "plea of 'not guilty' was ordered to be entered against all three prisoners, and a jury was empanelled for their trial." [149]

Edward Wilson was chosen foreman. The other members of the jury included Albert Frederick Hicks, William R. Gibbon, John Martin, Robert Wilson, John Forsythe, Robert P. Whear, James Gramslaw, William Loring, Robert Howe Austin, Thomas Gleed and Isaac Forley. [150]

Acting Attorney-General David Ring opened the case for the prosecution. He "stated the nature of the charges laid in the indictment, and gave an outline of the circumstances under which the crime was alleged to have been committed." [151]

The first witness to be examined was the Superintendent of Police, Horace Smith, who was sworn and gave his testimony which included the newly embellished "ambush story":

> I am the Superintendent of Police. I went in the Gunboat *Forward* to Kuper island—My object in going there was to apprehend the murderers of Marks and his daughter. The Gunboat was run in close enough to the shore to enable me to communicate with the people there. It was at the Lamalcha Village in Village Bay. We did not land because we had information that there would be an ambush. We saw some women and Boys. No men. We hailed them through a Interpreter. We told them that we wanted to communicate with their Chief. They asked us to come on shore. We refused to go. After some time they told us that they knew we had come

for the murderers but that they would not give them up. We explained the nature of our business in every way we could. This occupied about an hour and a quarter. I then called upon Lieutenant Lascelles the Officer in Command of the Gunboat for assistance. He then told them through the Interpreter that unless they (the Chiefs) appeared and communicated with us in a quarter of an hour he would fire on the Village. He then hoisted a red flag and said he would not fire until it was hauled down. They understood the signal because we lowered it half way as a trial and the Indians we saw, on seeing it going down, ran away. After the flag was hauled down a shot was fired from the Gunboat over the village—almost at the same time a sharp fire of musketry was opened from the shore close to us on the Gunboat. It was from an Ambush about a quarter of a mile from the village. As we neared the shore we saw Indians leaving the village with their Guns in the direction of the ambush. The firing continued and was like a fusillade, the Balls hitting the Gunboat and falling all around. There was a volley that raked her deck Fore and Aft. [152]

Chief Justice Cameron interrupted Smith at this point, "and the evidence here was interpreted to the prisoner Acheewun." The failure of the interpreter's method of translation, and the inability to communicate the detail of Smith's long testimony using Chinook, was indicated by Acheewun's short reply that "it was quite true that the women and children ran to the woods as soon as the flag was hauled down." [153]

Smith continued:

A man named Glyddon [sic] was on board standing near one of the howitzers. He was rated as a Boy and in the performance of his duty when a musket ball struck him in the head and killed him instantly. This ball came from the direction of the ambush. The firing had been going on for five or ten minutes before he fell. I afterwards assisted in arresting the prisoners. This was five or six weeks after. I have seen Otch-ee-wan [Acheewun] before. I have known him for three or four years. He was a leader of a small band. We could have recognized the features of the persons firing through a glass but not with the naked eye. I did not recognize the prisoners then. [154]

Once again Cameron interrupted Smith's testimony to allow it to be "translated," so that the accused would understand the crucial point in the indictments against them—that Gliddon had been killed during the firing. How well the interpreters succeeded is once more suggested by the brevity of Acheewun's reply: "It is true a number of shots were fired." [155]

Smith made his final statement to the court in answer to a question put to him by Cameron:

I was empowered by special instructions from the Governor to use every endeavour to arrest the murderers of Marks and his daughter and empowered to call upon the Naval Authorities if necessary to assist me. I used that authority by calling on the Commander of the Gunboat Lieutenant Lascelles for assistance to capture the murderers. Gliddon was under his command and was acting in the execution of his duty in my aid when he was killed. I am certain that the women and Boys knew when we went what we came for. We had two Interpreters and they both told us the same story "that they knew we had come for the murderers and that they would not give them up."[156]

The next witness called by Ring was Sheemaltun. Ashamed and afraid of his role as Crown witness, Sheemaltun "studiously avoided looking" at Acheewun.[157]After being sworn through the interpreters Sheemaltun said:

I remember seeing the gunboat at the Lamalcha village. The three prisoners were there. Squakim [Squ'acum] the Chief advised them to fire on the Gunboat. He is a powerful Chief. Otch-ee-wan [Acheewun] is not a Chief. Shenalsaluk is his brother.[The other prisoner is a common fellow]I saw the three prisoners fire on the Gunboat. They fired one shot only. All the people that were there fired one shot.[158]

When Sheemaltun's testimony, given in Chinook, was translated, Acheewun began to realize its implications. One observer noted: "On this being interpreted, Otcheewun said that he did not fire."[159] Qualataltun, on the other hand, "said that the witnesses' statement was correct ... Shenasaluk said he didn't know if it was true or false."[160]

Shacutsus "was then called and duly sworn as a witness thro' the Interpreter and being examined by Ring" said, "[I] remember the Gunboat coming to the Lamalcha Village. Know the Prisoners and saw them there at the time. They all had muskets and all fired on the Gunboat."[161]

"When asked if they had any questions to put to this witness, A-chee-wun said it was true; he took his musket but did not fire. Qualatultun said, "that he did not fire first; the witness fired before him."[162] His answer provoked laughter in the courtroom.

Commenting on Shacutsus' testimony, Shenasaluk "said that the witness was 'telling lies from first to last'."[163]

Ring then announced that Shacutsus' testimony "concluded the case on the part of the Crown."[164]

Chief Justice Cameron then addressed the interpreters who "were now directed by the Court to tell the Prisoners each separately that this was the time for their defence and if they had anything to say they would be heard." [165]

Acheewun was the first to speak. It is obvious from his statement that he partially understood the proceedings of the court despite the lack of legal counsel and the language barrier. He said: "I know that if I tell a lie I shall go to hell, and if I tell the truth I shall go to heaven; my heart is very good towards the white people; my brother is a witness to the fact that I did not fire. My defence is that my brother and myself were in the bushes away from the other prisoners." [166] He reiterated that "they had their guns but did not fire; there was no one with them ... His heart was very good towards white people." [167]

Shenasaluk said, "What my brother says is true. Neither of us fired." [168]

Qualataltun "admitted that he fired several times, but said that he went out originally to shoot birds, and Squa-cum induced him to fire upon the gunboat." [169]

Knowing that Acheewun and Qualataltun had incriminated themselves, Ring pronounced "that it was unnecessary for him to address the jury; he would only observe that where men were proved to be combined together for a common object, it mattered not by whose hand death was caused they were all equally guilty, whether of murder or manslaughter." [170]

After Ring spoke, Chief Justice Cameron addressed the jury. He "explained the nature of the indictment, and read extracts from the law relative to killing an officer armed with authority, or his assistant, in the execution of his duty, by which the jury were to be guided in their verdict. The law was stringent in the protection of its officers ... if they believed from the evidence that the prisoners were present in the ambush when the shot was fired which killed Glyddon [sic] and then knew that the Officers on board the Gunboat had authority to arrest the murderers of Marks and his daughter; their offence would be murder. But if while doing so they believed that the prisoners did not know that the officers had authority to arrest; their offence would be manslaughter only and that the fact of their being present in either case was sufficient to support the Indictment altho' none of the Prisoners may have fired the fatal shot." Cameron "then went through and commented on the evidence." [171]

The jury retired but, in contrast to the previous trials where a verdict was reached within minutes, in this case "the jury had some inkling of the weakness of the evidence of the crown." [172] The guilt of the accused hinged on whether or not they understood the mission of the *Forward* when it entered Lamalcha Bay, and this could not be proved. After forty minutes of deliberation, they re-entered the court where the foreman, Wilson, "stated that they could not agree." [173]

Cameron then "made some further quotations from the law books," virtually spelling out to the jury what he wanted them to do: "His Honor again explained to the jury that when an officer has proper authority to arrest and imprison and is using the lawful means for such purpose, any person resisting and killing such an officer or person is guilty of murder; and again, when any body of persons are assembled for an unlawful purpose, and in furtherance of such design, kill any person, whether police officer or otherwise, while so assembled, they are guilty of manslaughter." [174] The reporter for the *Victoria Daily Chronicle* considered that "the bias of the judge's summing up seemed to be in favour of the more serious charge." [175]

The foreman, "stated that one of the jurors was of the opinion that Captain Lascelles ought to have been examined," but Cameron replied "that they had to deal with the evidence before them." The Chief Justice, "after deliberating a few minutes [and] finding that the jury did not agree, adjourned the court to 3 o'clock." [176]

Finally, "after having been locked up two hours," the jury returned to the court-room "and gave by their Foreman a general verdict of Guilty against all the Prisoners with a strong recommendation to Mercy. The Judge then asked the Jury for the grounds on which their recommendation to Mercy was based when the Foreman answered that it was on the ground that none of the Prisoners may have fired the shot that killed Glyddon [sic]." [177]

The Chief Justice "thereupon adjourned the court" until Thursday, "at which time he directed the several prisoners who have been convicted during the session, to be brought up for sentence." [178]

Part of the way through the trial Sam, the Comiaken interpreter, had "refused to act" and was replaced by "another Indian," a friend of Garrett, who "completed the case." Garrett later claimed that Sam "was deeply interested in the escape of these men" and quit his role as interpreter "when he saw the case going against them." [179] Upon leaving the court, "indignant at what had happened and the result of the trial," Sam shouted:

> Let the whites hang us all; they will be sooner rid of us! Let them hang not only the men, but also our wives and children. [180]

When the court reconvened on Thursday morning, June 25th, the five hwulmuhw men that had been tried and convicted over the past ten days were brought before Chief Justice Cameron to receive sentence. Acheewun, Shenasuluk, and Qualataltun were the first to be brought forward.

> The prisoners, through the interpretation of the Rev. Mr. Garrett, were made to comprehend the nature of the offence of which they stood

convicted, and were asked if they had any reason to give why sentence should not be passed against them. [181]

Acheewun spoke first. He said, according to Garrett's translation, "that it was not his desire to fire upon the gunboat; it was at the instigation of the chief Squakum that the ambush was laid, and that they fired." [182]

When it was Shenasuluk's turn to speak it was reported that he "replied in the same strain." [183]

Qualataltun told the court that "his heart was right, and that it was at the urgent instigation of the same chief that he fired." [184]

The Chief Justice then addressed the prisoners:

> You, A-chee-wun, She-na-sa-luk and Qual-a-tal-tun, have been found guilty by the Jurors of our Sovereign Lady, the Queen, for the offence of murder. It appears by the evidence that you were each engaged with others assembled, in resisting the officers of justice in the execution of their duty, and following up that resolution you killed a man named Charles Glyddon [sic]. The law is clear in providing that officers of justice shall not be resisted with impunity.
>
> You perfectly knew the mission of that officer when you fired on the gunboat ... I cannot consider that as an excuse, that you did not know the officer's mission.
>
> You left your village to form an ambush, and fire on Her Majesty's gunboat. Even if (as some of you say) you did not fire, you were there, and countenanced the others in firing, which makes you equally guilty in the eye of the law.
>
> Against you, A-chee-wun, there are two other indictments for homicides, which the Crown Prosecutor has not gone into, because the present charge is, of itself, a capital offence ... So that even if you had escaped the present indictment you would have been indicted upon other serious charges.
>
> I cannot accept the excuse that you were instigated by your chief; you have been living long enough to know the laws. You have been to Victoria, and know the punishment awarded to persons whether white or colored who take the lives of their fellow creatures.
>
> The Jury have accompanied their verdict with a recommendation to mercy, that recommendation I shall be sure to forward to the Executive, but I cannot hold out hopes of mercy. It is my painful duty to pass the

sentence which the law requires for the crime of which you have been convicted. [185]

"His Lordship," reported the *Daily Evening Express*, "then passed sentence of death upon each of the prisoners in the usual form, naming Saturday, the 4th of July, as the day of execution. The prisoners listened patiently to the interpretation of the sentence, but displayed no emotion whatever upon learning the fate which awaited them." [186]

Allwhenuk was then brought forward and placed in the dock. Reverend Garrett interpreted the circumstances of his being found guilty "of assisting in the murder of Marks, and then consummating the enormity of his crime by plunging his knife into the breast of the unoffending girl, Caroline Harvey." [187]

In reply, Allwhenuk stated that:"His heart never had been bad; he was not guilty of the charge laid against him, but Sha-cut-sus, one of the witnesses brought against him, had belied him." [188]

After his reply was translated, Cameron addressed Allwhenuk and said:

You Um-wha-nuk [Allwhenuk] are now to receive the judgement of the court. You say that your heart is good, and accuse one of the witnesses on your trial with having belied you. It is too late to argue such an excuse. You with your comrade Palluck, after deliberately shooting the man Marks, went and cruelly killed his daughter. Your heart was not good then. You belong to the same tribe as those unfortunate men who have just been sentenced, and these offences have been going on for many years, until they culminated in the atrocious crime of which you have been convicted. It is high time to put an end to offences of the nature of which you have been convicted, and you now stand at the bar of justice to pay the penalty of forfeiting your life for taking that of another. [189]

Cameron passed "the sentence of death" upon Allwhenuk with "the same day being appointed for his execution as the others." [190] On receiving his sentence Allwhenuk "hung down his head, but evinced little or no concern." [191]

The last to be sentenced was Skiloweet, the Nanaimo elder found guilty of manslaughter "for the murder of a white man (name unknown) about five years ago." Skiloweet, "in reply to the question which had been submitted to the other prisoners said: 'I am an old man and have no wish to die, and would like to remain always in jail.'" [192]

Cameron, in passing sentence, said:

You Skiloweet, are charged in the indictment with murder. The jury have taken a merciful consideration of the evidence, and in consequence of mitigating circumstances, returned a verdict of manslaughter. Such a verdict saves your life; but it is necessary for the court to look at the nature of your offence, and to award a commensurate punishment, in order to deter others from perpetrating similar offences. You are an old man, and ought to have used influence with Palluck not to kill the white man. The jury have taken your statement that you did try to deter him, though unfortunately without success, into consideration; but it is my duty to inflict the heaviest punishment which the law permits. The court, therefore, sentences you to be imprisoned in Her Majesty's Jail for the term of four years with hard labor. [193]

After this, the Court of Assizes was adjourned and Skiloweet, with the four other condemned men, were marched back to the Police Barracks.

When the Court of Assizes ended, there was little public celebration in Victoria concerning the verdicts handed down by the court against the hwulmuhw defendants. Instead, judging from the editorials and letters which appeared in the colonial press, there was concern among many hwunitum that the accused had not been given a fair trial and that justice had not been served. As the *Victoria Daily Chronicle* observed:

> The severity of the sentence caused a very general feeling of dissatisfaction, and it was the opinion of many who had watched the proceedings that the prisoners had not been permitted those opportunities of defence which are never denied the poorest white man. [194]

The day after Acheewun, Shenasuluk, Qualataltun, and Allwhenuk were sentenced to death the *Victoria Daily Chronicle* published the following editorial which pleaded with Governor Douglas to act upon the jury's "strong recommendation for mercy," and commute their sentence. It questioned the fairness of conducting a trial without legal counsel for the defendants, who were convicted on the hearsay evidence of an interpreter who did not appear in court. The editorial writer contributed his own version of what Acheewun and his companions might have said in defence.

> The assizes are over—the special commission has fulfilled the business with which it was charged—the bench is deserted—the court room is emptied—and four criminals await in their cells the fatal morning which is to usher them into another world. If we are quite sure that before taking these men's lives we have carefully fulfilled every requirement of the law—that we have given them in every case the benefit of all those advantages which a merciful criminal code has provided—that we have not taken an unfair advantage of our brother's ignorance of our language and customs, we may without guilt on our souls leave them to their fate.

But if we have stinted these men of their just rights—if we have strained the text of the law against them—if we have inferred their criminality where it suited us—practiced upon their ignorance and fear—held out improper motives to witnesses, and neglected or refused to give them what Britons mean by a fair hearing, we are not clear of blame.

Had Otcheewon [Acheewun] and his two companions been able at the last moment to speak our language and learned something of our laws, when asked what they had to say, why sentence of death should not be passed, they might have replied:

"We have something to say which ought to alter your predetermination—which ought to mitigate that sentence which you are here to pronounce, and which we must abide. We are, compared to your nation, poor and ignorant—the laws in which we have been brought up are not as good as yours—we have not been trained to control our passions—we grew up to be men before you came among us—our law was that "might made right"—yours is better, but in passion we sometimes forget the new law. Some of our people have committed murder on yours—are we to be hanged for that, if it is not proved we did these things? We may ourselves have robbed white men—we have not been tried for that now. Are we to be condemned because there are rumours against our characters? Is that your Christian law?"

"We are charged with firing on the officers of justice on the gunboat, and put upon our trial. Your law says we must be heard in our own defence. We cannot speak your language and we are ignorant even to refrain from committing ourselves—you give us no friend to help us. We are told that in the great country where your Queen lives no man is ever tried for his life without counsel. We are far worse off to-day than the most ignorant men those learned judges ever tried.

"We are told that we are allowed a right of challenge. We could not tell from their faces whether the jurors were wise men, or whether they would say to themselves, "hang all the rascals," and not wish to think that we may not be all murderers. We were told we might cross-examine witnesses; we never witnessed trials and do not know how. Would any innocent white men ever be hung if there was no one wiser than themselves to ask questions?

"We are told the law will not take hearsay evidence, and everything must be proved; but you did not bring your interpreter to swear that he made himself understood when he talked from the ship to our women, and if you had proved that they understood him, how can you prove we did, when you did not know where we were until after the shots were fired? If we did not know what your officers came for, your own law says we were not guilty of murder. But if we did know what you came for, you only gave us too little time to think about what you wanted, and whether we were wrong; if you had waited even an hour or two, we are only like children, we might have done right in the end; we cannot think quickly—you should have been patient with us, and no one would have been killed."

"You fired upon our houses and near our women and children, because we would not come on board your ship, and we were provoked and fired back without thinking, but your law says that was not murder; we did not go away and think it over and come back again an hour afterwards and shoot at you. Two of us say we did not shoot at all, and the men you bring against us are as bad as ourselves; you make them swear on the Bible, but they do other things quite as bad as perjury, and your great courts where justice is done to rich and poor, do not believe wicked witnesses, and never hang men on such testimony."

"We know we have done wrong, but we have not been altogether well used; your officers assaulted and ill-treated us, contrary to your law. Had one of us died under the lash, that would have been murder. You know that this great wrong has been done by men who ought to know better; and yet you, who punish Indians for their crimes against you, have punished no one for this crime against us. We know your Queen never yet signed a death warrant for men condemned for a similar crime to ours, and if you hang us unjustly you will be worse than us, because you have knowledge and might study your law books better."

Such is a very imperfect sketch of what Otcheewon might have urged with truth. We admit all the difficulties, and the necessity of upholding the universal law—Salus populi—but we must beware of yielding to a clamour for bloody vengeance. We may not even for the benefit of the humblest individual; rather let these men escape the last penalty of the law than pollute the records of our courts in this country with a flagrant injustice.

A good counsel would have shivered the whole case in a few words; he would have shown the fatal defect in the prosecution,—the absence of the interpreter, the very man on whose testimony the whole case rested, was not produced and the fact which was the foundation stone upon which the fabric stood, the jury were asked to infer.

What an outrage upon justice to put these men to death on a finely drawn inference! The jury themselves without the advantages of the light counsel would have thrown upon the case, had some inkling of the weakness of the evidence for the Crown, and only brought in a verdict in accordance with the Judge's summing up, by overriding it with a strong recommendation to mercy.

The Governor, better informed of the present practice of British law courts, will listen to that recommendation, knowing that a refusal to do so would make it almost impossible to obtain similar verdicts from juries again in doubtful cases. He will remember that in his high office he holds for his sovereign the power of alleviation by mitigating the sentence where the law appears to bear rather hardly upon the convict. He will remember on this occasion that his oath binds him to execute judgement with mercy. [195]

The *Victoria Daily Chronicle* recognized the pivotal role of Smith's testimony for the prosecution regarding the evidence attributed to the interpreter before the fight at Lamalcha, namely that the Lamalcha knew why the British were there and knowingly resisted arrest. The interpreter who, curiously, is not named (he was, of course, Tomo Antoine), did not appear in court "to swear that he made himself understood when he talked to our women."

There was a very good reason why Tomo Antoine was not called upon to appear as a witness for the prosecution. At his homestead in the Shawnigan District on June 11th or 12th, shortly before the Court of Assizes were under way, Tomo, during a drunken argument with his wife Seenatoah (Jane Anthony), had "quietly wrung her neck ... and went off to hunt another." [196] The local Magistrate, John Peter Mouat Biggs, empanelled a jury of twelve men "to enquire into the cause of the death of Tomo, the interpreter's wife." From her fresh grave at Antoine's cabin, "the body was exhumed and from the evidence of a Mr. Davies, it appeared that death had resulted from violence." [197] Four hwulmuhw witnesses to the crime, including Tsosieten, the woman's aged father, had fled and the jury "returned a verdict of willful murder against some person or person's unknown." [198] Despite complaints "of the irregular manner in which the enquiry was instituted," Tomo Antoine was never charged with Jane Anthony's death. [199]

The *Daily Evening Express* also questioned the justice of the verdict against Acheewun, Shenasaluk and Qualataltun, and called upon the Governor to extend clemency to the condemned men.

In the recent trial before a Special Commission, the whole case for the crown rested upon one point, viz: whether the Indians understood the mission of the gunboat or whether they did not. If they did not know the reason of her presence, as the first shot was fired from her guns, the fact of returning the fire would not have constituted murder. The whole of the evidence on this vital point was the alleged assertion of an Interpreter, who was himself absent from the Court. Certainly the evidence of this man, had he been brought forward, might have strengthened the case against the prisoners, but even had he proved that he explained the *Forward*'s mission to the few women and children stated to have been on the beach, the guilty knowledge of the accused would not have been clearly established, though it might have been inferred. Would such a laxity as this have been suffered, had the life of a European been at stake!

Men of Victoria, your own hearts will answer for us! Was it because the accused were only Indians, ignorant of English customs, unread in English laws? Was it because a vague feeling existed that it was generally expedient these men should suffer? That such a feeling does exist we know full well, but on what principles of justice or humanity it is founded we have yet to learn. It is not our wish in any way to screen the Indians from a just punishment, but we demand that fairness and impartiality for them, which would never have to be asked for, were they white men.

We fully admit the necessity of impressing forcibly upon the minds of the native tribes the fact, that if they kill a white man they incur the penalty of death, but is it necessary in this case that all should suffer alike?

One of the three [Qualataltun] confessed to having fired upon the gunboat, but the two brothers, Atch-ee-wan and She-na-si-luck did not. If therefore, an example must be made, let him die who first confessed his guilt, but if we are to hand down to our posterity a record sustained by innocent blood—if we are to maintain in deed and in truth the character of a just people, let us endeavour to save these two men from the penalty of an unproved crime.

It is urged by some in justification of their sentence that as the Indians cannot comprehend the reasons for our forebearance when we have the offenders in custody, they will mistake clemency for weakness, and so evil will accrue from the act of mercy. In this reasoning we cannot concur, and we feel convinced that no danger can justify us in doing evil that good may come.

There is one in this Colony who holds the power of averting the last penalty of the law, even at the eleventh hour. He is not prejudiced against the natives of this land; his whole course has been characterized by fairness and impartiality towards them. To him we now appeal, in the earnest hope that he will exercise his prerogative on this occasion, remembering that clemency "is an attribute to God himself; and earthly power doth then show likest God's, when mercy seasons justice." [200]

As more of the hwunitum population learned of the irregularities of the recent trials, a petition "was got up by several clergymen and merchants of the town." It was addressed "to his Excellency asking him to commute the sentence of death passed on the three Indians, condemned for firing upon the gunboat, into such punishment as the merits of the case, in the Governor's estimation, shall demand." [201] The petition lay for signature at two Victoria businesses—that of grocer William Burlington Smith at 80 Government Street and Daniel Lindsay's china and glassware shop at 23 Fort Street. [202] As stated in the *Victoria Daily Chronicle*, "the reasons set forth in the memorial are such as will recommend themselves to all; and we trust every one who is interested in the execution of justice will call and read it, and if they approve of it sign their names. It will be presented to his Excellency some time tomorrow." [203]

The petition to the Governor was a succinct summary of the points regarding the miscarriage of justice at the June 24th trial of Acheewun, Shenasaluk, and Qualataltun. The text was as follows:

That these Indians could not have been aware that in the eye of English law resisting an officer in the execution of his duty, is, if the resistance prove fatal, punishable with death.

That they did not understand the nature of the law, which renders those present, but not actually engaged, participators in the crime.

That two at least, Atch-ee-wan and Shee-na-si-luck, though present, did not fire.

That no shot was fired by the Indians until the gunboat had made the attack.

That according to law, no officer is entitled to use violence until his authority be resisted with force.

That the evidence upon which they have been convicted is entirely the evidence of approvers unsupported by any other testimony whatever while the law requires that an approver's testimony must in all cases be supported by some independent witness.

That there is no satisfactory proof that the Indians clearly understood the nature of the demands actually made, as the interpreter who translated it was not produced in court.

That, while about to suffer the highest penalty of the law, they have not enjoyed the common priviledge of counsel to defend.

That their ignorance and moral degradation claim from civilization a wise and Christian forbearance. [204]

Within two days the petition was signed by one hundred and fifty hwunitum citizens of Victoria. [205]

On July 1st Cameron sent copies of his notes of the trials *Regina vs. Un Wha uck* and *Regina vs. Qual-ah-ilton She-nall-su-lik and Otch-ee wan* to Douglas, with the following additional comments regarding the jury's recommendation to mercy in the latter trial—a recommendation with which, as Cameron informed his brother-in-law, he did not agree.

> The notes will inform His Excellency of the facts elicited in each case. In the first the Jury arrived at their verdict in a very short time and gave it unqualified by any recommendation to mercy. In the second they took a much longer time to consider and although the second count of the Indictment against the prisoners was for Manslaughter which if they had found would have saved the Prisoners from the Penalty of Death they returned their Verdict of Guilty on the count for Murder accompanying it however with a recommendation of mercy to the Prisoners. This verdict clearly shows that the Jury believed from the evidence as I do that the Prisoners were aware at the time the Gunboat was fired on that the Officers on board were armed with a lawful authority to arrest. In such a case the homicide of Glyddon was legally Murder. I therefore thought it necessary as I concurred in their finding to ascertain their reasons for recommending to mercy and as I have stated in my notes the Foreman informed me that it was because they thought the fatal shot might not have been fired by any of the Prisoners. Such is the ground on which the Jury have recommended these Prisoners to His Excellency's clemency and I simply perform my duty in bringing it to his notice. I have however to say further for his information that the prosecution in consequence of this conviction did not press the other Indictments found against the Prisoners by the Grand Jury Viz. An Indictment against the three jointly for resisting an Officer in the execution of his duty and an Indictment against Otch-ee-wan singly for an Attempt to Murder and another for an attempt to shoot with an intent to wound. Under these circumstances and after a due consideration of all the facts attending these Murders I regret to say that I cannot join the Jury in their recommendation and therefore leave the consideration of it to his Excellency's discretion. [206]

The hwunitum population of Victoria were not alone in seeking to avert the death sentence against the three men. Hwulmuhw knew, as well, that the trial was "a gross violation of all law human and devine" [207] and they sought out their acquaintances amongst the hwunitum clergy, asking them to intercede on behalf of the condemned. On Tuesday, June 30th, a hwulmuhw delegation visited the Reverend Garrett at his octagonal-shaped schoolhouse adjacent to the Songhees village on Victoria Harbour. One of them was Allwhenuk's wife Koltenaht who, having failed to convince Chief Justice Cameron after the trial that she had been misled by Whisk's questioning during her testimony, came to ask Garrett's help in obtaining a commutation of her husband's death sentence. According to Garrett's recollection:

> I had a meeting of some thirty or forty Indians in my school, who came to me to plead for their friends. Among them was Koltenaught [Koltenaht] the wife of Un-when-uk [Allwhenuk] the murderer of Marks' daughter. A host of silly stories were then told to me by those who were interested in the culprits.
>
> I brought Koltenaught forward in the assembly and said in native Indian "did I ask you in the court, did you see Un-whun-nuck stab the girl?" She replied "yes." Did you say "yes! I saw him do it?" She replied "yes it is true!" She hung her head and said "yes." It is of little consequence said I, what any body may have said, you saw the deed committed that hangs the man. From that hour to the present no Indian has said one word to me in favor of Um-when-nuck."[208]

Another hwulmuhw delegation called upon Reverend Louis Joseph D'Herbomez, vicar of the Oblate Missions on the Pacific, at his residence at the St. Joseph's mission in Esquimalt.[209] These persons, whom D'Herbomez described as "disinterested Indians," recounted to the vicar their version of the court proceedings which included claims that witnesses and interpreters had lied, either for purposes of revenge or to avoid flogging. Based on what they told him D'Herbomez wrote a letter in French to Governor Douglas, asking him to reconsider the sentence against the condemned men. It was delivered to Douglas on July 2nd, and on the following day a translation appeared in the *British Colonist*.

> Your Excellency will I hope please pardon me, considering the importance of the circumstances I take the liberty to communicate officially to Your Excellency what has come to my knowledge in relation to the four Lamaltsha [Lamalcha] tribe sentenced to capital punishment.
>
> This information appeared to me of so much moment that I have made it my duty most humbly to submit it to Your Excellency's consideration, firmly persuaded as I am that Your Excellency is not unmindful that in a case of life and death too much cannot be done to become satisfied as to the guilt or innocence of the accused.
>
> I have, Your Excellency, always with pleasure heard it declared that the Indians of these colonies were considered the subjects of Her Majesty; that in this respect no distinction was made between them and the whites.

I loved to persuade myself that this principle would be adhered to, but the accounts which have been related to me are such as to make me fear that this wise and prudent impartiality has in practice not been at all times sufficiently acted up to, and more particularly so in this case.

It would appear from the following facts that the Indian interpreter and witnesses at the trial were likely to be influenced by motives calculated to render their evidence liable to suspicion, if not absolutely worthless before any tribunal.

It seems to be the fact that the Cowichan interpreter [Whisk] is the son of an Indian whose brother was killed by one of the condemned. It would also appear to be the fact that the young man [Sewholatza], the principal witness at the trial, had his father killed by a Lamaltsha in a quarrel.

Any one who knows the revengeful feelings which the savages cherish against their enemies is led to believe, and one can scarcely doubt, but that those two young men have with pleasure found in this affair the occasion of avenging the death of their parents. The Indians say that the two young men, animated by a revengeful spirit did every thing to procure the condemnation of the accused. They say that the interpreter (Gabriel) interpreted the very contrary to what the accused and witnesses deposed, or wished to say; that he made two of the witnesses answer yes, when they did not comprehend the substance of the question. He also told them that if they said yes, they would be pardoned and at liberty.

It is said also, that the witnesses gave their evidence to avoid flogging, choosing rather to give false evidence than to be beaten. If that was the case, may it not be asked, with good reason, if that is indeed the proper way to discover the truth? Who cannot perceive, that to employ threats or promises with Indians, who are natural liars, is to make them heap falsehood upon falsehood, and invent imaginary circumstances, to free themselves and inculpate others.

As in the sentence pronounced against the three Lamaltshas found guilty of having fired on the gunboat *Forward*, the generality of the Indians reason this way. "The whites, they say, kill three native for one man—why not kill them all? Are these three more guilty than the rest? If there is any of them guilty it is the chief who incited the others to fire. So let the chief be executed, and the death of the sailor avenged."

Your Excellency will, I am persuaded, pardon me, if I have, in some measure, undertaken the defence of the Lamaltshas. It is sufficient for me to see that they are unfortunate and abandoned by all, to believe it my duty to interest myself in their lot. Although they are to me unknown, that is no reason why I should be silent or not act in their favor.

I leave it to Your Excellency to judge as to what weight is to be attested to the representations above given and made to me by disinterested natives. Your Excellency has sufficient knowledge of the Indian character to be aware, that if it is dangerous to let them go unpunished for a crime, it is not the less dangerous to punish them unjustly. On one side we behold interested persons influenced by the different motives, vengeance, fear, or hope, bearing witness against the prisoners, while on the other hand, we hear the protests and comments of those whose opinion is unbiased. The conflict of opinion in so grave a treatise ought, it appears to me, to throw some doubt on the guilt of the prisoners. In this case I feel confident your Excellency will be inclined to extend clemency. This decision could not fail to win the affection of the natives, and so strengthen more and more your influence with all the tribes of the island and mainland.[210]

D'Herbomez's letter is significant because it contains additional insight into the irregularities of the trial as perceived by hwulmuhw people, particularly with regard to the damaging role played by hwulmuhw witnesses and interpreters. Unfortunately, not having been present at the trials of June 17th and 24th, D'Herbomez did not fully understand the context in which all his informant's statements were given and thus confused names and court sessions.

D'Herbomez focused the first part of his letter on the "two young men" whom his informants claimed had had a decisive effect on the outcome of the trial—the Cowichan interpreter whom he names Gabriel and "the principal witness at the trial" who "had his father killed by one of the Lamaltshas in a quarrel." The latter individual can only be Sewholatza whose Christian name was Gabriel, which D'Herbomez mistakenly cites as the interpreter's name.

Sewholatza was indeed "the principal witness" against Acheewun, but only at the hearing in the Police Court on June 11th. As a result of this testimony, Acheewun was charged with the murder of Sewholatza's father, Ashutstun, but the indictment "was ignored" by the Grand Jury. There is little doubt that Sewholatza was able to convince the colonial authorities that Acheewun and his men were involved in numerous "robberies" and "murders," thus ensuring that they would be convicted and executed, somehow. Although they may have been unappreciative of the finer points of legal process, the hwulmuhw who witnessed Sewholatza's testimony at the hearing of June 11th, cognizant as they were of his vendetta and his participation in the expedition against the Lamalcha, may be excused for having misconstrued his role in the conviction of Acheewun and his companions.

The irony is that although Sewholatza's eyewitness testimony against Acheewun, which accused him of the murder of his father, was supported by other witnesses and was admitted by Acheewun himself, the Grand Jury turned down an indictment on this charge only to commit him and others on the less tenable indictment for the death of Charles Gliddon. The death of a hwunitum, particularly a Royal Navy rating, was considered to be more significant than the death of a hwulmuhw.

It is D'Herbomez's revelation of the other "young man," "the Cowichan interpreter," and his participation in the trial, that best illuminates the iniquity of the trial and the inability, or unwillingness, of the court to overcome the language barrier and conduct a fair trial.

D'Herbomez's information was based on hwulmuhw observers who were familiar with the Hul'qumi'num language and therefore understood exactly the manipulation of statements between what the accused said and what the "Cowichan interpreter" translated to the court.

Based on the available evidence of the trial, the interpreter in question can only be Whisk, the Lamalcha man who was the "Cowichan interpreter" during the June 17th Court of Assize. He had been in custody since April 19th, when he was captured in Sansum Narrows by the *Forward* and arrested on suspicion of being concerned in the Marks' killings. He was never implicated in the assault, and when the authorities learned that his father's brother had been killed by one of the accused, as D'Herbomez reveals, evidently he, like Sewholatza, "found in this affair the occasion of avenging their parents." Since he was the only Hul'qumi'num-speaking interpreter at the June 17th trial of Allwhenuk, it can be assumed that the latter was the man who killed Whisk's uncle.

Before the revelations made by D'Herbomez about the manipulation of hwulmuhw court testimony by the interpreter Whisk, hwunitum criticism of the trials had focused on the lack of legal council for the defendants. Upon receipt of D'Herbomez's letter the day before the execution, with its allegations of fraudulent testimony, there was outrage.

> If the injustice of the sentence passed upon these men has been apparent before, and if humanity was shocked at the idea of men being convicted on hearsay evidence, how much more should we deprecate and protest against the execution of so extreme a sentence, when we learn that the agents employed in interpreting the thoughts and language of these poor Indians, and the witness brought forward to swear to their guilt, were alike influenced by motives which, had the trial taken place in England, would not only have rendered their testimony utterly worthless, but would have laid them open to a grave and serious charge themselves.

M. D'Herbomez announces that the uncle of the Cowichan interpreter was killed by one of the condemned, and that the principal witness on the trial was the son of a man who had met his death at the hands of a Lamalcho Indian. These are facts which speak for themselves. The deep and bitter spirit of revenge nurtured by savages could have had no better opportunity for wreaking itself than when those men were delivered, utterly defenceless and without the hope of aid, into the hands of their false and merciless enemies, burning with the deadliest hatred. That the interpreter had the power to place the accused in a false position cannot be doubted—that he had the will to ruin them will be admitted by all who know the Indian character—and that he really effected his purpose, deliberately and surely, is only too evident, if we are to believe the statements of the Indians mentioned in the letter of M. D'Herbomez.

If these statements are true and those Indians notwithstanding are executed tomorrow, the natives will cease to look for justice in the courts of this Colony for the future, and we must also be prepared to bear the penalty which so fearful a precedent will bring upon us, sooner or later.

If these statements are false, let them be proved so, but it behooves the Executive to enquire into and ascertain the facts, before a deed is done which can effect no good among the Indian tribes, and will certainly add nothing to the reputation of the Colony.[211]

The *Victoria Daily Chronicle* offered the following urgent appeal to the Governor to overturn "a verdict which was unfairly, illegally and inequitably arrived at." It appeared under the heading, "Is It Expedient?":

The three men who are convicted for firing on the gunboat *Forward*, unless the Governor at the last moment accedes to the request of that part of the community whose opinion being founded on reason ought to have most weight, will be beyond the reach of human justice four and twenty hours after this article meets our reader's eyes. In raising at the last moment a final prayer for these men, we do not rest our case on their innocence or private worth. We will admit, for the sake of argument, that they all have committed numerous other crimes, that is no reason they should die now, if the causes which led to the crime for which they have been tried and sentenced are enveloped in doubt. If the acts of the officials which provoked the alleged crime was itself criminal or contrary to either humanity or law, shall we dare to take life on a verdict which was unfairly, illegally and inequitably arrived at? Shall we wink at the crimes of flogging, torture and a hanging rehearsal which all but terminated fatally? Shall we allow a British Indian village—men, women and children, to be illegally fired upon, and take these wretched Indians' lives because in passion they fired back? All rumours about treachery and ambushes are idle, and have no bearing on the case at all. Had they not been worthless as evidence, they would have been produced at the trial. All that the men are said to have done before is nothing. If you can prove other murders against them, try them again—try them on another capital charge, and they shall have counsel, the fees will be raised by subscription, and the law shall be held immaculate. But there is no man in this country who has the authority—there is no man who has any sense of responsibility, dare even in the innermost reaches of his own heart, [to] justify taking human life on the ground of expediency. The men who have to sign death warrants must answer to God and their consciences even if they make an error in judgement.

The numerously signed petition for the commutation of the sentence of death passed upon the three men who fired upon the gunboat will be handed to the Governor today. Those gentlemen who think that they have not had a fair trial—that the interpreter's absence threw a doubt upon the nature of the crime—that they ought to have had counsel—will do well to sign the petition early this morning. By commuting the sentence to transportation for life every legitimate end would be answered. It is not the severity, but the certainty of the punishment, which deters men from crime. [212]

The day before the execution was to take place, Reverend Garrett collected the signed copies of the petition from the stores of the two Victoria merchants, Smith and Lindsay, and presented it to the Governor at one o'clock. [213] Douglas, however, was not prepared to grant executive clemency:

His Excellency stated that whilst it pained him to have to sign their death warrant, yet after weighing all the facts brought out on trial and finding no mitigating circumstances set forth in the petition, he could not with justice to the crown, the people, and the Indians, pardon them. [214]

Word of his refusal reached the publisher of the *Daily Evening Express* just as the evening edition was being prepared:

We have heard, just as we are going to press that His Excellency has expressed his determination to have the sentence upon the condemned Lamalchas carried out to-morrow morning. We have only to express our earnest hope that our informant may be astray and that we shall not hereafter have to look back upon what will be considered as a judicial murder. At least, let there be an inquiry into the truth of the statements which have now come to light in favour of the prisoners. This the public have a right to demand and we feel persuaded that his Excellency will concede it. [215]

There had, of course, been no error, and Douglas had no intention of reprieving the condemned men. He, in concert with the manufactured evidence of the Police, and through the connivance of his brother-in-law, Chief Justice David Cameron, ensured that Acheewun and his companions would die. The hwulmuhw were hanged not so much for the deaths of Marks, Harvey and Charles Gliddon (though no doubt their conviction and execution for the latter's death did much to satisfy the Royal Navy), but as a warning to all Hwulmuhw people of the futility of asserting their sovereignty in those areas where aboriginal title had not been extinguished. As Douglas himself explained:

These prompt and vigorous measures were necessary to address an apparently increasing mania amongst certain Tribes of Indians to become great and noted by the commission of crime. I am satisfied that the whole proceedings from first to last will not only tend to uproot such evil passions, but will materially conduce to the future of the white population, whether scattered in settlement around, or passing in solitary journey along the Coast. [216]

On the eve of the execution, after hearing that Governor Douglas had refused to commute the sentence of death, the *Victoria Daily Chronicle* unequivocally condemned what was about to take place. It was published under the heading, "The Judicial Murder," on the day Acheewun, Shenasaluk, Qualatultun and Allwhenuk were hanged.

Three men are to be hanged this morning for a murder which they did not commit—a murder which there is no pretense in either law or equity for saying that they committed. We have disgraced our humanity, our religion, our law, and our free constitution by staining our hands with innocent blood. We have dragged three defenceless Indians—who cannot speak our language, nor understand our forms of law, like dumb sheep to the slaughter. We have offered them a human sacrifice to our caprice, our judicial ignorance, our base expedience. We are hurrying fast down a course of illegality, which, if we continue to pursue, will swamp our liberties. We have tortured and flogged alike witnesses and prisoners to obtain circumstantial evidence. We have garbled the law, and curtailed the forms of justice. We have dictated to jurors, and disregarded their recommendations to mercy.

Indians have been hanged before this on charges of murder when the offence barely exceeded justifiable homicide. Here we have seen these Indians arraigned without counsel or defence—every merciful provision of the law disregarded—tried before a judge who however well meaning, is known to be, from want of knowledge, unfit to conduct a criminal trial where men's lives are at stake. Not one of the safeguards with which the law hedges in a prisoner was raised—hardly a question of cross-examination was asked—the statement of the law from the Court was both meagre and one-sided—no review of the merits of the evidence was attempted—the summing up in a judicial light was an entire failure, and the jury were all but directed in plain language to find the men guilty. The judge, and it is a grave fact worthy of remembrance, omitted to point out the absence of the interpreter on whose testimony the case hung. We think that the whole case will probably be reviewed—that the illegal conduct of the officials who captured these wretches will come to light.

The allegation is that men have been in several instances flogged to obtain confessions, and hung upon such evidence—that witnesses have been tied to guns on board one of Her Britainic Majesty's vessels, and then lashed with the cat-o-nine tails to compel them to give unwilling testimony. It has been openly alleged that grosser acts have been done, and however closely the secret may be kept, it will, it must come to light, and be blazoned on the broad page of a blue book, to the confusion of the authors.

The first beginning of this last wrong was sending officers on a mission requiring caution, patience and judgement, who were alleged to be themselves law-breakers, and the first result of the error was the death of one of the crew of the gunboat. It was said at the trial that the Governor had wisely given instructions that the Indians should be treated as British subjects, and yet the gunboat was laid opposite a British Indian village, and the male inhabitants ordered to come on board the vessel, upon pain of bombardment; that is, war was declared on these people, on their wives, on their children, and their property, unless they all surrendered themselves prisoners. They were asked to voluntarily surrender themselves on board a vessel on which they believed with reason that they would be flogged—flogged without trial, without mercy. Had the officers called to their aid those finer qualities which distinguish bravery from brute courage, they would have reasoned with the Lamalchas rather than threatened them—have remonstrated rather than exasperated them. They would neither have begrudged an hour nor a day to avoid bloodshed.

The first shot was fired from the gunboat at the Indian village, among the women and children. Then, and not until then, the Indians fired—fired in the heat of their passion upon their assailants, and the boy Glyddon fell dead upon the deck. Whether they understood the interpreter's demands or not, matters not now. If words and laws have any meaning, this was not murder. They were resisting, not arrest, but a wanton destruction of all they held dear.

Eventually these three victims were taken prisoners and are said to have been flogged. Mockery of Justice! First flogged, then brought up for trial, condemned and hanged! Such a tale of outrage needs no comment from us. Let it go as it is to that country where there are men more learned in the law—more tenacious of the liberty of the subject, whether he be white, black, or red—and who have the power to judge and the right to punish all concerned in this atrocious crime. [217]

The 4th of July dawned with the diffused light of overcast skies and ocean mist shrouding the distant hills of Sooke normally visible across the harbour from the square in front of the Police Barracks. Once again, a multiple gallows had been constructed inside the picket-fenced "small enclosure" in front of the building where "the concluding scene in the last act of the local tragedy of the "Mockery of Justice" would soon unfold. Due in part to the controversy generated during the week, "an immense concourse of citizens had assembled in front of the place of execution, among whom were many Indians." [218] An observer noted that "the concourse of spectators was large and various, even white women with children mixing in the throng." The police "appeared in full force, and a detachment of Marines under the command of Major McGuire was also upon the spot." [219]

Shortly after daylight the friends and relatives of the unhappy sufferers began to set up a pitiable wail which was continued until the closing of the scene of tragedy. The prisoners were accompanied to the platform by the priest, who had attended them during their last hours upon earth. They offered no resistance and met their fate with surprising fortitude. [220]

The two executioners who, according to hwunitum custom, were convicts from the jail, escorted Acheewun, Shenasaluk, Qualataltan and Allwhenuk up the steps to the gallows. An observer from the *Victoria Daily Chronicle* recorded the last mass execution in the Colony of Vancouver Island:

The doomed men looked self-possessed and ascended the scaffold with a firm step. The ropes were quickly adjusted, the black caps drawn over their faces, and at precisely thirty minutes past six o'clock, the drop was sprung. Two of the wretches died almost instantly; Ah-chee-wan's brother struggled violently for about half a minute; and Ah-chee-wan himself suffered for nearly twenty minutes, during which time the contortions of his body were fearful. The bungling manner in which the knot was adjusted caused it to slip from behind the ear to beneath the chin, and the miserable man was choked to death by a species of slow strangulation really horrifying to witness, and apparently most painful to experience. After hanging for an hour the bodies were cut down and handed to the friends. During the whole time that the bodies hung suspended several Indian women, among them the wives of two of the victims, each with an infant fastened to her back, cried and sobbed as though their hearts would break. It was a touching sight to behold. [221]

The reporter for the *Daily Evening Express* noted that the botched manner in which Acheewun was killed "was the subject of considerable horror among the spectators, and probably tended in a great measure to increase the distress of the relatives of the deceased. The male members of the tribe exhibited a stoical fortitude; but the wails of the Indian women who were assembled round the scaffold were heart-rending in the extreme." [222]

After the bodies of the four men were "cut down," they were "placed in coffins and delivered to their relatives, who, with the assistance of some members of the Songees people, conveyed them through Wharf street to the foot of Little's wharf, where they were transported to the Indian Reserve in canoes." [223] The rain began to fall in the afternoon. While "picnics, pleasure parties, and excursion parties" of American hwunitum made their way to various Fourth of July celebrations, in the Songhees village across the harbour from the town of Victoria, funeral rites were under way. [224]

Hwunitum reporters observed rites similar to the ritual treatment given the three Quamichan youths and other hwulmuhw victims of hanging. According to the *Victoria Daily Chronicle*, the bodies, "after being cut down, were taken to the Songish Indian village, where warm water was in waiting. The bodies were laid on their backs and the water poured over their faces, necks, and chests, in the vain hope of restoring them to life." The paper added that "an hour [was] spent in the fruitless effort." [225] The *British Colonist* reported that they "endeavoured by all the arts they could exercise to restore animation to the lifeless corpses." [226] While special rites administered to the victims of hwunitum justice may be indicated, there is also the possibility that the hwunitum observers were simply misinterpreting traditional hwulmuhw funeral rites—an important part of which was the washing of the body. [227]

Allwhenuk's body "was placed in a canoe and sent to Cowichan for interment," [228] but those of Acheewun, Shenasaluk and Qualataltun were to be buried nearby. According to hwulmuhw custom, the bodies after being washed, were:

> ... wrapped in a new blanket and bound in the position required for disposal before rigor mortis set in. Finally, it was placed on view and then, but not until then, friends and relatives came in to comfort the bereaved.

They wept together and in their anguish pulled their hair, beat their breasts, and scratched their faces. [229]

"Long after nightfall," reported the *Victoria Daily Chronicle*, "passers along Wharf Street could hear the sorrowful wail of the bereaved women coming from the Songish village." Finally, "the remains of Otcheewon, She-na-su-luk and Qual-al-tal-tun were interred near Hospital Point," on the Songhees Reserve at the entrance of the inner harbour overlooking the hwunitum city of Victoria.[230]

The Penelakut si'em, Hulkalatkstun, and some of his people, had witnessed the execution and afterwards met with an unidentified member of the Roman Catholic clergy:

> When all this was finished Hul-ka-latkstun returned to Penelakut, and for many days and nights talked to the [Penelakuts] and he told them that a good and wise man had told him many things, so that now he knew that wherever men who came from the great white chief across the water lived and made laws, there all would be cared for; but that no man must kill another, or, by the white man's laws, he also must die.
>
> And from that time Governor Douglas was a good friend to ... Pierre Hul-ka-latkstun, and every six months Governor Douglas gave him big presents of food, blankets and clothing for himself and his people.[231]

After the conclusion of the Court of Assize, the press was full of praise for the Reverend A.C. Garrett and "the valuable public service rendered by him during the recent trials." They were, of course, referring to his role as "a faithful interpreter" who fulfilled "the difficult and responsible office of explaining to the Indian prisoners in their own tongue the proceedings of the court, and impressing upon their minds the awfully solemn nature of their position."[232]

Of course, Garrett did not speak to the hwulmuhw defendants "in their own tongue." He only spoke Chinook, and had to rely on what the other interpreter, who spoke both Chinook and Hul'qumi'num, told him regarding the testimony of the accused. Consequently, Garrett had no way of knowing exactly what they said. During the course of the trials his ignorance of Hul'qumi'num was very apparent to hwulmuhw observers, one of whom "a young native who wanted no humbug in a matter of such importance, said to him in open Court, 'Speak Chinook, because one cannot understand you sufficiently when you speak the Indian tongue.'"[233]

When Father D'Herbomez's letter of July 2nd cast doubt on the reliability of the Hul'qumi'num interpreters during the trial, Garrett took personal offence.[234] After all the lavish praise for his work, he was not about to let "a foreigner" call attention to the fact that his inability to understand Hul'qumi'num could in any way diminish his effectiveness as a court interpreter. In keeping with his strong anti-Catholic bias, Garrett accused D'Herbomez of sedition:

> To impune, sir, the impartiality and in the justice of the Supreme Court of this Colony is a grave manner for a foreigner to attempt. Judge sir yourself the effect likely to be produced upon the native mind, when such open contempt of the Judiciary of this land gets spread abroad among the wild tribes of the Aborigines. At least before such a course be adopted by an alien, the crown and public have a right to expect that he will take the trouble to make himself acquainted with the facts, not as the savages, laboring to achieve the rescue of their friends, represent them, but as they are inscribed upon the records of the court. [235]

Garrett's backlash against prevailing opinion concerning the injustice of the trial and execution was shared by one of the jurors, who wrote the following letter in response to the *Victoria Daily Chronicle*'s July 4th "Judicial Murder" editorial:

> Editor: Assertions are not facts, nor is abuse argument. If such were the case, his Excellency the Governor and his Honor Judge Cameron had better resign in favor of yourselves. I now proceed to a review of the case. The Indians did aid and abet the murderers of Marks and his daughter; they did it knowingly and wilfully. Horace Smith deposed, "One of them told us they knew we had come for the murderers, but they would not let us have them." This evidence was interpreted to the prisoners, when Archewon [Acheewun] replied it was quite true; that the women and children ran to the woods as soon as the flag was hauled down. They did, while resisting her Majesty's officers in the execution of their duty, kill one of Her Majesty's subjects. So far, then, from their having been hung for nothing, and without sufficient proof; they were hung for an atrocious crime, and that on good evidence.
>
> But allowing that nothing was proved against them, why did not your reporter, when he went home with his notes and with the details of the case in his mind, speak his mind at once? Why wait till the *Topaze* was gone that contained the witnesses against the prisoners on another count? [236] When you have answered these questions so as to give general satisfaction, and not until then, will you have a right to attribute to his honor and his Excellency such gross mismanagement, nor make such sweeping assertions as appeared in your issue of the 4th instant. [237]

The juror's letter confirmed what the press had already asserted—that the three men charged in the death of Charles Gliddon were convicted and hanged on the basis of the testimony of an "absent interpreter."

Four days after the execution, the *Victoria Daily Chronicle* responded to the ongoing controversy with another "Judicial Murder" editorial:

> On Saturday morning last we offended some and pleased others of our constituents, by using plain language and calling a spade, a spade. There are occasions when loyalty to persons is inconsistent with loyalty to laws; we believe that we shewed [sic] more respect to the law than some whose business is to uphold it. If justice is brought into contempt it is not by us, but by the mal-practice of its paid servants. That the article shewed some traces of excitement we admit, but the man who could write calmly with such a theme must be made of different metal to ourselves. We have appealed from the law courts of Victoria to the people of England. Let them judge whether our undenied allegations are worth a Royal Commission of Inquiry. One of the jury failed to distinguish between hearsay testimony and sworn evidence on the most vital point. In his letter he places great weight upon the circumstantial evidence of the women leaving the beach when the red flag was hoisted. Mr. Garrett was hardly ingenuous when he kept back in his letter the fact that the assistant interpreter does not appear to have translated the message with which he was charged at all, but only warned the people to run out of the reach of the guns; and made known that the flag was a signal of grace while it was flying. This may be rumour, but as men have been hanged on rumour, it is right that it should be known that if this interpreter had been put in the box, he would have destroyed the slender case counsel for the prosecution had. [238]

The absence of Tomo Antoine, former Hudson's Bay Company hunter, guide, interpreter *par excellence* and suspected wife-killer, effectively doomed the warriors from Kuper Island.

Epilogue

The outrage of July faded into summer, as news of the defeat of the Confederate army at Gettysburg, Pennsylvania diverted hwunitum attention away from concerns of judicial impropriety and native land claims. In August, 1863, hwunitum colonists learned of the imminent retirement of James Douglas as Governor of the two colonies of Vancouver Island and British Columbia, an event which marked the end of an era, and created a widespread feeling of optimism and renewal amongst the hwunitum of the fledgling colonies.

Douglas was made a Knight Commander of the Most Honourable Order of the Bath. During his last few months in office, "Sir James Douglas enjoyed a popularity on Vancouver Island which he had never before experienced: knowing full well that he would soon discard his uniform, the colonists permitted themselves the luxury of a feeling of pride in the knighthood which a member of their own community had earned and expressed interest in his plans for a grand tour of Europe."[1] Criticism of Douglas and his regime all but disappeared as the two colonies looked forward to a prosperous future without him.

Douglas believed that the pacification of Hul'qumi'num First Nations was complete. In his opening speech to the House of Assembly on September 3rd he declared, "that the Indian tribes continue to evince a friendly disposition, and that nothing has occurred to disturb the peace of the outlying settlements which will be protected by the occasional visits of Her Majesty's ships."[2]

To ensure that there would be no further challenges to hwunitum colonization, Douglas punished the Lamalcha by confiscating the site of their village, the lelum'unup of six to eight hw'nuchalewum (house groups.) He gave verbal orders to the Superintendent of Police, Horace Smith, "not to allow any white man or Indian to settle there or cultivate the land."[3]

With the little time he had left as governor of the colony, Douglas made no more attempts to arrange formal land sale agreements with Hul'qumi'num First Nations, opting instead for an *ad hoc* system of creating reserves within the confines of lands already claimed by settlers in the pre-emption system.[4] On the Chemainus River, William Scott, without fear of reprisal, cleared the trees off his claim right up to the houses of the Upper Settlement.[5] In October 1863, Douglas instructed the acting Surveyor General, B.W. Pearse, to proceed to the Chemainus River with the gunboat *Grappler* to set aside both the alluvial cluster of islands at the mouth of the river, called Lulelqt, and the land surrounding the houses of the "Upper Settlement," as Reserve land.[6] Scott and Thomas Cunlan were forced to give up their claims in recognition of the rights of hwulmuhw owners who, as Pearse explained, were "very dissatisfied at having their lands taken away by the whites without any payment to them, and without proper Reserves being made for them for their Potato grounds."[7] These lands on the Chemainus River were the first official reserves established by Douglas among Hul'qumi'num First Nations, possibly to acknowledge the assistance given by various si'em, including Statumish, the father-in-law of Acheewun, to the colonial authorities during the late campaign against the Lamalcha.

Although it was not officially gazetted at this time, hwulmuhw families from Penelakut were confirmed in the possession of land at the north end of Galiano Island. Some of these people, it is said, "claimed [their] share of land in it as a direct gift from Governor Douglas himself."[8] Lamalcha and Penelakut rights to other locations on Galiano, including Montague Harbour and to the territories on the north end of Salt Spring Island, were not recognized although a Penelakut man named Swel-hul-ton, brother to Hulkalatkstun, claimed that he had been granted a small reserve on Salt Spring Island at Sansum Narrows.[9]

Hul'qumi'num First Nations continued to access their resources throughout the Gulf Islands and on Vancouver Island, including those lands claimed by hwunitum. In March 1864, a hwunitum settler on Salt Spring Island complained that "a large number of Cowichans have taken up their abode on the island and become very troublesome to the settlers by their thieving propensities. Mr. Hollins had his whole crop of turnips cleared out by them in one night."[10]

In August 1864, the Superintendent of Police Horace Smith, was sent to the Chemainus River to investigate a complaint by a Penelakut man named "Sausilion" that hwunitum cattle were destroying potato fields. Smith discovered that the Hul'qumi'num First Nations did not recognize the small reserves set aside for a few families. Smith wrote:

> The Chemainus Indians have a good piece of land set apart for reserve for them last year by Mr. Pearse, but many of them refuse to give up lands they have cleared and occupied for many years, unless they are recompensed in some way or other.[11]

Smith instructed the few hwumitum settlers to fence in their farms and cattle runs to prevent the cattle from destroying hwulmuhw crops but the settlers refused, and protested the "ridiculous regulations."[12]

With the Lamalcha warriors out of the way, growing numbers of hwunitum continued to pre-empt land throughout the territories of Hu'qumi'num First Nations, reassured that the Royal Navy would ultimately protect them from hwulmuhw retaliation. Sometime prior to October 1864, two hwunitum, Frank Walker and John Graves, made application to pre-empt two hundred acres on the south end of Kuper Island, including the site of Lamalcha. Because of "the ruins of an old Indian Rancherie remaining on the place" which disallowed pre-emption according to the Land Proclamation Act, their request was refused. [13] Frank Walker, however, continued to occupy the site. According to the late Eddy Edwards, Walker "fell in love with the chief's daughter from the Lamalchi tribe; and started farming on this said property, and years later his wife died [and] he evacuated this property." [14]

In the Cowichan valley some 3,500 acres of land had been provisionally set aside for the Cowichan people but the boundaries were vague and undefined. Hwunitum settlers, emboldened by the treatment meted out to the Quamichan and Lamalcha in 1863, encroached on hwulmuhw lands. Hwunitum pigs and cattle roamed freely and ruined hwulmuhw potato fields while the settlers denied Cowichan people access to traditional food gathering areas. As Bishop Demers observed:

> Berries and roots form a great part of their diet during the summer, and the latter article they can no longer gather on the land of the settlers, some of whom, on several occasions, have driven the women away from it after beating them most barbarously. [15]

Soon after the trials of 1863, Reverend Alexander Garrett pre-empted land in the Cowichan Valley, in hopes of establishing a mission there. Certain Cowichan people disliked his presence and in May 1864, five of them were arrested for shooting his horses and cattle. [16] Garrett wrote of unresolved land claims and the threat of more violence:

> When the Settlement was first established in Cowichan Valley in August 1862, certain definite promises were made to the Indians by Governor Douglas in person. He told them in the presence of the settlers that in the ensuing autumn he would return to Cowichan, have a gathering of all their tribes and make them suitable presents. This promise was never fulfilled. The Lamalchas unhappily became troublesome, three of their number were hanged, and the Governor did not think it would be expedient *then* to carry out his original intention. Nothing has since been done, and the matter is fast becoming complicated and more difficult of management ... The Indians do not understand the principle of expediency which led to the breach of promise already alluded to. However remote from the truth, the conviction in their minds is irresistible that there never was any intention to perform it.

They suffer positive and serious loss. The cattle and pigs of the whites, which are constantly on the increase, roam at pleasure over the potato crops and destroy their principle sustenance. And as the lease which Nature and first possession has given them over the whole country, has never been cancelled, they complain with some show of justice against the wholesale ruin of their labours. Last year they unquestionably suffered immensely in this way, as is evidenced by the very great decrease in the quantity of potatoes sold by them in comparison with previous years.

They have recently resumed their native "Tamanawis," or sacred science, have uttered loud threats … have exhibited an abundant supply of new muskets, and in many other ways shown a determination, gradually growing resolute, to take the law into their own hands and rid themselves of the cause of their sorrows. A blow, once struck, may lead to serious and melancholy consequences. [17]

Garrett's solution to the problem was for the government to fence one hundred acres around each of the five main villages and allow the remaining "three thousand acres of the best land on the Island" to be taken over by hwunitum settlers. He reasoned that proceeds from the sale of those lands "would yield an abundant revenue and settle forever the Indian Titles." [18] His suggestion gained currency among hwunitum in a colony in the midst of an economic depression.

After Douglas' retirement, delegations of Cowichan si'em approached his successor, Arthur Kennedy, in hopes that he would take steps to resolve the issue of unresolved land claims and prevent occupation of reserve lands. Although Kennedy "on several occasions, and in the strongest terms … promised them that their reserve would never be taken away from them," hwunitum continued their encroachment and unrestricted logging on the Cowichan River delta. [19] When the two colonies of Vancouver Island and British Columbia were united in 1866, a hwulmuhw delegation approached the new Governor, Frederick Seymour, "to accuse very bitterly Governor Kennedy of bad faith towards them." [20] Bishop Demers warned the new governor of the consequences of ignoring their requests:

A great deal has been said in connection with selling the Cowichan reserve. Public meetings, petitions, etc, have taught people to look upon the matter as if the welfare of the community and the general prosperity of the whole Colony depended on it. Whereas in reality that measure, if carried out, would only benefit some dozen more or less of individuals and possibly involve the Island in all the horrors of an Indian war … [The Cowichan] expect everything from his Excellency the new Governor and if they are once more to be put off with the same evasive answers, and behold their land quietly invaded by one man after another … there is no telling into what deeds of violence they may finally break out, peaceably disposed as they are at present. Indian threats, I know will hardly provoke a smile, for it would take but a short time to level down their villages and bring the miserable remnants of them to easy terms. But between *this* and *that* day, many a tale of horror would sadden the first pages of the history of Vancouver's Island.

The question of their lands is one of primary importance with the Indians, and it would be dangerous to the peace of the colony if the idea would spread among other tribes that the government has the intention of hunting them away from them.

... if the Indians were to resort to violence, the whole Island would be in a blaze. What has taken place more than once; and from similar causes, not so many years ago, and not so many miles from here, points out at least to the possibility of a similar result. [21]

Elsewhere amongst Hul'qumi'num First Nations, new opposition came from the ranks of former allies who saw the continued encroachment of hwunitum, particularly in light of their late assistance to the colonial armed forces, as a betrayal. An English immigrant, D.W. Mainguy, had pre-empted one hundred acres between the Chemainus River and Bonsall (formerly Someneos) Creek, where Penelakut families, including that of Hulkalatkstun, owned fishing stations, aerial duck nets and at least twenty acres of potato fields. [22]

The colonial government was quick to act to preserve the peace. In 1867, ignoring recommendations that the Penelakut potato fields be restricted to Kuper Island, the government proposed a land exchange in which Mainguy gave up his home and forty acres in exchange for the two delta islands (Lulelqt) of 126 acres, previously designated as reserve lands at the mouth of the river. [23]

The Halalt families who owned the confiscated delta islands were confirmed in their possession of a one hundred acre reserve further upriver, the site of the present day Halalt Reserve.

In 1867 and 1868 three qihuye' (black) settlers were killed on the west side of Salt Spring Island on lands owned and acessed by Cowichan, Halalt and Lamalcha families. [24] Their deaths were blamed on hwulmuhw people and, as usual, robbery was identified as the motive. However, it seems more likely that the men were killed in accordance with hwulmuhw justice because of their occupation of hwulmuhw lands. At least one of the men, William Robinson, may have been the victim of retaliatory violence. [25] Within a few years of their deaths, the sizeable black community of Salt Spring Island dispersed, with eleven of its fifteen families leaving the island. [26] Although historians have recently questioned the role of native people in this exodus, [27] the evidence from the black settlers themselves is unequivocal. Louis Stark, for example, applied for a new pre-emption to escape the violence on the island's western shores. In 1869, he wrote the Commisioner of Lands, Joseph Trutch, to explain:

> I beg leave to inform you that I have been obliged to move my family from my claim as the Indiens is daingeris. I cannot get any man to live on the place since Cirtice [Curtis] is killed ... [28]

The Cowichan reserves were officially surveyed by B.W. Pearse in 1867 but disputes continued, based upon "misunderstanding between Mr. Pearse and these Indians as to the exact limits of the lands to be held in reserve for them." [29] In the spring of 1869, in defence of his family's right to a particular tract of land claimed by a hwunitum settler, the Quamichan si'em, Te-cha-malt, "said that Governor Seymour could not take the land from him, that if the Governor sent his gunboat he would fetch his friends from all parts and hold the land against him. He also said that the governor was a liar and had not fulfilled his promise to pay for the land he had taken." [30]

Threats of retribution delivered in person by Commissioner of Police Augustus Pemberton, [31] and the intervention of si'em, such as Lohar of Comiaken, prevented violence. Lohar reminded the people of what befell the Lamalcha. According to Lohar's daughter Stokl-waht:

> The government began to mark out land for the Indians to live on, to be called their 'reserves,' and three men came here to mark the lands. This made the chiefs of the different tribes very angry, and they talked together and made plans to kill all the white people. My Pappa Lohar heard of this plan and he got very angry. He called all the chiefs of the tribes and talked to them, telling them that they must not touch the white men; that if they did so, the soldiers would come and would blow up all the houses and kill everyone. Two days and nights he talked to them, and at last they saw as he did, and said they would leave the white men in peace and would do them no harm. [32]

On July 15th, 1869, Joseph Trutch, the Chief Commissioner of Lands and Works, announced that the reserve boundaries were "finally settled and that no trespass will, in future, be permitted, either of Indians on lands outside of their reserves, or of white men on the land held by the Government in reserve for the use of the Indians in Cowichan Valley, and that any such trespass will be punished as the law directs." [33]

When British Columbia joined the Dominion of Canada in 1871, only 2,675 acres in the Cowichan Valley and 269 acres of the Chemainus Valley, had been reserved for Hul'qumi'num First Nations by the former British colonial government. [34] Within the next decade, bureaucrats from the Canadian Ministry of the Interior (the precursor to the Department of Indian and Northern Affairs), toured the territories of Hul'qumi'num First Nations, establishing the boundaries of many present-day reserves and further isolating the ancient winter villages from the larger traditional territory—a cartographic "final solution" of the "Indian Land Question," which completed the ideological and material integration of Hul'qumi'num First Nations into the "territorial orbit" of hwunitum governments.[35]

The hwunitum quickly forgot the contributions of their 1863 allies. Sewholatsa of Valdez Island, who was instrumental in defeating the Lamalcha warriors, soon found his island taken over by a Captain Wake who had recorded a pre-emption claim at the north end of Valdez Island. Under a law "permitting grants to be made to naval and military settlers," Wake recorded an additional military grant immediately south of the pre-emption claim securing for himself some 760 acres, almost a fifth of the island including some of the best arable land used by the Taitka for potato cultivation.[36]

Sewholatsa protested, and when the Indian Reserve Commissioners paid a visit to the village of Taitka on Valdez Island they were met by forty-nine villagers, including Sewholatsa, who, as a reminder of his loyal service to the colonial government, greeted them "arrayed in the cap and uniform of a Lieutenant in the Navy."[37]

> The Indians received the Commissioners well, and were not long in informing them that they desired to possess the whole of Valdez Island ... Their demand for the whole of the Island did not seem to be based on any reasonable ground, but on the feeling of petty chieftainship and tribal seclusion which it is necessary to discourage ... They did not wish white men, nor any other tribe of Indians to live on Valdez Island. The Commissioners rejected their claims.[38]

The Commissioners were also unsympathetic towards Penelakut claims on the Chemainus River. Claims to potato farms, house sites and other resources were ignored as the police, acting under the authority of the Canadian government, requisitioned gunboats such as HMG *Rocket* to intimidate the people into removing fences and houses from their traditional lands under threat of violence.[39]

All of Kuper Island, some 2,138 acres, was eventually set aside as reserve with one notable exception—the ancient village of Lamalcha. Despite Douglas' order "not to allow any white man or Indian to settle there or cultivate the land," hwunitum had occupied most of the village site, including the level land and stream at the head of the bay, off and on since 1864. Some of the Lamalcha people, presumably those who had little to do with the violence of 1863, had returned and rebuilt two large houses on the south side of the bay adjacent to the hundred acres confiscated by the hwunitum. William Conn occupied the site in 1867 and made

Lohar (1824 -1899) and a leading si'em of Comiaken counselled the Cowichan people not to wage war against Hwunitum settlers in the Cowichan Valley.

Royal British Columbia Museum, Photo PN 5935.

Lamalcha Bay, Kuper Island in the 1880s. The village of Lamalcha was confiscated and eventually pre-empted. This photograph shows the mission established by Reverend Robert Roberts after the confiscated land was bought by "The Company for Propagation of the Gospel in the New England and parts adjacent in America" in 1880. Lamalcha families who returned to their village after the war of 1863 lived in the two longhouses on the beach adjacent to the mission. British Columbia Archives and Records Service, Photo HP 11693.

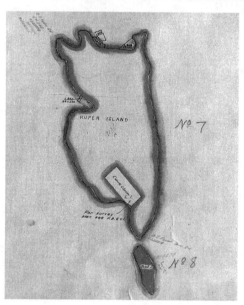

1877 Indian Reserve Commission map of Kuper Island showing the 100 acre pre-emption surrounding Lamalcha village. Courtesy of Surveyors General Branch, Victoria.

application for pre-emption in 1870. [40] According to elder Henry Edwards, the land was stolen.

> [The hwunitum] came when the people were away fishing on the Fraser River. When they came back, they found that he had stolen the land. [41]

In 1877 one of the reserve commissioners recorded in his journal that the Lamalcha "claim as theirs the land which Conn has pre-empted and improved." [42] There were also allegations that Conn had threatened some of the villagers. According to their testimony, Conn "treated us so badly that we were forced to remove from the old Village to Tent Island ... Conn took a gun and told [Quesquinum] he must go so he did remove to Tent Island." [43]

In 1880, after William Conn's death, Section 1 was purchased by "The Company for Propagation of the Gospel in the New England and parts adjacent in America," which, under the guidance of Reverend Robert James Roberts, established a mission on the site. [44] A gentle, compassionate man, Roberts "held a meeting with the [Lamalcha] tribe, in which he asked them that he wanted to build a church, [and the] request was granted; as he promised that whenever he should leave or died the said property for the church was to be reverted back to the Indians again." [45] Roberts died in 1905, and the land was sold. Testifying at a Royal Commission on Indian Affairs in 1913, Edward Hulbertson, the Penelakut Chief stated that the site of Lamalcha and its ancient burial ground "was taken away from us and we have never received anything for it." [46] Lamalcha families continued to access their lands and resources on the Fraser River, Chemainus River, Galiano Island and Salt Spring Island well into this century. [47] Henry Edwards, born at Lamalcha in 1919, came often with his people to various sites on the north end of Salt Spring Island to hunt, fish, gather plants and harvest clams.

> There never used to be any white people on the north end of Salt Spring. Just a few farms here and there. Then a store started in Ganges and more white people started coming because of the store. The white man stopped us from digging on the beaches. They said they owned the shoreline. They put these little sticks in the ground and say they own the land. The white man never lived on Salt Spring. That's Indian land. [48]

Various families have lived at Lamalcha intermittently during this century but, because of limited access to water, no hwulmuhw live there today. [49]

Hwunitum historians misconstrued what happened in 1863. The context of land alienation was forgotten, and the war was either ignored entirely or sensationalized by preoccupation with the attacks on Marks and his daughter, Brady and Henley as "treacherous acts of bloodshed" by "blood thirsty tribes," where "neither age nor sex was regarded, the murders being often carried out for the mere pleasure of killing human beings." [50] The errors and distortions of the historical record culminated in a series of unfortunate magazine articles published in the 1930s and 1940s, that were noteworthy for manipulation of facts and overt racism.[51] In these accounts, the war of 1863 becomes a crime story with the Superintendent of Police Horace Smith cast in the role of a super-sleuth, who outwits the "archcriminal," Acheewun. Smith is characterized as a hero with no mention of the fact that, in 1864, he was forced to resign in disgrace after being arrested and tried for taking bribes from Victoria saloons.[52] A year later he ended up on the west coast of Vancouver Island where Huu-ay-aht people claimed that "the former Superintendent tried to sell them demi-johns of liquor."[53]

In the intervening years, land claims of Hul'qumi'num First Nations continued to be ignored despite ongoing protests that their lands "were never ceded to or purchased by the Crown nor was the Indian title otherwise extinguished," and reminders that the si'em overall, since the Royal Proclamation of 1763, "continued to be firm and faithful allies of the Crown and have rendered important military service."[54]

Following the war of 1863, aboriginal lands continued to be alienated and aboriginal sovereignty and jurisdiction eroded throughout what is now British Columbia, leaving the inequity for us to resolve, almost a century and a half later.

> To be ignorant of what occurred before you were born is to always remain
> a child. For what is the worth of human life, unless it is woven into the life
> of our ancestors by the records of history?
>
> —Cicero, 46 B.C.

Notes

Chapter One: Tthu tumuhw 'i'tthu hwulmuhw 'i'tthu hwunitum (The Land, the People of the Land, and the Hungry People)

1. Hul'qumi'num Treaty Group, Opening statement, Lands, Main Table Meeting, Stage 4, Agreement in Principle, March 30, 1998, Chemainus.

2. Cryer, n.d., "Hy-Altz [Heel's] the Sun God." For a detailed account on the mainland see Simon Pierre in Jenness, 1955: 10.

3. Cryer, n.d., ibid.

4. Rozen, 1985: 180, 186, 190-191.

5. Rozen, 1985: 128-129, 191-194.

6. Cryer, op. cit. Rozen, 1985: 118, 120, 134, 244.

7. Hul'qumi'num is the name given to the Vancouver Island dialect of Halkomelem, a language of the Salishan language family spoken along the Fraser River and its tributaries from Sawmill (also known as Five Mile) Creek above Yale downriver to the mouth of the Fraser and across the Gulf of Georgia to the east coast of Vancouver Island from Nanoose to Malahat. It is also spoken along parts of the Nooksack river in the area of Everson and Deming in Washington State (Galloway, 1980: 1. Hukari and Peters, 1995: iii-iv.)

8. *Hul'qumi'num Treaty Group Newsletter*, Vol. 1, No. 10, May 1998: 2.

9. Peters, n.d.

10. Peters, n.d. Rozen, 1985: 120.

11. Henry Edwards, 1999, personal communication.

12. Suttles, 1987. See Mitchell, 1971, for an introduction to the archeology of the region. For botanical resources used by Hul'qumi'num First Nations see Turner and Bell, 1971. Turner (n.d.) refers to land used for the partial cultivation of certain rhizomes and bulbs as "a managed landscape."

13. Rozen, 1985: 155, 171, 190-194. Barnett, 1955: 21.

14. The mountain is called Tzouhalem by the hwunitum (Rozen, 1985: 141.)

15. Rozen, 1985: 144-189. Heaton, 1860. Garrett, 1863: 60.

16. Rozen, 1985: 118-119, 134, 135, 242-244. Barnett, 1955: 22.

17. *Hul'qumi'num Treaty Group Newsletter*, ibid.

18. Rozen, 1985: 123-124.

19. Rozen, 1985: 62-127.

20. Rozen, 1985: 123.

21. Rozen, 1985: 96-122.

22. Rozen, 1985: 113-114.

23. Rozen, 1985: 86, 104, 126. Peters, n.d. Roy Edwards, p.c., 1999.

24. *Hul'qumi'num Treaty Group Newsletter*, Vol. 1, No. 6, April 1997.

25. Barnett, 1955: 241-242. My transcription of the Hul'qumi'num word is derived from Suttles, 1987: 17. Kennedy (1995: 34) offers the translation "one blood or family."

26. Suttles, 1987: 219.

27. Ibid.

28. Suttles, 1987: 4-11.

29. Suttles, 1987: 17.

30. Suttles, 1987: 5-6.

31. Suttles, 1987: 30.

32. Suttles, 1987: 21-22.

33. Robert Akerman, personal communication.

34. Humphreys, n.d.

35. Robert Akerman, personal communication.

36. Hukari and Peters, 1995: 85. According to the missionary Thomas Crosby: "These inhabited certain mountains and headlands and rocky dangerous points, around which the waves raged and tossed their frail canoes, and sometimes upset them. A swirling eddy, a dangerous rapid, a lonely lake in the mountains, a steep precipice where perhaps at some time or other one of their people met with disaster and possibly death, was the abode of a "Stlaw-la-kum," or evil spirit." (1907: 112-113.)

37. Olsen, 1963: 7. Olsen, an historian from Chemainus, recorded the account from "an old Indian woman" who "recalled a story told by her grandmother."

38. Harris, 1997: 3-30.

39. Galois, 1994: 51-55, 234-235. Rozen, 1985: 78, 106-110.

40. Galois, 1994: 235.

41. Most notably Capilano's victory over "Fort Rupert Indians" at the First Narrows in Burrard Inlet. See Matthews, 1955: 415.

42. Suttles, 1951: 278.

43. Hayman, 1989: 48.

44. Cryer, n.d., "Memories of Tzouhalem."

45. Maud, 1978: 159. Tzouhalem's encounter with the warrior spirit is typical. Hwulmuhw warriors were called "mean" and they "were animated by horrendous spirits which they had sought by training and acquired by dream sanction just as did any other seeker after supernatural power. The yellow jacket and a few mythological monsters were special patrons of these mean men ... A war song was acquired at the time of spirit contact and the chanting of this song would put the possessor into a frenzied state in which he was exceedingly dangerous." (Barnett, 1955: 267.)

46. Cryer, op. cit.

47. Douglas, 1853. Heaton, 1860. Garrett, 1863: 60.

48. Cryer, n.d., "The Last Big Fight of the Cowichans." Maud, 1978: 160-162. Galois, 1994: 70, n. 87. Rozen, 1985: 130-131. Hwtlupnets, the Hul'qumi'num name for Maple Bay means "deep water behind [or on bottom of] bay." Rozen, 1985: 130. The orthography is Peters, n.d.

49. The allies used a special system of bird calls including the loon, small owl and big owl (Rozen, 1985: 131.) Different accounts of the battle are cited in 48 above.

50. See Ormsby, 1958: 84. The quote was by George Simpson.

51. Quoted in Akrigg and Akrigg, 1975: 358.

52. Ibid.

53. Ibid.

54. Suttles, 1987: 169.

55. Quoted in Akrigg and Akrigg, 1975: 370.

56. Ibid.

57. Akrigg and Akrigg, 1977: 19.

58. Hendrickson, 1980: I: 375.

59. Ibid.

60. Ibid.

61. Quoted in Hendrickson, n.d., 3.

62. Thackary, 1981: 4.

Chapter Two: The Entire Property of the White People Forever

1. Grant, 1857: 303-304.

2. Duff, 1969: 5-6. LaViolette, 1973: 102. Madill, 1981: 8. Berger, 1981: 50. Foster, 1996: 39-40.

3. Orange, 1987: 258.

4. Evison, 1993: 253-282.

5. Ibid.

6. Hendrickson, n.d., 6.

7. James Douglas to Archibald Barclay, September 3, 1849. Quoted in Bowsfield, 1979: 43.

8. Archibald Barclay to James Douglas, December 16, 1849. Quoted in Tennant, 1990: 18.

9. Quoted in Evison, 1987: 18.

10. Barclay to Douglas, op. cit.

11. James Douglas to Archibald Barclay, May 16, 1850. Quoted in Duff, 1969: 7-86, ibid.

12. The late Susan Lazaar Johnson recalled the story of how the 112 blankets were distributed among the Sooke people: "What they did was get there all together talking to whoever it was that signed the treaty. They brought the blankets in where they are meeting in the house and they shared it. When they found out it wasn't going to go around, they tore—halved it up and keep on passing it around until it was down to one quarter for each person. That's how they did that." (Johannesson, 1990: 3.)

13. Douglas to Barclay, op. cit.

14. Barclay to Douglas, August 16, 1850, AC 20 Vi7 M430, British Columbia Archives and Records Service, afterwards BCARS. See Evison, 1993: 271, 276, n. 50, for the original Maori text of "Kemp's Deed." For comparative purposes, Kemp's translation of the Maori text, which formed the basis for Douglas' land sale agreements, is as follows: "Know all men. We the Chiefs and people of the tribe called the "Ngaitahu" who have signed our names & made our marks to this Deed on this 12th

day of June 1848, do consent to surrender entirely & forever to William Wakefield the Agent of the New Zealand Company in London, that is to say to the Directors of the same, the whole of the lands situate on the line of Coast commencing at 'Kaiapoi' recently sold by the 'Ngatitoa' & the boundary of the Nelson Block continuing from thence until it reaches Otakou, joining & following up the boundary line of the land sold to Mr. Symonds; striking inland from this (the East Coast until it reaches the range of mountains called 'Kaihiku' & from thence in a straight line until it terminates in a point in the West Coast called 'Wakatipu-Waitai' or Milford Haven: the boundaries & size of the land sold are more particularly described in the Map which has been made of the same (the condition of, or understanding of the sale is this) that our places of residence & plantations are to be left for our own use, for the use of our Children, & to those who may follow after us, and when the lands shall be properly surveyed hereafter, we leave to the Government the power & discretion of making us additional Reserves of land, it is understood however that the land itself with these small exceptions becomes the entire property of the white people for ever. We receive as payment Two Thousand Pounds (2000) to be paid to us in four Installments, that is to say, we have this day received 500, & we are to receive three other Installments of 500 each making a total of 2000. In token whereof we have signed our names & made our marks at Akaroa on the 12th day of June 1848." Courtesy of Te Runananga o Ngai Tahu, Christchurch.

15. Barclay to Douglas, August 16, 1850, Ac 20 Vi7 M430, BCARS.

16. Ibid. See *Papers Connected with the Indian Land Question, 1850-1875*: 5-11 for edited versions of the so-called "Douglas Treaties."

17. Evison 1993: 1-19. Duff, 1965: 59-60.

18. Belich, 1988: 21.

19. Duff, 1969: 23-26, 55.

20. Douglas to Barclay, May 16, 1850. Quoted in Duff, 1969: 7.

21. Douglas to Barclay, September 3, 1849. Quoted in Bowsfield, 1979: 43217.

22. Elliot, 1990: 71.

23. Douglas to Barclay, March 18, 1852. Quoted in Pethick, 1969: 100-101.

24. The boy, who was employed by the Hudson's Bay Company, had been killed by a party of Cowichan in 1849. See Foster, 1996: 76, n. 77.

25. Elliot, 1990: 71-73.

26. Cryer, n.d., "Hyatz-A-Ha of Sna-na-mo."

27. Douglas to Barclay, September 3, 1849, op. cit.

28. The potato was introduced to hwulmuhw through contact with hwunitum at Fort Langley (Suttles, 1987: 137-151.) Already possessing a root-gathering tradition whereby the people lived a more or less sedentary life which allowed easy access to privately owned root patches and simple plant tending, hwulmuhw were quick to see the advantages the potato offered with respect to minimum labour and maximum yield. Within a short time potatoes came to be relied upon as a dependable food supply and a valuable trading commodity. Potato cultivation increased the number of privately owned plots of land in areas where food-gathering or other resource activities had been minimal or non-existent. By 1839, for example, a Hudson's Bay Company officer at Fort Langley observed that "the Cowegins [Cowichans] influenced by the counsel and example of the fort, are beginning to cultivate the soil, many of them having with great perseverance and industry cleared

patches of forest land of sufficient extent to plant, each ten bushels of potatoes." (Quoted in Suttles, 1987: 139.) On the shores of the Gulf of Georgia and Juan de Fuca Strait the same officer recorded "the very novel sight of flourishing fields of potatoes." (ibid.) The amount of land needed to grow potatoes grew exponentially due to the practice of shifting the potato patches when the fertility of the land declined. In 1860, a hwunitum visitor to the village of Comiaken on their Cowichan River delta observed that the people "have more than the average of cultivated potato land—and informed [me] that [a] thousand per cent was the usual return in these crops—on the other hand, it should be stated that they shift the ground every year or two, taking the benefit of successive virgin soils." (Heaton, 1860.) Over time extensive potato fields and patches of cleared land appeared in both the Cowichan and Chemainus Valleys as different families, some from great distances, staked out potato growing areas. Cultivation was mainly the work of women and slaves. Surplus potatoes were traded to hwunitum. Within decades of its introduction, potato cultivation became second only to salmon as a major food source in the hwulmuhw economy. Hwulmuhw land clearing activity and the success of their potato farming drew the envy of hwunitum observers who, as the maritime fur trade waned with the decline of the sea otter populations, began to turn their thoughts to land and agriculture.

29. Foster, 1996: 64.

30. Hayman, 1989: 26, n. 29, 49.

31. Douglas to Barclay, September 3, 1949, op. cit.

32. Down, 1983: 579

33. Douglas to Earl Grey, May 28, 1852, CO 305/3.

34. Ibid.

35. Fisher, 1977: 122-123.

36. Morice, 1910: 297-298.

37. James Douglas to Sir John Packington, August 17, 1852. Quoted in Olsen, 1963: 15.

38. Ibid.

39. Rozen, 1985: 135-136. Douglas' guide on this expedition is not known but it was likely Tomo Antoine.

40. Douglas to Packington, op. cit.

41. Ibid.

42. Ibid.

43. Douglas to Packington, quoted in Pethick, 1969: 104.

44. Douglas to Packington, op. cit.

45. Quoted in Lillard, 1986: 103.

46. Lillard, 1986: 104. Colvilletown was named after Hudson's Bay Company official, Eden Colvile, Associate Governor of Rupert's Land. The name was discontinued after 1860 (Walbran, 1909: 350.)

47. Douglas to Newcastle, October 24, 1853, CO 305/4.

48. Moresby, 1909: 107.

49. Douglas quoted in Olsen, 1963 a: 4.

50. Augustus Kuper to James Douglas, October 10, 1852. Quoted in Walter, 1943: 43.

51. James Douglas to Sir John Packington, November 11, 1852. CO 305.

52. Ibid.

53. Douglas Diary, January 3, 1853, "Private Papers of James Douglas, First Series," 31, BCARS.

54. Gough, 1984: 51. McKelvie, 1956: 226, 229-230. The Victoria Voltigeurs were formed in the spring of 1851, as McKelvie explains, "to act as a military police. Their numbers were largely recruited from French-Canadian half-breeds." Later their membership included Hawaiian and Black (West Indian?) recruits.

55. Douglas Diary, January 3-4, 1853, "Private Papers of James Douglas, First Series," 32, BCARS.

56. Ibid.

57. Ibid, 33.

58. Hudson's Bay Company records indicate £1/3/10 "paid to Indians by order of the Governor for secret service on the expedition to Cowetshin [Cowichan]" McKelvie, 1956: 229. The amount probably refers to the wholesale price of blankets and/or other goods. See note 77 below.

59. Douglas Diary, January 6, 1853, "Private Papers of James Douglas, First Series," 33, BCARS.

60. Ibid. Rozen, 1985: 155.

61. Douglas Diary, January 7, 1853. "Private Papers of James Douglas, First Series," 33, BCARS.

62. Douglas to Barclay, January 20, 1853. Quoted in McKelvie, 195: 226.

63. Moresby, 1909: 110.

64. Douglas Diary, January 7, 1853. "Private Papers of James Douglas, First Series," 34, BCARS.

65. Foster, Grove, and White, 1995,

66. James Douglas to John Todd, January 7, 1853, "Private Papers of James Douglas, First Series," 37, BCARS.

67. Douglas Diary, January 7, 1853. "Private Papers of James Douglas, First Series," 34-35, BCARS.

68. James Douglas to Sir John Packington, January 21, 1853. CO 305/4.

69. Ibid.

70. Ibid.

71. Walbran, 1909: 197.

72. McKelvie, 1956: 227. See Foster 1995: 61-64 for further discussion of the incident in the context of a clash between two "legal cultures."

73. Moresby, 1909: 107.

74. Douglas to Packington, op. cit.

75. Douglas to Todd, op cit.

76. James Douglas to Archibald Barclay, March 21, 1853. Quoted in Thackary, 1981: 35.

77. McKelvie, 1956: 229. As Thackary points out,"Payment for services such as that at Cowichan were not made in cash, but rather in Hudson's Bay trade goods, at full prices, thus effecting a "profit" for the Company:on this occasion, blankets, a gun, clay pipes, tobacco, and green baise." (1981: 37.)

78. Lamb, 1940: 51-58.

79. "Private Papers of James Douglas, First Series," 6, BCARS.

80. Cryer, n.d., "Memories of Tzouhalem."

81. Olsen, 1963: 40.

82. Pethick, 1969: 107.

83. Ibid.

84. Barnett, 1955: 22.

85. Lilliard, 1986: 104.

86. Hayman, 1989: 150, n. 124.

87. Quoted in Akrigg and Akrigg, 1977: 35.

88. See Duff, 1969: 23-27. The Saalaquun received 638 blankets, far in excess of the amounts distributed in the earlier treaties.

89. Cryer, n.d., "Hyatz-A-Ha of Sna-na-mo." Payments may have been made at least up until 1862. *British Colonist* (October 28, 1862) reported: "About 150 Indians assembled last Tuesday at the Hudson Bay Company's store to get pay for their lands."

90. Berger, 1981: 52.

91. MacFie, 1865: 468-469.

92. Duff, 1969.

93. *British Colonist*, May 2, 1863.

94. Lemert, 1954: 351.

95. Gough, 1984: 220.

96. *Victoria Daily Chronicle*, May 8, 1863. A notorious source of alcohol in the town of Nanaimo was an establishment known as "The Synagogue" (Crosby, 1907: 133-134.) Through the missionary Crosby's efforts the establishment was eventually shut down.

Chapter Three: The Imperial Chain

1. Gough, 1984: 59.

2. Quoted in Gough, 1984: 58-59.

3. Gough, 1984: 58-59.

4. James Douglas to the Right Hon. Henry Labouchere, February 24, 1857, CO 305/8.

5. Douglas to Labouchere, August 20, 1856. Quoted in Pethick, 1969: 140.

6. Ibid.

7. Douglas to Labouchere, July 22, 1856. Quoted in Pethick, 1969: 130.

8. Bruce to Wood, September 22, 1856. Quoted in Gough, 1984: 238-239, n. 37. Lieutenant Richard Mayne observed that, "whenever a white man takes up his residence among them, they will always supply him with a wife; and if he quits the place and leaves her there she is not the least disgraced." (Mayne, 1862: 248.)

9. Bruce Watson, personal communication.

10. Douglas to Labouchere, August 22, 1856, CO 305/7.

11. Ibid.

12. Bruce to Wood, op. cit.

13. Thackary, 1981: 70, 87, n. 71, states that the "medicine man," or shaman, received 7 blankets, biscuits, tobacco, a kettle and 8 yards of blue baize cloth.

14. Chemainus elder August Jack, quoted in Olsen, 1963a: 3.

15. Douglas to Labouchere, February 24, 1857.

16. James Douglas to Rear-Admiral Henry William Bruce, July 27, 1857. Quoted in Thackary, 1981: 71.

17. Entry in *Nanaimo Journal* for August 25, 1856. Thanks to Grahame Brazier for bringing this item to my attention.

18. Gough, 1984: 63. The naval forces included 254 sailors, 159 marines and 24 ambulance crew (Thackary, 1981: 89, n. 90.)

19. James Douglas to Rt. Hon. Henry Labouchere, September 6, 1856. Quoted in Akrigg and Akrigg, 1977: 89.

20. Interview with Chris Canute, paraphrased in Pickford, 1947: 251.Other sources state that the British only fired at targets set up on the flats (Norcross, 1959: 15.) Either way the aggressive display of military might had the desired effect.

21. Cryer, n.d., "Lohar, Chief of the Cowichans."

22. Probably a reference to the recent war waged by the American army against aboriginal people in Washington and Oregon (Thackary, 1981: 88, n. 79.)

23. Douglas to Labouchere, op cit. The villages in question were probably Comiaken, Clemclemalits and Somenos.

24. Cryer, n.d., "Lohar, Chief of the Cowichans."

25. Dennis Alphonse, personal communication.

26. Walbran, 1909: 310. Walbran's source was William MacDonald, captain of the Victoria Voltigeurs until his retirement in 1858.

27. Walbran, op. cit. Gough, 1984: 236, n. 31. According to Dennis Alphonse, the site of the trial and execution took place at the present-day intersection of Quamichan and Maple Bay Roads, behind the village of Quamichan.

28. Testimony of James Cooper, *British Colonist*, June 13, 1859.

29. Douglas to Labouchere, op cit.

30. Dennis Alphonse, personal communication.

31. Annie Deans, quoted in Gough, 1984: 236, n. 31.

32. Ibid.

33. Walbran, 1909: 31.

34. Douglas to Labouchere, op cit.

35. Testimony of James Cooper, op cit.

36. Douglas to Labouchere, op. cit.

37. Ibid.

38. Douglas to Bruce, August 25, 1856. Quoted in Thackary, 1981: 71.

39. Dennis Alphonse, personal communication.

40. Cryer, op. cit.

41. Chemainus elder August Jack, quoted in Olsen, 1963a: 3.

42. Gough, 1984: 67.

43. James Douglas to James Murray Yale, September 5, 1856, Colonial Correspondence, BCARS. Mackie, 1993: 37-38.

44. James Douglas to William Tolmie, September 6, 1856. Quoted in Gough, 1984: 67.

45. Rear Admiral Henry William Bruce to Sir Charles Wood, April 16, 1856. Quoted in Gough, 1984: 68.

46 Cryer, n.d., "Lohar, Chief of the Cowichans."

47. Olsen, 1963, b: 4.

48. Fisher, 1981: 116. Compare Kame'eleihiwa's analysis of the acceptance of Christianity over aboriginal beliefs by Hawaiian royalty in the early nineteenth century (1992: 81.)

49. Quoted in Pethick, 1968: 52.

50. Hill, 1953: 30.

51. Ibid.

52. Shaw, 1909:XI.

53. St. Onge, quoted in Shaw, 1909: XI.

54. Hill, 1953: 32-33.

55. Morice, 1910: 309. Unhappily, other "instruments" appear to have taken advantage of hwulmuhw "docility to the voice of God." In 1860, after the establishment of a resident priest at Comiaken, Anglican Bishop George Hills received reports that "there was no doubt of the fact of immoralities having been committed by the Romanist missionaries. He [the source, an "Indian Agent"] mentioned the Cowichans as one tribe amongst whom this is the case." (Bagshaw, 1996: 257.)

56. Demers, quoted in Olsen, 1963 a: 4.

57. Norcross, 1959: 29.

58. Cryer, n.d., "Lohar, Chief of the Cowichans."

59. Cryer, n.d., "The Good Priest, Father Rondeault."

60. Cryer, n.d., "Hul-ka-latkstun. Good Friend of Governor Douglas."

61. Cryer, n.d., "The Good Priest, Father Rondeault."

62. Norcross, 1959: 30.

63. *British Colonist*, March 26, 1861.

64. Cryer, op. cit.

65. Ibid.

66. MacFie, 1865: 473.

67. Cryer, op. cit.

68. Morice, 1910: 305.

69. See, for example, *Papers Connected with the Indian Land Question, 1850-1875*, 1987: 59. Hayman, 1989: 94.

70. Alexander Charles Garrett was born in 1832 in County Siglo "to one of the oldest families in Ireland" and the youngest of 15 children born to Reverend and Mrs. John Garrett. He arrived in the Colony of Vancouver Island in 1860. See Garrett, n.d., 10.

71. *British Colonist*, March 26, 1861.

72. MacFie, 1865: 474. Commenting on this particular incident, MacFie, a Congregationalist minister, wrote, "I feel we should look in vain for a display of similar zeal for the cause of morality and temperance in a white community of the same extent."

73. See for example Hayman, 1989: 140, n. 15, and Cryer, n.d., "Ye Olde and Merrie Game of Harltztzl" where Tzea-mntenaht states that the priests "gave my people seeds of vegetables for their gardens."

74. Manuel and Posluns, 1974: 61-62.

Chapter Four: After the Gold Rush

1. Suttles, 1951: 275.

2. Crosby, 1907: 68.

3. *British Colonist*, April 10, 1863.

4. Ibid.

5. *British Colonist*, June 12, 1863, describes a Lamalcha witness, Sayah, identifying Acheewun and Shacutsus, Sheemultun, Qualataltan, Allwhenuk, Seemak, Qu'salat, and Qualkais as having fired on the *Otter* in 1858. Walbran (1909: 299), writes that Montague Harbour was "known to the settlers as Stockade Harbour (Indians having attacked the Hudson's Bay vessel *Otter* near here)." See also reference in memorandum from Joseph D. Pemberton to to acting Colonial Secretary Wakeford, August 15, 1864, BCARS.

6. Regarding the influx of Hwunitum miners onto the mainland, Douglas informed the Colonial Office that "It will require the nicest tact to avoid a disastrous Indian War." (Quoted in Gough, 1978: 66, n. 60.)

7. Olsen, 1963: 19-21.

8. A list of their names appears in the July 11th, 1859 issue of the *British Colonist*.

9. *Vancouver Island Surveyor*, Papers relating to Cowichan Lands, 1858-1890, CAA 30.71, C83, BCARS.

10. *British Colonist*, July 22, 1862.

11. Joseph Pemberton to William Young, December 5, 1861, Colonial Correspondence, Department of Lands and Works, BCARS.

12. Oliver Wells, "Field Notes and Journal of the Cowichan Surveys," FB 12/59, Surveyors General Branch, Victoria.

13. Joseph Pemberton to James Douglas, July 22, 1859, Colonial Correspondence, Lands and Works Department, BCARS.

14. Wells, "Field Notes," op. cit.

15. D'Heureuse, 1860.

16. Pemberton to Wells, May 31, 1859, Colonial Correspondence, Lands and Works Department, BCARS.

17. Wells, 1859: 13-14.

18. Ibid.

19. Douglas to Lytton, May 25, 1859, CO 305/10.

20. *British Colonist*, July 11, 1859. Olsen, 1963: 19-20.

21. Pemberton to Young, July 17, 1862, Colonial Correspondence, Lands and Works Department, BCARS.

22. Mayne, 1862: 152.

23. MacFie, 1865: 73-74.

24. Thackary, 1981: 93-100.

25. Ibid. Hatch, 1955: 100. The police unit raised in Victoria was administered separately from that raised in the Colony of British Columbia. Pemberton's police were the forerunner of the Victoria City Police while its non-uniformed counterpart on the mainland became, in time, the British Columbia Provincial Police. (See Hatch, 1955: 101-102.)

26. Douglas to Lytton, April 15, 1859. Quoted in Hatch, 1955: 101.

27. Schofield and Howay, 1914: 97.

28. Thackary, 1981: iii.

29. Jonathan Begg to William and Margaret Chisholm, March 10th, 1860, Salt Spring Island Archives.

30. *British Colonist*, April 9, 1863.

31. *British Colonist*, July 4, 1859.

32. *British Colonist*, July 13, 1859.

33. Ibid.

34. Douglas to Newcastle, November 24, 1859, CO 305/11.

35. Pemberton to Douglas, June 1, 1859. Enclosure in Douglas to Newcastle, July 15, 1859, CO 305/10.

36. Douglas to Newcastle, ibid.

37. *British Colonist*, July 13, 1859.

38. *British Colonist*, July 18, 1859.

39. Begg to Chisholm, op. cit.

40. *British Colonist*, July 25, 1859.

41. Flucke, 1942: 167-168. See also Sandwell, 1997.

42. Rozen, 1985: 97, 122-126.

43. Flucke, 1942: 167, n. 17.

44. Flucke, 1942: 166.

45. Joseph Pemberton to John Copland, July 26, 1859, Colonial Correspondence, Lands and Works Department, BCARS.

46. *British Colonist*, July 27, 1859.

47. Begg to Chisholm, op. cit., Sampson, 1989: 1.

48. *New Westminster Daily Times*, September 24, 1859

49. Dennis Alphonse, p.c., identified Kwi'alhwat as the family head who owned the rights to the Burgoyne Valley. D'Heureuse(1860) shows that by 1860 the valley had been surveyed into 100 acre lots.

50. Interview with Robert Akerman, Salt Spring Island, July 27, 1998.

51. Sampson, 1989: 1. Walter, 1943: 24-25. According to Walter, Captain Peatson was the brother of Captain Verygood, whose hwulmuhw name was Swel'hultun. Swel'hultun was the brother of Hulkalatkstun or Pierre (Mary Rice interviewed by Cryer, n.d.) The physical description of Captain Peatson by Walter matches that of a photograph of Hulkalatkstun.

52. Bagshaw, 1996: 226. The influence of the Catholic missionaries amongst hwulmuhw was evident to Hills during his visit to the hwunitum settlement on the northeast side of the island. There he met "an old chief" who "had a chain round his neck to which was appended a crucifix. He had a roll of paper which he prized, amongst which were some scripture cards."

53. Cindy Johnny, personal communication. Henry Edwards (personal communication) questions the legitimacy of some marriages. When I mentioned the word "marriage" in this context, he replied, "If that's what you want to call it," in such a way as to suggest that not all of these "marriages" were culturally recognized or approved.

54. Kahn, 1998: 49. Michael Gyves, "a staunch Catholic," married Tehokwia, daughter of a high-ranking si'em at Clem'clemaluts. One of her cousins married John Maxwell, and another married Theodore Traige, both early settlers in the Burgoyne Valley. Interview with Robert Akerman, grandson of Gyves and Tehokwia, July 27, 1998.

55. Begg to Chisholm, op. cit.

56. Roy Edwards, personal communication.

57. Rozen, 1985: 97. Henry Edwards, personal communication. Numerous skeletons were uncovered during recent landscaping activities on a private property. Idol Island, off the west side of the island, was also a burial ground.

58. Mallandaine, n.d., 91.

59. The site was excavated by Simon Henson, an amateur archaeologist, in 1976. (Richards, 1976.)

60. See also, Rozen, 1985: 243. Hwulmuhw elders informed Rozen that the Ganges Harbour area was used in spring and summer for the raking of herring and the collection of herring spawn. In addition ling cod were fished, and during the summer a wide variety of beach foods were available, as well as sea mammal hunting.

61. Roy Edwards, personal communication. Henry Edwards (personal communication) states that the portage "... was used as a shortcut. In places, timbers were laid crosswise to act as skids for canoes. They'd use ropes to guide the canoe on some of the steeper sections."

62. On September 5th, 1860, Anglican Bishop George Hills "pulled up to the head of the harbour & walked up a winding trail through a deserted Indian village," the occupants of which were probably away at the Fraser River sockeye fishery. (Bagshaw, 1996: 223.)

63. Based on an interview with Lineker's daughter. (Walter, 1943: 31-32.)

64. Quoted in Sandwell, 1997: 129.

65. Sandwell, 1997: 274, Map 8.

66. Mayne, 1862: 164.

67. Audrey Ginn to author, April 11, 1987. Statement based on information provided by elders. Mrs. Ginn lived at Lamalcha Bay from 1953 to 1971, and was widely acquainted with Kuper Island elders.

68. Although Sandwell, 1997, does not emphasize this point, it seems obvious in light of hwulmuhw ownership of the land in question.

69. Wells, Field book "Survey of Chemainus District, 2/64," Surveyors General Branch, Victoria.

70. Olsen, 1963: 24.

71. *Daily Press*, April 19, 1861.

72. Ibid.

73. Cumming and Mickenberg, 1981: 191.

74. *Victoria Gazette*, April 13, 1860.

75. Commenting on the situation four years later, the *Victoria Daily Chronicle* of June 11th, 1863, observed that the colony needed prosperous farms: "but before these pleasing results can be obtained, before fields can be enclosed, prairies ploughed, crops sown and orchards planted, the Government must do their duty; certain measures must not only be talked about and promised, but done. The Indians must be compensated for their interest in their potato patches at Chemainus, before the willing settlers can begin to do the things which we all expect from them and for which the prosperity of the country is waiting. The settlers at Chemainus have serious ground of complaint against the Government. Some years ago farmers were invited to settle at Chemainus; farms were taken up and by this time the settlement would have obtained a prosperity that would have been invaluable in its effects on the whole colony. Through neglect and mismanagement troubles came, and the settlers were recalled."

76. Mayne, 1862: 164.

77. Ibid.

78. MacFie, 1865: 461.

79. Oshiane Mitchell, personal communication.

80. Cryer, n.d., "Hul-ka-lakstun, Good Friend of Governor Douglas."

81. Mary Joe, personal communication.

82. *British Colonist*, May 6, 1863.

83. Rozen, 1985: 96.

84. *British Colonist*, June 20, 1863.

85. Ibid.

86. Reid quoted in Foster, 1994: 53.

87. Foster, 1994: 52.

88. Jenness, n.d., 63.

89. *British Colonist*, June 12, 1863.

90. *Victoria Daily Chronicle*, June 12, 1863. "Swamuxum" may refer to Th'hwumksun (shining [or glittering] point), a small permanent winter village formerly located just east of Cayetano Point on Valdez Island. (See Rozen, 1985: 69-70.)

91. *British Colonist*, op cit.

92. *Victoria Daily Chronicle*, op. cit.

93. *British Colonist*, op. cit.

94. Ibid. Not all conflicts were resolved through violence. Where differences in rank were evident, aggrieved families could be compensated through the exchange of gifts or, as in the case of the killing of Peter Brown in 1852, substitution. (Barnett, 1955: 270-271, Foster, 1994.) Alcohol severely disrupted the delicate balance of reciprocal killing. Drunkenness led to aggressive behaviour and increased violence. The techniques of internal social control proved inadequate to restrain intoxicated individuals from irresponsibly precipitating inter-family conflict. Lemert writes that "the direct consequence of wholesale drunkenness was to multiply the mutual claims of clans and tribes to such a degree that the system of compensation for damages tended to break down and to be replaced by ruinous warfare. The possession of firearms undoubtedly combined with intoxication to multiply the number of more serious assaults and murders which were difficult to compensate. (1954: 349.)

95. Cryer, n.d., "Hul-ka-laktstun. Good Friend of Governor Douglas." Hulkalatkstun stated that Acheewun was "of my house" which was at Penelakut.

96. *Sergeant's Report Book*, Volume 1. Entry for June 11, 1863, reads: "Otchee-wun [Acheewun] an Indian of Porlier Pass." GR 426, BCARS. The major settlement on Galiano Island at Porlier Pass was Khinepsen "caught by the neck" or "caught in the neck." (Rozen, 1985: 112-115.) The name for this settlement is the same as that of Tzouhalem's birthplace at Green Point at the mouth of the Cowichan River (Rozen, 1985: 149.) Elders informed Rozen that the two villages "were actually occupied by the same extended families, perhaps simultaneously," suggesting that possibility that Tzouhalem and Acheewun may have been related.

97. Henry Edwards, personal communication. *British Colonist*, May 28, 1863. Hwunitum popular histories of Acheewun often refer to his cave of refuge on Galiano Island. According to De Bertrand Lugrin: "He had a secret cave on one of the mountains of Galiano, big enough to hold half a tribe. No one dared venture near except those of his chosen. It was said he used it for the pleasant purpose of imprisonment and torture, as well as in the testing of medicine men and young chiefs." (1936: 25.) During his survey of coastal waters between 1858 and 1864, Captain George Richards described Montague Harbour as "a snug and safe anchorage ... several Indian lodges are built on the shore of the bay." (Richards, 1864: 63.) Known as Sumnew ("inside [place], entering place"), Montague Harbour was a well-known clamming location and "a favourite camping place of the Cowichans and Chemainus." (Rozen, 1985: 119.) Archaeological investigations reveal occupation and intensive use of the area for at least three thousand years (Mitchell, 1971.)

98. See Chapter Nine.

99. See testimony of Superintendent of Police, Horace Smith, in the Police Court, *British Colonist*, June 12, 1863. Henry Edwards states that Acheewun, "was a leader. He gathered around him some people." (Personal communication.)

100. Rocky Wilson, personal communication. Acheewun's shamanic powers were alluded to frequently in hwunitum popular history. (See De Bertrand De Lugrin 1936 and Birch, 1940.)

101. Lamalcha represented the new economic order where persons of lower rank could gain wealth. As Jenness points out, the introduction of a wage labour economy had a significant impact on the social and political economy of the Hul'qumi'num First Nations: "when Europeans abolished

slavery, [they] furnished a labour market as open to the ex-slave and commoner as to the noble, and enabled one man to purchase with his year's wages as much food and goods as a whole village could have gathered previously in a year, then commoners and ex-slaves began to rival the nobles in the numbers and magnificence of their potlatches, and to assume titles to which they had no legitimate claim. This inevitably led to much friction and jealousy, but the nobles could no longer uphold their authority or stem the new economic and social currents that swirled around their doors." (Jenness, n.d., 58.) Squ'acum, the man considered to have the most influence at Lamalcha, bore "a middle name." (Tommy Paul, personal communication.)

102. *Victoria Daily Chronicle*, April 28, 1863.

Chapter Five: Pay the Indians for the Land or We'll Have an Indian War

1.   Hendrickson, 1980: II: 157.

2.   George Heaton to William Young, Colonial Secretary, June 16, 1860. Colonial Correspondence, F748/24a, BCARS.

3.   Ibid.

4.   Ibid.

5.   Ibid.

6.   Ibid.

7.   Henry Edwards, personal communication, Rozen, 1985: 96-97, 119-120, 243-245. The site of Lamalcha has yet to be examined archaeologically but the extent of the midden, some 800 by 25 meters, and an overall depth of a meter and a half, suggests a long occupation. Similarly, artifacts found at the site date from at least the last thousand years. (See for example, Duff, 1975: 64, 173.)

8.   Heaton to Young, op. cit.

9.   James Douglas to The Duke of Newcastle, March 25, 1861, Quoted in Berger, 1981: 55.

10. Fisher, 1977: 152.

11. Hayman, 1989: 116.

12. Cronin, 1960: 78.

13. Cronin, ibid. This occurred on April 11th, 1860, when the priests were almost killed in an ambush set up by Penelakut warriors anticipating another attack. As Chirouse and Fouquet approached the village, all was quiet. Suddenly dogs began to bark and "armed Indians ... sprang up from their hiding places." (Cronin, ibid.) According to Fouquet, disaster was averted when he "cried out 'Chilouse' (the name of my companion, Chirouse, whom they knew and loved.) A joyful voice replied, 'Pi Fouquet (and Fouquet too!) In no time they threw down their guns and came out of hiding. So glad were they to see us that, instead of waiting for us to land, they rushed into the water and drew our canoe up on the beach. Then the stories began. While they were congratulating themselves on not having shot at us one of them said he had his finger on the trigger to fire at us when the name of Chirouse disarmed him. Henry, the Saanich Indian who was visiting the tribe and had called out my name when he recognized my voice, was very ashamed to say that he too had just been going to shoot ..." (Cronin, ibid.) Besides illustrating the ongoing fighting between hwulmuhw and "northern Indians," the April 1860 incident demonstrates the affection and respect some Penelakut had at the time for the Roman Catholic clergy. Indeed, the pre-eminent

si'em of the village,Hulkalatkstun, was said to have been "the first chief to welcome Roman Catholic missionaries to the Pacific Coast." (Cryer, n.d., "Hul-ka-latkstun, Good Friend of Governor Douglas.") The notation was made by William Henry Lomas, Federal Indian Agent for the Cowichan Agency, in the 1880s underneath a photograph of the aged si'em which hung in his office.

14. Cryer, n.d., "Hul-ka-lakstun, Good Friend of Governor Douglas."

15. Bagshaw, 1996: 225. Marie Wallace, daughter of Sylvia Stark, a qihuye' woman who came to Salt Spring in 1860, states that the hwulmuhw were "local Indians" from Kuper Island. (Wallace, n.d., 19-20.)

16. Mayne, 1862: 246. Thomas Lineker to Charles Gowan, July 8, 1860. *British Colonist*, July 11, 1860. McCawley was a mysterious character (See Roberts, 1962: 22.) In 1861, a George McCauley was said to be the only hwunitum living in the Chemainus Valley (*British Colonist*, April 13, 1861) but there is no record of a pre-emption under that name.

17. Lineker to Gowan, op. cit.

18. Ibid.

19. Ibid.

20. In his initial reports of the battle, Lineker stated that of the fourteen Bella Bella, eight of the men were killed, one escaped and the three women and two boys were taken prisoner. However, two months later, his wife informed Bishop Hills that ten were killed and only one of the women "taken prisoner." (Bagshaw, 1996: 225.) The woman was apparently spared on account of her high rank. Her husband, the sole adult male survivor, was "a chief of the Kitzah-mat tribe." (*British Colonist*, July 17, 1860.) His identity as a "Kitzah-mat" (Kitimat) suggests that the northerners were not Bella Bella, but Tsimshian.

21. Lineker states, somewhat equivocally, that the "Cowichans [Lamalcha/Penelakut] did not, I believe, lose a man." (Lineker to Gowan, op. cit.)

22. Lineker to Douglas, July 9, 1860, Colonial Correspondence, BCARS.

23. Ibid.

24. Mayne, 1862: 248

25. Ibid.

26. Douglas to Newcastle, January 8, 1861. Quoted in Flucke, 1951: 182.

27. Lineker to Gowan, op. cit. Personal reminiscence from the Lineker's daughter to Walter (1943: 33.)

28. James Douglas to the Duke of Newcastle, January 8, 1861, CO 305/17.

29. Gough, 1984: 87-89.

30. Osborne, n.d.

31. Log, HMG *Forward*, May 9, 1863.

32. Osborne, op. cit.

33. Gough, 1984: 133-134.

34. Mayne, 1862: 246.

35. Akrigg and Akrigg, 1977: 154-155. The two companies were commanded by Captains Magin and George Bazalgette.

36. William Young to Joseph Pemberton, June 30, 1859, Colonial Correspondence, Lands and Works Department, BCARS. Young informed Pemberton that, "I am instructed by his Excellence the Governor to request you will cause the said Deeds to be made." No depot, however, was ever established.

37. Quoted in Berger, 1981: 54-55.

38. See Mayne, 1862: 461.

39. Berger, op. cit.

40. *British Colonist,* March 8, 1861.

41. Elliot, 1984: 4. Their employees may have been relations of Mayer's wife Matilda.

42. *British Colonist*, May 6, 1861.

43. *British Colonist*, October 20 and 28, 1861.

44. Hayman, 1989: 147, n. 102.

45. *Daily Press*, April 13, 1861.

46. Hendrickson, 1980: II: 291, n. 11.

47. Quoted in Berger, 1981: 55.

48. Minute by Newcastle attached to T.W.C. Murdoch (Emigration Office) to Rogers (Permanent Under-Secretary), June 12, 1861, CO 305/18.

49. Hendrickson, 1980: II: 446, 449.

50. Hendrickson, 1980: III: 566.

51. Akrigg and Akrigg, 1977: 231.

52. Flucke, 1951: 181-182. Roberts, 1962: 30, 35.

53. *British Colonist*, March 19, 1862.

54. *British Colonist*, May 13, 1862.

55. *British Colonist*, June 2, 1862.

56. Duff, 1965: 42-43.

57. *British Colonist*, June 12, 1862.

58. *British Colonist*, July 2, 1862.

59. *Daily Press*, June 27, 1862

60. *British Colonist*, July 12, 1862.

61. MacFie, 1865: 460.

62. *Victoria Gazette*, August 12, 1858.

63. Hendrickson, 1980: II: 345.

64. Hendrickson, 1980: II: 446.

65. See Akrigg and Akrigg, 1977: 213-214, 233-234. A native of Scotland, Donald Fraser was appointed to the Legislative Council by Douglas in 1858, and he held Cowichan Scrip on 10 sections of land in the Cowichan Valley. For a time he was "one of the largest holders of real estate on Vancouver Island." (Walbran, 1909: 190.)

66. Joseph Pemberton to William Young, July 17, 1862, Correspondence of the Lands and Works Department, BCARS.

67. *British Colonist*, June 8, 1862.

68. The notice was eventually published in the *British Colonist*, July 30, 1862, although the announcement was made earlier, on June 9.

69. Hendrickson, 1980: I: 395.

70. *British Colonist*, July 30, 1862.

71. Ibid.

72. Ibid. Pemberton was, of course, referring to the 1856 shooting of Thomas Williams by Tathlasut.

73. Garrett, 1863: 11. Elsewhere Garrett writes that, following the public meeting of July 29, "a number of prospective settlers gathered around Mr. Garrett and requested that he visit the country and bring them word as to its character." (Garrett, n.d., 20.)

74. Garrett, n.d., 20-21.

75. Pritchard, 1996: 82.

76. Ibid.

77. Garrett, n.d., 21.

78. *British Colonist*, August 12, 1862.

79. *British Colonist*, August 22, 1862.

80. Ibid. As one settler pointed out "the luxuries" were reserved only for "the Governor and suite." (*British Colonist*, August 26, 1863.)

81. *British Colonist*, August, 22, 1862. The majority of the Cowichan people, however, were absent at the Fraser River Fishery.

82. Garrett, n.d., 21.

83. Pritchard, 1996: 86.

84. Alexander Garrett to B.W. Pearse, March 10, 1865. Vancouver Island Colonial Surveyor Correspondence, CAA 30.71 KI2, BCARS.

85. Cryer, n.d., "Hul-ka-latkstun, Good Friend of Governor Douglas."

86. Re: The Lamalchas "dancing and making strange noises as though evil spirits were in them." Central to the acceptance of alcohol amongst aboriginal people was its recognition as a substance with strong transformative properties akin to spirit possession. As one ethnographer observed: "It is justifiable to assume that any people seeking visions or hallucinations as a means of acquiring supernatural power would have fewer inhibitions against surrendering to the effects of alcohol. Temporary loss of sanity or physical control would appeal subconsciously as a desireable end rather than a condition against which the will power should fight." (Quoted in Lemert, 1954.) Alcohol was the drug that gave the Hwunitum their power. Under its influence Hwulmuhw imitated the dress and actions of hwunitum in the belief that they might acquire that power. On two occasions in 1860, the Anglican Bishop George Hills observed a consistent pattern of intoxication by native people combined with imitation of hwunitum dress and speech. When Hills met intoxicated native people at New Westminster he witnessed that "[o]ne poor fellow was made frantic and was whirling himself round and in a circle uttering oaths in English. His words were 'G_d d_m son of a b_tch.'" (Bagshaw, 1996: 74.) On another occasion at Victoria, he observed, "a frightful scene of drunken confusion. The poor creatures were running about like crazy people in a lunatic yard. They were vociferating at each other and rolling and tumbling one against the

other. Some of them had on the most fantastic dresses, bright scarlet jackets, feathers and ribbons in their hair, all costumed to increase the bedlam look of the scene." (Bagshaw, 1996.)

87. Cryer, n.d., "Khul-stae-nun's Reminiscences."

88. *British Colonist*, November 14, 1862.

89. *British Colonist*, January 19, 1862.

90. *British Colonist*, November 14, 1862.

91. *Victoria Daily Chronicle*, May 10, 1863.

92. *British Colonist*, op. cit.

93. Pethrick, 1968: 208. *British Colonist*, November 17, 1862.

94. Olsen, 1963: 32.

95. *British Colonist*, April 9, 1863.

96. Wallace, n.d., 20.

97. *British Colonist*, December 17, 1862.

98. *British Colonist*, March 6, 1863.

99. *British Colonist*, February, 21, 1863.

100. Ibid.

101. *British Colonist*, January 3, 1863.

102. Diary of Bishop George Hills, November 4, 1862: 170-171, Ecclesiastical Archives of British Columbia, Vancouver.

103. *British Colonist*, March 6, 1863.

104. *British Colonist*, May 6, 1863.

Chapter Six: Another Atrocious Murder

1. *Hul'qumi'num Treaty Group Newsletter*, Vol. 1, No. 1, October 1995. Halibut and seals were taken in the nearby waters by Saanich and Hul'qumi'num First Nations (Rozen, 1985: 244.) Archaeological sites are found along the shoreline and a major midden at Breezy Bay contains evidence of sea-mammal, land-mammal hunting and shell-fish gathering (Wilson, 1991.)

2. Caroline Harvey had only recently married. On January 12th, 1863, she became the wife of Hosias Harvey of Waldron's Island in a ceremony performed by E.T. Hamblet, Esq., J.P., on San Juan Island. Their wedding was "the first marriage celebrated on San Juan Island." (*British Colonist*, January 29, 1863.) Thanks to Brenda Timbers for bringing this to my attention.

3. *British Colonist*, April 10, 1863.

4. Statement by Christian Mayer before A.F. Pemberton, April 10, 1863. Enclosure, Commodore John Spencer to Secretary of the Admiralty, May 4, 1863, Adm. 1/5829, Cap. S89. The man named "Henry" who lived on Pender Island is not further identified. There was a Saanich man named Henry who assisted Roman Catholic missionaries at this time. (See Cronin, 1960: 78.)

5. *British Colonist*, April 10, 1863.

6. Ibid. Walbran writes that that it was "a strong southeast wind." (1909: 298.)

7. Cameron, *Regina vs. Um—whan-uck [Allwhenuk]*, June 17, 1863, Notes of trial. Colonial Correspondence of David Cameron, F 260,8, BCARS.

8. *British Colonist*, June 6, 1863. The exact location of their temporary campsite is uncertain. Local tradition suggests that the place was Murder Point, named for the incident (Freeman, 1961: 158.) On the other hand, Walbran, drawing on local informants W.T. Collinson and John Briggs, writes that the Marks "landed on Saturna Island near Croker Point." (1909: 298.) Collinson and Briggs were said to be "residing on Mayne Island and in the neighbourhood at the time of the murder." (Ibid.) Dick (1961: 61) states that it was "a small cove." Contemporaneous accounts are equally vague. Smith, the Superintendent of Police, reported that the site featured "a high ridge that jutted out into the water," (Cameron, op. cit.), while Mayer states only that he found the remnants of the Marks' camp and equipment "on the beach at Saturna Island." (Mayer, op. cit.) Mayer's information suggests that the beach in question might have been Saturna Beach on Breezy Bay, a good location to wait out southeasterly gales. (See Obee, 1981: 193.)

9. *British Colonist*, June 6, 1863.

10. *Daily Evening Express*, May 8, 1863.

11. Captain John Pike to Commodore John Spencer, May 26, 1863, F1210/6, BCARS. See also Chapters 9 and 11.

12. This is according to the trial testimony of Semallee and Koltenaht who said that the bodies were disposed of in this manner, (see *British Colonist* and the *Victoria Daily Chronicle*, June 18, 1863.) Walbran records the unsubstantiated claim that, "the remains of the daughter, without clothing, and afterwards recognized by a comb left in the hair, were found by John Briggs some months after the murder, hidden in a crevice of the rocks about fifteen feet above high water mark, covered with large stones. The bones, &c., were taken to Victoria and buried in the old cemetery on Quadra Street." (1909: 298.) Briggs was a squatter on Mayne Island "at the time of the murder." (Ibid.) Briggs Point on Mayne Island was named after him.

13. Mayer, op. cit.

14. *British Colonist*, April 10, 1863.

15. Ibid.

16. Mayer, op. cit.

17. *British Colonist*, op. cit.

18. *British Colonist*, May 6, 1863. Horace Smith to Augustus Pemberton, April 22, 1863. Thalaston was also called Kaisue, and Oalatza bore another name, Swane-e-ya. Hwulmuhw of high status families may receive several names over the course of a lifetime. The names, accompanied by various rights and privileges, are recognized through the institution of the stlun'uq, or potlatch.

19. S'tayus means "wind drying," referring to drying salmon (Elliott, 1990: 33.) The area probably derived its name from the large earthworks used in the past to dry large quantities of salmon caught in offshore reef nets. (See Buxton, 1969. Suttles, 1974: 26.) Bedwell Harbour was used for porpoise and seal hunting, salmon, halibut and herring fishing, and the gathering of sea-urchins(Rozen, 1985: 244.) The water channel between the two islands have been used for millennia by hwulmuhw to access numerous resources particularly perch and ducks. (Hanson, 1995.)

20. Statement of John Henley before Augustus Pemberton, April 10, 1863. Enclosure in Spencer to Secretary of the Admiralty, May 4, 1863, Adm. 1/5829.

21. *British Colonist*, April 9, 1863.

22. Statement of John Henley, op. cit.

23. Fawcett, 1912: 86.

24. *British Colonist*, April 9, 1863.

25. Pritchard, 1996: 134.

26. Cameron, *Regina vs. Thalaston, Oalitza, Stalehum and Thask*, May 14, 1863, Notes of Trial. Colonial Correspondence of David Cameron, F260/8, BCARS.

27. *Victoria Daily Chronicle*, May 15, 1863.

28. *British Colonist*, April 9, 1863.

29. Statement of John Henley, op. cit.

30. Cameron, op. cit.

31. Statement of John Henley, op. cit.

32. *Daily Evening Express*, May 14, 1863. *British Colonist*, May 15, 1863.

33. *British Colonist*, May 15, 1863.

34. Statement of John Henley, op. cit.

35. Cameron, op. cit.

36. *British Colonist*, May 8, 1863.

37. Cameron, op. cit.

38. Fawcett writes that many of the Cherokee men who came to the Colony were "over six feet in height and powerfully built." (1912: 86.)

39. *British Colonist*, April 9, 1863.

40. Statement of John Henley, op. cit.

41. Cameron, op. cit.

42. Statement of John Henley, op. cit.

43. *Daily Evening Express*, May 5, 1863.

44. *British Colonist*, April 21, 1863. The Quamichan may not have been responsible for all the thefts. According to the newspaper report, "[s]uspicion points to the Eucultaw Indians in the neighbourhood; or as some think more likely, to two white men in a large northern canoe steered by a squaw, who, when asked where they were going to, replied [in true Salt Spring fashion] that 'they didn't know.'"

45. *British Colonist*, April 9, 1863. Statement of John Henley, op. cit.

46. *British Colonist*, op. cit.

47. Information of Horace Smith before Augustus Pemberton, April 9, 1863, File 1388, BCARS.

48. *British Colonist*, April 9-10, 1863.

49. *British Colonist*, April 10, 1863

50. *British Colonist*, June 6, 1863.

51. *Victoria Daily Chronicle,* June 6, 1863.

52. Humphreys, n.d. The killings on Saturna Island possibly had a combination of motives similar to the Nawhitti killings of three Hudson's Bay Company deserters near Fort Rupert on Vancouver Island in 1850. According to the Nawhitti version of events, the men were killed because "of a desire to act in accordance with the rules given by our forefathers which demand that our warriors kill all strangers they meet." (Quoted in Galois, 1994: 425.) Another possibility is that Palluk's attack on the Marks was a retaliatory move—a revenge killing—for earlier attacks by hwunitum against members of his extended family. For a warrior with a strong guardian spirit, such a situation would make it imperative that he kill someone, (see Barnett, 1955: 268.)

53. *British Colonist,* April 9, 1863.

54. *British Colonist,* May 15, 1863.

55. Barnett, 1955: 267-268.

56. *British Colonist,* May 15, 1863.

57. MacFie, 1865: 440-441. Barely 16 years had passed since the Cayuse of the Williamette Valley in Oregon had killed Marcus Whitman, his wife, and twelve others for practicing witchcraft at the Presbyterian mission at Waiilaptu. Many Cayuse had died from an epidemic of measles and dysentery and Whitman, a medical doctor, had tended the sick. When they died in his care, other Cayuse accused Whitman "of poisoning his patients" and he and others of the mission were subsequently slaughtered (Cronin, 1960: 12-13.) These killings precipitated a decade of inter-racial conflict in the Washington Territories. A similar, but poorly documented, incident is said to have occurred on Salt Spring Island in the early 1860s at the Ganges Harbour Settlement involving the death of a Doctor Hogg. Hogg lived amongst the hwunitum and qihuye' settlers and "was said to be peculiar in some way but trustworthy professionally." (Walter, 1943: 32.) He died in 1866 of "natural causes" according to the Cowichan Magistrate, but Walter (ibid.) writes that "an almost forgotten rumour told of his being killed by Indians because some child he had treated for illness did not survive."

58. *British Colonist,* April 9, 1863.

59. *British Colonist,* April 10, 1863.

60. The 47-year-old Spencer was the 6th son of Francis Spencer, the 1st Baron Churchill, and a grand-son of the 3rd Duke of Marlborough (Walbran, 1909: 467.)

61. *British Colonist,* April 10, 1863.

62. Ibid.

63. Ibid.

64. Ibid. After the war, however, he returned to his homestead at Miner's Bay where he and his hwulmuhw wife, Matilda, raised three sons, George, Joseph, and Frederick, the latter named for his late friend Frederick Marks (*British Colonist,* March 5, 12, 1867.)

65. Statement of John Henley, op. cit.

66. *Daily Evening Express,* May 5, 1863.

67. *British Colonist,* April 11, 1863. The Commissioner of Police was the second most powerful man in the colony. According to his biographers, Augustus Pemberton "settled disputes among the Indians for the government, in which position he was most zealous and never displayed the slightest fear. It is not too much to say that next to Governor Douglas there is no man to whom the

country is more greatly indebted for the establishment of a law abiding course than to Mr. Pemberton." (Howay and Schofield, 1914: 97.)

68. Douglas to Spencer, April 13, 1863. Enclosure in Spencer to Admiralty, May 4, 1863, Adm. 1/5829.

69. Ibid.

70. Ibid.

71. Log, HMG *Forward*, April 14-15, 1863.

72. William Young to Lieut. Commander the Hon. Horace D. Lascelles, April 15, 1863. Enclosure in Lascelles to Spencer, April 25, 1863, Adm. 1/5829. The memorandum was written April 14.

Chapter Seven: The Terror of the Coast

1. Lieut. Commander the Hon. Horace D. Lascelles to Commodore the Hon. John W.S. Spencer, "Letter of Proceedings," April 25, 1863. Enclosure in Commodore the Hon. John W.S. Spencer to Secretary to Admiralty, May 4, 1863, Adm. 1/5829, Cap. S89. Log, HMG *Forward*, April 15, 1863, Adm. 53/8028.

2. D.W. Higgins quoted in Reksten, 1986: 54. Pritchard, 1996: 113.

3. See Akrigg and Akrigg, 1977: 202.

4. *British Colonist*, April 15, 1863.

5. Log, HMG *Forward*, April 15, 1863, Adm. 53/8028.

6. *British Colonist*, April 14, 1863.

7. *British Colonist*, April 16, 1863.

8. Log, HMG *Forward*, April 16, 1863, Adm. 53/8028. The "settlement" referred to was Mayer's ranch.

9. Ibid.

10. This is probably the same Jack, identified as a "half Pennellicut [Penelakut]" whose name appears in a return of police receipts of expenses incurred during the war in which he served, off and on, for 48 days as a Voltigeur. Pemberton to Young, October, 5, 1863, File 1388, BCARS. The Jacks are a well-known family of Cowichan and, apparently, Penelakut ancestry who lived at Miners Bay. See Elliot, 1984.

11. Log, HMG *Forward*, op. cit.

12. Lascelles to Spencer, op. cit.

13. *British Colonist*, May 6, 1863.

14. *Victoria Daily Chronicle*, May 6, 1863.

15. Cameron, David. *Regina vs. Um-whan-uck [Allwhenuk]*, May 14, 1863, Notes of Trial. Colonial Correspondence of David Cameron, F260/8, BCARS.

16. *Victoria Daily Chronicle*, op. cit.

17. *British Colonist*, op. cit.

18. Log, HMG *Forward*, April 16, 1863, Adm. 53/8028.

19. Log, HMG *Forward*, April 17, 1863, Adm. 53/8028. Details of the weather in this and subsequent chapters are derived from the diary of Fitzgerald McCleery, an Irish immigrant, who settled on the north arm of the Fraser near its mouth in September, 1862 (Matthews, 1965.) McCleery was the first hwunitum to pre-empt land on what was to become the City of Vancouver.

20. Statement of John Henley before Augustus Pemberton, April 10, 1863. Enclosure in Douglas to Spencer, April 13, 1863.

21. Log, HMG *Forward*, April 17, 1863. Adm. 53/8028. Elliot, 1990: 28. Sqoqote is "crow" in English.

22. Matthews, 1965: 40.

23. Robert Brown, quoted in Olsen, 1963: 13.

24. Hayman, 1991: 49.

25. Lascelles to Spencer, April 25, 1863, op. cit.

26. Hayman, 1991: 19.

27. Olsen, 1963: 45.

28. Lascelles to Spencer, op. cit.

29. *British Colonist*, April 28, 1963.

30. Horace Smith to Augustus Pemberton, April 22, 1863, File 1388, Police Correspondence, BCARS.

31. Log, HMG *Forward*, April 19, 1963, Adm. 53/5028. Matthews, 1965: 41.

32. Lascelles to Spencer, op. cit.

33. Log, HMG *Forward*, op. cit.

34. *Victoria Daily Chronicle*, May 6, 1863. This account is essentially the same as that which appeared in the *British Colonist* on the same date undoubtedly originating from the same source (possibly Horace Smith.) "Chemainis" could refer to the village of Chemainus on Kulleet Bay or to the village of Halalt on Willy Island which was frequently identified, incorrectly, in correspondence and on maps, as "Chemainis," "Chemainos," or "Chemainus," by hwunitum of the day. (See Lascelles to Spencer, op. cit. D'Heureuse, 1860.)

35. *British Colonist*, May 6, 1863.

36. *Victoria Daily Chronicle*, May 6, 1863.

37. *British Colonist*, op. cit.

38. Lascelles to Spencer, op. cit.

39. Ibid.

40. Log, HMG *Forward*, op. cit.

41. *British Colonist*, op. cit.

42. *Victoria Daily Chronicle*, May 3, 1863.

43. This information is deduced from a letter written by Father Louis D'Herbomez in which he claimed that Whisk was "the son of a man whose brother was killed by one of the condemned." (*British Colonist*, July 3, 1863.) Whisk served as an interpreter at Allwhenuk's trial of June 17. (See Chapter 11.) Hwulmuhw observers claimed that Whisk, motivated by revenge, deliberately distorted and manipulated the testimony of witnesses to ensure Allwhenuk's conviction and execution, which leads one to believe that the man who killed his uncle was indeed Allwhenuk.

44. Elliot, 1990: 64. This account was given to Elliot by Lamalcha descendant Eddy Edwards.

45. Log, HMG *Forward*, April 20, 1863, Adm. 53/8028.

46. Ibid.

47. *Victoria Daily Chronicle*, June 25, 1863.

48. Smith to Pemberton, op. cit. It is Smith's reference to the blockhouse being constructed of "squared timbers," i.e. logs shaped with a broad-axe, which shows that the fortification was built according to hwunitum models, possibly along the lines of blockhouses built on Whidbey and San Juan Islands in the 1850s and still standing today.

49. *British Colonist*, May 6, 1863.

50. Squ'acum, in addition to being the pre-eminent si'em at Lamalcha, (Heaton, 1860) was also recognized by the Lamalcha families as the war leader (stomuhw) behind whom they united to resist attack. (See Carlson, 1997: 133-137.) Squ'acum was therefore both a si'em (high class person, respected person) and a stomex ('short tempered and likes to fight"), another indication of the unusual social structure at Lamalcha. See also *British Colonist*, June 25, 1863, and other newspapers of the same date for references to Squ'acum's role as the war leader and "a powerful chief."

51. Say'ah, a Lamalcha man, said "eight of the Indians fired on the gunboat." (*Victoria Daily Chronicle*, June 6, 1863), while John Humphreys, a hwunitum living at Quamichan, was told that "the Lemalchoes who fought the *Forward* on the 20th ult., numbered only twenty-two braves," (*Daily Evening Express*, May 20, 1863.)

52. *Victoria Daily Chronicle*, June 25, 1863.

53. Ginn to Arnett, April 11, 1987. During her many years of residence at Lamalcha Bay, Kuper Island elders pointed out to Audrey Ginn the locations of five "lookouts," two of which were situated on either side of the entrance to Lamalcha Bay.

54. The first Lamalcha volley was "fired simultaneously" from the two points of land which strongly suggest the use of a pre-arranged signal. See the account by the "*Topaze* sailor," who took part in the battle (*British Colonist*, May 2, 1863.)

55. Thanks to Bruce Rout of Chemainus who pointed this out to me on board the Kuper Island Ferry in March 1997, during a discussion of the battle.

56. *Daily Evening Express*, June 24, 1863. Elsewhere it was reported that Acheewun and his brother "were in a place apart from the rear; they had their guns but did not fire." (*British Colonist*, June 25, 1863.)

57. *British Colonist*, June 25, 1863. As will be seen in Chapter 11, Smith was not giving a truthful account of events. He also said in the same statement that the British "saw no men about" as they entered Lamalcha Bay.

58. Lascelles to Spencer, op. cit.

59. *Victoria Daily Chronicle*, May 6, 1863. *Daily Evening Express*, June 24, 1863.

60. Lascelles to Spencer, op. cit.

61. *British Colonist*, June 25, 1863.

62. *Daily Evening Express*, op. cit. *British Colonist*, May 6, 1863.

63. Lascelles to Spencer, op. cit.

64. *British Colonist*, May 6, 1863.

65. *Victoria Daily Chronicle*, June 6, 1863.

66. Lascelles to Spencer, op. cit.

67. *British Colonist*, July 2, 1862.

68. *British Colonist*, May 6, June 25, 1863.

69. Lascelles to Spencer, op. cit.

70. *Victoria Daily Chronicle*, July 8, 1863. Smith later testified that towards the end of the fifteen minute ultimatum "the flag was partly hauled down and pulled up again" in order to ascertain if the Lamalcha indeed knew what the flag meant (*British Colonist*, June 25, 1863.) According to Smith, "they perfectly understood the meaning of this signal, for when the time was up we lowered the flag a little, and at once the few Indians on the beach fled into the woods." (*Daily Evening Express*, June 24, 1863.) Smith may have made the story up. See Chapter 11.

71. *British Colonist*, May 6, 1863.

72. Elliot, 1990: 64. Elliot was told this version of events by the late Eddy Edwards of Kuper Island. Eddy Edward's son, Henry, p.c., states: "In that shelling of the Lamalchi village, the person that they were looking for wasn't there. They kept asking for somebody to bring this guy out but the people in the village didn't know what they were talking about."

73. Lascelles to Spencer, op. cit.

74. *Victoria Daily Chronicle*, June 6, 1863.

75. Lascelles to Spencer, op. cit. Lascelles' own account implies that he fired on the village while it was still occupied by women and children. A sailor from HMS *Topaze*, serving on board the *Forward*, also states that the British, "seeing that they [the women and children] were trying to get away, fired a shell into the ranch." (*British Colonist*, May 2, 1863.)

76. Log, HMG *Forward*, April 20, 1863.

77. Lascelles to Spencer, op. cit.

78. *British Colonist*, May 2, 1863. *Daily Evening Express*, June 24, 1863. *British Colonist*, April 27, May 2, June 25, 1863. According to Lascelles, Gliddon, a second class Boy, was killed "while acting as powderman at the Pivot Gun." (Lascelles to Spencer, op. cit.) Smith testified that Gliddon "was standing near one of the howitzers" when he was shot. (*Victoria Daily Chronicle*, May 6, 1863.)

79. Captain John Pike to James Douglas, May 26, 1863, F1210/6, BCARS. Following his capture, Pike wrote that "Ull-wheen—uck [Allwhenuk] boasts that it was he who shot the seaman on board the *Forward*."

80. *British Colonist*, May 2, 1863.

81. *Daily Evening Express*, June 24, 1863. *Victoria Daily Chronicle*, May 6, 1863.

82. *British Colonist*, May 6, 1863.

83. Log, HMG *Forward*, April 20, 1863.

84. Olsen, 1963: 14.

85. Log, HMG *Forward*, April 20, 1863. Since the 1880s solid shot and grapeshot have been found at Lamalcha Bay buried in the ground or lodged in trees by resident hwunitum. In a letter to the author, Audrey Ginn mentions that "one of the cannon balls was cut out of the large old maple tree near the beach." She found one "large iron powder cannon ball about 18 inches in circumference" in the field west of the present-day farm-house and several grape-shot "6 inches to 8 inches in circumference" in the vicinity of the old village site. (Ginn to Arnett, April 11, 1987.) Her finds were donated to the Royal British Columbia Museum, but were unfortunately not

catalogued. In his museum collection, Robert Akerman of Salt Spring Island has a handful of corroded grapeshot also found at Lamalcha Bay.

86. *British Colonist*, May 6, 1863.

87. *British Colonist*, June 24, 1863. Barnett, 1955: 268, writes that hwulmuhw warriors "believed that they were possessed, at least temporarily, by the spirits whose cries they uttered."

88. Smith to Pemberton, op. cit. *Victoria Daily Chronicle*, May 6, 1863.

89. *British Colonist*, May 12, 1863.

90. *Victoria Daily Chronicle*, May 6, 1863. Another, almost surreal, event which took place during the battle was told by Eddy Edwards of Kuper Island to Dave Elliot: "During the time of the shelling one old man had just returned to the village. He'd been out getting wood and he had returned with a canoe-load of wood. Just as he was starting to pack up his wood, the shelling started. That old man never stopped packing his wood up. But there was no village left." (Elliot, 1990: 64.)

91. Log, HMG *Forward*, op. cit.

92. *British Colonist*, May 6, 1863.

93. Smith to Pemberton, op. cit.

94. Log, HMG *Forward*, op. cit. Lascelles to Spencer, op. cit.

95. William Young to Lieut. Commander the Hon. H.D. Lascelles, April 16, 1863. Enclosure in Lascelles to Spencer, April 25, 1863.

96. Belich, 1988: 313.

97. Ibid.

98. See for example *Victoria Daily Chronicle*, April 26, 1863.

99. *Victoria Daily Chronicle*, May 6, 1863.

100. *Daily Evening Express*, May 18, 1863.

101. Log, HMG *Forward*, April 20, 1863, op. cit.

102. Lascelles to Spencer, op. cit.

103. *Victoria Daily Chronicle*, April 26, 1863. Rumours of others killed in the battle circulated through Victoria. On the 27th, the *British Colonist* published a the following short notice under the heading "Not true": "That Ben Griffin was shot in the fight with the Samalchas [Lamalchas] at Cowitchin. He still lives at the Boomerang."

104. MacFie, 1865: 469.

105. *British Colonist*, April 28, 1863, etc.

106. *Daily Evening Express*, May 2, 1863.

107. Henry Edwards, personal communication.

108. Log, HMG *Forward*, April 21, 1863, op. cit.

109. Lascelles to Spencer, op. cit. Lascelles says "most of the Indians" which implies that some of them were still present in the village.

110. Log, HMG *Forward*, op. cit.

111. Lascelles to Spencer, op. cit.

112. *British Colonist*, May 6, 1863.

113. *British Colonist*, May 2, 1863.

114. Log, HMG *Forward*, op. cit.

115 *British Colonist*, May 6, 1863.

116. Log, HMG *Forward*, op. cit.

117. *Daily Evening Express*, May 2, 1863.

118. Ibid.

119. *British Colonist*, April 27, 1863.

120. *Daily Evening Express*, op. cit.

121. Hayman, 1991: 41. Lemon (Lamont?) was one of the original Victoria Voltigeurs (McKelvie, 1956: 224.)

122. Smith to Pemberton, April 22, 1863, F 1388, Police Correspondence, BCARS.

123. Written notation by Augustus Pemberton, ibid.

124. Log, HMG *Forward*, April 23, 1863, Adm. 53/8028. Sxecoten is Saanich for "you can see where your mouth is," or, "dry mouth." (Elliot, 1990: 28.)

125. Log, HMG *Forward*, op. cit. Lo'le'cen means "place to leave behind," or "abandoned earth" in Saanich (Elliot, 1990: 28.)

126. Lascelles to Spencer, op. cit.

127. Ibid.

128. Log, HMG *Forward*, op. cit.

129. Lascelles to Spencer, op. cit. Lascelles wrote "I ... returned Mr. Marks' Boat &c ... "

130. Smith to Pemberton, May 8, 1863, F 1388, Police Correspondence, BCARS.

131. Smith to Pemberton, April 25, 1863, F 1388, Police Correspondence, BCARS.

132. Lascelles to Spencer, op. cit.

133. Log, HMG *Forward*, op. cit.

134. Smith to Pemberton, op. cit.

135. Lascelles to Spencer, op. cit. By "Chemainos Bay" Lascelles was referring to the area at the mouth of the Chemainus River and not Chemainus [Kulleet] Bay further north. See note 34 above.

136. Ibid.

137. Ibid.

138. *British Colonist*, May 2, 1863. Pritchard, 1996: 132.

139. *Victoria Daily Chronicle*, April 25, 1863.

140. Pritchard, 1996: 132.

141. *Victoria Daily Chronicle*, April 26, 1863.

142. Pritchard, 1996: 132.

143. Ibid.

144. *British Colonist*, April 27, 1863.

145. Douglas to Newcastle, May 21, 1863, CO 305/20.

146. *Daily Evening Express*, May 2, 1863.

147. *Victoria Daily Chronicle*, April 28, 1863.

148. *British Colonist*, April 27, 1863.

149. *Victoria Daily Chronicle*, April 28, 1863. According to the information given to the crew of the *Enterprise*: "The Indians, who were protected by a substantial stockade, were shelled from that position and took refuge in the woods. The stockade was entirely destroyed before the gunboat left the scene. The first shots were fired by the savages, one of which killed a young seaman, aged about 17 years and severely wounded another ... .It is believed that eight Indians were killed."

150. Ibid. The *Enterprise* crew had additional information about the disappearance of the Marks which paralleled that relayed in Smith's letter of the 25th. The information was said to have come from an unidentified hwulmuhw man at Nanaimo who "boasted of a connection with the crime"— possibly the Penelakut man who relayed similar information to Smith which he relayed in his April 25th letter to Pemberton. "There is said to be too much fear that the report that Marks and his daughter were massacred is true. An Indian, who boasts of having been concerned in the horrid deed, was seen at Nanaimo, and a portion of the clothes of the unfortunate woman were found on the beach of the island upon which her lifeblood is supposed to have been spilled. The Indian, in giving an account of the murders, says that Marks was first slain. His daughter fled to the high rock, whither she was followed by an Indian and a squaw. She was seized by the former and held while the latter plunged a knife again and again into the captive's breast until life was extinct— it being contrary to the custom of the tribe that a man shall kill a woman. A stove belonging to the murdered man and woman was then broken up, and large pieces attached to the necks of the victims and the bodies sunk in the water. This statement, it appears, was obtained from the fiend who boasted of a connection with the crime. We have not heard whether he was taken into custody; but presume that the authorities have taken care that he should not escape a punishment commensurate with his crime. The same man boasts of having killed eleven white persons within the past 4 years." This account is very similar to the information given to Smith by his informants at Plumper's [Active]Pass and Nanaimo who stated that a man shot Marks and a woman killed Caroline after which the bodies were weighted and sunk. The crew of the *Enterprise* may have only been repeating what they heard from Smith and the crew of the *Forward* which was anchored at Nanaimo at the same time. That the *Enterprise* had contact with the *Forward* is strongly suggested by their knowledge that parts of Caroline Harvey's clothing had been found on Saturna Island. Such information would only have been known by the members of the naval expedition.

151. *Daily Evening Express*, May 2, 1863.

152. *Victoria Daily Chronicle*, May 6, 1863.

153. Pike to Douglas, May 26, 1863, op. cit.

154. Pike to Douglas, op. cit. *Victoria Daily Chronicle*, May 21, 1863.

155. Walbran, 1909: 101.

156. *British Colonist*, April 28, 1863.

157. Smith to Pemberton, April 25, 1863, op. cit.

158. *Daily Evening Express*, April 29, 1863.

159. *Daily Evening Express*, May 2, 1863.

160. Ibid.

161. *British Colonist*, April 27, 1863.

162. *Daily Evening Express*, April 29, 1863.

163. Ibid.

164. *Daily Evening Express*, April 30, 1863.

165. Spencer to Secretary of the Admiralty, May 4, 1863, Adm. 1/5829.

166. Pemberton, Notation on Smith to Pemberton, April 22, 25, 1863, op. cit.

167. *British Colonist*, May 7, 1863.

168. *Daily Evening Express*, April 30, 1863. It is interesting to note that the newspaper uses the term "squatters" to refer to the hwunitum in the Cowichan Valley, a reference to the illegitimacy of their occupation of Cowichan land prior to any extinguishment of Cowichan title.

169. Ibid.

170. Spencer to Secretary of the Admiralty, May 4, 1863. Adm. 1/5829.

171. Ibid.

Chapter Eight: Much Indebted to the Roman Catholic Bishop

1. Log, HMG *Forward*, April 26, 1863, Adm. 53/8028.

2. *British Colonist*, May 6, 1863.

3. Log, HMG *Forward*, op. cit.

4. Commodore the Hon. John W.S. Spencer to Secretary of the Admiralty, May 4, 1863, Adm. 1/5829, Cap. S89.

5. Ibid.

6. Pritchard, 1996: 133. Spencer to Secretary of the Admiralty, op. cit.

7. Pritchard, 1996: 132.

8. *Victoria Daily Chronicle*, April 28, 1863.

9. Ibid.

10. *Daily Evening Express*, April 30, 1863.

11. *Daily Evening Express*, May 1, 1863.

12. *Daily Evening Express*, April 30, 1863.

13. *Daily Evening Express*, May 2, 1863.

14. Pritchard, 1996: 133. The "bishop" referred to was the Anglican Bishop George Hills.

15. Ibid.

16. Log, HMG *Forward*, April 29, 1863, op. cit. Verney, it seems, was jealous of Lascelles' influence over other naval officers, including the Commodore, who participated in drinking parties at Lascelles' cottage in Esquimalt to which Verney was not invited. Verney wrote that they "belonged to a set with which I have no sympathy, the horse-racing, fast set, the set with which I have merely an acquaintance … and which has no great love for me." (Pritchard, 1996: 112-113.)

17. Pritchard, 1996: 133. Log, HMG *Forward*, April 1863, op. cit.

18. Log, HMS *Devastation*, May 1, 1863, Adm. 53/8952.

19. *Daily Evening Express*, May 1, 1863.

20. Captain John W. Pike to Commodore the Hon. John W.S. Spencer, May 1, 1863. Enclosure in Spencer to Secretary of the Admiralty, May 4, 1863, Adm. 1/5829.

21. Horace Smith to Augustus Pemberton, April 25, 1863, F 1388, Police Correspondence, BCARS.

22. "Letter of Proceedings," Lieut. Commander the Hon. Horace D. Lascelles to Captain John W. Pike, May 5, 1863, Enclosure in Spencer to Secretary of the Admiralty, op. cit.

23. Pritchard, 1996: 133.

24. Pritchard, 1996: 133-134.

25. Pritchard, 1996: 134.

26. *British Colonist*, May 6, 1863. Log, HMG *Forward*, May 2, 1863, op. cit.

27. Lascelles to Spencer, May 5, 1863. Enclosure in Spencer to Secretary of the Admiralty, May 5, 1863, Adm. 1/5829.

28. *Victoria Daily Chronicle*, May 6, 1863.

29. Ibid.

30. *British Colonist*, May 6, 1863.

31. Lascelles to Spencer, op. cit.

32. Log, HMG *Forward*, May 2, 1863, op. cit.

33. Lascelles to Pike, May 5, 1863, op. cit.

34. Ibid.

35. Spencer to Secretary of the Admiralty, May 4, 1863, op. cit.

36. Draft of reply, on Pike to Douglas, April 28, 1863, F1210/5A, BCARS.

37. Log, HMG *Forward*, May 3, 1863, op. cit. Log, HMS *Devastation*, op. cit.

38. Pike to Spencer, May 8, 1863, Adm. 1/5829.

39. Log, HMG *Forward*, May 3, 1863, op. cit.

40. *British Colonist*, May 6, 1863.

41. Pike to Spencer, op. cit. With the removal of the land bridge joining the two Pender Islands in 1903, the name of Shark Cove has shifted to the cove on the north side of the former isthmus.

42. *Victoria Daily Chronicle*, May 5, 1863.

43. Pritchard, 1996: 134.

44. *Victoria Daily Chronicle*, May 6, 1863.

45. *Victoria Daily Chronicle*, May 3, 1863.

46. Pike to Spencer, op. cit.

47. *Victoria Daily Chronicle*, May 5, 1863.

48. *British Colonist*, May 6, 1863.

49. Log, HMG *Forward*, op. cit. Log HMS *Devastation*, op. cit.

50. Log, HMS *Devastation*, op. cit.

51. Lascelles to Spencer, op. cit. Log, HMG *Forward*, op. cit.

52. *Victoria Daily Chronicle*, May 5 1863.

53. Lascelles to Spencer, April 25, 1863. Adm. 1/8529.

54. *Daily Evening Express*, May 21, 1863.

55. Morice, 1910: 309.

56. *Victoria Daily Chronicle*, May 5, 1863. Pike to Spencer, May 8, 1863, op. cit.

57. Log, HMS *Devastation*, May 4, 1863, op. cit.

58. *Daily Evening Express*, May 5, 1863.

59. *British Colonist*, May 6, 1863.

60. Pritchard, 1996: 135.

61. *Daily Evening Express*, May 5, 1863.

62. Pritchard, op. cit.

63. Pike to Spencer, op. cit.

64. *Daily Evening Express*, op. cit.

65. Log, HMS *Devastation*, May 4, 1863, op. cit.

66. Pritchard, 1996: 135-136.

67. *British Colonist*, May 6, 1863.

68. Pritchard, 1996: 135.

69. *Daily Evening Express*, May 21, 1863.

70. *British Colonist*, op. cit. Newspaper accounts frequently refer to Thostinaht's attractive physical appearance.

71. *British Colonist*, op.cit, *Daily Evening Express*, May 5, 1863.

72. Spencer to Secretary of the Admiralty, May 6, 1863. Adm. 1/5829, Log, HMG *Forward*, May 5, 1863, op. cit.

73. *Victoria Daily Chronicle*, May 6, 1863.

74. Log, HMG *Forward*, May 5, 1863, op. cit. Bishop Demers located temporary lodgings for the Marks family in a house on Collinson Street owned by a Mr. Oughton (*British Colonist*, May 16, 1863.) The Victoria newspapers were quick to call upon their readers to assist the grieving family. (*Victoria Daily Chronicle*, May 6, 1863. *British Colonist*, May 7, 1863. *Daily Evening Express*, May 11, 1863.) Anti-Catholic factions in Victoria, while recognizing the importance of the fund-raising drive to assist the Marks family, expressed concern that the donations were to be placed solely in the hands of the Roman Catholic Bishop. When the amount of contributions, which included a sizeable donation to be forwarded from Nanaimo, reached in excess of a thousand dollars, Bishop Demers took steps to purchase a house and convinced three men, Samuel Nesbitt, P. O'Dwyer, and Jacob Sehl, to manage a trust fund for the Marks: "A full-sized lot, well fenced in, with a house and well of water on it, on Vancouver Street, between McClure and Collinson, has been purchased for six hundred and fifty dollars, and Mrs. Marks is left with a small capital which will be increased by a collection which I hope will soon be forwarded from Nanaimo. The property is held in trust by the committee for Mrs. Marks and in behalf of the children." (*Victoria Daily Chronicle*, May 28, 1863.)

75. *Daily Evening Express*, May 5, 1863.

76. MacFie, 1865: 79.

77. Ibid.

78. *British Colonist*, May 28, 1863

79. Sergeant's Report Book, Vol.1, Entry for May 5, 1863. GR 426, BCARS.

80. *British Colonist*, May 6, 1863.

81. Lascelles to Spencer, May 5, 1863, op. cit.

82. *British Colonist*, op. cit.

83. *Victoria Daily Chronicle*, May 6, 1863.

84. Log, HMG *Forward*, April 16, 1863, op. cit. Log, HMG *Forward*, April 23, 1863, op. cit., Smith to Pemberton, April 25, 1863, op. cit.

85. *Victoria Daily Chronicle*, op. cit.

86. *British Colonist*, op. cit.

87. Smith to Pemberton, May 8, 1863, F 1388, Police Correspondence, BCARS.

88. Douglas to Spencer, May 9, 1863, Adm. 1/5829.

89. Spencer to Secretary of the Admiralty, May 6, 1863, op. cit.

90. *British Colonist*, May 7, 1863.

91. Log, HMS *Devastation*, May 6, 1863, op. cit. *Daily Evening Express*, May 8, 1863.

92. *Daily Evening Express*, May 2, 1863.

93. *Victoria Daily Chronicle*, May 3, 1863.

94. Pike to Spencer, op. cit.

95. Pritchard, 1996: 136.

96. Pike to Spencer, op. cit. Civilians made similar observations. As one correspondent to a Victoria newspaper put it, "the Actual Indian Difficulties" were because "the Indians have repeatedly been promised payment for their lands, and that such promise yet remains to be performed" (*Victoria Daily Chronicle*, May 6, 1863.)

97. Pritchard, 1996: 210-211.

98. Pike to Spencer, op. cit.

99. Ibid. Pritchard, 1996: 136. Log, HMS *Devastation*, May 8, 1863, op. cit.

100. Captain John W. Pike to Lieut. Edmund H. Verney, May 8, 1863. Adm. 1/5829.

101. *British Colonist*, May 9, 1863.

102. *Victoria Daily Chronicle*, May 10, 1863. Another report stated that the presence of the *Grappler* "which lay in Cowichan Bay with her boarding nettings up and everything ready for immediate action appeared to have a salutary effect" and the Cowichan "no longer indulged in bombastic threats." (*British Colonist*, May 11, 1863.) The Anglican clergyman Alexander Garrett made his own reconnaissance and upon his return to Victoria, after an eight and a half hour ride on horseback along the trail from the Cowichan Valley, reported that the hwunitum in the Somenos District "are doing very well, and are busily engaged in planting and sowing." (*Daily Evening Express*,

May 15, 1863.) In Victoria Bishop Demers announced to the press "that the settlers are no longer alarmed at the chance of reprisals being made." (*Daily Evening Express*, May 4, 1863.)

103. *Daily Evening Express*, May 2, 1863.

104. *British Colombian*, May 20, 1863.

Chapter Nine: Suspended Between Heaven and Earth

1. *Victoria Daily Chronicle*, May 8, 1863.

2. *British Colonist*, May 8, 1863.

3. *Victoria Daily Chronicle*, May 8, 1863.

4. Statement by John Henley before A.F. Pemberton, April 10, 1863. Enclosure in Douglas to Spencer, April 13, 1863, Adm. 1/5829. *British Colonist*, May 8, 1863.

5. *British Colonist*, op. cit.

6. Ibid.

7. *Daily Evening Express*, May 12, 1863.

8. Cameron, *Regina vs. Thalaston, Oalitza, Stalehum and Thask*, Notes of Trial, in Cameron to William Young, May 20, 1863, F 260/8, Colonial Correspondence of David Cameron, BCARS.

9. *British Colonist*, May 13, 1863.

10. Cameron, op. cit.

11. *Daily Evening Express*, May 12, 1863.

12. Cameron, op. cit.

13. *Daily Evening Express*, op. cit.

14. *British Colonist*, May 13, 1863.

15. Ibid.

16. Mills, 1977: 8

17. Schofield and Howay, 1912: 655.

18. Ibid.

19. Ibid.

20. Loo, 1994: 43-44.

21. Loo, 1994: 41.

22. Loo, 1994: 44

23. Quoted in Ormsby, 1958: 120.

24. Quoted in Loo, 1994: 44.

25. Ormbsy, 1958: 190, 529.

26. Pritchard, 1996: 77.

27. MacFie, 1865: 461.

28. Shaw, 1909.

29. Crosby, 1907: 53.

30. Waddington, 1860.

31. Ibid.

32. Ibid.

33. Ibid.

34. Registrar's Record Book from Court of Assize, January 1862-June 1870: 40-42, CAA/30.3 P3, BCARS.

35. *Victoria Daily Chronicle*, May 15, 1863.

36. Ibid.

37. Cameron, op. cit.

38. Helmcken, May 14, 1863. In Douglas to Newcastle, May 22, 1863, CO 305/20.

39. *British Colonist*, May 11, 1863.

40. Douglas to Newcastle, op. cit.

41. Smith, 1974: 34.

42. Fawcett, 1912: 63.

43. *Daily Evening Express*, May 14, 1863.

44. Cameron, op. cit.

45. Hayman, 1996: 49.

46. *Victoria Daily Chronicle*, May 15, 1863.

47. Ibid.

48. *British Colonist*, May 15, 1863.

49. Ibid.

50. Cameron, op. cit.

51. Ibid.

52. *Daily Evening Express*, May 14, 1863.

53. *Victoria Daily Chronicle*, op. cit.

54. *Daily Evening Express*, op. cit.

55. Cameron, op. cit.

56. Ibid.

57. Ibid.

58. *Daily Evening Express*, May 14, 1863.

59. *British Colonist*, May 15, 1863.

60. *Daily Evening Express*, op. cit.

61. *British Colonist*, May 15, 1863.

62. *Victoria Daily Chronicle*, op. cit. *British Colonist*, op. cit.

63. *Victoria Daily Chronicle*, May 16, 1863.

64. *British Colonist*, May 16, 1863.

65. *Daily Evening Express*, May 15, 1863.

66. Ibid.

67. *British Colonist*, May 16, 1863.

68. Ibid.

69. *Victoria Daily Chronicle*, op. cit.

70. Douglas to Newcastle, May 21, 1863, CO 305/20.

71. Cameron, op. cit.

72. *British Colonist*, May 21, 1863.

73. *Victoria Daily Chronicle*, May 21, 1863.

74. *Daily Evening Express*, May 20, 1863.

75. *Daily Evening Express*, May 21, 1863.

76. Ibid.

77. *Victoria Daily Chronicle*, May 22, 1863. The "recent events" referred to by the newspaper was the second expedition under way against the Lamalcha, see Chapter 10.

78. *Victoria Daily Chronicle*, May 24, 1863. The *Daily Evening Express*, May 23, 1863, added that when Thalaston was hanged "by some mischance ... the hood fell from his face, it was, however, immediately replaced." The *British Colonist* (May 25) reported that "one white man is said to have been so much overcome by the solemn spectacle that he fainted away."

79. *British Colonist*, May 28, 1863.

80. Ibid.

81. Ibid.

82. *British Colonist*, May 29, 1863.

83. Jenness, n.d., Appendix: 11. The Hul'qumi'num term refers to the washing of the body of the deceased.

84. *British Colonist*, June 6, 1863.

85. Annie Deans, 1856, quoted in Gough, 1984: 236.

86. Jenness, n.d., Appendix: 14.

87. *British Colonist*, op. cit.

88. *Victoria Daily Chronicle*, June 5, 1863.

89. *Victoria Daily Chronicle*, May 30, 1863. The newspaper incorrectly identified her son as Thalaston (Kaisue.) All other accounts state that her son was Stalehum.

90. *Daily Evening Express*, May 30, 1863.

91. List of Prisoners, Victoria Gaol, GR 0305, Vol. 5, December 15th, 1863, BCARS.

92. *British Columbian*, May 23, 1863.

Chapter Ten: The Seat of War

1. *Victoria Daily Chronicle*, May 15, 1863.

2. *Victoria Daily Chronicle*, May 10, 1863.

3. Ibid.

4. *Victoria Daily Chronicle,* June 11, 1863.

5. *Daily Evening Express,* May 9, 1863.

6. *British Colonist,* May 1, 1863.

7. *Daily Evening Express,* May 9, 1863.

8. James Douglas to Commodore the Hon. John S. Spencer, May 9, 1863, Adm. 1/5829.

9. James Douglas to the Duke of Newcastle, May 21, 1863, CO 305/20.

10. *British Colonist,* May 9, 1863.

11. *Victoria Daily Chronicle,* May 10, 1863.

12. *Daily Evening Express,* May 12, 1863.

13. *British Colonist,* May 11, 1863.

14. *Victoria Daily Chronicle,* May 12, 1863.

15. *Daily Evening Express,* May 11, 1863.

16. *British Colonist,* May 12, 1863. Witnessing this display, one of the Englishmen present, W.C. Schoolbred, "made a proposition to the Government to enroll forty or fifty Englishmen at the rate proposed, with a corps of hunters and trappers detailed as sharpshooters to "beat up the game." (*Victoria Daily Chronicle,* May 12, 1863.) Schoolbred, who claimed that he had "seen service," had been arrested and charged the week before with threatening Captain Eastel Brico and challenging him to a duel. Douglas stated that he would take Schoolbred's proposal under consideration (*Victoria Daily Chronicle,* May 12, 1863.) The *British Columbia and Victoria Directory* for 1863 lists a Mrs. W.C. Schoolbred as proprietor of the New Millinery Store, 4 Fort Street. The business featured "dresses made to order" and carried "a large assortment of goods from Paris and London." (1863: 39.)

17. *British Colonist,* May 13, 1863.

18. Much of the sandstone shipped at this time was "intended for use in the construction of Messrs. Dickson, Campbell and Company's new building on Store Street" and their "new wharf." (*British Colonist,* April 15, 21, May 12.)

19. *British Colonist,* May 12, 1863.

20. *British Colonist,* May 20, 1863.

21. *Daily Evening Express,* May 18, 1863.

22. *Daily Evening Express,* May 12, 1863.

23. *British Colonist,* May 13, 1863.

24. *Victoria Daily Chronicle,* May 21, 1863.

25. *British Colonist,* May 12, 1863.

26. From his Somenos homestead, William Smythe observed that: "Certainly a few of our number are a little alarmed, it being rumoured that the natives have made a threat to exterminate the whole of the white men and take the land back to themselves; this however is generally believed to be a little 'blarney' on their part. It is, nevertheless, quite possible that a few mismanaged affairs, similar to the bomardment of that island upon which the Samalchas [Lamalchas] were living, might have a very pernicious effect on the Indian mind. As it is, they all laugh about the matter,

and call the man-of-war's men 'hyas piltons' [great fools]; they are certainly a little more saucy than they were, and in one or two cases have begun to encroach upon the settler's land. When remonstrated with they claim the first right to it; in fact, they say that we have no right to it at all, inasmuch as they have never received payment for it from the Government." (*Victoria Daily Chronicle*, May 12, 1863.)

27. *Daily Evening Express*, May 15, 1863.

28. *British Colonist*, May 16, 1863.

29. *Victoria Daily Chronicle*, June 10, 1863.

30. Smith, quoted in Augustus Pemberton to William Young, May 12, 1863, F 1388, Police, BCARS.

31. Ibid.

32. Douglas to Spencer, May 12, 1863, Adm. 1/5829.

33. Spencer to Secretary of the Admiralty, May 14, 1863, Adm. 1/5829.

34. *British Colonist*, May 14, 1863.

35. These names and the wages they received appear on a list of expenditures incurred by the Police during the war. (Pemberton to Young, October 8, 1863, F 1388, Police Correspondence, BCARS.) There may have been others; a news item in the *Daily Evening Express* of May 30th, 1863, mentions John Gowdy [Gowdie] (brother of James?), Thomas Mitchell and William Foley as having "lately accompanied Superintendent Smith in the expedition against the Lamalchoes [Lamalchas]."

36. Osborne, n.d.

37. *British Colonist*, May 11, 1863.

38. *Victoria Daily Chronicle*, May 21, 1863.

39. *British Colonist*, May 13, 1863.

40. *British Colonist*, May 14, 1863.

41. Augustus Pemberton to Horace Smith, May 14, 1863, F 1388, Police Correspondence, BCARS.

42. *British Colonist*, May 9, 1863.

43. Log, HMG *Forward*, May 9-13, 1863. Adm. 53/8028.

44. John W. Pike to His Excellency James Douglas, May 26, 1863, F 1210/6, BCARS.

45. Ibid.

46. Log, HMG *Forward*, May 15, 1863, Adm. 53/8028.

47. Pike to Douglas, op. cit., Pemberton to Young, October 8, 1863.

48. *Victoria Daily Chronicle*, May 27, 1863.

49. Pike to Douglas, op. cit.

50. Sumnuw is a descriptive place-name for Montague Harbour and has the meaning "inside place," or "place of entering." (Peters, n.d.: 4. Rozen, 1985: 119.) The area has a long history of occupation and use by Hul'qumi'num First Nations (Mitchell, 1971) and was "a favourite camping place of the Cowichans and Chemainus." (Rozen, 1985: 119.)

51. Pike to Douglas, op. cit.

52. Rozen, 1985: 120, gives the translation of the place-name as "measure penis place."

53. Pike to Douglas, op. cit.

54. Ibid.

55. According to Eddy Edwards (n.d.), Sewholatza, who was also known as Gabriel and George O'Shea, assisted the British because he "had a grudge and suspected the Lamalcha tribe for killing his people, so it gave him a chance to take revenge at this tribe."

56. Pike to Douglas, op. cit.

57. Log, HMG *Grappler*, May 15, 1863, Adm. 53/8159. Pike to Verney, May 7, 1863, Adm. 1/5829.

58. Log, HMG *Forward*, op. cit. Pike to Douglas, op. cit.

59. Log, HMG *Grappler*, May 16-20, 1863, Adm. 53/8159.

60. Log, HMG *Forward*, op. cit.

61. Pike to Douglas, op. cit. Log, HMS *Devastation*, May 15, 1863, Adm. 53/8592.

62. Rozen, 1985: 101-102. The village was almost twice as large as that of Lamalcha on the south end of the island.

63. Pike to Douglas, op. cit.

64. Rozen, 1985: 58-59. Peters, n.d., 5.

65. Crosby, 1909.

66. Pike to Douglas, op. cit., *Victoria Daily Chronicle*, May 27, 1863. Log, HMS *Devastation*, May 16, 1863, Adm. 53/8592.

67. Pike to Douglas, op. cit.

68. Log, HMG *Forward*, May 16, 1863, Adm.53/8028.

69. *British Colonist*, May 28, 1863. Log, HMG *Forward*, op. cit.

70. *British Colonist*, May 28, 1863. As Gough points out, "a well-manned canoe could do 7 1/2 knots and keep pace with one of Her Majesty's paddle-wheel sloops-of-war." (1985: 7.)

71. Log, HMG *Forward*, op. cit.

72. Ibid.

73. Log, HMS *Devastation*, op. cit.

74. Log, HMG *Forward*, op. cit.

75. Pike to Douglas, op. cit.

76. Pike to Douglas, op. cit.

77. *Victoria Daily Chronicle*, June 11, 1863.

78. Log, HMS *Devastation*, May 17, 1863, Adm. 53/8592.

79. Ibid.

80. Log, HMG *Forward*, May 17, 1863. Adm. 53/8028.

81. Log, HMS *Devastation*, op. cit.

82. Pike to Douglas, op. cit.

83. *Victoria Daily Chronicle*, May 27, 1863.

84. The "Upper Settlement" is the present-day site of Chemainus Indian Reserve No. 10. The old name of the place has yet to be recorded. "We're still trying to find that out," an elder told me. Brown,

in 1864, gave the name "Hap-hap-ye" for "a few lodges" on the Chemainus River that may correspond to the "Upper Settlement" mentioned by the British (See Hayman, 1989: 101.)

85. *Victoria Daily Chronicle*, May 27, 1863. Sk'wilu refers to the "men from who he received her." Suttles, 1987: 18.

86. *Victoria Daily Chronicle*, May 27, 1863.

87. *Victoria Daily Chronicle*, May 18, 1863.

88. Log, HMS *Devastation*, May 17, 1863, op. cit.

89. Pike to Douglas, op. cit.

90. Pemberton to Young, October 8, 1863, op. cit. In the return of expenses incurred during the expedition Statamish's name, spelled "Sta ta hiah," appears next to Voucher number 14a.

91. Log, HMG *Forward*, May 18, 1863, Adm. 53/8028.

92. Pike to Douglas, op. cit. Rozen, 1985: 82.

93. Pike to Douglas, op. cit.

94. *British Colonist*, May 27, 1863.

95. Ibid.

96. Log, HMS *Devastation*, May 18, 1863, Adm. 53/8592

97. Ibid. *British Colonist*, op. cit.

98. Pike to Douglas, op. cit. *British Colonist*, op. cit.

99. *British Colonist*, May 27, 1863.

100. Pike to Douglas, op. cit.

101. *Victoria Daily Chronicle*, May 28, 1863.

102. Pike to Douglas, op. cit.

103. Ibid.

104. *Victoria Daily Chronicle*, May 28, 1863.

105. Pike to Douglas, op. cit.

106. Log, HMG *Forward*, op. cit.

107. Pike to Douglas, op. cit.

108. Ibid.

109. Pike to Douglas, op. cit.

110. Ibid.

111. *British Colonist*, May 27, 1863.

112. *Victoria Daily Chronicle*, May 27, 1863.

113. *Daily Evening Express*, May 21, 1863.

114. Pike to Douglas, op. cit. The brother of Shacutsus was not identified by name.

115. *Victoria Daily Chronicle*, May 21, 1863. Another version stated that Shacutsus "was arrested and acknowledged that he held the defenceless girl until his brother's wife stabbed her with a knife." (*Daily Evening Express*, May 20, 1863.)

116. Log, HMG *Forward*, May 19, 1863, Adm. 53/8028. Log, HMS *Devastation*, May 19, 1863, Adm. 53/8592.

117. *British Colonist*, May 27, 1863.

118. Log, HMS *Devastation*, op. cit. Peters, n.d., 5.

119. Pike to Douglas, op. cit.

120. *Daily Evening Express*, May 20, 1863.

121. Log, HMG *Forward*, May 20, 1863. *British Colonist* published a more dramatic version of their capture based on information provided by the Captain of the *Emily Harris,* which was, apparently, not factual. (See *British Colonist*, May 27, 1863.)

122. Log, HMG *Forward*, op. cit.

123. *Daily Evening Express*, May 18, 1863.

124. The story was published the following day with the name of the *Devastation* substituted for the *Forward* (*Victoria Daily Chronicle*, May 21, 1863.) Douglas, on the same day, wrote the Duke of Newcastle to explain: "A paragraph which appeared yesterday in a local paper, reports a recent conflict with the Samalcha Indians, and that thirteen of the Seamen and volunteers had been wounded in the affray. This is mere fabrication, nothing of the kind having occurred, and every man of the expeditionary force being by late accounts, in perfect health." (Douglas to Newcastle, May 21, 1863, op. cit.) Called to account for the false report, *Victoria Daily Chronicle* published an explanation the following day: "On Wednesday afternoon we published an extra the contents of which were embodied in our morning addition of yesterday. The public has a right to an explanation for our reasons for making the statements alluded to. The facts are these, that we received from a person who, being a relative of an English nobleman, and an officer in Her Majesty's service, is generally received into society as a gentleman—a statement which, on further inquiry, we find was false, and that this person knew it was false when he uttered it. The Honourable Horace D. Lascelles having unenviably distinguished himself in an engagement with the Indians, has thought it politic on his part to perpetuate a hoax upon the residents of Victoria by inducing us to publish false news. He has had his jest or his revenge for a remark in a contemporary paper. It is now our turn." (*Victoria Daily Chronicle*, May 22, 1863.)

125. *Victoria Daily Chronicle*, May 22, 1863. The log of HMG *Forward* is silent concerning these events.

126. *Victoria Daily Chronicle*, May 22, 1863.

127. *British Colonist,* June 17, 1869. The trial, *Allen vs. Lascelles,* took place Tuesday November 24, 1863.

128. *Victoria Daily Chronicle*, May 22, 1863.

129. *Daily Evening Express*, May 21, 1863.

130. *Daily Evening Express*, May 22, 1863.

131. *British Colonist*, May 20, 1863.

132. Ibid.

133. Log, HMG *Grappler*, May 20, 1863, Adm. 53/8159.

134. Pike to Douglas, op. cit.

135. Log, HMG *Grappler*, op. cit.

136. Pike to Douglas, op. cit.

137. *British Colonist*, May 27, 1863.

138. Log, HMG *Grappler*, op. cit.

139. Pike to Douglas, op. cit.

140. Log, HMG *Grappler*, op. cit.

141. Pike to Douglas, op. cit.

142. Pike to Douglas, op. cit.

143. Ibid.

144. *British Colonist*, May 27, 1863.

145. Pike to Douglas, op. cit.

146. Ibid.

147. Pike to Douglas, op. cit.

148. Log, HMG *Grappler*. The captive woman's name was not recorded.

149. Ibid.

150. Log, HMS *Devastation*, May 21, 1863, Adm. 53/8592.

151. Ibid.

152. Ibid.

153. Ibid.

154. Ibid.

155. Log, HMG *Forward*, May 23, 1863, Adm. 53/8029. It would seem that these men were enlisted as "voltigeurs" in the service of the naval expedition. Pike was later reimbursed by the colonial government for a significant amount, $135, "for hire of Indians." (Pemberton to Young, op. cit.) This sum would cover five days of service by 26 men at the rate of a dollar a day each.

156. Pike to Douglas, op. cit.

157. Ibid.

158. Pemberton to Young, October 8, 1862. See Voucher 1, op. cit.

159. Pike to Douglas, op. cit. *British Colonist*, May 27, 1863.

160. *Victoria Daily Chronicle*, May 28, 1863.

161. *British Colonist*, op. cit. Log, HMG *Grappler*, May 23, 1863, Adm. 53/8159.

162. Pike to Douglas, op. cit. Rozen, 1985: 123.

163. Pike to Douglas, op. cit.

164. *British Colonist*, May 28, 1863.

165. Log, HMG *Forward*, May 23, 1863, Adm. 53/8029.

166. Pike to Douglas, op. cit.

167. Log, HMG *Forward*. Log, HMG *Grappler*, op. cit.

168. Log, HMG *Grappler*, op. cit.

169. Log, HMG *Forward*, op. cit.

170. Pike to Douglas, op. cit.

171. *British Colonist*, op. cit.

172. Ibid.

173. Pike to Douglas, op. cit.

174. *Victoria Daily Chronicle*, May 30, 1863.

175. Log, HMG *Forward*, May 24, 1863. Adm. 53/8029.

176. Log, HMG *Forward*, May 24, 1863. Adm. 53/8028.

177. Log, HMG *Grappler*, Log, HMG *Forward*, op. cit.

178. Log, HMG *Forward*, op. cit.

179. Ibid.

180. *British Colonist*, op. cit.

181. Pritchard, 1996: 138.

182. Log, HMG *Forward*, op. cit.

183. Pike to Douglas, op. cit.

184. *British Colonist*, May 27, 1863.

185. Ibid.

186. Ibid.

187. Sergeant's Report Book, June 5, 1863, GR 426, Vol. 1, BCARS.

188. Pike to Douglas, op. cit.

189. Log, HMG *Forward*, op. cit.

190. Log, HMS *Devastation*, May 25, 1863. Adm. 53/8592.

191. Slelum and Cawley are recorded as having received the reward for the capture of the individuals in the canoes (Pemberton to Young, op. cit.) They were identified in the newspaper as "Pemclicuh" [Penelakut]. (*Victoria Daily Chronicle*, May 27, 1863.)

192. Pike to Douglas, op. cit.

193. Ibid.

194. Log, HMS *Devastation*, op. cit. Pike to Douglas, op. cit.

195. Pike to Douglas, op. cit.

196. Pike to Douglas, op. cit. *Victoria Daily Chronicle*, June 20, 1863.

197. Pike to Douglas, op. cit.

198. *British Colonist*, May 28, 1863.

199. Ibid.

200. Pike to Douglas, op. cit.

201. *Victoria Daily Chronicle*, May 27, 1863.

202. See Vouchers 5 and 6 in Pemberton to Young, October 8, 1863, op. cit. *British Colonist*, May 13, 1863.

203. Pike to Douglas, op. cit., *British Colonist*, May 28, 1863.

204. Pike to Douglas, op. cit.

205. Ibid.

206. Log, HMG *Forward*, May 26, 1863, Adm. 53/8029.

207. Ibid.

208. *British Colonist*, May 27, 1863.

209. Log, HMG *Forward*, op. cit.

210. Log, HMS *Devastation*, May 26, 1863, Adm. 53/8592.

211. Pritchard, 1996: 138.

212. Pike to Douglas, op. cit.

213. Ibid.

214. Ibid.

215. Ibid.

216. Log, HMS *Devastation*, May 27, 1863, Adm. 53/8592.

217. Ibid., Log, HMG *Grappler*, May 27, 1863, Adm. 53/8159.

Chapter Eleven: Come! I, Hulkalatkstun go to kill um!

1. Fourteen adults were turned over to the police. Heaton's 1860 census showed 47 adults at Lamalcha village.

2. *British Colonist*, May 27, 1863.

3. Ibid.

4. *Victoria Daily Chronicle*, May 28, 1863.

5. *British Colonist*, May 28, 1863.

6. Ibid.

7. Ibid.

8. Ibid.

9. *Victoria Daily Chronicle*, May 29, 1863.

10. Augustus Pemberton to William Young, October 8, 1863, Vouchers 5-8, F 1388, Police Correspondence, BCARS.

11. Walter, 1943: 39

12. *Victoria Daily Chronicle*, May 29, 1863.

13. *Daily Evening Express*, May 30, 1863.

14. *Victoria Daily Chronicle*, May 29, 1863.

15. *British Colonist*, May 30, 1863.

16. *British Colonist*, May 27, 1863.

17. Horace Smith to Augustus Pemberton, April 25, 1863, F 1388, Police, BCARS.

18. James Douglas to Commodore the Hon. John W.S.Spencer, May 29, 1863, Adm. 1/5826.

19. Cryer, n.d., "Hul-ka-lakstan: Good Friend of Governor Douglas."

20. Douglas to Spencer, May 29, 1863, op. cit.

21. *Victoria Daily Chronicle*, May 30, 1863.

22. *British Colonist*, op. cit.

23. *Daily Evening Express*, op. cit. The four men were found passed out on the street.

24. *British Colonist*, May 20, 1863.

25. Log, HMG *Forward*, May 31, 1863, Adm. 53/8029. Matthews, 1965: 44.

26. Log, HMG *Forward*, May 31, 1863, Adm. 53/8029. The identities of the "Indian searchers" are not known, but one of them may have been Sewholatza. Tomo Antoine received his pay and discharge on May 27, 1863 (Voucher 2), His place as interpreter was apparently taken by John Lemon on May 31st or June 1st (Voucher 14a.) Pemberton to Young, op. cit.

27. Log, HMG *Forward*, op. cit.

28. *British Colonist*, June 1, 1863.

29. Captain Edward Hardinge to His Excellency James Douglas, June 8, 1863, "Letter of Proceedings," F 1208/2, BCARS.

30. Log, HMG *Forward*, op. cit.

31. *Daily Evening Express*, June 4, 1863.

32. Hardinge to Douglas, op. cit. The man referred to was Rowe, the "lunatic surveyor" from Salt Spring Island, killed in October of 1861.

33. Ibid.

34. *Victoria Daily Chronicle*, June 5, 1863.

35. Log, HMG *Forward*, op. cit.

36. Hardinge to Douglas, op. cit.

37. Ibid.

38. Ibid.

39. Cryer, n.d. "Hul-ka-lakstan: Good Friend of Governor Douglas," Young to Pemberton, op. cit. In the latter source Qual a quiea (Quoloquoi) is listed with two other names, Qu-she-lum and Gabriel, which may be other names for Hulkalatkstun and Whlumthat or different individuals. Qu-she-lum, Qual a quiea, and Gabriel were rewarded for their role in the subsequent capture of Acheewun, Shenasaluk and Sheemultun.

40. Ibid.

41. Ibid.

42. Log, HMG *Forward*, June 2, 1863, Adm. 53/8029.

43. Hardinge to Douglas, op. cit.

44. Ibid. This information was provided by Acheewun and Shenasaluk after their capture.

45. Ibid., Log, HMG *Forward*, op. cit.

46. Hardinge to Douglas, op. cit.

47. The cave, or "tunnel," is located on Mount Sutil, Galiano Island.

48. *British Colonist*, June 9, 1863.

49. Cryer, n.d., op. cit.

50. *British Colonist*, op. cit.

51. Hardinge to Douglas, op. cit.

52. Ibid.

53. Log, HMG *Forward*, op. cit.

54. *Victoria Daily Chronicle*, June 9, 1863.

55. *Victoria Daily Chronicle*, June 12, 1863.

56. *British Colonist*, op. cit.

57. Hardinge to Douglas, op. cit.

58. Ibid.

59. Ibid.

60. Ibid.

61. Log, HMG *Forward*, op. cit.

62. Hardinge to Douglas, op. cit.

63. Pemberton to Young, op. cit.

64. Hardinge to Douglas, op. cit.

65. Pemberton to Young, op. cit.

66. Log, HMG *Forward*, op. cit. Hardinge to Douglas, op. cit.

67. *Victoria Daily Chronicle*, July 3, 1863.

68. Hardinge to Douglas, op. cit.

69. Rozen, 1985: 120. Peters, n.d., 4, states that the name connotes "one island when the tide goes down, two islands when the tide goes up."

70. Rozen, 1985: 120-121.

71. Peters, n.d., 4. Rozen, 1985: 120.

72. Log, HMG *Forward*, June 3, 1863, Adm. 53/8029.

73. Hardinge to Douglas, op. cit. "Wall-e-shuk" was another name given to Sheemaltun.

74. Ibid.

75. Ibid. Log, HMG *Forward*, op. cit.

76. Hardinge to Douglas, op. cit.

77. Hardinge to Douglas, op. cit.

78. Ibid., Log, HMG *Forward*, op. cit.

79. Hardinge to Douglas, op. cit.

80. Ibid. *British Colonist*, June 9, 1863.

81. *British Colonist*, June 8, 1863.

82. Hardinge to Douglas, op. cit.

83. *British Colonist*, op. cit.

84. Hardinge to Douglas, op. cit.

85. Ibid.

86. Ibid.

87. Ibid.

88. Ibid. The two hwunitum settlements were the workings of the Salt Spring Stone Company on Houston Passage, and the Saltspring Settlement at present-day Fernwood.

89. Ibid.

90. Ibid.

91. Ibid. The "tribe" in question referred to people living at Yuhwala'us, site of the former Residential School and the present-day Penelakut Band offices.

92. Ibid.

93. *British Colonist*, June 6, 1863.

94. *British Colonist*, June 8, 1863.

95. Ibid.

96. Hardinge to Douglas, op. cit.

97. Log, HMG *Forward*, June 7, 1863, Adm, 53/8029. Hardinge to Douglas, op. cit.

98. Hardinge to Douglas, op. cit.

99. Ibid.

100. Pemberton to Young, op. cit.

101. Hardinge to Douglas, op. cit.

102. Ibid.

103. Log, HMG *Forward*, June 8, 1863, Adm. 53/8029.

104. Hardinge to Douglas, op. cit.

105. Cryer, n.d., op. cit.

106. *British Colonist*, June 8, 1863.

107. *Victoria Daily Chronicle*, June 8, 1863.

108. Log HMG *Forward*, op. cit.

109. *British Colonist*, June 9, 1863.

110. *Victoria Daily Chronicle*, June 9, 1864

111. Hardinge to Douglas, op. cit.

Chapter Twelve: Judicial Murder

1. *Victoria Daily Chronicle*, July 4, 1863.

2. *British Colonist*, July 3, 1863.

3. *Victoria Daily Chronicle*, June 6, 1863.

4. *British Colonist*, June 6, 1863.

5. Ibid.

6. Ibid.

7. Ibid.

8. Ibid.

9. Ibid.

10. Ibid.

11. *Victoria Daily Chronicle*, June 6, 1863.

12. *British Colonist*, op. cit.

13. Ibid.

14. *Victoria Daily Chronicle*, op. cit.

15. Ibid. Koltenaht, "wife of Al-whan-ock said that Palluck killed both Marks and his daughter ... Al-whan-ock made a similar statement."

16. *British Colonist*, op. cit.

17. *Victoria Daily Chronicle*, op. cit. *British Colonist*, op. cit.

18. *British Colonist*, op. cit.

19. Pike to Douglas, May 26, 1863, F 1210/6, BCARS.

20. *Victoria Daily Chronicle*, June 6, 1863.

21. Ibid.

22. *British Colonist*, op. cit.

23. *Victoria Daily Chronicle*, op. cit.

24. Ibid. Sergeant's Report Book, Vol. 1: 491, GR 426, BCARS.

25. *Victoria Daily Chronicle*, op. cit.

26. Ibid.

27. Ibid.

28. Ibid.

29. Ibid.

30. Sergeant's Report Book, op. cit.

31. *Victoria Daily Chronicle*, op. cit. *British Colonist*, June 12, 1863, states that their names "corresponded with those who fired on the *Otter* in 1858."

32. Ibid.

33. Sergeant's Report Book, op. cit.

34. *Daily Evening Express*, June 11, 1863.

35. Ibid.

36. *Daily Evening Express*, June 12, 1863.

37. In a list of trades and professions in Victoria at this time, MacFie (1865: 90) notes five barristers and five solicitors.

38. *Victoria Daily Chronicle*, June 9, 1863.

39. *British Colonist*, June 9, 1863.

40. *Victoria Daily Chronicle*, June 12, 1863.

41. *Victoria Daily Chronicle*, June 9, 1863.

42. *Daily Evening Express*, June 9, 1863.

43. *British Colonist*, op. cit.

44. *Victoria Daily Chronicle*, June 11, 1863,

45. *British Colonist*, June 12, 1863.

46. Ibid.

47. *Victoria Daily Chronicle*, June 12, 1863.

48. *British Colonist*, op. cit.

49. Ibid.

50. Ibid.

51. Ibid.

52. Ibid.

53. Ibid.

54. Sergeant's Report Book, Vol.1: 499, op. cit.

55. *British Colonist*, op. cit.

56. Ibid.

57. Ibid.

58. Ibid.

59. Ibid.

60. Ibid.

61. Sergeant's Report Book, op. cit.

62. *Victoria Daily Chronicle*, June 16, 1863.

63. *British Colonist*, June 18, 1863.

64. Ibid.

65. Ibid.

66. Ibid.

67. *Victoria Daily Chronicle*, June 18, 1863.

68. *British Colonist*, op. cit.

69. Loo, 1994: 212, n. 103.

70. *British Colonist*, June 6, 1863. *Victoria Daily Chronicle*, June 19, 1863.

71. *Victoria Daily Chronicle*, June 18, 1863.

72. *British Colonist*, June 18, 1863.

73. Ibid.

74. Ibid.

75. Ibid.

76. Ibid.

77. *British Colonist*, June 19, 1863.

78. *Daily Evening Express*, June 18, 1863.

79. See letter by Pere Louis D'Herbomez, *British Colonist*, July 3, 1863.

80. Ibid.

81. *Daily Evening Express*, op. cit.

82. Smith, 1974: 14.

83. *Daily Evening Express*, June 18, 1863.

84. *Victoria Daily Chronicle*, op. cit.

85. Cameron, *Regina vs. Un-whan-uck [Allwhenuk]*, Notes of Trial. In David Cameron to William Young, Colonial Secretary, July 1, 1863, Colonial Correspondence of Vancouver's Island, File 260/8, BCARS.

86. *Daily Evening Express*, op. cit.

87. *Victoria Daily Chronicle*, op. cit.

88. *Daily Evening Express*, op. cit.

89. *Victoria Daily Chronicle*, op. cit.

90. *British Colonist*, June 19, 1863.

91. *Victoria Daily Chronicle*, op. cit.

92. *Daily Evening Express*, op. cit.

93. *Victoria Daily Chronicle*, op. cit.

94. See Foster, 1994: 68.

95. Cameron, op. cit.

96. *British Colonist*, op. cit. *Victoria Daily Chronicle*, op. cit.

97. Letter from D'Herbomez, *British Colonist*, July 7, 1863.

98. *Victoria Daily Chronicle*, op. cit.

99. Cameron, op. cit.

100. Ibid.

101. Ibid.

102. *Victoria Daily Chronicle*, op. cit.

103. Cameron, op. cit.

104. Cameron, op. cit.

105. *Victoria Daily Chronicle*, op. cit.

106. Cameron, op. cit.

107. *British Colonist*, op. cit.

108. *Victoria Daily Chronicle*, op. cit.

109. Cameron, op. cit.

110. *Daily Evening Express*, op. cit.

111. *British Colonist*, op. cit.

112. Ibid.

113. *Daily Evening Express*, op. cit.

114. See Letter from D'Herbomez, *British Colonist*, July 7, 1863

115. *British Colonist*, June 20, 1863.

116. Ibid.

117. *Victoria Daily Chronicle*, June 20, 1863.

118. Ibid.

119. Ibid.

120. *British Colonist*, op. cit.

121. Registrars Record Book from Court of Assize, January1862-June 1970, 45, C/AA/30.3P3, BCARS.

122. *Victoria Daily Chronicle*, op. cit.

123. Ibid.

124. Ibid.

125. Ibid.

126. Ibid.

127. Ibid.

128. *British Colonist*, op. cit. "Five years since" would place he killing in 1858. Other accounts state that the killing took place three years earlier (1860.)

129. *Victoria Daily Chronicle*, op. cit.

130. Ibid.

131. *British Colonist*, op. cit.

132. *Victoria Daily Chronicle*, op. cit.

133. Ibid.

134. Ibid.

135. *Victoria Daily Chronicle*, op. cit.

136. Ibid.

137. *Victoria Daily Chronicle*, June 21, 1863. Semallee's fate has yet to be determined. She may have moved back to Lamalcha.

138. *Daily Evening Express*, June 22, 1863.

139. *Daily Evening Express*, June 23, 1863.

140. *British Colonist*, June 24, 1863.

141. Horace Smith to Pemberton, April 25, 1863, File 1388, Police Correspondence, BCARS.

142. Cameron, *Regina vs. Qual ah ilton [Qualataltan], She Nall su luck [Shenasaluk]and Otch-ee-wan [Acheewun]*, Notes of Trial in Cameron to William Young, Colonial Secretary, July 1, 1863, Colonial Correspondence of David Cameron, File 260/8, BCARS.

143. *Victoria Daily Chronicle*, June 25, 1863.

144. Ibid.

145. Ibid.

146. Ibid.

147. Cameron, op. cit.

148. *British Colonist*, June 25, 1863.

149. *Victoria Daily Chronicle*, op. cit.

150. Cameron, op. cit.

151. *British Colonist*, op. cit.

152. Cameron, op. cit.

153. *British Colonist*, op. cit.

154. Cameron, op. cit.

155. *British Colonist*, op. cit.

156. Cameron, op. cit. As discussed earlier, Palluk and Semallee were not present at the village.

157. *Victoria Daily Chronicle*, op. cit.

158. *Victoria Daily Chronicle*, op. cit. *British Colonist*, op. cit. Referring to Qualataltan: despite Sheemaltun's statement that Qualataltan was "a common fellow" he bore a "high name" (Personal communication, Tommy Paul.)

159. Cameron, op. cit.

160. *Daily Evening Express*, June 24, 1863.

161. *Victoria Daily Chronicle*, op. cit.

162. *British Colonist*, op. cit.

163. Ibid.

164. Ibid.

165. Cameron, op. cit.

166. *Victoria Daily Chronicle*, op. cit.

167. *British Colonist*, op. cit.

168. Cameron, op. cit.

169. *Daily Evening Express*, op. cit.

170. *British Colonist*, op. cit.

171. Ibid.

172. *Victoria Daily Chronicle*, June 26, 1863.

173. *British Colonist*, op. cit.

174. Ibid.

175. *Victoria Daily Chronicle*, op. cit.

176. *British Colonist*, op. cit.

177. Cameron, op. cit.

178. *British Colonist*, op. cit.

179. Letter from A.C. Garrett, *British Colonist*, July 7, 1863.

180. Letter from D'Herbomez, op. cit.

181. *British Colonist*, June 26, 1863.

182. Ibid.

183. Ibid.

184. Ibid.

185. Ibid.

186. *Daily Evening Express*, June 25, 1863.

187. *British Colonist*, op. cit.

188. Ibid.

189. Ibid.

190. *Daily Evening Express*, op. cit.

191. *British Colonist*, op. cit.

192. Ibid.

193. *Victoria Daily Chronicle*, June 26, 1863.

194. Ibid.

195. Ibid.

196. *Victoria Daily Chronicle*, June 17, 1863.

197. *British Colonist*, July 1, 1863.

198. Ibid. Horace Smith to William Young, June 16, 1863, File 1388, Police Correspondence, BCARS.

199. See Hayman, 1989: 49.

200. *Daily Evening Express*, June 30, 1863.

201. *Victoria Daily Chronicle*, July 1, 1863.

202. *British Columbia and Victoria Directory*, 1863

203. *Victoria Daily Chronicle*, op. cit.

204. *Daily Evening Express*, July 3, 1863.

205. *British Colonist*, July 4, 1863.

206. Cameron, op. cit.

207. Letter from "Brutus," *British Colonist*, July 3, 1863.

208. *British Colonist*, July 7, 1863.

209. Letter from D'Herbomez, *British Colonist*, July 3, 1863.

210. Ibid.

211. *Daily Evening Express*, July 3, 1863.

212. *Victoria Daily Chronicle*, July 3, 1863.

213. Ibid.

214. *British Colonist*, July 4, 1863.

215. *Daily Evening Express*, op. cit.

216. James Douglas to the Duke of Newcastle, July 4, 1863, CO 305/20: 223.

217. *Victoria Daily Chronicle*, July 4, 1863.

218. *Victoria Daily Chronicle*, July 5, 1863.

219. *Daily Evening Express*, July 4, 1863.

220. *British Colonist*, July 5, 1863.

221. *Victoria Daily Chronicle*, op. cit.

222. *Daily Evening Express*, op. cit.

223. Ibid.

224. *British Colonist*, July 6, 1863.

225. *Victoria Daily Chronicle*, July 5, 1863.

226. *British Colonist*, op. cit.

227. Among the native people of southern Vancouver Island were "special functionaries who had inherited the proper ritual (si'win) to protect themselves from being contaminated by the dead." (Barnett, 1955: 216.) As soon as a death occurred these undertakers, who were paid for their services, prepared the body for burial. Their duties "included undressing the body, placing it on a bed platform ... so that it faced east, and washing it." (Ibid.)

228. *Victoria Daily Chronicle*, op. cit.

229. Barnett, op. cit.

230. *Victoria Daily Chronicle*, op. cit. Hospital Point was an old name for Songhees Point, named for a smallpox treatment centre, but as Grant Keddie has pointed out (p.c.), it was located within the old Songhees village site and was probably not used as a burial ground. Lime Bay, further up the harbour, was the more likely location of their interment. A number of burials dating from the colonial period have been excavated at Lime Bay in recent years.

231. Cryer, n.d., "Hul-ka-lakstan, Good Friend of Governor Douglas."

232. *British Colonist*, June 25, 1863.

233. Letter from D'Herbomez, *British Colonist*, July 12, 1863.

234. *British Colonist*, July 7, 1863.

235. Ibid.

236. The witnesses referred to by the writer were the sailors of the *Topaze* involved in the capture of Acheewun, Shenasaluk, and Sheemaltun at Montague Harbour on June 2nd. They were to testify against Acheewun for attempting to fire on them during the incident.

237. *Victoria Daily Chronicle*, July 5, 1863.

238. *Victoria Daily Chronicle*, July 8, 1863.

Epilogue

1. Ormsby, 1958: 197.

2. Hendrickson, 1980: III: 7.

3. Smith to Wakeford, August 3rd, 1864, Colonial Correspondence, Acting Colonial Secretary, BCARS. Smith writes that he received these orders "when the village was destroyed."

4. Tennant describes this as the "Douglas system" whereby lands were set aside for aboriginal people prior to settlement and without land sale agreements (1990: 27-38.) The system was complicated on Vancouver Island by the fact that the colonial government had surveyed and sold lands prior to establishing defined reserves. Any pretense that the colonial government would settle land claims with fair and equitable treaties vanished with Douglas' retirement. His successor, Kennedy, delegated others such as Joseph Trutch to deal with the problem. Regarding the Cowichan, Trutch claimed that he could find "no record of any promise having been made to these Indians that they should be paid for the lands in the Cowichan Valley which they may have laid claim to, nor can I learn that any such promise has ever been made. But it is probable that the Cowichans, when the white people began to reside among them, may have expected and considered themselves entitled to receive for the lands, which they held to be theirs, similar donations to those which had been presented to their neighbours, the Saanich Indians, years previously (as before mentioned) on their relinquishing their claims on the lands around their villages. It is further very likely that it was Governor Douglas' intention that such gratuities should be bestowed on this tribe, although no direct promise to that effect had been made." (British Columbia, 1875, Appendix II.) Whether or not Trutch deliberately distorted historical events is unclear but his extreme prejudice towards aboriginal people and culture is evident throughout his career in which he used his position "to reduce or eliminate the elements of Douglas' Indian policy legacy that were beneficial to Indians." (Tennant, 1990: 39.)

5. Pearse to Wakeford, October 7, 1863, Colonial Correspondence, Department of Lands and Works, BCARS.

6. Ibid.

7. Ibid.

8. Walter, 1945: 14.

9. Ministry of the Interior, RG 10, Volume 3611, File 3756-11, 28, 29. Swel-hul-tun is identified by his hwunitum name, Captain Verygood.

10 *British Colonist*, June, 1864.

11. Smith to Wakeford, op. cit.

12. Hayman, 1989: 100.

13. Walker and Graves to Pearse, August 2nd, 1865, Colonial Correspondence, Department of Lands and Works, BCARS.

14. Edwards, n.d.

15. Bishop Modeste Demers to Governor Seymour, November 17th, 1866, Diocese of Victoria Archives, Victoria.

16. Thackary, 1981: 172. Regarding this incident, Augustus Pemberton wrote that there was "a want of harmony in the workings of the Roman Catholic and Protestant Missions." (Quoted in Thackary, ibid.)

17. Alexander Garrett to B.W. Pearse, March 10, 1865, Vancouver Island Surveyor, CAA 30.71KI2, BCARS

18. Ibid.

19. Demers to Seymour, op. cit.

20. Ibid.

21. Ibid.

22. Cryer, n.d., "Hul-ka-latksun Part IV," "Ye Olde and Merrie Game of Hawltz-tzl."

23. Hayman, 1989: 149, n. 114. This land is now Penelakut Indian Reserve No. 6, (Tsussie.)

24. Lutz and Sandwell, 1997.

25. Crosby, 1907: 138. This was the opinion of Thomas Crosby, a Methodist missionary fluent in the Hul'qumi'num language, who wrote that, as a result of the killing of a Nanaimo chief by hwunitum liquor traders, "poor innocent Robinson, a coloured man, was shot in his cabin on Salt Spring Island." A Halalt man, Tshuanahusset, was hanged for the death of Robinson. There were numerous instances of interracial conflict during this period, the details of which would fill another book. An anonymous letter to a Victoria newspaper in 1877 stated that "for every Indian you hear of being hanged for murder, you hear of ten white men being shot and hacked to pieces." (Olsen, 1963: 53.)

26. Sandwell, 1997: 274.

27. Lutz and Sandwell, 1997.

28. Quoted in Sandwell, 1997: 194.

29. British Columbia, *Papers Connected with the Indian Land Question*, 1875: 61.

30. Ibid., 59.

31. Ibid.

32. Cryer, n.d., "Lohar, Chief of the Cowichans."

33. British Columbia, *Papers Connected with the Indian Land Question,* op.cit, 62.

34. Ibid., 104.

35. Brealey, 1995: 149. Present-day (1999) reserve lands total 5,503 hectares for approximately 5,000 people. The Cowichan Tribes, with a population of over 3,000, have a land base of nine reserves totalling 2,493 hectares. 40% of the land is located within the environmentally sensitive Cowichan River, while 600 hectares are inaccessible by road. As a result, over 1,000 Cowichan are forced to live off reserve. The 175 member Lyackson First Nation has three reserves totalling 745 hectares on Valdez Island. A lack of roads and dock facilities force the majority of these people to live elsewhere. The 1,000 member Chemainus Tribe has four reserves of 1,225 hectares on Ladysmith Harbour and Stuart Channel. The 200 member Halalt First Nation has two reserves covering 166 hectares of land on the Chemainus River, including the uninhabited Willy Island at the river's mouth. The Penelakut First Nation consists of four reserves covering 645 hectares, including most of Kuper Island, a small reserve (Tsussie) at the Chemainus River mouth, and another on the north end of Galiano Island. (Information from: Hul'qumi'num Treaty Group, "Statement of Interests, Land and Resources" presented to Main Table, December 11, 1996. H. Olsen, 1963: 49.)

36. Gilbert Malcolm Sproat to the Minister of the Interior, January 8, 1877, Record Group 6, Ministry of the Interior, Public Archives of Canada.

37. Ibid.

38. Ibid.

39. Sproat to the Minister of the Interior, February 15th, 1877, op. cit. The Chemainus tribe was awarded the largest acreage possibly in recognition of the alliance between various si'em and the colonial government during the 1863 war. After the war, cerain si'em were recruited as Indian Police, (see Olsen, 1963: 47-49.) Sproat also indicates that the Chemainus families were given a larger reserve to force the Penelakut to agree to hwunitum demands, with the threat that further resistance would result in no reserve being granted to them.

40. Journal, Archibald McKinley, Indian Reserve Commissioner, E/MC/M21/ pt. 1, BCARS. William Conn was from Dalry, Scotland. His first wife was related to people from Kuper Island and he may have been allowed to occupy the land through this relationship. She died in childbirth after 1873. Conn's second wife was a Nanaimo woman. (Harry Conn, personal communication.)

41. Henry Edwards, personal communication, 1999.

42. Journal, op. cit.

43. Ibid.

44. Ginn, 1978. Robert James Roberts lived peacefully with the Lamalcha people administering to them and Hwunitum settlers in the Chemainus Valley and on Thetis, Galiano, and Salt Spring Islands. (See Roberts Diaries, 1881-1905, BCARS.) The mission church built by him in the early 80s still stands near the site of the Lamalcha blockhouse. An indication of the respect accorded to Roberts and his family by the Lamalcha people is the fact that his daughter Mary "was the only white child to ever be given an Indian name by the Lamalcha tribe." (Ginn, 1978: 71.)

45. Edwards, n.d.

46. Testimony to Royal Commission on Indian Affairs, 1913.

47. Diary of Robert Roberts, Entries for Friday, April 7, 1882; June 29, 1885; December 10, 1885; BCARS. Roy and Henry Edwards, personal communication.

48. Henry Edwards, personal communication, 1999.

49. The site (1999) is the subject of a Specific Land Claim by the Penelakut Band.

50. Walbran, 1909: 117.

51. See De Bertrand Lugrin, 1936, MacDonald, 1939 and Birch, 1940. These and later accounts (McKelvie, 1949) relied heavily on the *British Colonist* for source material. For recent, more balanced accounts of "the Lamalcha incident," compare Gough, 1984 and Laronde, 1993.

52. *British Colonist*, November 4, 1864

53. *British Colonist*, September 18, 1865

54. Petition of Coast Salish Chiefs presented to King George, Quoted in *Hul'qumi'num Treaty Group Newsletter*, Vol. 1, No.3, April 1996.

Bibliography

Newspapers and Newsletters

British Colonist, Victoria.

British Columbian, New Westminster.

Daily Evening Express, Victoria.

Daily Press, Victoria.

Hul'qumi'num Treaty Group Newsletter, Ladysmith.

Victoria Daily Chronicle, Victoria.

Victoria Gazette, Victoria.

Archival Materials

British Columbia Archives and Records Service. *Colonial Correspondence*. Victoria: British Columbia Archives and Records Service.

Osborne, G.A., compiled by. *Notes on Royal Navy Vessels*, L Series. Vancouver: Maritime Museum of British Columbia.

Public Archives of Canada. *Record Group 6*, Ministry of the Interior. Ottawa: Public Archives of Canada.

Public Record Office. *Admiralty Papers*, Adm. 1, Adm. 53 series. London: Public Record Office.

Public Record Office. *Colonial Office Series*, CO 305, Vancouver Island. London: Public Record Office.

Surveyors General Branch. *Surveyor's Field Books*. Victoria: Surveyors General Branch.

Unpublished Materials

Begg, Jonathan. "Letters 1860." Ganges: Salt Spring Island Archives, 1860.

Buxton, Judith. "Earthworks of Southwestern British Columbia." M.A. Thesis, University of Calgary, 1969.

Douglas, Sir James. "Private Papers, including a census of the Indians of Vancouver Island." Second Series. Victoria: British Columbia Archives and Records Service.

Edwards, Eddy. "Letter, July 26th, 1963." Kuper Island: Penelakut Band Office, 1963.

Garrett, Alexander C. "Reminiscences." Victoria: British Columbia Archives and Records Service.

Hendrickson, James. "The Aboriginal Land Policy of Governor James Douglas, 1849-1864." Paper delivered at the B.C. Studies Conference. Burnaby: Simon Fraser University, November 1988.

Hatch, Frederick J. "The British Columbia Police, 1858-1871." M.A. Thesis, University of British Columbia, 1955.

Hills, Bishop George. "Diaries 1860." Vancouver: Archives of the Anglican Provincial Synod of British Columbia and Yukon.

Humphreys, John. "Cowichan Indian Stories and Legends" and "History of the Cowichan Indians." Victoria: British Columbia Archives and Records Service.

Jenness, Diamond. "The Saanich Indians of Vancouver Island." Victoria: British Columbia Archives and Records Service.

Kennedy, Dorothy I. "Looking for Tribes in all the Wrong Places: An examination of the Central Coast Salish Social Network." M.A. Thesis, Department of Anthropology, University of Victoria, 1993.

Lutz, John and Sandwell. "Who Killed William Robinson?" *Race, Justice and Settling the Land,* at website http://web.uvic.ca/history-robinson/index.html, University of Victoria, n.d.

Mallandaine, Edward. "Reminiscences." Victoria: British Columbia Archives and Records Service.

Osborne, George. "The British Gunboats *Forward* and *Grappler.*" Vancouver: Maritime Museum of British Columbia.

Peters, Mary. "Quwutsun Place Names." Collection of the author, n.d.

Roberts, Robert James. "Diaries 1881-1905." Victoria: British Columbia Archives and Records Service.

Rozen, David L. "Place-names of the Island Halkomelem." M.A. Thesis, University of British Columbia 1985.

Sampson, Rocky. "A Short History of the Sampson Family." Ganges: Salt Spring Island Archives, 1989.

Sandwell, Ruth. "Reading the Land: Rural Discourse and the Practice of Settlement, Salt Spring Island, British Columbia, 1859-1891." Ph.D. Thesis, Department of History, Simon Fraser University, 1997.

Thackary, William S. "Keeping the Peace on Vancouver Island: The Colonial Police and the Royal Navy, 1850-1866." M.A. Thesis, Department of History, University of Victoria, 1981.

Turner, Nancy J. "Post-contact Landscape Change on First Nations' Resources and Cultures." Paper given at the Colonial Conference, Fulford Harbour, January 9-10, 1999.

Wallace, Marie A. Stark. "Sylvia Stark's Story." Ganges: Salt Spring Island Archives.

Wilson, Ian. *DeRt 8 Heritage Resource Assessment, Land Subdivision, Saturna Island, Breezy Bay, Saturna Beach.* Permit 1991-84. Victoria: Heritage Conservation Branch, 1991.

Articles and Books

Akrigg, G.P.V. and H.B. Akrigg. *British Columbia Chronicle, 1778-1846.* Vancouver: Discovery Press, 1975.

———. *British Columbia Chronicle, 1847-1871.* Vancouver: Discovery Press, 1977.

Bagshaw, Roberta L., Ed. *No Better Land: The 1860 Diaries of the Anglican Colonial Bishop George Hills.* Victoria: Sono Nis Press, 1996.

Barnett, Homer G. *The Coast Salish of British Columbia.* Eugene: University of Oregon Press, 1955.

Belich, James. *The New Zealand Wars and the Victorian Interpretation of Racial Conflict.* Auckland: Penguin Books, 1988.

Berger, Thomas R. "Wilson Duff and Native Land Claims." *The World Is As Sharp As A Knife: An Anthology in Honour of Wilson Duff.* Victoria: British Columbia Provincial Museum, 1981.

Birch, C. "Capture of Ah-Chee Wun." *The Shoulder Strap,* Winter 1940.

Bibliography

Bowsfield, H., ed. *Fort Victoria Letters, 1846-1851*. Winnipeg: Hudson's Bay Record Society, Vol. 32.

Brealey, Ken G. "Mapping Them 'Out': Euro-Canadian Cartography and the Appropriation of the Nuxalk and Ts'ilhqot'in First Nations' Territories, 1793-1916." *The Canadian Geographer*, 39, no.2, 1995: 140-156.

British Columbia. *Papers Connected with the Indian Land Question, 1850-1875*. Victoria: R. Wolfenden 1875

Carlson, Keith Thor, Ed. *You Are Asked To Witness: The Sto: lo in Canada's Pacific Coast History*. Chilliwack: Sto: lo Heritage Trust, 1997.

Cronin, Kay. *Cross in the Wilderness*. Vancouver: Mitchell Press, 1960.

Crosby, Thomas. *Among the An-ko-me-nums or Flathead Tribes of Indians of the Pacific Coast*. Toronto: W. Briggs, 1907.

Cumming, Peter and Neil Mickenberg. "Native Rights in Canada: British Columbia." *British Columbia: Historical Readings*. Compiled and Edited by Peter Ward and Robert MacDonald. Vancouver: Douglas and McIntyre, 1981.

D'Heureuse, R. *Map of the Cowichan Valley and Chemainus, Comprising Six of the Eastern Districts of Vancouver Island*. Victoria: British Columbia Archives and Records Service, 1862.

Cryer, Beryl M. "Indian Legends of Vancouver Island." 3 volumes. Old Manuscript Catalogue, F/8.2/C88.1. Victoria: British Columbia Archives and Records Service, n.d.

De Bertrand Lugrin, N. "The Capture of A-Chu-Wun." Policing B.C. Series No. 4, *Maclean's Magazine*, January 15, 1936.

Dick, Geraldine. "A Gulf Island Tragedy." *A Gulf Islands Patchwork: Some Early Events On The Islands of Galiano, Mayne, Saturna, North and South Pender*. Pender Island: Gulf Islands Branch, B.C. Historical Association, 1961.

Down, Edith E. "The History of Catholic Education in British Columbia." *Canadian Catholic Historical Association Report* 50, 1983.

Duff, Wilson. "The Fort Victoria Treaties." *B.C. Studies* 3, Fall, 1969.

———. "Prehistoric Stone Sculpture of the Fraser River and Gulf of Georgia." *Anthropology in British Columbia*, Memoir No.5. Victoria: British Columbia Provincial Museum, 1956.

———. "The Indian History of British Columbia, Vol. 1, The Impact of the White Man." *Anthropology in British Columbia*, Memoir No. 5. Victoria: Provincial Museum of British Columbia, 1964.

Elliot, David. *Saltwater People*. Janet Poth, Ed. Saanich: School District 63, 1990.

Elliot, Mary. *Mayne Island*. Mayne Island: Gulf Islands Press, 1984.

Evison, Harry C. *Ngait Tahu Land Rights and the Crown Pastoral Lease Lands in the South Island of New Zealand*. Ko Roimata Whenua Series, No.1. Christchurch: Ngai Tahu Maori Trust Board, 1987.

———. Te Wai Pounamu. *The Greenstone Island: A History of the Southern Maori during the European Colonization of New Zealand*. Christchurch: Aoraki Press, 1993.

Fawcett, Edgar. *Some Reminiscences of Old Victoria*. Toronto: 1912.

Fisher, Robin. *Contact and Conflict: Indian-European Relations in British Columbia, 1774-1890*. Vancouver: University of British Columbia Press, 1977.

Bibliography

————. "Missions to the Indians of British Columbia." *British Columbia: Historical Readings.* Compiled and Edited by W. Peter Ward and Robert MacDonald. Vancouver: Douglas and McIntyre, 1981: 113-126.

Flucke, A.F. "Early Days on Saltspring Island." *British Columbia Historical Quarterly* 15, 1951.

Foster, Hamar. "The Queen's Law is Better than Yours: International Homicide in Early British Columbia." *Essays in the History of Canadian Law: Crime and Criminal Justice.* Jim Phillips et al, Eds. Toronto: University of Toronto Press and The Osgoode Society, 1994.

————. "Indian Title in British Columbia." *Essays in the History of Canadian Law, Volume IV: British Columbia and the Yukon.* Hamar Foster and John McLaren, Eds. Toronto: The Osgoode Society of Canadian Legal History, 1995.

Foster, Hamar, Alan Grove and Bill White. "The First Hanging." *Islander Magazine,* April 23, 1995. Victoria: Times Colonist.

Freeman, Beatrice J.S. "Origin of Place Names on Galiano." *A Gulf Islands Patchwork: Some Early Events on the Islands of Galiano,Mayne, Saturna, North and South Pender.* Pender Island: Gulf Islands Branch, B.C. Historical Society, 1961.

————. "Saturna Island Place Names." *A Gulf Islands Patchwork: Some Early Events on the Islands of Galiano, Mayne, Saturna, North and South Pender.* Pender Island: Gulf Islands Branch, B.C. Historical Society, 1961.

Galloway, Brent. "The Structure of Upriver Halq'emeylem: A Grammatical Sketch." *To:lmels Ye Siyelyolexwa / Wisdom of the Elders.* Sardis: Coqualeetza Education Training Centre, 1980.

Galois, Robert. *Kwakwaka'wakw Settlements, 1775-1920: A Geographical Analysis and Gazetteer.* Vancouver: UBC Press and Seattle: University of Washington Press, 1994.

Garrett, Alexander C. *The Mission Field Monthly Record of the Proceedings of the Society for the Propagation of the Gospel at Home and Abroad.* March 1, 1863. London: 1863.

Ginn, Audrey. "The Mission." *Memories of the Chemainus Valley: A History of People.* Chemainus: Chemainus Valley Historical Society, 1978.

Gough, Barry M. *Gunboat Frontier: British Maritime Authority and Northwest Coast Indians, 1846-1890.* Vancouver: University of British Columbia Press, 1984.

Grant, Walter C. "Description of Vancouver Island." *Journal of the Royal Geographic Society,* Vol. XXVII. London: 1857: 268-320.

Hanson, Diane K. "Subsistence During The Late Prehistoric Occupation Of Pender Canal, British Columbia (DeRt-1.)" *Canadian Journal of Archaeology* 19, 1995.

Harris, Cole. "Voice of Disaster: Smallpox around the Strait of Georgia in 1782." *Ethnohistory* 41, 1994: 4.

Hayman, John, Ed. *Robert Brown and the Vancouver Island Exploring Expedition.* Vancouver: University of British Columbia Press, 1989.

Hendrickson, James. *Journals of the Colonial Legislatures of the Colonies of Vancouver Island and British Columbia 1851-1871.* 5 vols. Victoria: Provincial Archives, 1980.

Hill, J.M. "The Most Reverend Modeste Demers, D.D. First Bishop of Vancouver Island." *Canadian Catholic Historical Association Report,* 1953.

Howard, Frederick P. and George Barnett. *British Columbia and Victoria Directory for 1863 under the Patronage of His Excellency Governor Douglas, C.B. and the Executive of both Colonies.* Victoria, 1863.

Hukari, Thomas and Ruby Peters, Eds. *The Cowichan Dictionary of the Hul'qumi'num Dialect of the Coast Salish People.* Duncan: Cowichan Tribes, 1995.

Jenness, Diamond. "The Faith of A Coast Salish Indian." *Anthropology in British Columbia*, Memoir No. 3. Victoria: British Columbia Provincial Museum, 1955.

Johannesson, Kathy, Ed. *That Was Our Way Of Life: Memories of Susan Johnson, T'Sou-ke Elder.* Sooke: Sooke Region Museum, 1990.

Kahn, Charles. *Salt Spring: Story of an Island.* Madeira Park: Harbour Publishing, 1998.

Kame'eleihiwa, Lilikala. *Native Land and Foreign Desires.* Honolulu: Bishop Museum, 1992.

Lamb, W. Kaye. "The Census of Vancouver Island." *The British Columbia Historical Quarterly* 8, 1940.

Lemert, Edwin M. *Alcohol and the Northwest Coast Indians.* University of California Publications in Culture and Society. Berkeley and Los Angeles: University of California Press, 1954.

Laronde, Les. "The Gulf Islands Crisis of 1863." *More Tales from the Outer Gulf Islands.* Pender Island: Gulf Islands Branch, B.C. Historical Society, 1993.

LaViolette, F.E. *The Struggle for Survival: Indian Cultures and the Protestant Ethic in British Columbia.* Toronto: University of Toronto Press, 1961.

Lillard, Charles. *Seven Shillings A Year: The History of Vancouver Island.* Ganges: Horsdal & Schubart, 1986.

Loo, Tina. *Making Law, Order, and Authority in British Columbia, 1821-1871.* Toronto: University of Toronto Press, 1994.

MacDonald, Resy. "Murder on Saturna." *Victoria Daily Times*, Saturday, June 17, 1939.

MacFie, Matthew. *Vancouver Island and British Columbia.* London: Longman, Green, Longman, Roberts and Green, 1865.

Mackie, Richard S. "The Colonization of Vancouver Island, 1849-1858." *B.C. Studies*, No. 96. Winter 1992-93: 3-40.

Madill, Dennis. *British Columbia Treaties in Historical Perspective.* Ottawa: Research Branch Corporate Policy, Indian and Northern Affairs Canada, 1981.

McKelvie, B.A. "The Defiance of Otcheewun." in *Tales of Conflict.* Vancouver: Vancouver Daily Province, 1949.

McKelvie, B.A. and W.E. Ireland. "The Victoria Voltigeurs." *The British Columbia Historical Quarterly*, 20. 1956.

Manuel, George and Michael Posluns. *The Fourth World: An Indian Reality.* Don Mills: Collier MacMillan Canada Ltd., 1974.

Matthews, Major J.S. *Conversations with Khatsalano 1932-1954.* Vancouver: City of Vancouver Archives, 1955.

———. "The McCleery Diary 1862-1866." *Vancouver Historical Journal*, No.5. August, 1965.

Maud, Ralph. *The Salish People: The Local Contribution of Charles Hill-Tout.* 4 Vols. Vancouver: Talonbooks, 1978.

Bibliography

Mayne, R.C. *Four Years in British Columbia and Vancouver Island*. London: J. Murray, 1862.

Mills, Edward. *The Early Court Houses of British Columbia*. Ottawa: Parks Canada, Manuscript Report Series No. 288, 1977.

Mitchell, Donald H. "Archaeology of the Gulf of Georgia Area, A Natural Region and Its Cultural Types." *Syesis*, Vol.4, Supplement 1. Victoria: The British Columbia Provincial Museum, 1971.

Moresby, Admiral John. *Two Admirals: Sir Fairfax Moresby, John Moresby: A Record of a Hundred Years*. London: Methuen, 1913.

Morice, A.G. *History of the Catholic Church in Western Canada*. 2 Vols. Toronto: The Mission Book Company, 1912.

New, Donald. "Random Notes on Galiano." *A Gulf Islands Patchwork: Some Early Events on the Islands of Galiano, Mayne, Saturna, North and South Pender*. Pender Island: Gulf Islands Branch, B.C. Historical Society, 1961.

Norcross, E.B. *The Warm Land*. Duncan: Island Books, 1959.

Obee, Bruce. *The Gulf Islands Explorer: The Complete Guide*. North Vancouver: Whitecap Books, 1981.

Ormsby, Margaret. A. *British Columbia: A History*. Toronto: MacMillan, 1958.

Orange, Claudia. *The Treaty of Waitangi*. Wellington: Allen and Unwin Port Nicholson Press, 1987.

Olsen, W.H. *Water Over The Wheel*. Chemainus: Chemainus Historical Society, 1963.

————. "The Face of Tomo Antoine. Part III. Missionary and Man-Hunter." *Ladysmith Chronicle*, January 24, 1963.

————. "The Face of Tomo Antoine. Part V. The Pathfinder of the Colony." *Ladysmith Chronicle*, February 7, 1963.

Pethick, Derek James. *Douglas: Servant of Two Empires*. Vancouver: Mitchell Press Ltd., 1969.

Pickford, A.E. "Prehistoric Cairns And Mounds British Columbia: With a Report on the Duncan Burial Mound." *British Columbia Historical Quarterly* , Vol. XI, No.4, 1947.

Pritchard, Allan, Ed. *Vancouver Island Letters of Edmund Hope Verney 1862-65*. Vancouver: University of British Columbia Press, 1996.

Reksten, Terry. *"More English than the English": A Very Social History of Victoria*. Victoria: Orca Book Publishers, 1986.

Richards, Captain George G. *The Vancouver Island Pilot 1864*. Compiled from the Surveys made by Captain G.H. Richards, Royal Navy in Her Majesty's Ships *Plumper* and *Hecate* between the years 1858 and 1864. London: Hydrographic Office, Admiralty.

Richards, Valerie. "Stone-cutter's cabin is found at Southey Point." *Gulf Islands Driftwood*, Wednesday, February 1, 1976.

Roberts, Eric. A. *Salt Spring Saga: An Exciting Story of Pioneer Days*. Ganges: Driftwood, 1962.

Scholefield, E.O.S. and F.W. Howay. *British Columbia from the Earliest Times to the Present*. 4 vols. Vancouver: S.J. Clarke, 1914.

Shaw, George C. *The Chinook Jargon and How to Use It*. Seattle: Rainier Printing Company Inc., 1909.

Smith, Dorothy B. *Lady Franklin Visits the Pacific Northwest: Being Extracts from the Letters of Miss Sophia Cracroft, Sir John Franklin's Niece, February to April 1861 and April to July 1870*. Victoria: Provincial Archives of British Columbia Memoir No. XI, 1974.

Bibliography

Suttles, Wayne. "Economic Life of the Coast Salish of Haro and Rosario Straits." *Coast Salish and Western Washington Indians*. New York and London: Garland Publishing, 1951.

————. *Coast Salish Essays*. Vancouver: Talonbooks, 1987.

Tennant, Paul. *Aboriginal Peoples and Politics: The Indian Land Question in British Columbia, 1849-1989*. Vancouver: University of British Columbia Press, 1990.

Turner, Nancy J. and M.A.M. Bell. "The Ethnobotany of the Coast Salish Indians of Vancouver Island." *Economic Botany*, 25 (1): 63-104.

Waddington, Alfred E. *Judicial Murder*. Victoria, 1860.

Walbran, John T. *British Columbia Coast Names: 1592-1906*. Ottawa: Government Printing Bureau, 1909.

Walters, Margaret. *Early Days Among the Gulf Islands of British Columbia*. Victoria: Hebden Printing, 1945.

Wells, Oliver. *Vancouver Island: Survey of the Districts of Nanaimo and Cowichan Valley*. Victoria, 1859.